MAN–COMPUTER INTERFACES

COMPUTER SCIENCE TEXTS

COMPUTER SCIENCE TEXTS

Man–Computer Interfaces

R. B. COATS
and
I. VLAEMINKE
Both Principal Lecturers
in Computing
Leicester Polytechnic

BLACKWELL SCIENTIFIC PUBLICATIONS

OXFORD LONDON EDINBURGH

BOSTON PALO ALTO MELBOURNE

© 1987 by
Blackwell Scientific Publications
Editorial offices:
Osney Mead, Oxford OX2 0EL
 (*Orders*: Tel. 0865 240201)
8 John Street, London WC1N 2ES
23 Ainslie Place, Edinburgh EH3 6AJ
52 Beacon Street, Boston
 Massachusetts 02108, USA
667 Lytton Avenue, Palo Alto
 California 94301, USA
107 Barry Street, Carlton
 Victoria 3053, Australia

First published 1987

Set by V & M Graphics Ltd,
 Aylesbury, Bucks
Printed and bound in Great Britain by
 Mackays of Chatham, Kent

DISTRIBUTORS

USA and Canada
 Blackwell Scientific Publications Inc
 PO Box 50009, Palo Alto
 California 94303
 (*Orders*: Tel. (415) 965-4081)

Australia
 Blackwell Scientific Publications
 (Australia) Pty Ltd
 107 Barry Street
 Carlton, Victoria 3053
 (*Orders*: Tel. (03) 347 0300)

British Library
Cataloguing in Publication Data
Coats, R. B.
 Man–computer interfaces: an
 introduction to software design
 and implementation.
 1. Computer interfaces
 I. Title   II. Vlaeminke, I.
 004.6   TK7887.5

ISBN 0–632–01542–X

Library of Congress
Coats, Robert B.
 Man–computer interfaces: an
 introduction to software design and
 implementation/R. B. Coats & I.
 Vlaeminke.
 Includes index.
 ISBN 0–632–01542–X
 1. Computer software—
 Development.   2. Electronic
 data processing—Psychological
 aspects.   3. System design.
 I. Vlaeminke, I.
 II. Title
 QA76.76.D47C63   1987
 005—dc19   87–16110

Contents

Preface

The last ten years have seen an increasing recognition of the important role played by the man–computer interface in the success of a computer system. Interest in this aspect of systems development has grown not only amongst computer scientists but also amongst ergonomists, psychologists, sociologists and graphic designers, reflecting its multi-disciplinary nature. Indeed, it has frequently been suggested that for many applications, successful development requires a design team whose members represent these various disciplines.

This text is aimed at undergraduates following a course in Computer Science, the future providers of the software expertise in such a multi-disciplinary team. It focuses on the facilities which can be provided by software in the interface and on how they can be implemented, and proposes a strategy for this aspect of systems design. It provides an introduction to the basic facilities and concepts of text-based interfaces in the conviction that competence in these basics is a prerequisite to an understanding of more advanced interfaces and to an appreciation of the possibilities for further advances. In the authors' opinion, graphical interaction deserves a separate treatment and is not covered, other than in the obvious overlap in window-based systems.

The major theme underlying the book is that the interface software can be identified as a distinct element which can be separated from the task processing in any system. Furthermore, the interface can be subdivided into a number of layers, whose functions can be represented by generalised abstractions. The concept of abstraction is introduced by deriving abstractions for basic input and output processes, and illustrating their practical implementation. A common abstraction is then developed for the traditional dialogue structures (Question and Answer, menus, forms and commands) to demonstrate that these represent simple variants of the same basic structure. This interpretation is used to explain the features of each structure and to justify accepted guidelines on their use.

The dialogue abstractions are extended to incorporate techniques which ameliorate the impact of system response on users of the system and which permit a limited form of adaptation, within a system, to the requirements and preferences of different users. The input and output abstractions are extended to systems which support multiple, overlapping windows and a direct manipulation style of interface.

The identification of these abstractions is fundamental to the proposed design strategy since, by encouraging the modularisation of the interface and the development of module libraries, it improves consistency and portability and permits a prototyping approach to development. Transition network and production system representations are described to illustrate that dialogues based on the abstractions can be generated automatically.

Although the emphasis is on software techniques and a design strategy for their utilisation, accepted guidelines for other aspects of interface design are explored, and an attempt is made to explain the rationales which underpin them. The level of detail is based on the criterion that the 'software member' of the design team must be capable of appreciating inputs from other disciplines in deciding the data values to be supplied to the abstractions in different situations. The final chapter provides a brief introduction to more advanced interfaces which extend the range of input/output channels or the adaptation to different user characteristics.

Practical illustration of how the abstractions can be implemented requires a choice of programming language and of workstation facilities. The language chosen is PASCAL, not because it represents the optimal choice for implementation, but because it is commonly used to teach programming and because its syntax is easily readable by someone familiar with other procedural languages; the ideas illustrated in PASCAL are easily transferred to other langauges such as Modula-2, C or APL. The workstation assumed in most examples is one with facilities equivalent to a PC-compatible equipped with a mechanical mouse. Again this choice is dictated by popularity, rather than innate virtue, and because these facilities can be considered a base standard for a typical workstation; examples are given of the facilities offered both by dumb terminals and by more sophisticated workstations.

The practical exercises which accompany a course on programming typically require some design of input and output, but programming language texts necessarily concentrate on the mechanics of the input and output functions provided within the particular programming language. This book is designed to complement a programming course by discussing the enhancements to these raw input and output functions, both in structure and in facilities, which are necessary for a successful interface, and by giving practical illustrations of how they can be accomplished. Most chapters are followed by sets of discussion and programming exercises to provide practical exposure to the concepts. A design exercise for a simple transaction processing system runs through the early chapters. The Appendices contain two other case studies and listings of all machine-independent code referenced in the text.

The book is intended as an introductory text; it is not a summary of the latest research findings. The bibliographies which accompany each chapter are not comprehensive but are intended to provide a next step in following up the concepts introduced. It is the authors' conviction that an appreciation of the published guidelines for interface design is best achieved by experimenting with different types of interface; for example, the reader should experience for himself the confusion which results when a screen is filled with a multiplicity of different highlights. For this reason, the text includes only a limited number of illustrations drawn from commercially available systems; these are used to illustrate specific techniques rather than as exemplars of interface design. Interaction with a system is a dynamic process whose characteristics are not easily assessed from a static snapshot; at the end of various chapters, the reader is specifically encouraged to try out examples of typical packages to experience these dynamics.

The authors gratefully acknowledge the assistance of Apollo Computer Inc., CASE plc., City Business Systems and Digital Research Ltd. for their permissions to copy illustrations. Thanks are also due to a number of colleagues, and in particular to Ian Marshall, for their suggestions on revisions to the text.

Acknowledgements

Apollo and Domain are registered trademarks of Apollo Computer Inc.
CP/M, GEM and Desktop are registered trademarks of Digital Research Inc.
IBM is a registered trademark of International Business Machines Corp.
Lotus and 1-2-3 are registered trademarks of Lotus Development Corp.
MS-DOS is a registered trademark of Microsoft Corp.
UNIX is a registered trademark of Bell Laboratories.
WordStar is a registered trademark of MicroPro International Corp.

Chapter 1

The significance of the man–computer interface

1.1 What is the Interface?

Every computer system can be measured against two criteria:

Correctness and **Convenience**

With the traditional concept of a computer system as illustrated in Fig. 1.1, correctness means that if suitable input values are supplied to the process it will produce the desired output values.

Input ⟶ Process

Output ⟵

Fig. 1.1.

Systems staff have traditionally emphasised this computational correctness; much effort has been applied to ways both of producing software and of testing it in an attempt to achieve correctness. Whilst few, if any, of these would claim to have produced commercial software which operates 100% correctly, the majority of systems perform reasonably well against this criterion, and most are at least consistent in the results they produce.

Much less effort has been devoted to the concept of convenience. Although any computer system includes at least one human user within its boundary, systems have been viewed as undertaking a task — such as maintaining a sales ledger — rather than as a tool used by a human to assist in achieving that task. *Locus of Control.* It is the sales clerks who maintain the company's sales ledger not the computer system! The emphasis on the correctness of the values has tended to be at the expense of considering exactly how these values should be input or output; function has been the significant factor rather than form.

The input and output elements are too often viewed by software producers as a series of rather tedious read and write operations which must be gone through before one gets to 'the interesting bit of the program'; have you ever heard a programmer claim that they 'produced a really great write statement today'? However, the results of these read and write operations, and the

1

terminal devices on which they occur, are often all the human user sees of the computer system.

The user of a computer-based system has a right to expect not only that the system produces correct values but also that it is easy to use. This implies that the human does not have to alter his natural work pattern significantly in order to use the computer system. In most cases, the actual processing of the input values to produce the output values has no impact on this since the user does not experience it directly and has no need, or desire, to know how it is done. The actual mechanics by which the steering of a car is transferred from steering wheel to the road wheels is of little consequence to the motorist; on the other hand, the shape and position of the steering wheel has an enormous impact on him. Similarly, the nature and positioning of the workstation, the format in which input is requested, and the layout of messages produced by the system, have an enormous impact on the human user of the computer system.

The *man–computer interface* encompasses all those aspects of a computer-based system which the user experiences directly.

1.2 What Factors Affect Convenience?

For his usage to be 'convenient', the user must feel 'comfortable' when interacting with the system. Thus, the factors which affect convenience are those which influence this feeling of comfort. They can be divided into the three broad classifications of Fig. 1.2.

Classification	Affected by	Influences
social factors	organisational climate	emotional comfort
physical ergonomics	hardware	physical comfort
psychological ergonomics	software design	cognitive comfort

Fig. 1.2. Factors influencing a user's comfort.

The general climate within the organisation — such aspects as management style and job security — and the way in which a prospective system is introduced, can build preconceptions long before the actual system is encountered. The functions which are allotted to the user by the system, and the way in which these human functions must be carried out, can disrupt traditional social groupings in the workplace, isolate the user from normal social interaction or disturb relationships with superiors. These *social factors* will tend to reinforce or to allay a user's fears about a system. A great deal has been written about this aspect of system development and about the involvement of users in the development process. We will be concerned only with how the use of a particular software design strategy can facilitate this involvement.

Assuming that a user approaches a system with no negative preconceptions, the *ergonomics* or usability of the actual system can significantly improve or worsen his attitude towards it. The main aspects of ergonomics are shown in Figure 1.3.

— design and arrangement of equipment
— design of the dialogue
— availability and reliability of the system
— responsiveness of the system

Fig. 1.3. The ergonomic aspects.

The way in which the equipment, both computer hardware and any ancillary equipment, is designed and arranged into a workstation will affect the *physical comfort* of the user when using the system. Can the user read the characters on the screen easily, or has it been positioned so that the sun causes a glare which makes the user peer at the screen through half-closed eyes? Can the keyboard be positioned so that the user can reach the keys and any other items required without having to stretch unnaturally? For example, in some supermarkets the checkout tills are positioned in such a way that the cashiers have to twist and reach for each item being purchased — resulting in a lot of tired cashiers at the end of a day! Has the system designer given as much thought to the seating and worktop as to the terminal which rests upon it, or did he just use any old table and chair which happened to be spare? The design of equipment is the province of ergonomics; with most computer systems, the systems designer selects off-the-shelf equipment rather than designing it from scratch.

The second aspect of the interface might be termed *psychological ergonomics*; just as physical ergonomics is concerned with matching the system to human physical processes, psychological ergonomics is concerned with matching it to human cognitive processes. To illustrate the difference, consider the process of reading a message from a screen. A user who cannot physically discern the characters because of glare or poor contrast will suffer physical discomfort. The user who manages to read the characters but who cannot comprehend the message because it is phrased in computer jargon, or because it is laid out in some eccentric fashion, will suffer psychological discomfort. There is little point in sparing a user the discomfort of back ache or eye strain if the system makes his brain ache instead! This aspect, called the *dialogue*, is an area of systems design which software producers can very easily influence for good or ill, and its design is the major concern of this book.

Two aspects closely related to psychological ergonomics, but sufficiently important to warrant individual treatment, are the *availability* and the *responsiveness* of the system.

Can the user gain access whenever and wherever he needs to? The designer should ensure that the times when the system can be expected to be available match the hours when the user will require it. Furthermore, the reliability of the system must be such that the user can reasonably expect it to be available when it is supposed to be. It is not only the total amount of time lost due to faults which is significant but also the number of faults; a series of losses in a network link, each lasting no more than a few seconds, can be much more frustrating than a single failure lasting an hour. The number of workstations must be adequate to support the number of prospective users. Unless usage is very casual or work patterns are not affected if a workstation is not immediately available, this generally implies individual workstations located within the user's normal work area. There are a surprising number of systems which provide users with an instantaneous answer to a query after they have walked up two flights of stairs and queued for ten minutes for a workstation to become free. Economising on the number of workstations is a false economy.

Almost as frustrating as being unable to access the system at all, is being expected to wait 20 seconds or longer for the system to respond to the last input. Even worse is the case where some days it takes two seconds to respond and other days it takes 20 seconds; variable response is a marvellous way to keep the user guessing whether the system has crashed or not! The provision of acceptable response is one of the more technically demanding and costly aspects of interactive system development, and is discussed in Chapter 8.

1.3 Why is Convenience Significant?

In the 1960s and early 1970s the user's convenience was largely ignored by systems designers. The large mainframe was a precious item to be cosseted with air conditioning and an army of operators; humans fitted in with the machine rather than vice versa.

With the demise of batch processing came an increasing realisation that convenience was a major factor in the success or failure of a system; this awareness was heightened as systems development moved away from the clerical bread-and-butter data processing applications into the area of decision-support for management. For the system to be effective, it is not sufficient for the hardware and software to produce the correct output values for given input values — the human's performance is critical to success.

Humans have emotional, physiological and psychological needs which must be met in any activity if that activity is to be performed effectively. A user who is confused, frustrated or stressed physically or psychologically *cannot* perform well. The component of a system which causes the presence or absence of stress is the man–computer interface — that is what the user experiences when interacting with the system. Some cynics might observe that this awareness has yet to dawn on the designers of many microcomputer operating systems!

The human body is a mechanism which has limitations and tolerances within which it must work. Our eyes require images to be within a particular size range, of a certain level of brightness, to contrast sufficiently against their background, and to be located a suitable distance away if they are to be viewed in comfort. Some colours are perceived more easily than others, some colour juxtapositions aid discrimination whilst others are confusing. We can move our limbs only over certain ranges, our reach is limited, and our hands have limits on their dexterity. If we are to maintain a particular position for any length of time our bodies need adequate support, and so on.

These physical limitations are commonly recognised. However, the limitations of our brains are less well understood and are more often overlooked. Whilst we have an extremely capacious *long term memory*, we have a very limited *short term memory*. Short term memory is often considered as a series of input and output buffers in which intermediate data can be stored during any activity. Like the buffers in a computer system, this memory has a very limited capacity and can be easily overloaded. Long term memory seems to have an unlimited capacity and humans can retrieve information from it very rapidly. If we undertake an activity regularly, we can easily 'remember' it without overloading the short term memory; if we do it often enough, it becomes almost subconscious. However, if we carry out an activity irregularly, our short term memory is fully occupied throughout the activity.

Even if the basic activity itself is familiar, we can overload the short term memory with a particular instance of that activity. Consider the case of a clerk looking up the details of an invoice. These details are displayed across two screens because there is too much detail to fit onto one. The clerk may have carried out the task many times, and may well be able to tell you without difficulty which fields are on which screen, since he will have seen the same field captions many times. Remembering the values for a particular invoice from one screen to the next will be much more difficult, if not impossible.

Humans bring to every activity a set of expectations of how that activity should proceed. These expectations — a mental *model* of the activity — are based on their previous experience. Long term memory is often viewed as a store of patterns representing different models against which humans seek to match mental stimuli; rather than storing low level details, humans reconstruct this detail information from higher level patterns. Most people expect to read a screen from left to right and from top to bottom, just as they read a printed page. They look for order and structure in a display, and seek clues as to the relative importance of different items.

Humans are remarkably adaptable. They can contort themselves into weird positions and operate under the most unfavourable conditions — just look at programmers at their workstations! They can supplement their short term memory with pieces of paper. They can adapt the way in which they undertake a task. They can acquire new models which run contrary to their previous expectations and impose order in a display where none existed. But this adjustment causes stress which may exhibit itself in confusion, frustration or physical aches and pains.

The results of this stress can take various forms. Where usage is discretionary the user may simply opt not to use the system. For example, take the situation where a manager could use a financial planning system or he could do the exercise manually using a calculator. If his perceptions of the system are unfavourable because of poor availability, response, physical discomfort, or whatever, he might choose the manual solution. Where the user has no choice, for example a clerk operating a sales ledger or order processing system, it might result in illness or persistent absence, or in an unacceptable level of errors. These errors are not deliberate attempts to sabotage the system — it is possible to arrange the inputs and outputs of a computer system so that it is difficult to get them right!

Many systems in use today exhibit problems caused by failure of the interface to meet the users needs in these areas. They were not deliberately designed to do so. Thus, one must examine why so many have failed.

1.4 What are the Difficulties in Designing the Interface?

Very few systems are used by a single user, and very few are designed to support a single task. Since the interface must match both the physiological and psychological needs of a user if it is to succeed, an obvious problem arises in its design and implementation:

PEOPLE ARE DIFFERENT!

It is obvious that different individuals have different physical characteristics and capacities. A comfortable keying position for one user could be extremely uncomfortable for one of a very different physique. The brightness level necessary for one user to discern characters on the screen may be uncomfortably bright for another.

In the same way, humans have different psychological needs which vary both with the individual and the task being undertaken. A novice user who is unacquainted with a system, or who uses it infrequently, will require system messages to be much more explanatory than an experienced user who accesses the system regularly. It is extremely irritating to have described each time in great detail an input which you have entered a hundred times a day for the last six months — almost as irritating as not having it described at all the very first time you encounter it! A complex task which requires a sequence of coded responses obviously imposes a much higher memory loading, and requires more support from the interface, than a simple query.

Expectations and tolerance also vary with the user and the task. A manager requiring an answer to a query about stock levels as part of a larger task on which he is engaged is less likely to be patient than a clerk whose main function is to query stock levels. Expectations are a major problem since humans tend to compare the computer's capabilities with their own, which can sometimes give rise to false expectations. Humans are very impressed by the number-crunching capability of computers — something at which humans are poor — and are frequently disappointed when computers perform badly at tasks in which humans excel. As an example of this difference, consider a financial analysis system which can provide answers to queries of the form:

What products have a profit margin less than $x\%$?

Suppose there are 100 products, and only products with numbers 3 and 86 have margins above $x\%$. What format should the answer take? A human would almost certainly reply:

All except products 3 and 86

whereas nearly all computer systems would produce a lengthy list of the form:

products 1 2 4 5 ... 85 87 ... 100

Humans might lack in calculating power (the system can calculate the profit margins much quicker) but they have a marvellous capacity for interpretation and discrimination. In spite of many false expectations raised by literature and the media, most present-day computer systems are totally lacking in these capacities.

Although our knowledge is improving, we understand how people tick much less well than we understand how the computer in the system ticks. The interface designer has nonetheless to try to apply this incomplete knowledge to potential users who cannot be fully known to him, no matter how familiar he is with the organisation. He has not only to match their user requirement in terms of computational mechanics but also to match their physical and psychological needs in the interface.

To compound the complexity of this venture, humans have a further characteristic — they are exceptionally adaptive. Humans learn very readily; both the way they operate and their psychological needs change as they adapt in the light of this learning. The novice user of Monday morning may have become an expert user by Tuesday afternoon, and the interface which was ideal on Monday morning may be frustrating to the same user by Tuesday afternoon!

1.5 A Strategy for Design of the Man–Computer Interface

The reader might justifiably reply that it cannot be impossible to implement an effective interface. Car manufactuters have been making cars for a wide range of customers for many years, and most of these customers have not only been able to drive their cars without suffering discomfort but have even enjoyed it! The same is true of computer games. Although their popularity has declined somewhat of late, these games — the classic example of discretionary usage — have enjoyed an enormous appeal which cannot be explained solely by novelty value. It might be illuminating to examine some characteristics of the interfaces in these two examples.

Car manufacturers take great pains to find out as much as possible about their potential customers. Whilst they seldom know the individual customer, they have a very clear idea of their target. They make use of a number of general guidelines, for example in the positioning and labelling of controls and instruments, and call on individual experts in these particular aspects. To cater for the requirements of individual customers above this basic requirement, many of the elements of the interface — seating, steering column, mirrors — are designed to be adjustable. They spend a great deal of effort on testing their products with typical customers in typical environments, and they adjust the design in the light of user reactions. A final point worthy of mention is that although they try to make their models as distinctive as possible, they mostly adopt consistent interface standards (layout of pedals, controls) so that a driver can readily adapt to driving any other type of car. If you consider the computing equivalent of driving to be interacting with the operating system, it is certainly not true that someone who can 'drive' one computer can readily 'drive' another type of computer.

The designers of computer games spend a great deal of effort on the design of the man–computer interface; in fact, a computer game is almost all interface. The use of colour, sound and graphics is not fortuitous but is a conscious design decision. Games include an element of adaption so as to maintain the user's interest; as the user's familiarity with the game grows, and his level of skill increases, the game changes, for example by speeding up. Games designers have to be aware of the capabilities of the hardware and software that is available, and are imaginative and innovative in its application. Yet, in spite of the importance of originality, the operations required by a user to run games have a basic consistency.

Why should the design and implementation of an operating system or an applications package differ radically from the above examples? How many accounts clerks find using their sales ledger system pleasant? Is it inevitable that they should not? Surely we can draw a number of conclusions from these examples which would be applicable to any computer system.

1.5.1 Treat the Man–Computer Interface as a Distinct Component of the System

Just as the data structures within a system can be isolated from the processing algorithms which are applied to those data structures, we can to a certain extent isolate the man–computer interface from the computational task processing. In Chapter 2, we examine the elements which make up this component of the system.

The interface deserves a specific design activity in the same way that the files maintained by a system are designed; the nature and format in which input is requested from and output presented to the user should be the result of conscious design decisions.

1.5.2 Be Aware of the Capabilities of Hardware and Software

Systems designers, like everyone else, have a natural tendency to stick with what they know. If anything, this innate conservatism has been strengthened rather than weakened by recent rapid advances in hardware and software capabilities. However, it is impossible to design a component without an understanding of the possibilities and limitations of the basic building blocks from which it can be constructed. In Chapter 3, the basic processes which are supported by common input and output devices are examined and, in Chapter 12, the capabilities of more advanced mechanisms are outlined.

1.5.3 Be Consistent

Whilst innovation in design is necessary for progress, some care must be taken to ensure that innovation does not degenerate into gimmickery and an unnecessary proliferation of approaches. Nowadays, many users access a variety of systems and it is unreasonable to expect them to adjust their approach each time they change system. Since these systems are probably designed by different systems staff, consistency is not achieved easily.

The development of software 'families' where a range of different applications all operate in the same manner is desirable. It has been suggested that this can be encouraged by the maintenance of a *house style book* containing recommendations for interface design; such books are often maintained by newspapers and periodicals, to ensure that copy produced by a number of different journalists will all match the paper's 'style'. It can also be encouraged by the provision of module libraries which can be used in the development of software interfaces for different systems. We examine this approach in Chapters 4, 5 and 10.

1.5.4 Make Use of Accepted Guidelines for Interface Design

The physical interaction between user and workstation has much in common with any other interaction between man and machine. Thus, there are a large number of established results in ergonomics which can be readily applied to the design and organisation of a workstation. Similarly, the display of information is not unique to computer systems; many parallels can be drawn from graphic design with regard to the layout of information on the screen, the phrasing of messages, the use of highlighting features, and so on.

Designers should be aware of such guidelines, and be willing to draw on expertise from related fields when faced with difficult design decisions in these areas. In Chapters 6 and 7, we consider some of these guidelines in relation to the provision of user support facilities in the interface and in the layout of displays.

1.5.5 'Understand' the Task and the User

Not only must the designer be aware of the computer processing required to support the task, he must also appreciate the other activities required from the user in order to achieve the goal of the task. He must be aware of the characteristics of potential users of the system.

It is interesting to note the progress that has been made over the years in software development environments — the man–computer interfaces of programmers. By comparison, the interfaces of many packages produced by programmers using such environments are very primitive; one might speculate on the improvements which would result if programmers had to operate the software they produce day in and day out as their users have to!

1.5.6 Involve the Users

The exhortation to 'understand' the task and the user is one that is easier given than complied with. A systems analyst or designer cannot be expected to be intimately acquainted with all the application areas which he will encounter, nor to have a deep understanding of the psychological needs of all potential users.

There are guidelines which can be followed and which are described in any systems analysis text. Typically, these involve the analyst drawing the required information from prospective users by judicious questioning. One useful technique for deciding what questions are judicious is for the analyst/designer to imagine himself in the role of the user operating the system.

However, the only way that the acceptability of an interface can be assessed is by a user actually interacting with it in his normal working environment. It is unreasonable to expect a user to judge an output by examining patterns of Xs and 9s on the pieces of squared paper which, in many system specifications, represent screen layouts. Similarly, the implications of an input cannot be judged by reading a narrative — the user must press real keys in response to actual messages on the screen.

This requirement runs contrary to the traditional view of software development as a linear process with discrete stages:

$$\text{Analysis} \longrightarrow \text{Design} \longrightarrow \text{Construction} \longrightarrow \text{Implementation}$$

An iterative approach is required, in which prototype interfaces are developed, tried by the user, and modified in the light of his reactions until an acceptable product is produced. This implies a construction approach which permits rapid changes. Software techniques which facilitate this are described in Chapter 11.

1.5.7. Incorporate Adaptation Within the Interface

Whilst general guidelines can provide a basis for the design and implementation of the interface, they can never fit an individual user's requirements; design for the average is a lowest common denominator approach. Similarly, involvement of users in the development process cannot guarantee continuing acceptability; even if task requirements remain fairly constant, the needs of a user, or even the users themselves, will change.

A truly successful interface, as in the car and computer games examples, must be capable of being tailored to the needs of different users, and to the same user over a period of time. The problem of adaptation in man–computer interfaces has been a major area of research in recent years; some aspects of this are outlined in Chapter 12. Much remains to be done, but a number of techniques have emerged which permit some measure of adaption to be implemented fairly simply; these are considered in Chapter 9. Adjusting the driver's seat is hardly the height of automobile technology but is none the less a worthwhile feature!

1.6 Measuring the Success of the Design

Assuming that the strategy above is adopted, how will the designer know when he has achieved a suitable design? A number of criteria have been suggested for judging the success of the interface; these measure three basic aspects:

ease in learning and in remembering how to operate the system;
performance in accomplishing task goals by use of the system;
subjective satisfaction in operating the system.

It may be possible to set targets for the amount of *time it takes a given type of user to learn* enough about the system to achieve a specified level of proficiency. The criterion may also specify the type of training which will be provided to help him achieve this. Such a criterion might be phrased in the form: 'after two days of hands-on training with a self-instruction course, a user who is new to the system will be familiar with all the operating system commands necessary to maintain files in hierarchical directories on disk'.

The *retention of this learned information over time* is a related criterion which measures how much retraining is necessary to refresh this knowledge following periods when the system is not used.

Task performance may be measured in terms of *speed* or in terms of *accuracy*. Note that the speed is measured in terms of achieving task goals and not in terms of performing system actions. Thus, rather than a keystroke rate, the target for a data entry system might be expressed as: 'an invoice clerk will be capable of clearing 20 purchase invoices per hour, with a subsequent query rate of below 1%'.

Subjective satisfaction criteria attempt to reflect how the user views the system and his comfort when operating it. Targets for such criteria are hard to quantify but, for example, might be specified in terms of the extent of voluntary usage of an optional system. In a clerical system, such as invoice clearance, they might be specified in terms of changes in absenteeism or staff turnover rates.

Although all these criteria are appropriate to any application, those that are particularly significant to the success of an individual application will vary with the nature of the application. It would be reassuring to believe that accuracy and speed of performance were the major criteria in interfaces to systems such as air traffic control. Systems which are to be accessed by the general public must require no training before use since there is no opportunity to provide such training. Users must feel as comfortable using a system like electronic mail as they do with the alternatives; otherwise they will resort to these alternatives.

Establishing targets for the criteria is only the first of the difficulties; the designer must be able to measure the system's actual performance against the targets. A number of techniques have been used for these experiments. Systems may automatically maintain transcripts of particular interactions, or log the times taken to complete different task activities, or the number and nature of errors. Users may be interviewed or asked to complete questionnaires in order to determine their subjective satisfaction. Usage of the system may be observed or videotaped for subsequent analysis.

With all these techniques, it is difficult both to be sure that you are measuring the correct thing, and that any variations you observe are attributable to the system rather than to some external factor; the statistical methods, which are often used, make rather stringent assumptions about the nature of the sample and about how the measurements are made. The design of questions which will elicit an accurate and precise response, either in an interview or on a questionnaire, is notoriously difficult. People can alter their behaviour dramatically when they know that they are being observed or 'tested'.

These problems have faced researchers in other fields for many years and the literature contains numerous descriptions of experiments which attempt to measure these factors, both for man–computer interfaces and in other areas. We will not be concerned with them further in this book, but will concentrate on software design techniques which facilitate modification of the interface, both to permit experimentation and to reflect the results of such experiments.

1.7 Summary

The man–computer interface encompasses those aspects of a computer system which a user experiences directly.

It is a significant factor in the success of the computer system since the ergonomics (both physical and psychological) of the interface have a major impact on a user's performance.

To minimise stress, the system must match both the user's physical processes and his mental model of the task; this requirement is complicated by the variety of users which most systems must support and by the fact that an individual user's requirement will change with usage of the system.

There is a strategy for design of the interface which can produce systems which are usable by humans.

It is not the aim of this book to provide a detailed recipe for the design and implementation of the ideal user interface; no such panacea exists. Interface design, like all design processes, requires flair as well as formulae. The aim is to describe techniques which have proved themselves successful in practice (and some which have not), and to provide the reader with an appreciation of the factors which should be considered during the design and implementation of the interface of a computer system if some common pitfalls are to be avoided.

Discussion Exercises

Read Appendix A which describes a commercial computer system, 'Mailsale', a telephone sales system for a mail order company.

D1.   Outline the 'tasks' which must be carried by a clerk operating the system. You may find it useful to imagine yourself in the role of a clerk and follow through an imaginary interaction with an agent from when an incoming call is received until the call is terminated.

D2.   What conclusions can you draw from the specification about the characteristics of a typical user? What are the requirements suggested by the tasks above — e.g. is keyboard skill a prime requirement? Will the system need to cater for untrained operators?

D3.   In the light of your answers to 1 and 2 above, what aspects of physical and psychological ergonomics will be particularly significant in reducing stress on a user in this application?

Further Reading

Bailey R.W. (1982) *Human Performance Engineering: A Guide for Systems Designers* (chapters 6–10) Prentice Hall.

Damodoran L.and Eason K. (1981)'Design Procedures for User Involvement and User Support', in Alty J.L. and Coombs M.J. (Ed) *Computing Skills and the User Interface* Academic Press.

Gaines B.R. (1984) 'From Ergonomics to the Fifth Generation: 30 years of Human–computer Interaction', *INTERACT84*.

Gould J.D. and Lewis C. (1985) 'Designing for Usability: Key Principles and What Designers Think', *Comm.ACM*, **28** 3.

Keen P. (1981) 'Information Systems and Organisational Change', *Comm.ACM*, **24**, 1.

Nickerson R.S. (1981) 'Why Interactive Systems are Sometimes Not Used by People who Might Benefit From Them', *Int.J. Man–Machine Studies*, **15**, 4.

Potosonak K.M. and Koffler R.P. (1986). 'Testing for Usability', *AFIPS*, **55**.

Thomson N. (1984) 'Human Memory: Different Stores with Different Characteristics'; Thompson P. 'Visual Perception: An Intelligent System with Limited Bandwidth'; both in Monk A. (Ed) *Fundamentals of Human–Computer Interaction*, Academic Press.

Chapter 2

The constituents of the man–computer interface

2.1 What Does the Interface Comprise?

The design strategy proposed in the previous chapter exhorts the designer to treat the man–computer interface as a distinct component of the system. To do this, the designer must be able to recognise those elements of the system which make up the interface.

Consider a trivial computing exercise — calculating the mean of a set of numbers; no programmer should have any difficulty in writing a program to do this. Clearly there is little point in developing a routine which will operate only for a fixed set of numbers. A general routine is required which will work for any set of numbers supplied as a parameter. One possible approach is to define a function, *mean*, as in Fig. 2.1; there are obviously other approaches.

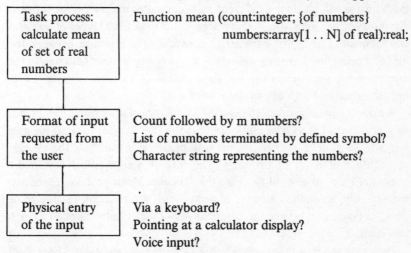

Task process: calculate mean of set of real numbers	Function mean (count:integer; {of numbers} numbers:array[1 . . N] of real):real;
Format of input requested from the user	Count followed by m numbers? List of numbers terminated by defined symbol? Character string representing the numbers?
Physical entry of the input	Via a keyboard? Pointing at a calculator display? Voice input?

Fig. 2.1.

How will the user of a system which incorporates this routine specify the necessary input values? Hopefully, no one would suggest that the user should be required to count the number of items first so that the input will directly satisfy the format of the parameter list of the function! A far better approach

17

would be for the user simply to enter the numbers as a list, and use some special terminator to indicate the end of the list. This can be converted by the system to the format required by the function.

Should the input values be defined as of type real? If so, how will the terminator be specified? A moment's thought should suffice to identify the problems in doing this. What character can be used as the terminator since anything which satisfies type real will be treated merely as another number in the list? What happens if the user mistypes and hits a non-numeral key? With a language like PASCAL, the program will crash. This suggests that any program which calls *mean* should request the input as a character string and convert it to real only when it has been validated.

How will the user physically enter the character string? The obvious answer is by typing it through a keyboard. There are, however, many alternative methods. The system could draw a calculator pad on the screen, with the user 'pressing' the relevant 'keys' via a pointing device. The user could speak the digits into a microphone attached to a speech analysis chip, and so forth.

Thus the same computer *process* (the sequence of operations represented by the function *mean*) can be invoked in a variety of formats and via a variety of input and output mechanisms. Each combination of formats and mechanisms will produce a different man–computer interface — a different direct experience for a user — and will be suited to different types of user and environment. The list of parameters constitute the interface between the function mean and any program calling it. Any programmer who knows the format of the parameters can use the function (with no knowledge of its internal structure) with any of these interfaces.

We use the term 'process' to describe a sequence of operations carried out by a processor. Let us now introduce the term *task* to refer to what the user wants to be done. For example, the task might be to calculate the average profitability of a set of products. The task is accomplished within the computer by a process, in this case the CalculateMean process. There are, theoretically, an endless number of tasks which a user might require to be done; in practice, most systems comprise only a very limited number of such processes.

Each task will be accomplished by one or more task processes. There is not a one-to-one correspondence between tasks and processes. One process might be used by several tasks; one task may involve several processes. In this book we are not concerned with the details of these processes — we simply treat them as black boxes. In general, we will refer to these processes as *task processes*.

The man–computer interface provides the communication channel between the human user and these task processes. It enables the user to specify which tasks are to be activated, to supply data values upon which they can act, and to receive the results of these actions. From a software viewpoint, the interface comprises two distinct components — a set of input/output processes and a dialogue process. This general structure is illustrated in Fig. 2.2.

The user of a computer system interacts with the interface — he sends input to it, and receives output from it. Behind the scenes are the 'task processes' which are invoked by the interface at appropriate times. Hence, from a user's viewpoint, the interface appears to be in the foreground, and the 'task processes' appear to be in the background. For this reason, many authors refer to task processes as *background tasks*.

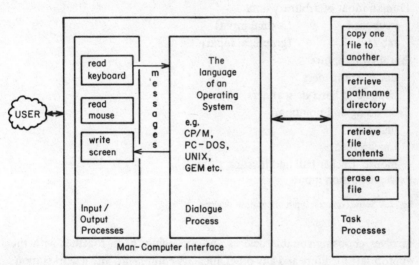

Fig. 2.2. Constituents of the man–computer interface (as exemplified by an operating system interface).

2.2 Input/Output Processes

The *input/output processes* are concerned with receiving raw input from, and presenting raw output to, the user via various physical devices. The growth of interactive computing has been accompanied by the development of numerous input and output devices through which the user can interact directly, more or less, with a computer. Figure 2.3 lists some of the more common devices. In most applications the design of the physical interface

Output device types
Transient text and graphics
   monochrome and colour CRT screens
Hardcopy
   character printers (text output)
   laser printers   (text and graphical output)
   plotters   (graphical output)
Aural output
   speech synthesisers (voice output)
   tone generators   ('music' output)
Photographic output
   interactive video
Input device types
Human input of arbitrary data
   keyboard   (textual input)
   tablet   (graphical input)
Automatic capture
   document readers
   badge and barcode scanners
Positioning and pointing
   lightpen
   touchscreen
   mouse, tracker ball and joystick
Voice and vision input

Fig. 2.3. Some common input and output devices.

involves choosing suitable devices and arranging them, together with the appropriate furniture and any other ancillary equipment, into a workstation.

The choice of devices is governed by:

The nature and format of the information to be exchanged. Some applications require only a limited range of text characters, others require a high resolution graphics facility. Some require the user to supply a set of arbitrary values, others merely selection from a small set of possible values.

The volume of input and output. High volumes of input suggest an indirect input mechanism such as automatic data capture.

The constraints of the user and his environment. A standard keyboard has limited success in an oily workshop, or where a user's hands are constrained by disability, or the requirements of auxiliary tasks.

The constraints of other hardware and software with which the system must operate.

We will not describe the mechanical operation of the various devices in detail; the reader is referred to a text on the operation of computer peripherals for such a description. Nor will we discuss in detail the ergonomic criteria which should govern the choice between particular examples of a device type for a particular type of user. Although there are still glaring (literally) examples of poor ergonomic design on the market, the necessary criteria are being recognised more and more by manufacturers, and incorporated into their equipment. Often, however, the good work of the manufacturer is undone by installing the equipment on any old table and chair which happen to be available, or by giving inadequate thought to arranging the equipment on the worktop or within a room.

Each device will have its own input or output process whose purpose is to take the input entered by the user (e.g. depressing the 5 key on the keyboard) and to transform it into an internal representation which the 'dialogue process' can use (e.g. 0011 0101, the bit pattern of ASCII 5). If the user opted to use a 'speech input unit' to enter his data, then the sound produced by speaking 'five' would be transformed by the 'speech input unit' process to the same internal representation in memory. This is illustrated in Fig. 2.4.

Obviously the 'keyboard' process and the 'speech input unit' process are different, each catering for its own physical device. By separating the physical I/O processing from the dialogue processing, the input or the output device can be changed without the need to change the dialogue process, simply by adopting a different input/output process.

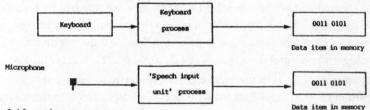

Fig. 2.4 Input/output processes.

2.3 The Dialogue Process

A dictionary defines a *conversation* as an 'exchange of information governed by agreed conventions which takes place between two or more persons via the spoken word'.

The conventions are important. The participants must understand the same language. A conversation cannot take place between an Englishman and a Frenchman if neither understands the other's language (unless they employ an interpreter). It is also a convention of conversation that people do not speak at the same time. One person speaks, and the others listen. When the speaker has finished, then one of the others will become the speaker. The information which emanates from the new speaker is usually related to the information provided by the previous speaker. The items of information exchanged during a conversation are not just sequences of unrelated utterances. For example:

Jones: I'm sorry I'm late. I took my car to the garage this morning to be repaired, and they delayed me.
Smith: Which garage do you use?
Jones: Autorepairs Unlimited.
Smith: I've used them before. They are quite expensive, but do a good job.

Problems can arise when the accepted conventions are not followed. The most professional of interviewers can be embarrassed by an interviewee who gives very terse answers, or replies only after an inordinately long pause. Clients are frequently irritated by bureaucrats who expect everyone to appreciate the significance of P763/97 or other jargon. Most customers are offended by the salesman who is patronisingly familiar.

A *man–computer dialogue* can be defined as an exchange of information governed by agreed conventions which takes place between a computer-based system and its users via an interactive terminal.

The *dialogue process* is the mechanism by which this exchange of 'information' is effected and can be considered as the framework which holds together all the individual 'task processes' making up the system. The input/output processes support communication at the 'grunt' level; it is the responsibility of the dialogue to interpret the 'grunts'. The dialogue process is concerned with:

Determining what task the user requires the system to carry out.
Obtaining logical input data from the user, and depositing it in the correct format in the 'input data items' of the relevant task process.
Invoking the task process.
On completion of the task process, returning the logical results from the task process to the user in the appropriate format.

The exchange of information between a person and an interactive computer system is in many ways similar to the exchange of information which occurs in normal conversation. For this reason, the adjective 'conversational' is often used to describe such an exchange. The words 'dialogue' and 'conversation' are synonymous, but 'dialogue' is used more often than 'conversation' in the computing context. We will follow this trend and use 'dialogue' for the remainder of the book.

The conventions are equally important. It was explained in Chapter 1 that the conventions must be chosen to suit the human's rather than the computer's ease of processing. If they are not, similar problems to those that occur in human–human conversations will arise; in fact, each of the problems we used as illustrations earlier in this section have a precise counterpart in man–computer dialogues.

Workstation design is concerned with maximising the physical comfort of the user by ensuring that the physical processes required to interact with the system are convergent with the human's physical capabilities. Dialogue design is concerned with maximising the psychological comfort of the user by ensuring that the dialogue style is convergent with the human's needs and expectations. By separating the dialogue processing from the task processing, the same task processes (e.g. add a record to a linked list file) can fulfil very different user tasks (e.g. record a customer's order, or update a bank account) simply by being used with different dialogues.

2.4 Messages

A dialogue involves an exchange of information between the participants. This information is conveyed in the form of messages and, in any dialogue, these messages can be classified into several different types (see Fig. 2.5). Consider the following fictitious telephone dialogue between a customer and a salesman.

Salesman:	Good morning. Autobits Ltd.	(*Status*)
	Can I help you?	(*Prompt*)
Customer:	I'd like to know the price of some parts	
	for a '73 Mud Buggy, please.	(*Input control*)
Salesman:	Which part?	(*Prompt*)
Customer:	A castellated widget, part number P12347.	(*Input data*)
Salesman:	I'm afraid that's not a current Mud Buggy	
	part number. They all start Q7…	(*Error message*)
	(Pause, implying what part.)	(*Prompt*)
Customer:	What parts are there in the rear sprudgeon	
	assembly?	(*Input control*)
Salesman:	Well, there's the ………………………	
	…………………………	(*Help message*)

Customer: It must be the crenellated sprodget Q7914.   (*Input data*)
Salesman: Just checking the price for you.   (*Status*)
            They're £13.95 for the pair.   (*Output data*)
            Anything else?   (*Prompt*)

Thus, a message exchanged in a dialogue between humans may fulfil any of several possible functions which are required to maintain the interaction. These same functions are required to maintain an interaction between a user and a computer system, and a similar classification of message types is possible.

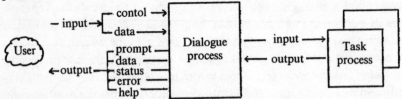

Fig. 2.5. Classification of messages according to function.

A *prompt* is a message output by the system to indicate that an input is required from the user. In human dialogues, a prompt may be anything from a raised eyebrow to a recited list of possible choices and, as we shall see, a similar variety of formats exists in man–computer dialogues.

The user's reply to the prompt may invoke a particular task process (looking up a price list) or activity by the dialogue process (such as the provision of assistance in responding to the prompt) or it may supply data values to a task process. For example, the input message may select a task which displays the contents of a file, or it may specify the name of the file which is to be displayed. We will call the first type *input control messages* since they control the way in which the dialogue proceeds, and the second type we will call *input data messages*. It is also possible to have a compound message which, in a single input, both selects the required task process and supplies the relevant data values.

It is usually necessary for the dialogue process to check that the input from a user represents a valid message at that point in the dialogue. The nature of the check will vary with the format of the input message, but might typically include matching the contents of an input control message against a list of possible task processes, or the contents of an input data message against a range of possible data formats. In many cases, the amount of checking which can be carried out by the dialogue process is limited. For example, if the name of a file is input, the dialogue processor can check that the input conforms to the required format, but a task process would have to be executed to determine whether such a file exists. An *error message* is an indication from the dialogue process that it is unable to continue because it, or the requested task process, cannot process the user's input message.

The dialogue process acts as a go-between for the user and the various task processes in the system available to that user. Thus, the user's input messages to the dialogue process will frequently result in corresponding input messages, possibly in a standardised format, from the dialogue process to a task process. The task process will respond to (or at least acknowledge) these input messages by sending output messages to the dialogue process. The dialogue process in turn conveys these, in a suitable format, to the user as either output data or as output status messages.

Output data messages contain data values returned by the task process. For example, if the user has sent input messages to request a display of the contents of a file, he would expect to receive one or more output data messages showing the contents of that file. The task process supplies the output data in a standard form which the dialogue process converts to a suitable format for presentation to the user.

Status messages are acknowledgements from the system to the user that something has happened, or is happening. For example, if the user is asked to input a coded data value, the system may respond with a confirmation of the data item. When you dial a telephone number, you expect the answering party to quote their name or number; if the person at the other end just says 'hello', you may experience some anxiety as to whether you have dialled correctly. Similar confirmation is required if a user inputs a coded identifier such as a part number. The system may confirm that a particular task process has been completed (e.g. sales ledger updated) or, where there is going to be a long delay before the system can respond with the output data, it may provide a message confirming that it is still active ('just checking the price for you').

The final type of output message arises in situations where the user is unable to respond to the system's request for input, either because he does not understand the prompt or because he has forgotten precisely what input message is required. In response to a particular input control message, the dialogue process may output a *help message* to provide further information on what is required, and why.

We will look further at the requirements of error and help messages in Chapter 6; data and status messages are covered in Chapters 7 and 8. For the

remainder of this chapter, we will consider the implications of different forms
of input message and of prompts.

2.5 Input Messages

A dialogue may be categorised by the format of its input messages and by the
flexibility allowed the user as to when a particular input message must be
supplied. An input message may:

select a dialogue process activity, such as help;

select a particular task process;

supply data values for a task process.

A *system-driven* dialogue is one in which the dialogue process strictly
controls when a particular task process can be selected or data value supplied.
It does this by leading the user through the various facilities by means of
explicit prompts which determine what information is to be supplied at each
point. The sample dialogue in the previous section is an example of a system-
driven dialogue, with the salesman performing the role of the system.

A *user-driven* dialogue is one in which the user takes the initiative and
instructs the system directly on the task to be undertaken at each point.
Typically, the user will do this by means of a compound input message which,
in a single input, both selects the task and supplies the necessary data values.
The majority of operating systems have user-driven dialogues.

Further to illustrate the difference between the two approaches, consider
the interaction between a customer (user) and a shopkeeper (system) in the
purchase of some apples. A system-driven dialogue would proceed along the
lines:

shopkeeper : What would you like?

  customer : Some apples, please.

shopkeeper : Granny Smith? Golden Delicious? Sturmers?

  customer : Sturmers.

shopkeeper : How many?

and so on. By contrast, in a user-driven dialogue, the customer would walk
into the shop with an instruction such as:

2lb of Sturmers, please

to which the shopkeeper would respond.

A system-driven dialogue is more supportive since it guides the user's
progress; by virtue of this, it is also more restrictive than a user-driven
dialogue. It also implies that the background task processes are structured,

typically into a hierarchy, and that the dialogue will always proceed by following this structure.

The format in which the user can supply the input messages might be called the dialogue *grammar*. There are a number of different possibilities:

Codes
Program-like keyword strings
Limited English
Natural English

Codes provide a concise way of identifying particular data items or particuar task processes, and are an intrinsic part of most computer systems. For example, 153H might be the code for customer J.H.Smith. At its most basic, the input process may be coded into the simple operation of pointing at a specific area on the screen. The input may be coded onto function keys, or the user may be required to key in a particular mnemonic identifier. Codes can be used for input control messages in either system- or user-driven dialogues and, by reducing the volume of input, can increase the speed of the interaction and reduce the number of errors occurring during input.

In a *program-like* grammar, the user communicates with the system in a form which resembles the source statements of a high level programming language. Such statements provide a means of generating compound input messages which permit both task selection and supplying data values in a single input. It is commonly used in user-driven dialogues such as operating systems and report selection in database packages. A typical example is an operating system command of the form

COPY destination = source

Both the syntax and the semantics are very restricted; no variations in the above statement are permitted, except perhaps for the inclusion of some additional spaces. Such a grammar can accommodate a large number of functions, and can provide a powerful interface for an experienced user. However, it imposes a high memory load since the user must remember the precise syntax and phrasing. Program-like grammmars also tend to be unnatural, a tendency often exaggerated by the phrasing chosen. Those who are not familiar with the UNIX operating system might not immediately associate the input:

mv myfile1 myfile2

with a request to rename a file.

Limited English (or French or German) is the most commonly used grammar with computer-driven dialogues, although it can be implemented so as to mimic user-driven dialogues, as we shall see later. It is 'limited' in the sense that only a small range of 'words' are recognised, and that an input message consists of a very small number of words (typically one) at any point (for example, the input of the word 'sales' to select an update of the Sales Ledger). Since these 'words' can be identifiers of particular tasks or data values (words can be numerics) it can be used for both input control and input data messages.

The aim of *Natural language* is to allow the user to communicate with the system as though it were another human. The system would respond to any phrasing and to any syntax which a human could reasonably be expected to understand. It differs from Limited English not only in the size of the subset of 'words' permitted but also in how those words can be combined in an input message. Supporters of this approach claim that it is the only way of ensuring a dialogue which is both natural and flexible. Although there are several impressive attempts to implement such grammars, particularly for database queries, a number of reservations exist about both the practicality and the desirability of such an approach. These are discussed in Chapter 12.

2.6 Validating the Input

Regardless of the format in which they are entered, all input messages represent an explicit or implicit selection from a (possibly infinite) set of acceptable responses. In some cases, particularly for input control messages, the set of possible responses is small enough to be explicitly stated. For example, the set of operations allowed by an operating system might be as shown in Fig. 2.6.

DATE : to set the current date
DIR   : to list the directory
ERA   : to erase a file or files from the disk
PIP   : to copy files
REN   : to rename a file
STAT : to show the usage of the disk space
TIME : to set the current time
TYPE : to list a source file on the screen

Fig. 2.6. The operations permitted by an operating system.

In such cases, validation of the input involves matching the user's input message against the list of possible task names. We can define the list of possible responses as an array of target strings. The input string is matched against these target strings by a function such as that illustrated in Fig. 2.7.

```
const MaxTargets      = 10;
type  TargetListType  = array[1..MaxTargets] of string;
var   NumberOfTargets : integer;
      TargetList      : TargetListType;

function MatchString(subject:string;
                     TargetList:TargetListType;
                     NumberOfTargets:integer):integer;
var k,match : integer;
begin
match:=0;
k:=1;
while (k<=NumberOfTargets) and (match=0) do
   if TargetList[k]=subject then match:=k
                            else k:=k+1;
MatchString:=match;
end; {MatchString}
```

Fig. 2.7. Matching against an explicit list.

A simplistic implementation of selection from the options illustrated in Fig. 2.6 might be as follows:

```
var NumberOfTargets : integer;
    TargetList      : TargetListType;
    reply           : string;
    choice          : integer;
    ....................................
    ....................................

begin
NumberOfTargets:=8;
TargetList[1]:= 'DATE';      TargetList[2]:= 'DIR';
TargetList[3]:= 'ERA';       TargetList[4]:= 'PIP';
TargetList[5]:= 'REN';       TargetList[6]:= 'STAT';
TargetList[7]:= 'TIME';      TargetList[8]:= 'TYPE';
choice:=0;

repeat
   write('option : ');
   readln(reply);
   choice:=MatchString(reply,TargetList,NumberOfTargets);
   if choice=0 then writeln('unrecognised option ',reply);
until choice<>0;
case choice of
   1: {DATE processing}
   2: {DIR  processing}
      ................
   8: {TYPE processing}
end; {case}
end;
```

We shall see later that this simplistic approach can be considerably improved to provide a more general and flexible matching mechanism; the reader may well be able to suggest a number of improvements. However it serves for the present to illustrate the basic structure of any dialogue input process, i.e.

```
repeat
    issue a request for input
    receive an input string
    validate the input
until valid input
take action on input
```

An input control message will typically cause a branch in the dialogue process; for example, an input of 'DATE' may cause the dialogue process to request the current date whereas an input of 'STAT' may request the user to supply a valid disk drive.

The range of values may be too extensive for an explicit list to be practical, especially for an input data message which specifies the value of a data item such as a date or the name of a file. All possible dates and filenames could be listed but it would be much more sensible to specify the format to which the input had to conform. For example:

dd/mm/yy   for a date with day, month and year defined as 2 digits, and separated by slash characters.

{<drive>:} <name> {.<ext>} for a filename comprising
an optional single letter drive followed by a colon;
a name of up to 8 characters;
an optional extension of up to 3 characters preceded by a period.

In such cases the input checking that can be carried out by the dialogue process consists of matching the input message against the template provided by the format specification. It is relatively easy to develop a procedure which will validate an input string against a given template. To generalise this to validate a string against any supplied template is very much more difficult.

Note also that such a check does not ensure that the input is correct, only that it is *feasible*. For example, if the input consisted of an identifier for a particular part, the dialogue could confirm that the input denoted a possible Part Identifier; whether such a part actually *existed* would presumably require a task process to look up a Parts File to determine whether there was a record with that identifier. Similarly, it may be necessary for a background task to check that a particular data value is *consistent* with other data values which may have been supplied.

Finally, the input may be totally arbitrary. For example, the input of a description such as the name of a part is not susceptible to any check other than perhaps on length; the input data value may contain any combination of characters. This is one obvious reason for the use of codes rather than names as identifiers of data items.

In later chapters, we will return to the problem of matching the user's input against the set of acceptable inputs. For the present, we assume that such a matching procedure exists.

2.7 Prompts

There are a number of ways in which a human can indicate that he is ' expecting a message from another participant in a dialogue. Similarly, there are a number of possible formats for displaying prompts in man–computer dialogues.

The most elaborate format is the *menu* which, as well as indicating that an input message is expected, also explicitly lists what inputs are allowed. An example is shown in Fig. 2.8.

```
DATE  : to set the current date
DIR   : to list a directory
ERA   : to erase a file or files from disk
PIP   : to copy one file onto another
REN   : to rename a file
STAT  : to show the usage of disk space
TIME  : to set the current time
TYPE  : to list the contents of a character file

option?
```

Fig. 2.8. An example of a menu.

The menu need not be displayed as a text message. Pictorial representations (*icons*) of the various options available could be displayed with the user making his selection by 'pointing' at the one required.

A menu format is only possible where the range of valid inputs is small enough to be listed explicitly; it is a common mechanism for requesting the input of control messages. It can be very useful in guiding an inexperienced user through the system. On the other hand, it can be very tedious for a user already familiar with the possibilities.

The system can indicate what type of input is required without explicitly listing all the possibilities, by means of a *question*. The prompt can also include an indication of the format the input message must take. For example,

Invoice Date (dd/mm/yy):

Where a series of data values are required for a particular task, the prompt may be displayed as a *form* which the user completes. An example is shown in Fig. 2.9.

Invoice number	[ ]
Invoice date	[/ /]
Supplier code	[ ]
Invoice total	[.]
VAT amount	[.]

Fig. 2.9. An example of a form.

Finally, there is the computer equivalent of the non-committal 'Yes, can I help you?' This simply indicates that the system is expecting input without in any way indicating the possible input messages which can be entered. The system always displays the same prompt, such as:

A>   or   ?

Such an output message is called a *command* prompt. Clearly the user must be familiar with what input messages are acceptable at that point, and the mechanism is therefore appropriate to user-driven dialogues.

Traditionally, the various prompt formats have been used to subdivide the system-driven and user-driven dialogues, as shown in Fig. 2.10.

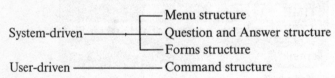

System-driven ──────── ┬── Menu structure
                       ├── Question and Answer structure
                       └── Forms structure
User-driven ────────────── Command structure

Fig. 2.10. User-driven and system-driven dialogues.

2.8 Summary

The man–computer interface comprises two basic constituents:

• A dialogue process which provides the framework to bind the background tasks into a coherent system.

• A set of input/output processes which provide for physical communication between the user and the dialogue process.

Just as in human–human communication the dialogue must observe certain conventions. Dialogue design is concerned with ensuring the convergence of these conventions with human psychological needs and expectations.

Information is exchanged between the human and the dialogue process by messages. A number of functions must be fulfilled by these messages in order to sustain the dialogue.

Dialogues may be classified in terms of the format of input messages supported (the grammar) and into system-driven and user-driven styles. These broad classifications may be further subdivided by the format of the prompts by which input is requested.

Regardless of the dialogue grammar or style, the basic make-up of each input stage in the dialogue process consists of a loop:

an explicit or implicit request for input
receipt of input via a physical input process
validation of the input

which is repeated until an acceptable input is received. If the request is for an input control message, the stage to which the dialogue process next progresses will be dependent on the control which is input.

In Chapter 4, we discuss some general guidelines for assessing a man–computer dialogue and examine how each of these dialogue styles measures up to the criteria which these guidelines suggest. First, however, we examine the input and output processes which provide the basic building blocks from which all logical dialogue styles are constructed.

Discussion Exercises

D1   Reread the description of the *Mailsale* system in Appendix A. In Chapter 1, you were asked to outline the 'tasks' which must be carried out by a clerk operating the system. Outline the computer 'task processes' which are necessary to support these tasks.

What type of dialogue grammar and style do you consider would be appropriate for the task of entering a customer order? Give reasons for your choice.

D2   Investigate different pieces of software to see examples of the types of man–computer interface which have been implemented. A demonstration pack is often supplied with commercially available software. Ideally the software should include examples of different types of:

- operating systems;
- line-based editors of the type typically provided as operating system utilities;
- screen-based editors, i.e. those in which you indicate changes in the current position by moving the cursor rather than by quoting a line number;
- word processing packages; these typically provide additional facilities to simple text editing;
- packages for typical commercial transaction processing such as accounting and order processing;
- information retrieval packages which enable users to examine the content of databases either in a fixed format, such as viewdata systems, or by formulating their own queries;
- packages aimed at assisting planning and forecasting such as spreadsheet and outlining systems;
- desktop accessory packages which provide utilities such as a notepad, telephone directory, clock, calculator, etc;
- window-based operating environments.

Identify, for each example, the structure of the dialogue and the type of grammar which it supports. Which ones do you find comfortable and easy to use? Why?

D3   Suggest a suitable dialogue structure for the following applications, giving reasons for your choice.

(a) The entry of details of a holiday reservation by a clerk in a travel agents.

(b) Access to a Prestel database by the general public for everyday information such as news, weather, sports results, and so on.

(c) Selection by a clerk in an estate agents of a list of houses meeting a client's requirements from a database of properties for sale. The properties are accessed by six fields: type of house, age of house, number of bedrooms, size of garden, area, and price range.

(d) Access by users of a local network who can connect to or disconnect from any other workstation, or list the status of the connection.

Programming Exercises

P1.   A customer code is defined as a array of 5 characters. The first 4 characters are numeric digits padded with leading zeros and the fifth is an alphabetic check digit; for example, 1234J or 0007B. Implement a procedure which will accept the input of a customer code without the need for the user to enter leading zeros, and return the full 5 character code padded as necessary.

P2.   Implement a function

   function ValidDate (date:string;format:DateType): boolean;

which will return true or false depending on whether <date> denotes a valid date between January 1,1985 and December 31,1995 for the <format> as follows:

DateType = (Julian,US,Alpha);
where   Julian is of the form dd/mm/yy
        US   is of the form mm/dd/yy
and   Alpha is of the form dd mmm yy

   Amend your function so that it returns an integer value corresponding to:

   yymmdd if the string denoted a valid date
   zero otherwise

P3.   Figure 2.1 uses the calculation of the mean of a set of numbers to illustrate how the processing associated with a task and that associated with the interface can be separated. Develop a program, Average, which enables a user to enter a set of integer numbers and to calculate either the mean, or the median or the mode of this set.

   The procedures which calculate each of these averages should be separate from any procedures for reading the input of the numbers or writing the result and should communicate with them via parameter lists. Assume that there will not be more than 100 numbers in the set.

P4.   The specification of the procedure Mean in Figure 2.1 requires a maximum number of input numbers to be defined; it is possible to respecify mean such that it is unnecessary to define this maximum.

   Amend your solution to question P3 so that the program will calculate the mean of an unlimited number of input numbers whilst preserving the separation between the procedure which calculates the mean and those which read the input and write the output.

Further Reading

Berzins V. *et al.* (1986) 'Abstraction-Based Software Development', *Comm.ACM*, **29**, 5.

Coutaz J. (1985) 'Abstractions for User Interface Design', *IEEE Computer*, **18**, 9.

Edmonds E.A. (1982) 'The Man–Computer Interface: a Note on Concepts and Design', *Int.J.Man–Machine Studies*, **16**, 3.

Gaines B.R. and Shaw M.L. (1984) *The Art of Computer Conversation*, Prentice Hall.

Hebditch D. (1979) in Shackel B. (Ed) *Man Computer Communication*, vol 2, Infotech.

Wilkinson B. and Horrocks D. (1980) *Computer Peripherals*, Hodder & Stoughton.

Chapter 3

Input/output processes

3.1 Introduction

In Chapter 2, the messages exchanged between a user and the system were classified in terms of the functions they performed within the dialogue. In this chapter, we concentrate on how the nature of the information exchanged impinges on software design. For this purpose we classify the basic input/output processes which support these message functions into the categories of Fig. 3.1.

Output of a text message
    at the current postition on the device
    at a particular position on the device
    with particular format attributes
Input of a text message
    using standard high level input routines
    character-by-character
    where 'special characters' are involved
Input of a Point and Pick message
    relative pointing to scroll round a list
    absolute pointing anywhere on the device
Output of a graphical message
Input of a graphical message

Fig. 3.1. A classification of common input and output processes.

A *text message* is defined as a string of *characters*; these characters may be upper or lower case alphabetics, numerals, or even the basic graphics characters (such as playing card suit symbols) available as alternate character sets on many microcomputers. A *graphical message* is defined as a message which cannot be represented as a string of characters; typically it must be described at the 'bit' rather than at the 'character' level. *Point and pick* is a special case of an input message for selecting from a set of possible options; as we shall see, it has characteristics which deserve individual treatment.

The simple dialogue examples in Chapter 2 utilise the standard PASCAL input and output procedures for the input/output processes. In this chapter

37

we consider other features which are available to enhance these processes. These features have typically been considered in terms of the processing required to effect them on a particular device. However, we also saw in Chapter 2 that the dialogue process deals with logical entities and should be separated from the precise mechanics of a particular device. Therefore, whilst considering how the features can be effected, we will attempt to develop generalised 'abstractions' for the processes which the dialogue process can assume.

3.2 Output of a Text Message

3.2.1 Output of Text at the Current Position of the Device

My Message Displayed Here

Fig. 3.2.

An output text message, like that illustrated in Fig. 3.2, can be specified by defining:

> *what* is to be output, i.e. a string of characters identifying the content of the message;
> *where* it is to be output, i.e. the position on the output device;
> *how* it is to be output, i.e. a list of attributes, such as colour, which define how the content is to be formatted; we will assume that the attributes are constant for a given message.

We define an output message as an entity which is represented by a data structure of type:

```
OutputMessageType = record
                    content    : string;          {what}
                    slot       : SlotType;        {where}
                    attributes : AttributesType;  {how}
                    end;
```

Content is of type 'string' by virtue of our definition of a text message.

However, the definitions of SlotType and AttributesType require further consideration.

The most common input/output device in the early days of interactive computing was the *teletype*, which resembles a golfball typewriter. A teletype only provides the facility to output the message content at the current position of the device; the current position can be advanced to a new line by the output of suitable control characters. Most programming languages contain procedures for teletype operation.

The WRITE and WRITELN statements of PASCAL operate in this way; thus,

write ('write this without advancing to a new line')

displays the specified character string and leaves the output device positioned at the next character position and

writeln ('write this and skip to a new line')

displays the character string and positions the output device at the first character position on the next line.

The teletype has largely been superseded by the Visual Display Terminal (VDT) consisting of a monochrome or colour display and keyboard. Early VDTs operated merely as 'glass teletypes' with the same *line* scrolling mode. Nowadays, the vast majority provide *page* mode operation, in which the output can be considered a screen at a time rather than a line at a time; a message can be written at any position on the screen.

We will concentrate on output to a screen since it is the most common device; similar considerations apply for a printer. The basic approach is also appropriate for other output devices, such as a speech synthesiser, although the features will obviously differ.

3.2.2 Output of Text at a Particular Position on the Device

The text of an output message is displayed in a slot — a rectangular area on the device w character positions wide and h character positions high. There are three possible cases, as shown in Fig. 3.3. Thus, the Slot can be defined by a data structure of type

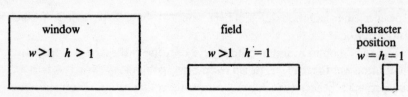

Fig. 3.3. Slots.

```
byte      = 0..255;
SlotType  = record
              row,col      : byte;   {starting position}
              width,height : byte;   {size}
            end;
```

The current (that is, the next available) output position on the screen is indicated by a *cursor* symbol — frequently a flashing block or underline character. The commonest way of causing a message to be output in a particular slot is to

• move the current position to the starting (row,col) of the slot;
• use the 'teletype' functions provided by the programming language to output the content, suitably justified, at the new position.

Some programming languages, such as the various BASIC dialects, provide facilities within the language itself for repositioning; others, including PASCAL, do not. However, most microcomputers, dumb VDTs and printers will reposition the cursor in response to the output of a specific string of characters.

The sequence may be a single ASCII character. Most devices will respond to the statement

write (chr(12))

by 'form feeding', i.e. skipping to a new page on a printer, or clearing the screen and positioning the cursor in the top left corner on a screen. Linefeed (ASCII character 10) and Carriage Return (ASCII character 13) are other examples of such special characters. Normally, a sequence of characters is needed to control positioning; since the first character is usually Escape (ASCII character 27), they are commonly called *Escape sequences*.

The precise sequence for a particular operation varies with the device. A standard has been produced — the ANSI terminal specification — to which many devices conform. It defines sequences for particular operations, including cursor positioning and clearing areas of the screen; a subset is illustrated in Fig. 3.4. (<ESC> is the ASCII character Escape and the notation <j> means that <j> should be replaced by the relevant value expressed as a character sequence. For example, <ESC> followed by the characters [15A will move the cursor up 15 lines.)

<ESC> [<n> A   move cursor up n lines
<ESC> [<n> B   move cursor down n lines
<ESC> [<n> C   move cursor right n columns
<ESC> [<n> D   move cursor left n columns
<ESC> [<m> ; <n> H   move cursor to column n of line m
<ESC> [1 K   erase from current position to end of line
<ESC> [2 K   erase all of current line

Fig. 3.4. Typical ANSI terminal Escape sequences.

Thus cursor positioning on a device which conforms to the ANSI standard can be accomplished by a procedure of the form:

```
procedure CursorTo(row,col:byte);
begin
write(chr(27),'[',row:1,';',col:1,'H');
end;
```

There is nothing magical about the Escape character. The operating system contains procedures which effect the repositioning and which are invoked in response to these strings. These procedures may also be invoked directly from the application software by suitable low level system calls. Most operating systems will provide the facilities of Fig. 3.5.

procedure CursorTo(row,col:byte)
    positions cursor to (row,col)
procedure CursorAt(var row,col:byte)
    returns the current cursor position (row,col)
procedure SwitchCursor(switch:OffOn)
    causes the cursor symbol to be hidden/displayed
function   TestCursor:OffOn
    test whether the cursor symbol hidden/displayed

Fig. 3.5. Cursor control procedures.

3.2.3 Output of Text with Particular Format Attributes

Most VDTs provide more display facilities than just the ability to output at any point on the screen. In particular, they often provide a range of *highlighting* features which can be used to enhance the text of a message. Common highlighting features include:

Colour. The text characters (or foreground) can be displayed in a different colour from the background. On some monochrome screens, a similar effect is produced with different shades of the screen's base colour. *Inverse video* is a special case of this feature where the background and foreground colours or shades are swapped.

Blinking. An area of the screen may be made to flash by displaying it alternately in normal and in inverse video. This is commonly used to highlight the cursor position.

Bold Intensity. The ability to support different contrast levels and make an area of foreground appear brighter than surrounding areas.

Highlighting facilities vary from device to device. Some provide only inverse video; others provide a wide range of colour tones and intensity levels. Several provide a number of different fonts (type size and face) for the text characters. In fact, the same device may provide a different range of features depending on the *mode* to which it has been initialised; for example, an IBM-PC may be set to display 40 or 80 columns, colour or monochrome and in various resolutions. In Chapter 6, we discuss guidelines on where and when highlighting features should be used. For the present, we will concentrate on how they are implemented.

In the general case, we may represent the video attributes associated with an output text message by a data structure of type

```
AttributesType = record
                    foreground  : colours;
                    background  : colours;
                    blink       : OffOn;
                    bold        : OffOn;
                    font        : TextStyles;
                    end;
where
  colours     = (black, blue, green . . . . . . . . . . . );
  OffOn       = (off,on);
  TextStyles  = (roman, . . . . . . . );
```

Highlighting facilities may often be invoked by means of escape sequences similar to those for positioning. The range of facilities, and the sequences which invoke them, should be included in the documentation for your particular device. For example, an IBM-PC Escape sequence may be used to switch inverse video on or off with a procedure of the form:

```
procedure inverse(switch:OffOn);
begin
if switch=on then write(chr(27),'[7m')
            else write(chr(27),'[0m');
end;
```

Once a feature has been 'switched on, it remains on until it is 'switched off'. Thus, to output a particular message in inverse at row 10, column 16 requires a sequence of statements of the form:

```
CursorTo(10,16);
inverse(on);
write('this message in inverse at (10,16)');
inverse(off);
```

How does the device know what highlighting features are in force when a particular character is to be displayed? In most microcomputers the screen is *memory-mapped*. For each position on the screen there is a corresponding area of memory which specifies what is to be displayed at that position and in what format; we will refer to this area as the *video map*. In a *character-mapped display*, the smallest addressable position on the screen is a complete character. On an IBM-PC, highlighting features are accommodated by reserving two bytes for each character position on the screen — the first, called the *attribute byte*, specifies how it is to be displayed and the second, called the *content byte*, specifies the character itself — as in Figure 3.6.

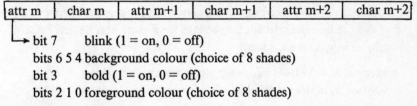

attr m	char m	attr m+1	char m+1	attr m+2	char m+2

bit 7   blink (1 = on, 0 = off)
bits 6 5 4 background colour (choice of 8 shades)
bit 3   bold (1 = on, 0 = off)
bits 2 1 0 foreground colour (choice of 8 shades)

Fig. 3.6. Character video map.

There are 3 bits for both background and foreground colour to correspond to the 3 phosphors (red, green, blue) from which the colours are produced. 'Black' is generated with all 3 bits set to off and 'white' with all 3 bits set to on.

In the example of Figure 3.6, a memory area of $2 \times 80 \times 25$ bytes (approximately 4K) is required for the video map of a standard 80 column by 25 line display. The organisation of the memory map may not correspond directly with the layout of the screen in the way that Fig. 3.6 suggests. Column 1 of row n+1 may not immediately follow column 80 of row n in the map. With a smaller video map, less features can be accommodated; with a much larger map, the system may maintain copies of several physical screens simultaneously or provide a large 'virtual' screen only part of which appears on the physical screen at any one time. We shall see in Chapter 10 that this feature of modern microcomputers can be used to provide an interface technique called *windowing*.

The interpretation of the Escape sequences which set attribute values is supported by routines in a microcomputer's operating systems which write directly into the video map (and hence to the screen). Often system calls are provided which can be invoked directly from the application software; these may provide the programmer with access to more highlighting features than are available with the Escape sequences. For example,

PutChar(content,attribute:byte)

might be an assembler routine which causes the operating system to write the character specified by *content* into the video map at the current cursor position, set the attribute bits to correspond with the value specified by *attributes*, and finally advance to the next position. Most operating systems will support an equivalent to PutChar and a corresponding procedure, GetChar, which returns the content of the current position on the device, and the value of its attributes.

Defining the attributes in terms of actual bit patterns in the video map is both unwieldy and inflexible; it is preferable to specify them in terms of the attribute data structure which we defined earlier. The low level routines can be incorporated into procedures which convert the enumerated types of this data structure into the relevant bit patterns for a particular device. Suitable procedures would take the form

procedure WriteVideoMap(ch:char;attributes:AttributesType)
procedure ReadVideoMap(var ch:char;var attributes:AttributesType)

A string can be displayed with particular attributes by repeated calls to WriteVideoMap, as illustrated by the DisplayString procedure of Fig. 3.7.

```
procedure DisplayString(content:string;
                        attributes:AttributesType);
var size,k : byte;
begin
size:=length(content);
for k:= 1 to size do WriteVideoMap(content[k],attributes);
end;
```

Fig. 3.7. Displaying a message with given attributes.

3.2.4 A Generalised Output Process for Text Messages

We are now in a position to generalise the output of a text message to a device such as a screen. An output message is represented by a variable, *field* (of type FieldType), whose structure is defined by the type declarations of Fig. 3.8.

```
byte            = 0..255;
colours         = (black,blue,green,cyan,red,magenta,yellow,white);
OffOn           = (off,on);
LeftCentreRight = (left,centre,right);

SlotType        = record
                  row             : byte;
                  col             : byte;
                  width           : byte;
                  end;

AttributesType  = record
                  foreground      : colours;
                  background      : colours;
                  blink           : OffOn;
                  bold            : OffOn;
                  justification   : LeftCentreRight;
                  end;

FieldType       = record
                  content         : string;
                  slot            : SlotType;
                  attributes      : AttributesType;
                  end;
```

Fig. 3.8. Type declarations for the output message process.

For simplicity, we restrict our discussion in this chapter and the following chapters to the display of a field, i.e. a message which starts at a specified (row,col) character position and extends for a specified number of character positions. In other words, we have omitted 'height' from the SlotType declaration.

Also, for simplicity and because it is a feature which is not available on a number of devices, we have omitted text fonts. It is not difficult to incorporate this facility, although different font sizes may make it tricky to operate in fixed integral character positions.

We have introduced a new attribute — *justification*. The reason for this attribute is merely to make the display of *field.content* more convenient. The number of 'significant' characters in the content string may be less than *field.slot.width*; for example, we may wish to display a short string of black text characters centred within a longer band of blue background. We could assign a string, suitably padded with leading and trailing spaces, to content. Introducing a justification attribute merely saves the designer the trouble of calculating the number of padding spaces required. The string will be displayed automatically with the appropriate number of padding spaces.

We require a mechanism for assigning values to an output field. This is done by the CreateField procedure, which takes the form:

procedure CreateField (var field:FieldType;
                          message:string;
                          row,col,width:byte;
                          AttributeString:string);external;

The field represented by Fig. 3.9 can be initialised by the statement:

CreateField (Figure 3_9, 'My Message Displayed Here',6,10,31,
            'fore=black,back=blue,just=centre');

My Message Displayed Here

Fig. 3.9.

Let us examine CreateField more closely. Assigning values to content and slot raises no queries but the assignment of attributes deserves some attention. We have already seen that it is desirable to specify the attributes at a conceptual level rather than in terms of how they are implemented. It is tedious to specify a value for each attribute every time we define a field; we will frequently want the same set of values. More significantly, we will 'bake' this set of attributes into our application software since, if we add a new attribute, we will have to amend all existing software to include the additional value.

Therefore we specify the desired attributes as a string of characters. This string consists of a series of settings separated by commas, and with each setting having the form

keyword = value

where *keyword* identifies a particular attribute (fore, back, blink or bold) and *value* the enumerated type value which the attribute is to take. Any attributes which are not specified explicitly take a default value. In our example, the blink and bold attributes take their default values of 'off' because they are not specified explicitly. The default values for background and foreground are 'black' and 'white' respectively, and the default value for justification is 'left'.

In order to manipulate the field data structures we assume a library of procedures of the form detailed in Fig. 3.10. These procedures utilise the low level routines for positioning and attribute setting described in the preceding sections. Appendix G contains a library of suitable PASCAL procedures. Note that these procedures are not restricted to any particular screen device — device dependence is localised within the low level routines.

The field in Fig. 3.9 can be output to the screen by a statement of the form

DisplayField(Figure3_9);

The content of the field in Fig. 3.9 can be 'cleared' by a statement of the form

ClearField(Figure3_9);

```
procedure ChangeFieldContent(var field:FieldType;
                          NewContent:string);external;
procedure ChangeFieldSlot(var field:FieldType;
                          row,col,width:byte);external;
procedure ChangeFieldAttributes(var field:FieldType;
                          NewAttributes:string);external;
procedure ClearField(field:FieldType);external;
procedure CreateField(var field:FieldType;
                          message:string;
                          row,col,width:byte;
                          AttributeString:string);external;
procedure DisplayField(field:FieldType);external;
procedure HideField(field:FieldType);external;
```

Fig. 3.10. Field manipulation procedures.

This temporarily sets the foreground to the same colour as the background of the field and redisplays it. If the background colour of the field is different from that of the rest of the screen, the area occupied by the field will still be visible but the content will be invisible. This can be used to indicate the location of a message but without displaying the message content.

There are occasions when the dialogue process wishes to draw a user's attention to a message which has already been displayed i.e. to repeat the message with greater emphasis. Rather than creating a new message, this can be done by changing the specification of an existing message and redisplaying it. For example, the statements

    ChangeFieldAttributes(Figure3_9,'fore⁵white');
    DisplayField(Figure3_9);

will redisplay the field in the same position but with white text on a blue background. There are corresponding procedures to change the content or the slot.

Finally, we may wish to hide the area of the screen occupied by the display of a field. This is accomplished by a statement of the form:

    HideField(Figure3_9);

Figure 3.11 illustrates the use of these procedures to display the range of shades available on an IBM-PC colour screen. The program ShowColours outputs a pyramid with shades lightening from black at the top to white at the bottom; each row of the pyramid contains the shade caption in the same colour as the background but in bold intensity.

3.3 Input of a Text Message

3.3.1 Standard Input from the Keyboard

The *keyboard* is the archetypal input mechanism of interactive computing. It can be used for the entry of any text-based input and is appropriate for low to moderate volumes, depending on the proficiency of the user. Where large volumes of input from fairly standard source documents are involved, an automatic data capture device such as an *optical character reader* should be considered; these devices are widely used by public utilities for processing customer account payments and by banks for processing cheques.

```
program ShowColours;
type
{include field Type definitions of Figure 3.8}

var
  OutField        : FieldType;
  row,col,width : byte;
  k               : byte;
  shade           : array[1..8] of string;

{include field Procedure declarations of Figure 3.10}
procedure ClearScreen;external;

begin
shade[1]:='black' ; shade[2]:='blue' ; shade[3]:='green';
shade[4]:='cyan' ; shade[5]:='red'  ; shade[6]:='magenta';
shade[7]:='yellow'; shade[8]:='white';
ClearScreen;
CreateField(OutField,'Colours Available',2,1,80,
                     'back=white,fore=black,just=centre');
DisplayField(OutField);
row:=3; col:=35; width:=10;
for k:=1 to 8 do
  begin
  ChangeFieldContent(OutField,shade[k]);
  ChangeFieldAttributes(OutField,
            concat('bold=on,back=',shade[k],'fore=',shade[k]));
  row:=row+1; col:=col-2; width:=width+4;
  ChangeFieldSlot(OutField,row,col,width);
  DisplayField(OutField);
  end;
end. {ShowColours}
```

Fig. 3.11. A colour pyramid.

Other equipment which can be used to substitute or supplement keying includes badge readers (into which you insert your bank service card at the automatic till) and barcode scanners (used to identify products at retail checkout desks). In both cases, their use eliminates the need for the user to enter a long and meaningless string of digits to identify the customer or product code.

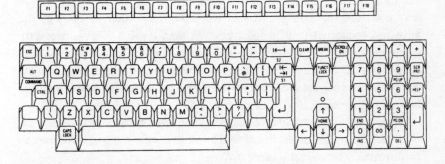

Fig. 3.12. Olivetti M24 keyboard.

In certain systems a full keyboard is unnecessary or undesirable and a customised keyboard may be used, e.g. the numeric keyblock on an automatic bank till. However, unless they are to be produced in large numbers, customised keyboards are expensive. Many improvements on the traditional QWERTY layout, illustrated in Fig. 3.12, have been proposed and shown to reduce the physical strain on the user; thus far it has withstood all competitors.

The basic mechanism by which input is received by a program is the same for all keyboards. Most high level languages provide a procedure to read input delimited by an end of line marker such as Carriage Return. Thus in PASCAL, the statement

    read (x)

reads a value from the keyboard and assigns it to variable x.

The use of a standard input facility, like READ, has a number of implications for the interface. The processing which occurs to effect the input is as follows:

repeat
  – *wait* for input to become available;
  – *interpret* any control sequences for editing (such as Backspace or Delete) or screen positioning;
  – *echo* the edited/interpreted input to an attached screen;

until end of input is indicated by the user pressing the Carriage Return key.

In a language such as PASCAL, the input will then be checked for type consistency with the input variable and *converted* as appropriate, or will cause an error.

For many text-based applications, the processing described above may be exactly what is required. However, it does have limitations. The application may not want the dialogue to wait for input, but rather to examine the keyboard to see whether or not a key has been pressed. This is necessary where the system repeatedly carries out a process until the user presses a key to terminate it. A common example occurs when a source file is listed on the screen. Lines from the file scroll up the screen until the user causes a pause, typically by pressing control-S.

It may be undesirable to echo what the user types onto the screen. Obviously password protection would be of little use if the password were to be displayed whenever it was entered.

The application may interpret editing keys in a non-standard manner.

During execution of a PASCAL read instruction, the Backspace key is interpreted as a *destructive backspace*, i.e. the previous character is overwritten. With a form displayed on the screen, the dialogue may want to interpret the Backspace key as 'position the cursor at the preceding field'.

If the dialogue is expecting a single character reply, the user should not be required to press the return key; the input should terminate when one character has been entered.

3.3.2 Character-by-Character Input

To support these variations, many languages allow *character-by-character* input. Even if the language (as with PASCAL) does not include it, many operating systems provide the facility via a low level routine which can be linked with the language's procedures. The essentials of such input are that:

The application software can interrogate the keyboard to see if a key has been pressed. If it has, the character code corresponding to the key will be returned; otherwise an indicator such as ASCII NUL (**ascii 0**) will be returned.

The majority of input codes will not be interpreted to see if they represent control sequences (it may not be possible to trap some Resets). In particular, a Backspace will appear as the ASCII character BS (**ascii 8**).

The input will not be echoed automatically onto the screen.

This facility gives the designer the ability to control the way in which input is received from the keyboard. A program can wait for input by repeatedly scanning the keyboard until a non-null character is obtained. Input can be echoed by displaying characters as they are received; in fact, numeric input can be echoed right-justified, and alphabetic input can be echoed left-justified.

Since control sequences are not interpreted by the operating system, the dialogue process can interpret any character, or sequence of characters, in any way. The corollary of this freedom is that it must undertake any editing functions required.

A final point to note is that this mechanism only supports input of type Char. Although this may seem a disadvantage, a little thought should suggest that all text input (including that of numbers) should be as characters which are then converted explicitly by the application software. No system should crash because a keying error caused a type mismatch in a PASCAL program!

Handling character-by-character input requires the existence of an external procedure of the form

function GetKeyChar(WaitSwitch:WaitType;EchoSwitch:EchoType):byte;

where WaitType = (Wait,NoWait) and EchoType = (Echo,NoEcho) and the byte value returned contains the ASCII code of the character corresponding to the key.

3.3.3 Handling 'Special' Keys

Most keyboards contain a number of 'special' keys in addition to the alphabetics and the numeric digits. These 'special' keys include editing keys such as Backspace, cursor control keys and function keys. If GetKeyChar returns the corresponding ASCII code when an alphabetic or numeric is pressed, what does it return if a special key such as the cursor ↑ or function key F1 is pressed?

Keys such as Backspace and CarriageReturn also return a single ASCII code. On some devices, all the keys operate in this manner; that is you can test for function key F1 by a statement of the form

if key = n for some $0 < n < 256$

Unfortunately, not all devices are so helpful. Many terminals and microcomputers (such as the IBM-PC) return a sequence of several characters for the depression of a single function or cursor control key. Often this sequence starts with the ASCII NUL character which is also used to indicate that no key has been pressed; a function like GetKeyChar will not handle special keys on these devices.

There is a solution to this problem. Each key on the keyboard (even ShiftLock) has a unique numeric code, a *scan code* associated with it. The scan codes for the keyboard illustrated in Fig. 3.12 are shown in Fig. 3.13. When a key is depressed, the corresponding scan code is generated. Some keys (Shift, Control, CapsLock, etc.) do not produce an input 'character'. They

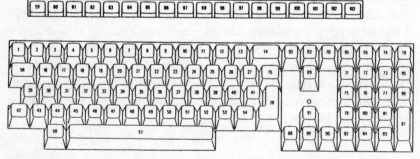

Fig. 3.13. Olivetti M24 scan codes.

have no meaning except when combined with a 'character' key and merely set a KeyBoard State flag. If the 'c' key is depressed, the keyboard handler translates it as 'C' or 'c' or 'control-C' and generates the corresponding ASCII code by interpreting the scan code in light of the Keyboard State flags. A sequence of ASCII codes for a function key or cursor control key is generated in a similar manner.

Many operating systems provide entry points which enable low level routines to access the scan codes rather than just the translated ASCII codes.

Consider an external procedure of the form

procedure GetKeyScan(WaitSwitch:WaitType;EchoSwitch:EchoType;
var scan,ascii:byte); external;

This operates in a similar way to GetKeyChar except that it returns values for both the scan code and an ASCII interpretation of this code. The scan code will be non-zero if and only if a key has been pressed. For a normal key, the scan code will be interpretable as an ASCII value which will be returned in the variable ASCII; for special keys, no such interpretation will be possible and so the value of ASCII will be zero.

By associating with a single key an action which might otherwise require several keystrokes, the amount of keying required from the user can be minimised. The existence of a procedure like GetKeyScan enables the dialogue to interpret function and cursor keys in any way it wants. Since the normal 'character' keys produce ASCII codes in the range 0..127, one simple way of doing this is to assign special keys a number in the range 128..255, and to translate their scan codes on input as in the general keyboard input procedure, GetAnyKey, illustrated in Fig. 3.14. Appendix F contains a list of the keycodes used in this book to represent special keys.

There is a further refinement which we can incorporate into the process. Suppose that the dialogue requests the user to enter a customer code which is all numeric. If the user keys a character other than a digit from 0 to 9, it is obvious that a typing error has occurred. The input process could accept the field with this error and let the dialogue process validate it, reject it, output an

```
function GetAnyKey(WaitSwitch:WaitType;EchoSwitch:EchoType):byte;
var  scan,ascii : byte;
begin
GetKeyScan(WaitSwitch,EchoSwitch,scan,ascii);
if (scan<>0) and (ascii=0) then ascii:=scan+128;
GetAnyKey:=ascii;
end; {GetAnyKey}
```

Fig. 3.14. Character-by-character input of any key.

error message and request re-input. This is a long-winded approach to such a trivial mistake; it would be easier if the input process simply ignored the miskeyed character.

This facility can be incorporated by specifying a *filter* which defines the set of keys to which the input process is sensitive. Any characters entered which are not in this filter are ignored; a suitable procedure, GetFilterKey, is illustrated in Fig. 3.15.

```
type
    WaitType  = (wait,NoWait);
    EchoType  = (echo,NoEcho);
    SetOfByte = set of byte;
function GetFilterKey(WaitSwitch:WaitType;
                      EchoSwitch:EchoType;
                      filter     :SetOfByte):byte;
var  scan,ascii : byte;
begin
ascii:=0;
repeat
    GetKeyScan(WaitSwitch,EchoSwitch,scan,ascii);
    if (scan<>0) and (ascii=0) then ascii:=scan+128;
    if not (ascii in filter) then ascii:=0;
until (ascii<>0) or (WaitSwitch=NoWait);
GetFilterKey:=ascii;
end; {GetFilterKey}
```

Fig. 3.15. Character-by-character input via a filter.

3.3.4 A General Input Process for Text Messages

In the previous sections, we were concerned with input only at the level of individual characters. In practice, a general input text message will consist of a string of characters up to a given length. This introduces further requirements.

First, the process requires a variable in which to return the content of the input message; by definition, this will be of type string. If the input is to be echoed to the screen, there must be a definition of the slot on the screen where this content will be echoed and a definition of the format (attributes) in which it is to be echoed. This appears a remarkably similar requirement to that for an output text message, and indeed an input field has the same type declaration:

var InputField : FieldType

where
FieldType = record
           content   : string;
           slot   : SlotType;
           attributes : AttributesType;
           end;

Note that the slot defines not only where the input is echoed. By specifying a width, it also defines a maximum length for the input.

The user may make a keying mistake; a *rubout* character must be defined to permit editing of the input. If a user can abort the system at any point, a *RequestAbort* character must also be defined. An *EchoSwitch* is required to specify whether the input is to be echoed. A *RequestHelp* character is needed to permit the user to request help.

The input process must be able to determine when to terminate. As we discussed earlier this can be signalled either by the input of a special terminator character or by the input of a fixed number of characters. An *AcceptField* character can be defined to cater for the first case; the process will continue until this character is input, regardless of the number of characters which have been entered. If more characters are entered than the slot can contain, any excess will be ignored. In the second case, there is no explicit terminator character and so AcceptField will be defined as null; the process will continue until exactly slot.width characters have been entered.

The number of such 'switches' which are required to control the input process would result in a very unwieldy parameter list if they were all passed as individual parameters. We will collect them all into a single data structure which we will refer to as a *Dialogue Information Block* (DIB). Because this structure contains settings which control the input process we will call it a control DIB.

The complete structure of the control DIB is illustrated in Fig. 3.16. It contains a number of other elements in addition to those which we have already described. The purpose of these additional elements will be described as they are required.

Combining all these requirements results in a procedure of the form:

procedure ReadField (var field:FieldType;
                         DataSet:SetOfByte;
                         var ControlDIB:ControlDIBtype)

where DataSet is a filter defining the 'keys' to which the process is sensitive.

```
ControlDIBtype = record
                ControlBuffer        : byte;
                (input of text message)
                rubout               : byte;
                EchoSwitch           : OffOn;
                AcceptField          : byte;
                (standard controls)
                RequestAbort         : byte;
                RequestHelp          : byte;
                (picking & pointing controls)
                reserved1            : byte;
                reserved2            : byte;
                reserved3            : byte;
                (form positioning controls)
                reserved4            : byte;
                reserved5            : byte;
                reserved6            : byte;
                reserved7            : SetOfByte;
```

Fig. 3.16. The Control DIB data structure.

To accept the input of a numeric field of up to 6 digits terminated with a CarriageReturn and to echo right-justified in inverse video starting at (20,10) requires a program fragment of the form:

```
var ControlDIB : ControlDIBtype;
    InField     : FieldType;
    DataSet     : SetOfByte;

with ControlDIB do
   begin
   rubout:=BS;                 (keycode 8)
   EchoSwitch:=on;
   AcceptField:=CR;            (keycode 13)
   RequestAbort:=ESC;          (keycode 27)
   end;
(display blank slot for answer in inverse video)
CreateField(InField,'',20,10,6,'fore=black,back=white,just=right');
DisplayField(InField);

DataSet:=[ord('0')..ord('9')]; (filter only allows digits 0-9)
ReadField(InField,DataSet,ControlDIB);
```

To accept an input of exactly 6 alphabetic characters without echo behind a mask of asterisks starting at (20,10) requires a program fragment of the form:

```
with ControlDIB do
   begin
   rubout:=BS;                 (keycode 8)
   EchoSwitch:=off;
   AcceptField:=null;          (keycode 0, no explicit terminator)
   RequestAbort:=ESC;          (keycode 27)
   end;
```

```
{display slot for answer filled with asterisks}
CreateField(InField,'******',20,10,6,'');
DisplayField(InField);
DataSet:=[ord('a')..ord('z'),ord('A')..ord('Z')];
ReadField(InField,DataSet,ControlDIB);
```

In both cases, the user's input will be returned in InField.content. Although in the second case the input characters are not echoed, the cursor will still track the input position along the asterisks. Of course, the user may decide not to enter a text message but may choose instead to press the RequestAbort key. ReadField will terminate immediately but this is unlikely to be a sufficient response by the system; the dialogue needs to know that the user has aborted the process. The ControlBuffer in ControlDIB provides the means for this; when ReadField returns, ControlBuffer will contain the keycode of Request-Abort. We shall see later that there are other occasions when this ControlBuffer is used for communicating 'control' inputs to the dialogue.

A suitable ReadField procedure is detailed in Appendix G. It makes use of the low level routines which were discussed in the previous section.

3.4 Positioning, Pointing and Picking

3.4.1 Targets

In Chapter 2, we saw that an Input Control message typically involves selection from a limited set of options; an Input Data message may also involve such a selection. It can be accomplished by keying a text message which identifies the option desired. It can also be accomplished if the list is reasonably small, by the system displaying the choices available and the user 'pointing' at the one required.

The alternatives are represented by a list of targets. These targets may be individual characters; in editing a piece of text, the selections possible are the character positions on the screen. They may be a set of character strings; such as a list of task processes which can be executed, or a list of file names which may be opened. In the more general case, they may be a series of targets represented pictorially on the screen, as in Fig. 3.17.

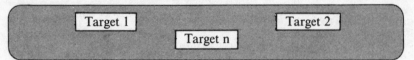

Fig. 3.17. Targets on a screen.

Each target is specified by

A *content* which describes the target; each target should be clearly labelled so that a user knows where to aim.

A *slot* in which it appears on the device; targets should be as large and as widely separated as possible. Different pointing devices have different resolutions ('fineness of pointing') but it will always be easier to point at a large target than a small one.

A *set of attributes* which describe its format. Target areas should be clearly distinguished; one way of doing this is by painting the target area with given attributes.

This is simply the specification of any output text message; thus, we can specify a set of targets as an ordered list of output text messages. If, as in previous sections, we restrict ourselves to messages which are of type FieldType, any set of up to N targets can be displayed by a program fragment of the form

```
const MaxTargets    = N;
type
    TargetListType = array[1..MaxTargets] of FieldType;
var
    k                  : byte;
    NumberOfTargets : byte;
    TargetList         : TargetListType;

for k:= 1 to NumberOfTargets do DisplayField(TargetList[k]);
```

The number of targets should be kept small so that the user is not confused by a multiplicity of target areas. The next stage is to define how a user can point at the targets. There are two basic mechanisms.

Absolute pointing allows the user to point anywhere on the display, regardless of whether a target is located there or not. It implies that the corresponding input process will receive precise positioning information from the input device and is most commonly used with a specialist pointing device such as a mouse or a touchscreen.

In *Relative pointing*, the range of positioning is restricted merely to scrolling round the target list. The user will always be pointing at some target from this list; typically, the process is initialised with the user pointing at the first. Scrolling is commonly implemented with keyboard input; particular keys (typically the cursor control keys) are interpreted as a request to scroll to the next or previous target in the list.

A user needs clear and immediate confirmation of where he is pointing. A common method of providing this feedback is by changing the attributes of the CurrentTarget to highlight the corresponding slot on the device. Appendix G details a suitable PASCAL procedure:

procedure HighlightField(field:FieldType;highlight:AttributesType)

which temporarily changes the attributes of an output field and redisplays it.

Finally, a mechanism is required to terminate the input process — we must define how a user 'picks' the target he is pointing at. This is usually accomplished by defining a particular key or mouse button as an explicit *AcceptTarget* character; the input process terminates when this character is entered. It is possible for a target to be picked as soon as it is pointed at. This implicit picking implies the use of a pointing device (such as a touchscreen) which does not require the user traversing other targets to reach the one required.

3.4.2 Relative Pointing — Scrolling Around a Target List

Any keys on a standard keyboard can be used for pointing at a list of targets, though it is more common to use 'special' keys such as the cursor control or function keys. The processing of input from these keys was discussed in Section 3.3.3.

One key will be needed by the user to point to the next target. The chosen key is specified by assigning *PointNextTarget* a value in the range 0..255 (every key is assigned an unique keycode, Appendix F). Each time the corresponding key is pressed, the system will position at, and highlight, the next target in the list. When it gets to the end of the list it wraps around to the beginning.

Being able to scroll in both directions eases the users task; if he overshoots the required target, it is not necessary to cycle through them all again. Another variable, *PointPriorTarget*, is required. At any stage, the user can indicate that he has reached the target he wants by entering the character specified as *AcceptTarget*. A means of aborting the mechanism without making a selection is also desirable.

Where are these characters to be defined? In Section 3.3.4, we introduced the concept of a Dialogue Information Block (the ControlDIB) which contained the various controls for the input process for a text string. PointNextTarget, PointPriorTarget and AcceptTarget are corresponding controls for the Relative Pointing process; these are also stored in the controlDIB data structure as shown in Fig. 3.18.

The procedure in Fig. 3.19 illustrates the use of this mechanism; it returns in *CurrentTarget* the ordinal number of the target picked. The target at which the user is currently pointing is highlighted with the attributes specified in the corresponding input parameter. SwitchCursor is an external routine which switches the normal screen cursor on or off. Why is this necessary? (The reader may note that the reassignments of CurrentTarget in response to the input of PointNextTarget or PointPriorTarget could be coded more elegantly, if less transparently, using the MOD function to cycle CurrentTarget through the values 1..NumberOfTargets.)

3.4.3 Absolute Pointing

Cursor control keys can be used to move, one character at a time, to any position on the screen. However a series of crablike vertical and horizontal

```
ControlDIBtype = record
                ControlBuffer      : byte;
                (input of text message)
                rubout             : byte;
                EchoSwitch         : OffOn;
                AcceptField        : byte;
                (standard controls)
                RequestAbort       : byte;
                RequestHelp        : byte;
                (picking & pointing controls)
                PointNextTarget    : byte;
                PointPriorTarget   : byte;
                AcceptTarget       : byte;
                (form positioning controls)
                reserved4          : byte;
                reserved5          : byte;
                reserved6          : byte;
                reserved7          : SetOfByte;
```

Fig. 3.18. The Control DIB data structure with Pointing Controls.

```
procedure RelativePick(TargetList:TargetListType;
                       NumberOfTargets:byte;
                       highlight:AttributesType;
                       var ControlDIB:ControlDIBtype;
                       var CurrentTarget:byte);
var
   complete : boolean;
   filter   : SetOfByte;
begin
with ControlDIB do
   begin
   filter:=[RequestAbort,RequestHelp,
            PointNextTarget,PointPriorTarget,AcceptTarget];
   SwitchCursor(off);
   if (CurrentTarget<1) or (CurrentTarget>NumberOfTargets) then
      CurrentTarget:=1;
   HighlightField(TargetList[CurrentTarget],highlight);
   complete:=false;
   repeat
      ControlBuffer:=GetFilterKey(Wait,NoEcho,filter);
      {ControlBuffer cannot be zero}
      if ControlBuffer=RequestAbort then
         complete:=true
      else
      if (ControlBuffer=PointNextTarget)
      or (ControlBuffer=PointPriorTarget) then
         begin
         DisplayField(TargetList[CurrentTarget]); {turn off old highlight}
         if ControlBuffer=PointNextTarget then
            if CurrentTarget=NumberOfTargets then CurrentTarget:=1
                                       else CurrentTarget:=CurrentTarget+1
         else
            if CurrentTarget=1 then CurrentTarget:=NumberOfTargets
                             else CurrentTarget:=CurrentTarget-1;
         HighlightField(TargetList[CurrentTarget],highlight);
         ControlBuffer:=0; {because it has been actioned}
         if AcceptTarget=0  then complete:=true;
         end
      else
      if ControlBuffer=AcceptTarget then
         begin
         complete:=true;
         ControlBuffer:=0; {because it has been actioned}
         end
      else
         {terminated by a higher level control input}
         complete:=true;
   until complete;
   SwitchCursor(on);
   end;
end; {RelativePick}
```

Fig. 3.19. Scrolling round a set of targets.

motions is hardly natural or speedy. Free pointing anywhere on the screen
really requires a specialist pointing device. The operating system will contain
low level routines to support the operation of the device; a PASCAL program

will typically access these routines via calls to external procedures. The format in which these routines report device activity varies from device to device. However, it should be possible to produce a generalised procedure of the form:

procedure ReadPointer(var row,col:byte;var action:byte)

action specifies what activity, if any, has occurred; for example, we need to be able to tell if the user has picked a target, requested an abort and so forth. The position of the device is specified by (row,col); most pointing devices report position in terms of pixel co-ordinates but these can easily be converted to row and column values for use in text-based applications.

In order to determine which target, if any, is being pointed at, these row and column co-ordinates must be matched against the co-ordinates of the target areas. A target is pointed at if the character position (row,col) lies with the target slot. The point and pick procedure must try all targets in the list, as illustrated in Fig. 3.20, until a match is found; if the list is exhausted before a match is found, then the user is not pointing at any target.

The mouse (Fig. 3.21) is the pointing device in vogue. Although developed more than a decade ago, recent dramatic reductions in cost have resulted in its incorporation in most modern workstations. It consists of a box about the size of a cigarette packet attached to the keyboard or processor; set into the top are a number (1 to 4) of buttons which operate rather like function keys. As the mouse is moved in the palm of the hand over a convenient surface (a desktop or a tablet), its position is tracked relative to some preset origin using

```
function MatchPosition(row,col:byte;
                       TargetList:TargetListType;
                       NumberOfTargets:byte):byte
var k,match : byte;
begin
match:=0;
k:=1;
while (k<=NumberOfTargets) and (match=0) do
    if  (row=TargetList[k].slot.row)
    and (col>=TargetList[k].slot.col)
    and (col< TargetList[k].slot.col+TargetList[k].slot.width) then
       match:=k
    else
       k:=k+1;
MatchPosition:=match;
end; {MatchPosition}
```

Fig. 3.20. Matching a target area.

Fig. 3.21. An Olivetti mouse.

one of two methods. The cheaper and more common mechanical mouse rolls on a ball bearing; the motion of the ball bearing is transferred to two rollers which are perpendicular to each other and which track motion in the x and y planes. The optical mouse which is common in graphical applications uses an optical crosshair over a special tablet upon which a very precise grid has been etched.

It was mentioned in Section 3.2.3 that the output features provided on some screens depend on the *mode* to which they have been initialised. Similarly, many mice exhibit different operating characteristics depending on the mode to which they have been *configured*. This configuration involves supplying values for a variety of parameters which control the mouse operation; for example, one parameter will specify the sensitivity of the mouse i.e. the scale of physical movement necessary to effect one unit of movement on the screen.

A common facility used with text-based dialogues is *keyboard emulation*. Movements of the mouse and presses and releases of the buttons are converted to associated key character strings. Typically, a mouse movement to the left is converted to the character generated by the cursor left key, a press of Button 1 is converted to a CarriageReturn character, and so forth. The key strings which are 'emulated' for each mouse action can be set by the configuration routines.

The dialogue has no need to know of the existence of a mouse operating in keyboard-emulation mode. Use of the mouse imposes no special software requirements since its inputs will be processed correctly by any of the keyboard routines which we have discussed previously. Therefore we will concentrate on the case where the mouse operates as a independent device, often called *real mouse* mode.

There are no intrinsic procedures in most high level languages for processing real mouse input i.e. there is nothing that corresponds to the Read and Readln procedures for the keyboard. All input/output from auxiliary devices like the mouse must be handled via low level routines called *drivers*; in fact, the routines like WriteVideoMap and GetKeyScan which we discussed in Sections 3.2 and 3.3 are examples of Screen and Keyboard drivers. The precise implementation of the Mouse driver depends on the particular mouse. We will consider the types of facility provided by the driver of a typical mechanical mouse. These are listed in Fig. 3.22.

Movement of the mouse is tracked on the screen by a mouse cursor symbol. A number of different cursor symbols may be supported — a block, a character attribute setting or a symbol such as an arrowhead or sightmark. The cursor symbol can be set by a statement of the form:

SetMouseCursor(inverse);

It may be desirable to turn the cursor off; for example, when a particular target is highlighted, a flashing cursor is an unnecessary distraction. This requires a statement of the form:

```
procedure SetMouseCursor(cursor:CursorType);external;
procedure SwitchMouseCursor(switch:OffOn);external;
procedure SetMouseLimits(limits:rectangle);external;
procedure MouseTo(row,col:byte);external;
procedure MouseAt(var row,col:byte);external;
procedure ReadPress(button:ButtonType;
                    var report:ReportType);external;
procedure ReadRelease(button:ButtonType;
                      var report:ReportType);external;
```

Fig. 3.22. Typical real mouse facilities.

SwitchMouseCursor(off);

The area of the screen over which the mouse can travel can be restricted, for example, to constrain the user to positioning within a given rectangular area such as a list of options. This requires a statement of the form:

SetMouseLimits(TargetListArea);

Just as the normal screen cursor can be initialised to a given position, the mouse cursor can be set to any given position by a statement of the form:

MouseTo(10,25);

On many systems, the designer must take care to avoid conflicts between the mouse cursor and the normal text cursor. The system may well treat these as different entities. In particular, the fact that the mouse cursor is displayed at a particular position on the screen does not necessarily imply that an output to the screen will occur at this position; output will take place at the position pointed at by the text cursor.

Various mouse actions can be reported. The application software can determine the current mouse position and whether the buttons are currently up or down. As well as these absolute reports, the mouse can provide relative reports of activity since it was last interrogated, such as the relative movement or the number of times a button has been pressed or released and the absolute position at which this last occurred. The second of these is useful for checking whether the user has 'clicked' (i.e. pressed and released a button) in a particular target area.

A report on the current mouse position (row,col) can be read with a statement of the form:

MouseAt(row,col);

Reading 'clicks' from the mouse requires statements of the form:

ReadPress(LeftButton,report);
ReadRelease(RightButton,report);

where *report* is a variable of type

```
ReportType = record
             count : byte;   {count of presses or releases}
             row   : byte;   {row of last press or release}
             col   : byte;   {col of last press or release}
             end;
```

and returns the number of presses (releases) of the specified button and the position at which the last one occurred. Button is an enumerated value from

ButtonType = (LeftButton,RightButton)

The way in which a button is pressed can also be coded. A common convention is that a single 'click' selects/deselects a target, holding the button down drags a target across the screen, and a 'double click' (i.e. two clicks in quick succession) indicates some operation on the target, such as opening a file.

Alternatives, which operate in a similar manner to the mouse, include the *tracker ball* and the *joystick*. The *touchscreen* and the *lightpen* both differ from the mouse in that a user can point and pick in a single operation. The dialogue process should not be concerned with which of these particular devices is being used; therefore we need to define an abstraction for absolute pointing which generalises to all of these. We will illustrate this by considering the process for a mouse with two buttons which are 'single clicked'.

The ReadPointer abstraction must provide sufficient information to decide which target, if any, is currently pointed at; this can be accomplished if its implementation returns the (row,col) position. It must also indicate whether a target has been picked or an abort has been requested. For relative pointing, we defined a particular keycode for each of these in ControlDIB; the mouse input routine, which knows about buttons, implements this by converting clicks (releases of a button) to keycodes which the dialogue knows about. Fig. 3.23 illustrates the mechanism.

Similar generalisations are required for the cursor control procedures of Fig. 3.22. The dialogue requires an abstraction for any pointing device with the same parameter format; for example:

MouseTo(row,col:byte) => PointerTo(row,col:byte)

These can be incorporated into a generalised procedure for absolute picking as illustrated in Fig. 3.24. The boolean function equal(a,b:byte):boolean returns the value 'true' if and only if (a=b) and (a<>0). It is required to prevent a zero result in the ControlBuffer matching an undefined (and hence zero value) control variable (for example RequestAbort) in ControlDIB.

Point and pick devices can be used very sucessfully provided the user is not continually having to alternate between the device and a keyboard. The mouse and the touchscreen in particular have both proved very acceptable to and easily used by a wide range of users. The touchscreen has the disadvantage at present of being very expensive relative to the other

```
procedure ReadPointer(var row,col:byte;var action:byte);  {mouse}
type ReportType = record
                     count : byte;
                     row   : byte;
                     col   : byte;
                     end;
var  report : ReportType;
{include Mouse procedure declarations of Figure 3.22}

begin
ReadRelease(RightButton,report);
if report.count>0 then        {right button release = abort}
   begin
   row:=report.row;
   col:=report.col;
   action:=ESC;               {keycode 27}
   end
else
   begin
   ReadRelease(LeftButton,report);
   if report.count>0 then     {left button release = pick}
      begin
      row:=report.row;
      col:=report.col;
      action:=CR;             {keycode 13}
      end
   else
      begin
      MouseAt(row,col);       {no clicks but check position}
      action:=0;              {keycode 0}
      end;
   end;
end; {ReadPointer for a Mouse}
```

Fig. 3.23. Checking for pointing device activity.

mechanisms, but with the advantage of not impeding keyboard use in any way.

3.5 Input and Output of Graphical Messages

We defined a graphical message as one in which the information exchanged must be described at the 'bit' level rather than at the 'character' level. It is not our intention to discuss graphics in this book but we will mention a few of the factors which are similar to text input and output.

A screen memory map need not store the screen contents as characters; it may hold them instead as *pixel* (short for picture element) information. A

```
procedure AbsolutePick(TargetList:TargetListType;
                       NumberOfTargets:byte;
                       highlight:AttributesType;
                       var ControlDIB:ControlDIBtype;
                       var CurrentTarget:byte);
var
    complete     : boolean;
    PriorTarget  : byte;
    row,col      : byte;

begin

with ControlDIB do
    begin
    SwitchCursor(off); SwitchPointerCursor(on);
    if (CurrentTarget>=1) and (CurrentTarget<=NumberOfTargets) then
        begin
        PointerTo(TargetList[CurrentTarget].slot.row,
                  TargetList[CurrentTarget].slot.col);
        HighlightField(TargetList[CurrentTarget],highlight);
        end;
    complete:=false;
    repeat
        PriorTarget:=CurrentTarget;
        ReadPointer(row,col,ControlBuffer);
        if equal(ControlBuffer,RequestAbort) then
            complete:=true
        else
            begin
            (ControlBuffer may be zero)
            CurrentTarget:=MatchPosition(row,col,TargetList,NumberOfTargets);
            if (CurrentTarget<>0) and (AcceptTarget=0) then
                complete:=true
            else
            if CurrentTarget<>PriorTarget then
                begin
                if PriorTarget<>0 then DisplayField(TargetList[PriorTarget]);
                if CurrentTarget<>0 then HighlightField(TargetList[CurrentTarget
                                                          ,highlight);
                end
            else
            if  (ControlBuffer<>0)
            and (ControlBuffer in [AcceptTarget,RequestHelp]) then
                complete:=true;
            end;
    until complete;
    SwitchPointerCursor(off); SwitchCursor(on);
    end;
end; (AbsolutePick)
```

Fig. 3.24. Absolute pointing at a set of targets.

pixel is the smallest addressable element of the screen. Pixels might be considered as the dots which are combined to create the normal character set. On a monochrome screen, one bit is required to specify each pixel (it is either on or off) and thus such displays are often referred to as *bit mapped displays*;

on a colour screen, a number of bits representing the basic phosphor colours are required for each pixel.

Analogous to the WriteVideoMap and ReadVideoMap procedures for characters discussed in Section 3.2.3, the operating system may include WriteDot and ReadDot procedures which write or read a pixel value at the current position. Frequently, these basic facilities are incorporated into procedures which support the drawing of basic shapes such as a straight line betweeen two points, a circle or a rectangle. Graphic input may be obtained via a mouse. Another common input device is the tablet which consists of a flat slab used in conjuction with a pen-like stylus. The position of the stylus can be detected by a variety of techniques; a common mechanism utilises the pressure of the stylus to vary the electrical properties of a membrane coating on the tablet. A pressure sensitive tablet can be used both for freehand drawing and for tracing.

The tablet can also be used for point and pick operation. Rather than display the targets on the screen, they are printed onto a transparent overlay which rests on the pad. Both because of the smaller typography which is possible and because of the greater precision of the stylus, targets can be smaller and more cluttered than with other devices.

3.6 Summary

The dialogue process treats input and output messages at a logical level, i.e. in terms of the functions they fulfill.

The input/output processes deal with the raw material of the messages. They are not concerned with their function only with their format which, for text-based dialogues, can be classified into

the output of a text message
the input of a text message
point and pick input

The intrinsic procedures of most high level languages only support 'teletype' operation. Low level routines provide many facilities which can enhance the quality of the dialogue but introduce device-dependence. To facilitate *portability* of the system, it is important to localise this dependence.

The input/output processes are split into two levels. The Dialogue Process calls the higher level which represents *abstractions* concerned with what is to be effected rather than how it is implemented.

This higher level calls lower level physical device *drivers* which implement the abstractions on a particular device. Implementation for a different device involves the 'linking' of a different library of driver routines.

An input process must be able to distinguish inputs which represent data from those which control the input process itself; an example of a control input is the rubout key. A data structure, which we have called ControlDIB, parameterises the control inputs of the abstractions; any given dialogue can assign its own particular keycodes to these parameters.

This layering of the processes into different libraries of routines is described further in Appendix D. The library of input/output handling abstractions developed in the chapter are described in more detail in Appendix G and the driver routines for the screen, keyboard and mouse are listed in Appendix F.

Discussion Exercises

D1.   An application which was developed for use on a device with a colour screen is to be 'ported' to a device with a monochrome screen which only supports inverse video. The dialogue abstractions assume that colour and blink are available. How should the driver for the monochrome screen interpret different colour settings and blink? (Consider examples such as a white foreground on a blue background and a black foreground on a green background.)

D2.   Some applications use sound as a highlighting feature; when a field is displayed the associated sound is produced, for example to indicate that the dialogue expects input. Most devices provide a mechanism to 'ring the bell' and several support tone generators which can produce quite elaborate tunes. What extensions to the abstractions described in the chapter would be necessary to incorporate this facility?

D3.   In question D2 of Chapter 2 you were asked to investigate different types of software package in terms of their basic dialogue structure and grammar. Re-examine these packages in terms of the input/output processes they support; for example, what devices are supported, whether they utilise pointing, what video attributes are used.

What benefits or disadvantages do these features bring to interface in each example? Why? Most packages must be *installed* for the particular devices which are used. Determine what type of information about the devices must be specified during installation of these packages.

Programming Exercises

P1. Determine how the cursor control and attribute settings discussed in Section 3.2 can be implemented on the device you are using. In many cases (such as IBM compatibles), this can be done by writing suitable control sequences. Implement the library of screen driver routines listed in Appendix F.

P2. Implement the library of keyboard driver routines discussed in Section 3.3 and listed in Appendix F. On many devices, the keycodes which are produced by a given key (such as the function keys) can be set via particular Escape sequences. This can be considered as setting the *mode* for the keyboard in the same way that the operating mode of a screen or a mouse must be initialised.

P3. What field definitions are required to produce the following 'boxed' list of options? The text is white on a blue background. The character set of most microcomputers includes line segment symbols which can be used to 'draw the box' in text mode.

(8,21)

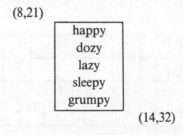

```
happy
dozy
lazy
sleepy
grumpy
```

(14,32)

Use the procedures described in the chapter to display the box on the screen and to scroll around it.

P4. Repeat the previous question but instead of scrolling around the screen use the ReadField procedure to request the user to type one of the letters h,d,l,s or g. This input will not be echoed but the corresponding adjective in the list will be highlighted by 'inversing' it.

P5. Develop a

procedure SaveSlot(slot:SlotType:var buffer:BufferType);

where BufferType = array[1..80] of BufferEntry
and   BufferEntry = record
                                    ch   : char;
                                    attributes : AttributesType;
                                    end;

which copies the contents of the video map corresponding to *slot* into the
variable *buffer*.

P6.   Although absolute pointing using cursor keys is cumbersome, it is
perfectly possible to point absolutely with a mouse which is operating in
keyboard emulation mode. To the system, this is equivalent to pressing the
cursor keys. Figure 3.23 illustrated the implementation of ReadPointer for a
mouse in real-mouse mode. Implement a corresponding driver for cursor key
input.

P7.   Display a keyboard layout on the screen as illustrated below. Each key
will be represented as an individual field and initially the key captions will be
blank. Implement a procedure which will scan the keyboard for an input
keystroke and will display a suitable caption on the relevant key. Thus for an
input of

    c = c will appear on the C key
    C = C will appear on the C key and RS/LS on the shift keys
  Ctl+c = ^C will appear on the C key and Ctl on the control key

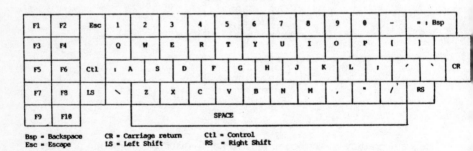

Further Reading

Biggerstaffe T. (1986) *System Software Tools* (chapter 3), Prentice Hall.

Cakir A. *et al.* (1980) *The VDT Manual*, Wiley.

Carroll A.B. (1984) 'Three Types of Touch Technology Simplify
Man–Machine Interface', *Computer Tech. Rev.*, Winter.

Lopiccola P. (1983) 'Meet the Mouse', *Popular Comp.*, **2**, 5.

Montgomery E.B. (1982) 'Bringing Manual Input into the 20th Century', *IEEE Computer*, **15**, 3.

Pfaff G. *et al.* (1982) 'Constructing User Interfaces Based on Logical Input Devices', *IEEE Computer*, **15** 11.

MicroSoft Corp. (1984) MS–DOS Programmer's Reference.

Olivetti (1984) M24: Hardware Architecture and Function.

Chapter 4

Dialogue structures – question and answer and the menu

4.1 Introduction

As we saw in Chapter 2, a common way of classifying the man-computer interface is in terms of the *dialogue structure*. The dialogue structure determines the extent to which control over the progress of the interaction lies with the user or with the system; it also determines the basic format in which this control is exercised. Interactive dialogues are traditionally classified into four main structures:

Question and answer structure
Menu structure
Form structure
Command structure

each of which is based on an analogy with a particular class of human–human interaction. In this chapter we examine how the first two of these structures

- present information to and receive information from a user;
- match the psychological requirements of differing types of user for differing types of application;
- can be implemented using the input/output processes described in Chapter 3.

There are dangers in basing human–machine dialogues too closely on human–human models since the machine cannot fulfil the role a human would perform. However, the suitability of a dialogue structure can, to a large extent, be gauged by considering the situations in which the analogous human–human structure is used. To make this assessment more explicit, we will first consider five general criteria — naturalness, consistency, non-redundancy, supportiveness and flexibility — by which any dialogue's suitability can be assessed.

4.2 What Makes a 'Good' Dialogue?

4.2.1 Naturalness

A natural dialogue is one which does not cause the user significantly to alter his normal approach to the task in order to interact with the system. It does *not* mean that the computer should pretend to human attributes. At a minimum, it implies that the dialogue should utilise the user's native tongue; it is unreasonable to expect a French clerk to 'update an order' rather than 'mettre à jour une commande'.

The tone used should be that of the spoken rather the written language - look at how instructions are printed on cartons. Both long-winded pomposity and the 'matey' tone typical of junk mail should be avoided. Appending a user's name to every question the system asks is a cheap technique which palls very rapidly for even the most inexperienced user. A concise prompt of the form:

option?

is as informative and more comfortable than the mock politeness of:

JAMES, please enter the option which you require

Phrasing should be as self-explanatory as possible. Words like 'print', 'end' and 'copy' have obvious meanings, whereas 'pip' (the CP/M keyword for copy) and 'mv' (the UNIX keyword for rename) do not. The use of jargon is desirable, giving a nice idiomatic feel to the dialogue, provided that it is the jargon used everyday in the user's department and not that used in the computer department. A designer might consider the task to be 'updating the expense file' but if the users call it 'posting P47s', that is how the dialogue should refer to it. Note also that some phrasing can carry strong emotional connotations. Our intended readership should not be offended by common computing jargon but the use of words like 'abort' and 'kill' in a dialogue may disturb some individual users.

Another major aspect of naturalness is the order in which the system requests information. This should always be geared to the order in which the user would normally have the information available; systems have been designed in which the user has to input data from random parts of a clerical document because the programmer failed to recognise the significance of the ordering. Human preprocessing of input, or postprocessing of output, so as to make the computer processing or programming easier, should be avoided.

One microcomputer accounting system requires the user to sort documents which arise naturally in reference number order into customer number order before input; of course, it does simplify programming the printing of customer totals!

The designer should also be careful to ensure that a nonsensical (in human terms) sequence of questions is avoided. Consider the two examples:

sex : female	surname : Bloggs
surname : Bloggs	forename : Mabel
forename : Mabel	sex : ???

As you might imagine, it was not unknown for the second sequence of questions to elicit answers other than 'male' or 'female'!

An unnatural dialogue is frequently the result of a designer's unfamiliarity with how the users would normally undertake the tasks supported by the system and should be detected by the prototyping approach. For example, human pre- and postprocessing will be apparent if the user finds a need for paper and pencils to note down input or output at the workstation.

4.2.2 Consistency

A consistent dialogue ensures that expectations which the user builds up through using one part of a system are not frustrated by idiosyncratic changes in the conventions used in another part.

A consistent *phrasing* implies that a coded input, such as a keyword, always has the same effect. It is very easy when implementing a dialogue to introduce small inconsistencies. For example, 'list' means display on the screen on most occasions, but occasionally it means output to a printer. The two most common line editors used with CP/M both use 'q' to mean quit; unfortunately, it means 'quit and scrap the changes' in one editor and 'quit and save the changes' in the other.

Standard responses should be truly 'standard'. If the user can get help by pressing function key F1 in response to one prompt, he should be able to request help at every prompt by pressing F1; ideally F1 should have no other function other than to provide help. Similarly the conventions for pointing and picking should be the same throughout the dialogue.

A consistent *format* implies that similar fields will always be accepted by the system in the same format. If one date field has the form dd/mm/yy, then all date fields should use that format. If users can abbreviate input, they should always be able to abbreviate to the same extent, e.g. first character, most significant characters.

A consistent *layout* for screens which fulfil a similar function ensures that a user knows where to look for instructions, error messages, and so on. Highlighting techniques should be used consistently, so that, for example, when a user sees an area of inverse video, its significance is immediately apparent.

The maintenance of published guidelines for dialogue implementation has been recommended as an aid to consistency. However, even with the best intentions, it is very easy for small inconsistencies to creep in. One computer package accepts some dates as 'dd/mm/yy' but requires others as 'ddmmyy'; this was not a design feature to keep the user on his toes but almost certainly the result of the different routines being developed by different people. The establishment of libraries of dialogue processes, similar to the libraries of input/output processes in Chapter 3, reduces the risk of this occurring.

4.2.3 Non-Redundancy

A non-redundant dialogue requires the user to input only the minimum information for the system's operation. It has the merit of making the interaction both quicker and less error-prone, since both time and errors increase with the number of keystrokes required.

Probably the classic failure in this area is where an identifier such as a customer code is defined, for technical reasons, as alphanumeric but has a numeric value. There are many systems where the user continually undergoes the tedium of typing '00010' instead of '10', just to save a programmer the one-time effort of writing a routine to pad out the field with leading zeros. A user should *never* be required to enter pad characters in an interactive dialogue.

The dialogue should not request information which the system can derive automatically, or which has been entered previously, such as the current date. Once a description has been associated with a code (for example, 153H is customer J.H.Smith), only that code is required for identification; in almost all cases, it is pointless to have the user type both code and description, since an automatic cross-check of code and description is seldom feasible. Equally, information that is not used by the system should not be requested.

Default values are a useful means of minimising input; the user may press the return key to indicate the default is required. Allowing abbreviations serves the same purpose, although the designer must resist the temptation of choosing phoney or unnatural keywords so as to permit unique identification by a single character abbreviation.

Information should not be output just because the system has it available. The output messages should contain just the information requested/required by the user, in a directly usable form and with the minimum highlighting to achieve the desired emphasis.

A dialogue which fails this criterion will often do so because the programmer who produced it was trying to make his task 'easier' or more 'interesting'. It may be fun to code a program which paints the screen with random blocks in many assorted colours; it is considerably less fun to use such a program!

4.2.4 Supportiveness

The supportiveness of a dialogue is a measure of the amount of assistance the dialogue provides to the user in running the system. It has three major aspects:

the quantity and quality of instructions provided
the nature of the error messages produced
confirmation of what the system is doing.

Instructions to the user are provided both by the the system's prompts and by any additional 'help' facilities. The nature and the amount of instruction provided should obviously vary according to the user's familiarity with the system, and with what he is trying to do. It is counterproductive to provide instructions which are not required by the user, or which do not relate to the user's specific problem. Help must be available at the time it is required, and at the relevant level. Has the user no idea why the system is asking this question, or has he just forgotten the precise format required for the answer?

Error messages are another area where few system designers can take much pride in their work. An error message should explain exactly what is wrong and detail what corrective action is needed, not quote some general phrase like 'syntax error', or obscure code like 'OC1'. Error handling is discussed further in later chapters.

Confirmation messages are required so that the user can check whether the system has or is about to carry out the action requested. Although they are

essential in some areas, they should be used sparingly. It is infuriating to be
continually asked to confirm trivial inputs such as

date? (dd/mm/yy) : 17/11/85
date is 17 November 1985. OK? (Y/N) :

Inputs should be confirmed if their acceptance would result in an
irreversible action by the system (such as deleting a record or a file), or when
a code has been entered, and the user needs to check, by inspecting its
description, that the correct item (such as customer or product) has been
selected. It may also be desirable to confirm that an action has taken place (for
example, a record has been added to a file).

In systems with a deep hierarchical structure, users may forget where they
are. It may be desirable not only to confirm particular actions as they occur,
but also to provide a Status message indicating what point in the system the
user has reached. This can be provided by reserving an area of the screen to
indicate the path which the user has taken to reach the current position.

The essence of a supportive dialogue is that it should provide adequate
support, neither too little nor too much. A dialogue may fail this criterion
because the designer has failed to assess the users' support needs correctly or
because the dialogue has been unable to reflect the changing support
requirements of different users.

4.2.5 Flexibility

The flexibility of a dialogue is a measure of how well it can cater for or tolerate
different levels of user familiarity and performance. Such flexibility implies
that the dialogue is able to adapt either its structure or the inputs it will accept.

The concept of adaption in dialogues is one of the most popular research
areas in man–computer interaction, and a number of techniques for
facilitating simple adaption are discussed later. The main problem lies not in
the technical provision to effect the change in the dialogue but in identifying
what usage characteristics might signal when a change is required and the
nature of that change.

The four traditional dialogue structures all meet these general criteria in
different ways. Some are more natural than others for user/application
combinations. They provide different levels of explicit support. We will now
examine these structures in detail.

4.3 The Question and Answer Structure

4.3.1 Features

The Question and Answer structure (Q&A) is based on an analogy with human–human interaction during an interview. The system takes the role of an interviewer and draws the required information from the user, an answer at a time, by explicit questions. It is the oldest of the dialogue structures since it requires only 'teletype' input and output processes for its implementation; it was originally called Conversational Mode.

The term 'question and answer' is something of a misnomer, since all computer-driven dialogues consist of the system posing questions in one form or another, to which the user responds by supplying answers. However, this process is explicit in the Q&A structure. At each point in the dialogue, the system issues a single explicit question as the prompt, to which the user responds with a single answer. Depending on the answer given, the system can decide what question to ask next. A typical session might proceed as in Fig. 4.1.

Which Ledger	? **sales**
What Option	? **post**
Type of Item	? **invoice**
Invoice number	? **123456**
Customer	? **c123**

Fig. 4.1. A question and answer session.

If an interviewee gives an inappropriate answer, the interviewer normally provides feedback indicating that it is inappropriate and reposes the question. Similarly, if an erroneous response is entered in a Q&A structure, the system displays an error message and reissues the prompt; the process is repeated until an acceptable response is received. The answer will normally be supplied by the user keying a text string. This string may represent either a choice of one of a set possible responses (targets as we have called them), or an arbitrary data item.

4.3.2 Design Criteria

Q&A provides a natural mechanism for requesting both Input Control and Input Data messages; an interviewer can elicit both what somebody wants to do and what they want it done to! There is no restriction on the range or type of input data which can be accommodated. It has been implemented with natural language responses but a 'one word' Limited English grammar is more common.

How natural the interviewee finds the process depends very much on how the questions are asked. If an interviewer asks very long questions, the interviewee will have forgotten what he is to answer by the time he reaches the end of the question; he must also be able to tell easily what is a question and what is not. The same holds true for the Q&A structure.

To facilitate reading, the display width should be restricted to about 40 columns centred in the left-hand two-thirds of the screen. Prompts should be clearly distinguished from the user's responses; this can be achieved by using different cases, contrasts or colours, or by means of punctuation symbols such as colons.

Q&A is moderately supportive since even a concise prompt can be made self-explanatory by judicious phrasing. If necessary, additional assistance such as the format of the input can be incorporated within the prompt, for example:

Invoice date (dd/mm/yy) :

The supportiveness is not increased by verbosity or over-politeness in the phrasing of the prompts. You would soon feel uncomfortable in an interview where the interviewer used very stylised speech or prefixed every question with 'please'. However, Q&A can be made highly supportive for a user who requires this. If a user can reply to any question with a request for help, the system can supply assistance specifically detailing what information is required for that question, e.g.:

Which Option? : **help**
The possible options are:
    post   to post transactions to the ledger
    report   to produce trial balances, statements
                       or aged analyses
    monthend   to roll the ledgers to a new month

Q&A does not necessarily provide the minimum input in terms of keystrokes but, with the use of suitable abbreviation, need not impose any redundancy. Even though input is relatively quick, answering a series of questions one at a time can be tedious for the expert who already knows the questions to be asked and the answers he will give. What is required is a mechanism which enables the user to supply, in a single response, the answers to a string of questions. Such a mechanism, known as *answer-ahead*, can be easily implemented to improve the flexibility of Q&A dialogues and is discussed in Chapter 8.

4.3.3 Implementation

The Q&A structure can be easily implemented in PASCAL using the 'teletype' procedures, Write and ReadLn. However, this mode of operation makes poor use of the facilities provided by a screen so we will consider implementation using the input and output processes discussed in Chapter 3.

There are three basic steps in the structure: the output of the Question, the input of the Answer and the Validation of this answer.

The *question* is a data item of type FieldType — it has a content, a slot on the screen where it is displayed, and a set of attributes which specify how it is to be displayed. It can therefore be created and be displayed using the CreateField and the DisplayField processes.

CreateField(question,'Which Ledger ?',12,1,15,'');

The answer will normally be a text string. We may or may not require that the input is echoed, that it is possible for the user to edit the input string prior to entry, that only certain keys are acceptable, or that input is terminated by a specific character. These are precisely the facilities supported by the ReadField process of Chapter 3.

procedure ReadField (var InField:FieldType;
DataSet:SetOfByte;
ControlDIB:ControlDIBtype)

Thus we must define an *answer* data item of type FieldType, a *filter* specifying a dataset of active keys, and suitable values of keyboard controls in a ControlDIB (Fig. 4.2) data structure:

```
CreateField(answer,'',12,17,9,'fore=black,back=white');
filter:=[ord('a')..ord('z')];
with ControlDIB do
   begin
   rubout:=BS;                  {keycode 8}
   EchoSwitch:=on;
   AcceptField:=CR;             {keycode 13}
   end;
```

The above code fragment specifies that the answer contains a maximum of 9 lower-case alphabetics terminated by a Carriage Return. It will be echoed in a left-justified inverse video field starting at position (12,17). The user may edit his input using the backspace key.

```
ControlDIBtype = record
                 ControlBuffer    : byte;
                 rubout           : byte;
                 EchoSwitch       : OffOn;
                 AcceptField      : byte;
                 RequestAbort     : byte;
                 RequestHelp      : byte;
                 PointNextTarget  : byte;
                 PointPriorTarget : byte;
                 AcceptTarget     : byte;
                 reserved1        : byte;
                 reserved2        : byte;
                 reserved3        : byte;
                 reserved4        : SetOfByte;
                 end;
```

Fig. 4.2. Input process Control DIB.

If the answer represents a choice from a list, the possible answers can specified as a *TargetList*. The MatchString routine described in Fig. 2.7 matches the input against string values; the MatchPosition routine described in Fig. 3.20 matches against Slot values. To accommodate both, we will define each target in the list as a field:

TargetListType = array[1..MaxTargets] of FieldType

When matching an input text string, we will use the content of each target field; when matching an input position report, we will use the slot information for each target field. The MatchString routine of Fig. 2.7 must be modified slightly (as in Fig. 4.3) to reflect this.

In the cases we have considered so far, the input is accepted only if it matches one of the target strings exactly; we shall see that other *matching* strategies are possible:

TypeOfMatching = (exact,abbreviated,partial)

For the present, we deal only with *exact* matching; abbreviated and partial matching are considered in Chapter 9.

If the answer represents an arbitrary data value, some *validation* procedure

```
function MatchString(subject:string;
                     TargetList:TargetListType;
                     NumberOfTargets:byte):byte;
var k,match : byte;
begin
match:=0;
k:=1;
while (k<=NumberOfTargets) and (match=0) do
   if TargetList[k].content=subject then match:=k
                                    else k:=k+1;
MatchString:=match;
end; {MatchString}
```

Fig. 4.3. Matching an input text string.

will be executed, possibly to check the input against a string which specifies a format template.

In either case, if the input is unacceptable an *ErrorMessage* will be displayed; this error message is also of FieldType. There must also be some mechanism for 'undisplaying' this message when the user has seen and acted upon it, presumably when he enters a revised answer. The user may request help in answering the question; a *HelpMessage* must therefore be associated with the question.

For an input data message (such as the invoice number in Fig. 4.1), the system needs to know what the user actually entered; this will be returned as the *content* of the answer field. For an input control message (such as 'Which Ledger' in Fig. 4.1), the actual text string is less likely to be significant; the system is concerned that the user selected the first option rather than that the string 'sales' was entered. The matching process will determine this value — the *CurrentTarget*, allowing the relevant task process to be invoked by a control structure of the form

case   CurrentTarget of
    1: {execute sales ledger task}
    2: {execute purchases ledger task} ....

Thus we can abstract any Q&A process by defining a data structure, a *QandA_DIB*, which specifies all the variables associated with the process. Such a data structure is illustrated in Fig. 4.4 and the Q&A process which utilises it in Fig. 4.5. The input process is complete when either a text string has been entered or any control keycode, other than RequestHelp, has been entered. The function *equal* tests that ControlBuffer contains a non-zero value equal to the keycode for RequestHelp. It is necessary to prevent a zero

```
QandA_DIBtype = record
                question        : FieldType;
                answer          : FieldType;
                filter          : SetOfByte;
                HelpMessage     : FieldType;
                validation      : string;
                ErrorFlag       : OffOn;
                ErrorMessage    : FieldType;
                NumberOfTargets : byte;
                TargetList      : TargetListType;
                matching        : TypeOfMatching;
                CurrentTarget   : byte
                end;
```

Fig. 4.4. A Q&A Dialogue Information Block (Q and A_DIB).

```
procedure ArbitraryData(var QandA_DIB:QandA_DIBtype;
                        var ControlDIB:ControlDIBtype);
var complete : boolean;
begin
with QandA_DIB,ControlDIB do
    begin
    if ErrorFlag=on then DisplayField(ErrorMessage);
    ErrorFlag:=off;
    complete:=false;
    repeat
        DisplayField(question);
        ReadField(answer,filter,ControlDIB);
        HideField(ErrorMessage);
        HideField(HelpMessage);
        if equal(ControlBuffer,RequestAbort) then
            complete:=true
        else
        if equal(ControlBuffer,RequestHelp) then
            begin
            DisplayField(HelpMessage);
            answer.content:='';
            ControlBuffer:=0;      {because it has been actioned}
            end
        else
            complete:=true;
    until complete;
    end;
end; {ArbitraryData}
```

Fig. 4.5. The Q&A process for input of an arbitrary data value.

value in ControlBuffer, which occurs if there is no explicit terminator for text input, matching an undefined (zero) RequestHelp value.

The reason for coding the display of the error message before rather than after the display of the question deserves some comment. It is possible that validation of an arbitrary data item is an application task rather than a dialogue task; for example, it may be necessary to check existence rather than just format. In this case, the validation lies outside the process of Fig. 4.5 but it will still be necessary to keep requesting input until an acceptable answer is entered. This can be achieved by entering the process on the second and subsequent occasions with ErrorFlag set; hence the ErrorFlag parameter is held in the QandA_DIB.

If the answer represents selection from a set of alternatives, i.e. the NumberOfTargets in the QandA_DIB is non-zero, the answer content is matched against the contents of the target fields; the process is repeated until a matching string is entered. The process is illustrated by the procedure, ChooseByID, of Fig. 4.6. If the user requests an abort in response to the

```
procedure ChooseByID(var QandA_DIB:QandA_DIBtype;
                     var ControlDIB:ControlDIBtype);
var complete : boolean;
begin
with QandA_DIB,ControlDIB do
   begin
   complete:=false;
   repeat
      ArbitraryData(QandA_DIB,ControlDIB);
      if (ControlBuffer=0) and (length(answer.content)<>0) then
         begin {a text string has been entered}
         CurrentTarget:=MatchString(answer.content,TargetList,
                                    NumberOfTargets);
         if CurrentTarget<>0 then
            begin
            answer.content:=TargetList[CurrentTarget].content;
            complete:=true;
            end
          else
            ErrorFlag:=on;
         end
      else
      if (ControlBuffer=0) and (length(answer.content)=0) then
         {a null string followed by AcceptField - do nothing}
      else
         {a control character has caused completion}
         complete:=true;
   until complete;
   end;
end; {ChooseByID}
```

Fig. 4.6. Selection from a set of possible options.

question, the ControlBuffer in ControlDIB will contain the keycode for RequestAbort when ChooseByID terminates; the dialogue can test for this and proceed as appropriate.

The following program fragments illustrate the use of these structures to implement the first question and answer step of Fig. 4.1. The user is asked to select one of three possible ledgers, sales, purchases or nominal.

```
with ControlDIB do {initialise the keyboard controls}
   begin
   rubout:=BS;          {keycode 8}
   EchoSwitch:=on;
   AcceptField:=CR;     {keycode 13}
   RequestAbort:=ESC;   {keycode 27}
   RequestHelp:=F1;     {keycode 187}
   end;

with QandA_DIB do {initialise the QandA parameters}
   begin
   CreateField(question,'Which Ledger   : ',12,1,15,'');
   CreateField(answer,' ',12,17,9,'bold=on');
   filter:=[ord('a')..ord('z'),ord('A')..ord('Z')];
   CreateField(HelpMessage,'sales,purchases OR nominal',
               24,10,40,'fore=black,back=white,just=centre');
   validation:='';
   ErrorFlag:=off;
   CreateField(ErrorMessage,'ledger name not recognised',
               24,10,40,'fore=black,back=white,just=centre');
   NumberOfTargets:=3;
   for k:=1 to NumberOfTargets do
      CreateField(TargetList[k],' ',0,0,0,'');
   TargetList[1].content:='sales';
   TargetList[2].content:='purchases';
   TargetList[3].content:='nominal';
   CurrentTarget:=0;
   end;

ChooseByID(QandA_DIB,ControlDIB);
if ControlDIB.ControlBuffer=RequestAbort then
   {processing required for abort}
else
   case QandA_DIB.CurrentTarget of
      1: {sales ledger}
      2: {purchases ledger etc}
```

4.3.4 Summary

Although the Q&A structure rather went out of fashion with the ascendency of the VDT as the input/output processor, it does have a number of virtues. It is very much a middle-of-the-road structure which can cope with a wide variety of user and data types and is moderately supportive and moderately flexible. It is particularly appropriate to dialogues with a great deal of 'branching' i.e. where each question has a large number of possible replies, and the reply influences which question is posed next. For this reason it is often used as the dialogue structure of expert systems.

4.4 The Menu Structure

4.4.1 Features

The menu is probably the most common mechanism for requesting input in computer-driven dialogues. It was an ever-present feature of the early low-cost microcomputer application packages, and was usually what a salesman meant when he described a package as 'user friendly'. Its popularity has increased further with the advent of mouse-based interfaces.

The use of the term *menu* derives from an analogy with the interaction which takes place between a diner and waiter in a restaurant. The essence of the menu structure is that the user is provided with an explicit list of possible inputs from which to select his requirement. There is a variety of formats in which this list may be displayed; some examples are illustrated in Fig. 4.7.

The menu *block* is the traditional format. The other formats have become popular with the 'windowing' techniques now common on microcomputers and are discussed in detail in Chapter 10. The menu *bar* may appear at either the top or bottom of the screen and frequently remains in position throughout the dialogue. It is thus a convenient way of displaying options which are available at all points in the dialogue. Another common technique is for subsidiary menus to be presented as blocks which *pop up/drop down* or are *pushed up/pulled down* from the bar. *Icon* menus appear as a set of target blocks scattered across the screen; frequently the target contains a pictorial representation of the option.

The operation of a Menu dialogue follows the restaurant analogy very closely. The waiter hands the menu to the customer who scans the menu and indicates his choice. There is no need for an explicit question by the waiter to elicit this choice although he may give some indication that he is ready. Similarly, there is no need for an explicit question to be displayed in a Menu dialogue.

The customer may indicate his choice in two ways:

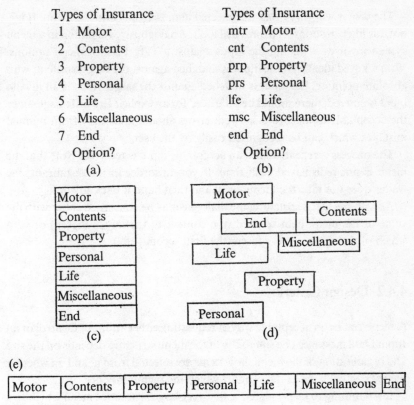

Fig. 4.7. Some examples of different menu formats.
(a) Block with numeric codes; (b) block with mnemonic codes; (c) menu block; (d) 'icon' format; (e) menu bar.

- by quoting the identifier of a menu item
- by pointing at an item; he may point at the item directly or he may run his finger down the list until he gets to it.

Similarly, the user may select in a menu dialogue by entering a text string which identifies an item, by pointing at it directly, or by scrolling through the list.

It is possible for the system to step through the items on the list, with the user pressing a key to confirm when the current item is the one required. This is equivalent to the waiter reciting the courses available, and the diner nodding when the required item is reached. In a computer-based dialogue, this method has problems since the waiter is usually better able to judge the speed at which to step through the list than is the system.

The waiter will check that the selected item is actually on the menu. If it is not, his likely response is a quizzical look. Analogously, validation in a menu system involves matching the input against a TargetList of menu options. With a keyed identifier, the input is matched against the target content; with absolute pointing, the input is matched against the target slots. If an invalid input is entered, there should be little need for an explicit ErrorMessage; since the acceptable inputs are displayed, errors should arise only from manual mistakes which can be recognised easily by the user.

The process is repeated until an acceptable input is received. Note that the menu is not redisplayed each time. If you misorder in the restaurant, the waiter does not take the menu away and then hand it back to you!

As with the Q&A structure, the dialogue may be concerned either with the value of the menu item selected (the content of the target chosen) or with which of the options was chosen (the first, second, etc.)

4.4.2 Design Criteria

A menu can be an acceptable way of requesting either an Input Control or an Input Data message. The suitability of the menu structure depends on the size and organisation of the menu, how items are selected from it, and on whether the user actually needs the support which the menu provides.

It is daunting to be presented with a very large restaurant menu which you can hardly read let alone comprehend. The same is true of a large list on a screen, with the added complication that it is harder to read than the printed page. Ideally, a screen menu should contain 5–6 alternatives; lists of 10 or more items should generally be avoided. A menu which is too small is equally unnatural. There is no need of a menu in the Monty Python restaurant serving only

> spam
> spam and spam
> spam, spam and spam

Some designers have even implemented traditonal block menus when YES and NO were the only options!

If a large number of choices exist, they should be organised into a hierarchy of smaller menus, just as a large restaurant menu is split into hors d'oeuvres, fish, entrées and deserts. Figure 4.8 shows the menu that might be presented after the user chooses 'Motor' in the insurance menu shown in Fig. 4.7. If you

Motor
New Risk
Renewal
Amendment
Cancellation
Claim
End

Fig. 4.8. A subsidiary menu in the hierarchy.

cannot easily derive a natural hierarchical grouping, it suggests very strongly that a menu structure is the wrong approach. For this reason, menus are seldom appropriate for input data messages (such as entering a customer code or a filename) where the range of options is very large.

Some authors have demonstrated exceptions to the above generalisations. On slow speed terminal networks, a flat hierarchy of large (multicolumn) menus may be preferred to a deep hierarchy of smaller menus; this helps to overcome time lags in redrawing the screen for successive menus. Providing a consistent scrolling mechanism for all selection inputs throughout the system may also result in menus containing a large number of items, such as filenames in a directory, which cannot be subdivided; it may also result in yes/no menus.

Within each menu of a hierarchy the ordering of the items in a list is significant — the entrées on a restaurant menu do not appear in a random order but are listed by type of meat, price, or some other classification. Similarly, in a dialogue menu, the items should follow a natural ordering, if such can be identified. If there is any doubt about a 'natural' order, or where the list is relatively long, the items should be listed in alphabetical order. Take care not to imply an ordering of priorities where none exists, or to imply a wrong ordering. People tend to believe that Item 1 on a list should be undertaken before Item 2. For this reason, the exit option is often the last item on a menu.

The menu structure is the most natural mechanism for use with a point and pick input; the menu display provides the targets at which the user aims. If the dialogue consists exclusively of menus, a consistent interface can be provided in which the user needs to utilise only the pointing device; this total consistency can seldom be achieved in practice. It should also be noted that although these mechanisms place less stress on keyboard skills, they may not be the quickest way for an experienced user to select an item.

All the considerations for point and pick discussed in Chapter 3 apply. The menu should consist of a limited number of relatively large, well spaced and clearly labelled targets so that the user can readily identify where to aim, and easily move to that position; it is common to provide this identification by 'boxing' the item with a particular attribute feature. The currently selected target should be identified by a consistent highlight.

Instead of pointing, the user may indicate his choice by entering an identifier. The identifier may be the name of the option as shown on the screen, e.g. 'Property' if he was dealing with property insurance. Two problems arise: first, he must type exactly what appears on the screen, or the dialogue must make allowances for slight deviations (such as not starting with a capital P); secondly, this process involves pressing several keys, which increases the likelihood of error. The keying can be reduced either by allowing the user to enter an *abbreviated name*, or by using *coded identifiers* for the options.

Item names can often be chosen so that the first letter of each is unique. In this case, a single letter is sufficient to identify the selection. This would not work for the examples in Fig. 4.7 (Property/Personal and Motor/Miscellaneous), where a two- or three-letter abbreviation is better. However, the designer must guard against sacrificing naturalness by using opaque phrasing to provide one-character abbreviation; a well-known word processing package uses E to identify rEname, because R has been used to identify Run.

Identifiers may be coded using function keys, mnemonic codes or numeric identifiers. *Function keys* can be 'customised' so that one function key is allocated to each option, and the user only needs to press one key to select an option. This approach is used in automatic bank tills where different buttons are assigned meanings such as cash, balance, etc. Their use is particularly approriate where keys can be assigned the same value throughout the system, i.e. where the same items appear on several menus.

Where the user types a coded identifier such as a mnemonic or numeric code, it should be immediately apparent from the menu display precisely what is to be input. The codes should be distinguishable from any associated description either by their attributes or by leaving two or three spaces between identifier and description.

Mnemonic identifiers are useful where natural abbreviation is not easy (for example, you could use MTR for MOTOR), but care must be taken to ensure that they are both commonsense and sufficiently distinct to avoid being sensitive to common keying errors. If the rules for forming the mnemonic are straighforward and result in a code which is readily associated with the item, users will find it easy to remember. As they become familiar with the system, they will not need consciously to read the menu display.

Numeric identifiers have been a very popular way of coding options in menu structured dialogues, particularly with programmers! Outside computing, numbers are used in chinese restaurants and on wine lists, where it is undoubtedly easier to ask for Item 41 than for a bottle of Gewürztraminer. The criteria for naturalness suggests that they would be appropriate to a computer dialogue where no other means of identification is easily available. Numeric identifiers are not memorable since there is no natural association between the identifier and the item itself. They can suggest priorities where none exist, and can lead to problems of consistency: if 'end' is the last option on each of a group of different menus, it may be variously identified by 4, 9, 6, 8, and so on.

One rationale for their widespread use is that it reduces both the number of keystrokes and the set of keys from which they are drawn. Whilst it is true that a numeric key is easier for the inexperienced typist to locate than an alphabetic, a cynic might point out that their use makes life easier for the programmer too! Perhaps a pointing technique would be more suitable for a poor typist. Designers considering the use of numeric identifiers should take care to avoid the absurdity (drawn from an actual system) of Fig. 4.9.

4.4.3 Implementation

The menu structure has two basic steps — a single display of the menu followed by a repeated request for input until a valid selection has been made.

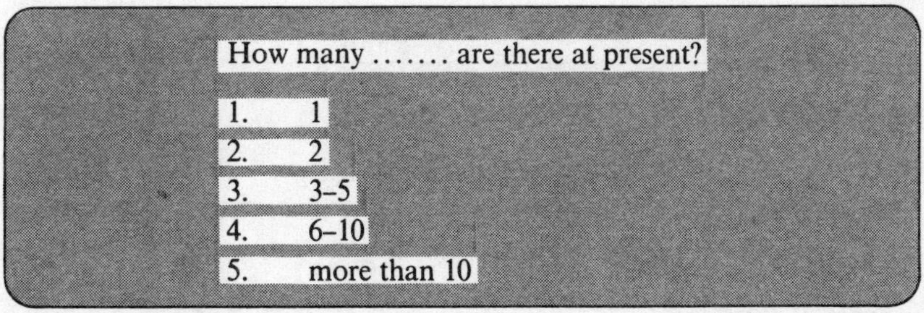

Fig. 4.9. A problem with numeric identifiers?

4.4.3.1 Displaying the Menu

The display of any menu is merely the output of a text message. This text message, the menu, comprises a set of fields; amongst this set of fields are the targets against which the input is to be validated. The various display formats illustrated in Fig. 4.7 look quite different but can in fact be specified by simple variations of values in a common data structure.

As illustrated in Fig. 4.10, each menu consists of

An optional Menu Header; this can be defined as a data structure of FieldType since it has a content, a slot in which it appears, and a set of attributes specifying how it appears.

An optional Menu Trailer also of FieldType.

A Menu Body consisting of a list of targets. Each target identifies a particular menu item; there may also be supplementary text providing a further description of each item. Both target and supplementary text are of type FieldType.

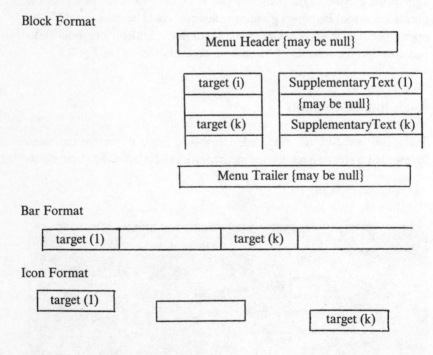

Block Format

Menu Header {may be null}

target (i)	SupplementaryText (1)
	{may be null}
target (k)	SupplementaryText (k)

Menu Trailer {may be null}

Bar Format

target (1)		target (k)	

Icon Format

target (1)		target (k)

Fig. 4.10. Commonality of menu structures.

A menu block may or may not have a Header and/or a Trailer. If selection is by a keyed identifier, the target content contains the identifier and the target slot and attributes identify how and where this is displayed; usually a supplementary text field is necessary to describe or complete the description of the item corresponding to the identifier. If selection is by pointing, the target itself describes the item and no supplementary text is necessary. The block display is achieved by specifying

target[i+1].slot.row   = target[i].slot.row + n
target[i+1].slot.col   = target[i].slot.col
target[i+1].slot.width = target[i].slot.width

where n is the number of rows by which the targets are separated on the screen.

A menu bar has a null Header field, a null Trailer field and null Supplementary text fields. The bar format is produced by specifying

target[i+1].slot.row = target[i].slot.row
target[i+1].slot.col = target[i].slot.col + target[i].slot.width

In the icon format, the Header is usually null; the Trailer and all supplementary text fields are null. The targets are usually displayed in a regular fashion initially (along the bottom or down one side of the screen), but the user can often move them to wherever he wishes. Since this may result in targets scattered randomly around the screen, there is no specific relationship between the target slots.

A menu can be defined by a data structure of type MenuDIBtype as illustrated in Fig. 4.11. It is quite common to enhance the display of the menu by actually drawing boxes around it, as in Fig. 4.8; in text-based dialogues the boxes can be created with the line segment symbols which appear in the extended character sets of many microcomputers. The use of these *decorators*

```
MenuDIBtype = record
             MenuHeader          : FieldType;
             NumberOfOptions     : byte;
             TargetList          : TargetListType;
             SupplementaryList   : TargetListType;
             MenuTrailer         : FieldType;
             end;
```

Fig. 4.11. A menu Dialogue Information Block (MenuDIB).

can be included in the MenuDIB data structure by incorporating another list
of fields to specify them.

Once suitable values have been assigned to a menu variable (for example,
using the CreateField procedure), the menu can be displayed by a procedure
of the form illustrated in Fig. 4.12. Note that the screen is cleared before the
menu is displayed; in Chapter 10 we consider cases where only that portion
of the screen occupied by the menu display is cleared.

Selection from a menu block is normally achieved by keying an identifier
or by scrolling. Menu Bars are usually associated with scrolling and the Icon
format with absolute pointing. However, any of these input techniques may
be used with any of the formats.

4.4.3.2 Selection by Identifier

Selection by keying an identifier is essentially the same as for the Q&A
structure. A data structure of type ControlDIBtype must be initialised with
suitable values for the rubout and AcceptField characters and the Echo-
Switch. An answer field which will hold the input must be initialised with the
echo characteristics, and a filter specifying the active keys must be defined. A
TargetList must be initialised with the target values.

Thus we can abstract the process of selection by keying an identifier into the
same QandA_DIB, illustrated in Fig. 4.4, that was used for the Q&A
structure. For selection from a menu, the question and ErrorMessage fields
will typically be null since there is normally no need for either an explicit
question or error message. The input can then be accepted with the procedure
ChooseByID illustrated in Fig. 4.6.

procedure ChooseByID(var QandA_DIB:QandA_DIBtype;
var ControlDIB:ControlDIBtype)

```
procedure DisplayMenu(MenuDIB:MenuDIBtype);
var k : byte;
begin
ClearScreen;
with MenuDIB do
   begin
   DisplayField(MenuHeader);
   for k:=1 to NumberOfOptions do
      begin
      DisplayField(TargetList[k]);
      DisplayField(SupplementaryList[k]);
      end;
   DisplayField(MenuTrailer);
   end;
end; {DisplayMenu}
```

Fig. 4.12. Displaying the menu.

Selection from the menu illustrated in Fig. 4.7(b) can then be implemented with program fragments of the form:

```
with ControlDIB do {initialise the keyboard controls}
    begin
    rubout:=BS;            {keycode 8}
    EchoSwitch:=on;
    AcceptField:=CR;       {keycode 13}
    RequestAbort:=ESC;     {keycode 27}
    RequestHelp:=F1;       {keycode 187}
    end;


with QandA_DIB do {initialise the QandA parameters}
    begin
    CreateField(question,'',0,0,0,'');
    CreateField(answer,' ',15,16,3,'bold=on');
    filter:=[ord('a')..ord('z')];
    CreateField(HelpMessage,'enter the 3 character code',
                24,10,40,'fore=black,back=white,just=centre');
    validation:='';
    ErrorFlag:=off;
    CreateField(ErrorMessage,'',0,0,0,'');
    NumberOfTargets:=7;
    CreateField(TargetList[1],'mtr',7,10,3,'');
    CreateField(TargetList[2],'cnt',8,10,3,'');
    CreateField(TargetList[3],'prp',9,10,3,' ');
    CreateField(TargetList[4],'prs',10,10,3,' ');
    CreateField(TargetList[5],'lfe',11,10,3,' ');
    CreateField(TargetList[6],'msc',12,10,3,' ');
    CreateField(TargetList[7],'end',13,10,3,' ');
    CurrentTarget:=0;
    end;


with MenuDIB do
    begin
    CreateField(MenuHeader,'Types of insurance',5,8,18,'');
    NumberOfOptions:=7;
    for k:=1 to NumberOfOptions do
        MenuDIB.TargetList[k]:=QandA_DIB.TargetList[k];
    CreateField(SupplementaryList[1],'Motor',7,15,13,'');
    CreateField(SupplementaryList[2],'Contents',8,15,13,'');
    CreateField(SupplementaryList[3],'Property',9,15,13,'');
    CreateField(SupplementaryList[4],'Personal',10,15,13,'');
    CreateField(SupplementaryList[5],'Life',11,15,13,'');
    CreateField(SupplementaryList[6],'Miscellaneous',12,15,13,'');
    CreateField(SupplementaryList[7],'End',13,15,13,'');
    CreateField(MenuTrailer,'Option?',15,8,7,'');
    end;


DisplayMenu(MenuDIB);
ChooseByID(QandA_DIB,ControlDIB);
if ControlDIB.ControlBuffer=RequestAbort then
    {processing required for abort}
else
case QandA_DIB.CurrentTarget of
    1: {processing for motor}
    2: {processing for contents etc}
```

4.4.3.3 Selection by Scrolling

Selection by scrolling is a straightforward utilisation of the RelativePick process which was described in Chapter 3.

> **procedure RelativePick(TargetList:TargetListType;**
> **NumberOfTargets:byte;**
> **highlight:AttributesType;**
> **var ControlDIB:ControlDIBtype;**
> **var TargetChosen:byte);**

A ControlDIB data structure must be initialised with the character values that denote a scroll forward, a scroll backward, and picking of the current target:

```
with ControlDIB do
   begin                   {since no data characters are entered}
   rubout:=0;              {editing is inappropriate}
   EchoSwitch:=off;  {there is nothing to echo}
   AcceptField:=0;   {and there is no text string to terminate}
   PointNextTarget:=CursorUp;        {keycode 200}
   PointPriorTarget:=CursorDown;     {keycode 208}
   AcceptTarget:=CR;                 {keycode 13}
   end;
```

Each menu item field is a *target* in the TargetList. The RelativePick procedure returns the ordinal in the TargetList of the users choice but the dialogue may need the data value which corresponds to this choice. We define an *answer* data structure of FieldType whose content will return this value. The attributes of answer specify the highlight to be applied to the current target; this seems a logical usage since they would define the echo for a keyed identifier.

A very common way of highlighting is by reversing the foreground and background colours. To facilitate the coding of such a feature we will include a procedure

procedure InvertField(field:FieldType)

which swops the foreground and background colours of a field. The answer field can then be initialised by statements of the form:

CreateField(answer,″,0,0,0,″);   {default attributes}
InvertField(answer);   {inverse video}

We can also abstract this process using our QandA_DIB data structure. It is hard to imagine how the user can make an error when scrolling, hence there is no use for the ErrorFlag and ErrorMessage items with this mechanism. Selection from the menu by scrolling can be accomplished via the procedure ChooseByScroll illustrated in Fig. 4.13.

Selection from the menu bar illustrated in Fig. 4.7(e) can then be implemented with program fragments of the form:

```
with ControlDIB do {initialise the keyboard controls}
    begin
    rubout:=0;
    EchoSwitch:=off;
    AcceptField:=0;
    RequestAbort:=ESC;              {keycode 27}
    RequestHelp:=Fl;               {keycode 187}
    PointNextTarget:=CursorRight;  {keycode 203}
    PointPriorTarget:=CursorLeft;  {keycode 205}
    AcceptTarget:=CR;              {keycode 13}
    end;

with QandA_DIB do {initialise the QandA parameters}
    begin
    CreateField(question,'',0,0,0,'');
    CreateField(answer,' ',0,0,0,''); InvertField(answer);
    filter:=[];
    CreateField(HelpMessage,'-> forward  <- backward  <-] pick',
                24,10,40,'fore=black,back=white,just=centre');
    validation:='';
    ErrorFlag:=off;
    CreateField(ErrorMessage,'',0,0,0,'');
    NumberOfTargets:=7;
    CreateField(TargetList[1],'Motor    ',1,1,8,'');
    CreateField(TargetList[2],'Contents  ',1,9,10,'');
    CreateField(TargetList[3],'Property  ',1,19,10,'');
    CreateField(TargetList[4],'Personal',1,29,10,'');
    CreateField(TargetList[5],'Life',1,39,10,'');
    CreateField(TargetList[6],'Miscellaneous',1,49,14,'');
    CreateField(TargetList[7],'End',1,63,3,'');
    CurrentTarget:=1;
    end;

with MenuDIB do
    begin
    CreateField(MenuHeader,'',0,0,0,'');
    NumberOfOptions:=7;
    for k:=1 to NumberOfOptions do
        begin
        MenuDIB.TargetList[k]:=QandA_DIB.TargetList[k];
        CreateField(SupplementaryList[k],'',0,0,0,'');
        end;
    CreateField(MenuTrailer,'',0,0,0,'');
    end;

DisplayMenu(MenuDIB);
ChooseByScroll(QandA_DIB,ControlDIB);
if equal(ControlDIB.ControlBuffer,RequestAbort) then
    {processing required for abort}
else
    case QandA_DIB.CurrentTarget of
        1: {processing for motor etc}
```

```
procedure ChooseByScroll(var QandA_DIB:QandA_DIBtype;
                           var ControlDIB:ControlDIBtype);
var complete : boolean;
begin

with QandA_DIB,ControlDIB do
   begin
   complete:=false;
   repeat
      DisplayField(question);
      RelativePick(TargetList,NumberOfTargets,answer.attributes,
                   ControlDIB,CurrentTarget);
      answer.content:=TargetList[CurrentTarget].content;
      HideField(HelpMessage);
      if equal(ControlBuffer,RequestAbort) then
         complete:=true
      else
      if equal(ControlBuffer,RequestHelp) then
         DisplayField(HelpMessage)
      else
         complete:=true;
   until complete;
   end;
end; {ChooseByScroll}
```

Fig. 4.13. Selection from a menu by scrolling.

```
procedure ChooseByPosition(var QandA_DIB:QandA_DIBtype;
                             var ControlDIB:ControlDIBtype);
var complete : boolean;
begin
with QandA_DIB,ControlDIB do
   begin
   complete:=false;
   repeat
      DisplayField(question);
      AbsolutePick(TargetList,NumberOfTargets,answer.attributes,
                   ControlDIB,CurrentTarget);
      HideField(ErrorMessage);
      HideField(HelpMessage);
      if equal(ControlBuffer,RequestAbort) then
         complete:=true
      else
      if equal(ControlBuffer,RequestHelp) then
         DisplayField(HelpMessage)
      else
      if CurrentTarget<>0 then
         begin
         answer.content:=TargetList[CurrentTarget].content;
         complete:=true;
         end
      else
         DisplayField(ErrorMessage);
   until complete;
   end;
end; {ChooseByPosition}
```

Fig. 4.14. Selection from a menu by DirectPointing.

4.4.3.4 Selection by Pointing

Selection from a menu by direct pointing is a straightforward utilisation of the AbsolutePick procedure described in Chapter 3.

> **procedure AbsolutePick(TargetList:TargetListType;**
>   **NumberOfTargets:byte;**
>   **highlight:AttributesType;**
>   **var ControlDIB:ControlDIBtype**
>   **var TargetChosen:byte);**

It can be abstracted by the same QandA_DIB. Selection from the menu can be implemented by the procedure ChooseByPosition of Fig. 4.14. The parameters for this procedure are initialised in a similar way to that described for ChooseByScroll. The values in ControlDIB will differ since there are no values for PointNextTarget and PointPriorTarget. There may or may not be a value for AcceptTarget. The presence of a non-null AcceptTarget character implies the user must pick explicitly (by pressing a mouse button for example); its absence implies that a target is to be picked as soon as the user points to it.

Selection by explicit picking from the icon menu illustrated in Fig. 4.7(d) can then be implemented with program fragments of the form

```
with ControlDIB do {initialise the keyboard controls}
    begin
    rubout:=0;
    EchoSwitch:=off;
    AcceptField:=0;
    RequestAbort:=ESC;              {keycode 27}
    RequestHelp:=F1;                {keycode 187}
    PointNextTarget:=0;
    PointPriorTarget:=0;
    AcceptTarget:=CR;               {keycode 13}
    end;

ObjectFormat:='back=blue,fore=white,just=centre';
with QandA_DIB do {initialise the QandA parameters}
    begin
    CreateField(question,'',0,0,0,ObjectFormat);
    CreateField(answer,' ',0,0,0,ObjectFormat); InvertField(answer);
    filter:=[];
    CreateField(HelpMessage,
                'position to option required and press <-] ',
                24,10,40,ObjectFormat);
    validation:='';
    ErrorFlag:=off;
    CreateField(ErrorMessage,'not pointing at any option',
                24,10,40,ObjectFormat);
    NumberOfTargets:=7;
    CreateField(TargetList[1],'Motor',2,60,10,ObjectFormat);
    CreateField(TargetList[2],'Contents',4,70,10,ObjectFormat);
    CreateField(TargetList[3],'Property',6,30,10,ObjectFormat);
    CreateField(TargetList[4],'Personal',8,40,10,ObjectFormat);
```

```
CreateField(TargetList[5],'Life',10,70,10,ObjectFormat);
CreateField(TargetList[6],'Miscellaneous',12,10,14,ObjectFormat);
CreateField(TargetList[7],'End',14,50,10,ObjectFormat);
CurrentTarget:=0;
end;

with MenuDIB do
   begin
   CreateField(MenuHeader,'',0,0,0,'');
   NumberOfOptions:=7;
   for k:=1 to NumberOfOptions do
      begin
      MenuDIB.TargetList[k]:=QandA_DIB.TargetList[k];
      CreateField(SupplementaryList[k],'',0,0,0,'');
      end;
   CreateField(MenuTrailer,'',0,0,0,'');
   end;

DisplayMenu(MenuDIB);
ChooseByPosition(QandA_DIB,ControlDIB);
if equal(ControlDIB.ControlBuffer,RequestAbort) then
   {processing required for abort}
else
   case QandA_DIB.CurrentTarget of
      1: {processing for motor}
      2: {processing for contents etc}
```

4.4.4 Summary

Using a menu in a restaurant presupposes a range of courses with which you are not particularly familiar. If you eat regularly at a pizza restaurant offering five or six different pizzas, with all of which your stomach is intimately acquainted, you will not use the menu. Their ease of implementation has resulted in traditional menus being rather over-used for any man–computer dialogue involving selection from a set of options.

Menus are a natural mechanism for use with pointing. They can also provide a consistent interface with a device like the mouse.

The menu is the most supportive structure for novice users. Note however that a menu does not necessarily provide all the support required. It may tell you that 'Rillettes de Veau' is a possible main course; this may not give you any idea of its impact on your stomach!

The converse of its supportiveness is that it can become tedious for an experienced user. The traditional menu structure is inflexible and not very compatible with the use of techniques, such as AnswerAhead, to speed selection by experienced users. Prestel was intended as an information service for the general public and uses a menu hierarchy with numeric identifiers to select the information required. The slowness of this technique caused frustration in many business users who always accessed the same types of information. A mechanism for direct access to any particular area of information was overlaid on the menu structure to alleviate this problem.

4.5 The Supressed Menu

Both the Q&A structure and the menu structure request a single answer to a single question. In the menu structure, this answer always involves choosing from a list; in the Q&A structure, the answer may involve choosing from a list or it may involve supplying an arbitrary data value. A menu provides additional support to an inexperienced user by displaying the list explicitly before the question is asked.

The basic similarity between the two structures is emphasised by the fact that an abstraction for the input process in both can be defined in terms of the same data structures:

- A ControlDIB which contains values controlling the operation of the input/output process.
- A QandA_DIB which contains values specifying the question to be asked, what to do with the answer, what constitutes a valid answer, and how to respond to exceptional inputs such as an invalid input or request for help.

A number of different processes operate on these structures depending on how the user is expected to enter the answer. Selection from a menu may utilise a keyed identifier (procedure ChooseByID), scrolling (ChooseBy Scroll) or absolute pointing (ChooseByPosition). Q&A may be used for selection (ChooseByID) or to supply data (procedure ArbitraryData). Selection is involved in a Q&A structure if the NumberOfTargets in the QandA_DIB is non-zero. For a menu, the dialogue needs to know which selection mechanism is to be used. This can be accomplished by extending the QandA_DIB, as illustrated in Fig. 4.15, to include a SelectionType indicator.

A single procedure, Q&A, will then handle all the possibilities; this is illustrated in Figure 4.16.

This general dialogue input process suggests another variant. Selection in a Q&A structure usually involves keying a text string; this is not the only mechanism, however. Obviously direct pointing is impossible (there is nothing to point at), but consider the following program fragments:

```
with ControlDIB do
   begin                       {define a scrolling mechanism}
   rubout:=0;
   EchoSwitch:=off;
   AcceptField:=0;
   PointNextTarget:=CursorRight;      {keycode 205}
   PointPriorTarget:=CursorLeft;      {keycode 203}
   AcceptTarget:=CR;                  {keycode  13}
   end;

with QandA_DIB do {initialise the QandA parameters}
   begin
   CreateField(question,'Which Ledger   :',12,1,15,'');
   CreateField(answer,'  ',12,17,9,'bold=on');
   filter:=[];
   CreateField(HelpMessage,'-> next   <- previous   <-] select',
               24,10,40,'fore=black,back=white,just=centre');
   ErrorFlag:=off;
   CreateField(ErrorMessage,'',0,0,0,'');
   NumberOfTargets:=3;
   for k:=1 to NumberOfTargets do
       CreateField(TargetList[k],'',12,17,9,'');
   TargetList[1].content:='sales';
   TargetList[2].content:='purchases';
   TargetList[3].content:='nominal';
   SelectionBy:=scroll;
   CurrentTarget:=0;
   end;

QandA(QandA_DIB,ControlDIB);
```

This mechanism is like a scroll menu. However, the display of the menu has been supressed and replaced with an explicit question. Furthermore, the answer field and each target all have the same slot i.e. would be displayed in the same position on the screen. The user by pressing the cursor left and right keys can echo the possible answers in turn through the answer field; when the

```
SelectionType = (id,scroll,position);

QandA_DIBtype = record
                question        : FieldType;
                answer          : FieldType;
                filter          : SetOfByte;
                HelpMessage     : FieldType;
                validation      : string;
                ErrorFlag       : OffOn;
                ErrorMessage    : FieldType;
                NumberOfTargets : byte;
                TargetList      : TargetListType;
                matching        : TypeOfMatching;
                CurrentTarget   : byte;
                SelectionBy     : SelectionType;
                end;
```

Fig. 4.15. The general Q&A Dialogue Information Block.

```
procedure QandA(var QandA_DIB:QandA_DIDtype;
                var ControlDIB:ControlDIBtype);
begin
if QandA_DIB.NumberOfTargets=0 then
   ArbitraryData(QandA_DIB,ControlDIB)
else
   case QandA_DIB.SelectionBy of
      id       : ChooseByID(QandA_DIB,ControlDIB);
      scroll   : ChooseByScroll(QandA_DIB,ControlDIB);
      position : ChooseByPosition(QandA_DIB,ControlDIB);
   end; {case}
end; {QandA}
```

Fig. 4.16. A general dialogue input process.

Which Ledger	:	**sales**	{user presses -> to produce}
Which Ledger	:	**purchases**	{user presses -> to produce}
Which Ledger	:	**nominal**	{user presses <- to produce}
Which Ledger	:	**purchases**	{user presses CR to select}

Fig. 4.17. The suppressed menu.

desired answer is reached, pressing CarriageReturn selects whatever is currently displayed. This is illustrated in Fig. 4.17.

This *suppressed menu* mechanism provides a useful alternative to a linear set of traditional block menus, i.e. in cases where a fixed number of selections each from a limited range of options is required, there is no space to display a menu for each and it is difficult to design suitable keyed identifiers. The inputs can be obtained via a series of questions all displayed on the same screen and without imposing a significant keying load.

4.6 Summary

The quality of any dialogue may be assessed against five main criteria:

   naturalness
   consistency
   non-redundancy
   supportiveness
   flexibility

Dialogues are traditionally classified into four basic structures, each based on a different analogy with human–human interaction, and which meet the criteria in different ways and are therefore suited to different types of user and of application.

The menu structure displays an explicit list of options and invites the user to select one by:

keying an identifier
scrolling
pointing at it.

It suits selection, particularly by pointing, from a small set of options; it is highly supportive of inexperienced users and can be made very consistent.

The Question and Answer dialogue is suitable for both selection and data entry; there is no restriction on the range of data values but the structure does not fit with pointing techniques as well as the menu. It is not automatically very supportive but can provide any level of support on request.

There is considerable commonality between the two structures; the menu structure is effectively Q&A with an automatic help facility: Q&A with Help Ahead. The input process for both mechanisms can be abstracted into a common QandA_DIB data structure.

In fact there is also considerable overlap within the selection procedures ChooseByID, ChooseByScroll and ChooseByPosition; all contain similar facilities for handling errors, aborts and help requests. Appendix H details a common dialogue input procedure which recognises these similarities.

Both the Question and Answer and the Menu structure deal with a single answer at a time. In the next chapter, we consider the remaining two traditional structures – the Form and the Command – which supply a series of answers at each input step.

Programming Exercises

P1. A block menu may be boxed with line segment characters as in

Header
Targets
Trailer

Boxing may be indicated by including in the MenuDIB another attribute, boxed : boolean. Develop an amended version of the DisplayMenu procedure to cater for boxed or unboxed menus. Note that the header and trailer fields are optional.

P2. Develop a procedure, SeeField, which utilises a Q&A dialogue structure to request a definition of the contents, slot and attributes of a field and then displays the results of this definition. The attributes should be selected with a supressed menu mechanism.

P3. Implement a 'Job Title Generator' which displays three fields in a row, each containing one word of a three word job title, e.g.

Finance	Project	Manager
Production	Support	Analyst
Marketing	Project	Programmer
Software	Team	Leader
....	....	Director

Each box will contain one word chosen at random from the list of words below it. The combination of words will appear for about one second and then 'spin' to a new combination. This process will be repeated until the user presses the space bar. The first time the space bar is pressed, the left hand box will be 'held'. The remaining two boxes will continue to spin until the space bar is pressed again to hold the second box. The process terminates when the space bar is pressed the third time. Such a program uses the 'NoWait' type of keyboard input.

Some cynics believe that such a program is actually responsible for some of the job titles dreamed up in DP departments.

P4. Develop a procedure NeonSign which fills the screen with the string 'neon'. The string is intially output at position (1,1), and advanced 4 characters each time it is output, i.e.

(1,1) (1,5)....(1,77) (2,1)............(24,77) (1,1)........

The process continues until the user presses a specified key, whereupon a bar menu of colours is displayed in row 25 of the screen. The user selects a colour from the menu by scrolling and line 25 is cleared. The display of the string 'neon' continues from the point at which it was interrupted but using the selected colour as the foreground attribute.

P5. Amend the procedure of P4 such that the menu bar is replaced by a block menu which 'pops up' in the middle of the screen. The area of screen occupied by the menu must be saved before the menu is displayed and restored afterwards. (See question P5 of Chapter 3.)

This is a common technique in recent interfaces. A utility package is loaded into memory and an application package is loaded adjacent to it. The keyboard interrupt routine is amended to trap key sequences which invoke the utility package. The user runs the application package normally but if he enters one of the special key sequences, the utility program springs into life. As soon as the requested function has been executed, it goes back to sleep.

Further Reading

Kiger J. I. (1984) 'The Breadth/depth Trade-off in the design of Menu-driven User Interfaces', *Int. J.Man-Machine Studies*, **20**, 2.

Koved L. and Shneiderman B. (1983) 'Embedded Menus: Menu Selection in Context', *Comm.ACM*, **26**.

Morland V.D. (1983) 'Human-factors Guidelines for Terminal Interface Design', *Comm.ACM*, **26**, 7.

Norman D. A. (1984) 'Stages and Levels in Human-machine Interaction', *Int. J.Man-Machine Studies*, **21**, 4.

Perlman G. (1984) 'Making the Right Choice with Menus', *INTERACT '84*.

Shneiderman B. (1986) *Designing the User Interface*, Addison Wesley.

Smith S. and Mosier J. L. (1984) *Design Guidelines for User Interface Software*, MITRE Corporation.

Spence R. and Apperley M. (1983) 'Hierarchical Dialogue Structures in Interactive Computer Systems', *Software Prac. and Exp.*, **13**, 9.

Stewart T. (1980) 'Communicating with Dialogues', *Ergonomics*, **23**, 9.

Thimbleby H. (1980) 'Dialogue Determination', *Int.J.Man-Machine Studies*, **13**, 3.

Chapter 5

Dialogue structures – forms, commands and hybrids

5.1 Introduction

In Chapter 4 we examined the characteristics of the Question and Answer and of the menu structures. Both request a single answer to a single question and we saw that the same abstraction can be used to define the input process in either structure. In this chapter, we consider two structures which request a series of answers and will see that this same abstraction applies to the processing of each individual answer in the series.

The four structures represent a broad classification of a single step in a dialogue. Each is suited to a particular class of user or type of input message. However, the dialogues for most applications must handle a variety of input message types and different levels of familiarity; no one dialogue structure is suitable for the whole of the dialogue. We examine how these basic structures may be combined to cater for differing requirements in different areas of the system. We will refer to these combinations as *hybrid* structures.

5.2 The Form Filling Structure

5.2.1 Features

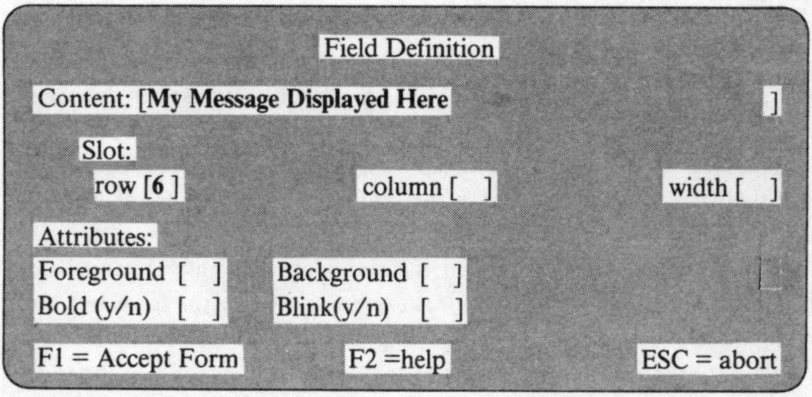

Fig. 5.1. A form dialogue.

One way of obtaining information from other people is to ask them questions and listen to their replies, an approach reflected in the Question and Answer structure. Another approach is to have them fill in the information on a form, such as the one shown in Fig. 5.1.

Forms are widely used for ordering goods, making reservations or payments, completing insurance proposals, as questionnaires and so forth. The clerical procedures in most companies are based on standard forms such as invoices, sales orders and purchase orders; in fact forms are generally used where the recording of an activity (*transaction*) requires the entry of a fairly standard set of data items.

The form dialogue structure is based on an analogy with this way of collecting information. Unlike the Q&A structure which presents questions one at a time, the user is presented with a set of questions. This set is relatively standard in the sense that answers to previous questions in the set do not normally influence whether a particular question is asked.

A clerical form is usually filled in by working from left to right and top to bottom. The person completing the form can make alterations whilst entering an answer, skip over questions temporarily, go back and change the answer to a previous question, or even tear up the form and start again. He maintains control up to the point when the form is handed over to the recipient.

Form dialogues typically provide the same facilities. A user may edit an individual answer as it is being entered. He may also move around the form, skipping questions or going back to answer a previous question. The user retains this ability until he indicates that he is satisfied with the input, either by pressing a particular key to accept the form or by answering a final question equivalent to

OK to process (y/n)

If the recipient of the form is present whilst the form is being completed, he can point out errors as they occur. This approach may distract the person completing the form and may lead to an increase in the number of errors; the alternative is to wait until the form has been completed before checking it. He will then indicate all the items which are wrong and ask for them to be corrected.

If the computer system is present, it can validate each answer immediately it is input, or it can wait and report errors only when the form has been completed. With some hardware configurations, the user's input is only available to the system when he presses an 'enter' key, typically at the end of the form. Whether to validate immediately or to defer is not a trivial decision;

reporting errors immediately may be distracting but immediate confirmation of a coded value as a result of a validation may also be desirable. As a rule of thumb, in cases where the input comes from a source document, validation is deferred to the end of the form to avoid disrupting the keying process; where there is no source document, validation is immediate.

If any errors are encountered, the dialogue does not redisplay a new blank form; the form with the previous answers is shown with any erroneous items indicated. In the human–human analogy, you only get a new form if you have made such a complete mess of the previous one that it is simpler to start again from scratch.

As with the Q&A and menu structures, an individual answer may represent either selection from a list of possible replies or an arbitrary data value. It is traditionally entered as a text string but, as we saw in Chapter 4, a selection input may be made by scrolling round a supressed menu; this is analogous to 'delete as appropriate' on clerical forms.

5.2.2 Design Criteria

Forms are a natural mechanism for the entry of transaction data since a transaction, by definition, comprises a relatively standard set of data values. Thus, the structure is particularly appropriate where the source of the data is an existing clerical form. In the example of Fig. 5.1, the dialogue knows in advance precisely what data items are required since a field is defined in terms of content, slot and attributes.

The criteria discussed in Section 4.3.2 for Q&A apply to the phrasing and display of the individual questions on the form. Answer fields should be clearly differentiated from the rest of the form by boxing with a particular attribute or by delimiting them with 'decorators' such as the brackets in the example of Fig. 5.1; the remainder of the screen should be *protected* so that input echo is restricted to these areas. The fact that the screen contains a number of questions imposes additional requirements which complicate the design of the screen layout; layout considerations are discussed in Chapter 7.

It is essential that the form displayed on the screen should match any clerical form from which information is to be taken. It need not have exactly the same physical appearance, indeed this can result in a very cluttered screen, but all input items must appear in the *same relative order* and have the *same format* as the source data. The reasons for this are obvious if you consider the input process.

Often, all the items required cannot be displayed on a single screen but must be broken into sections which are displayed on successive screens. It is essential that this breakdown preserves a *logical grouping* so that related items are not split over different screens. An existing clerical form will provide strong clues as to where such breaks should occur; Chapter 7 provides an example of this process.

The forms structure is highly supportive. Where a physical form provides the source of the input, little additional support is required from the dialogue. Since the user is required merely to transcribe the information, the screen can be relatively full, with the questions merely terse captions. The minimum requirement is that the user can read his input to check it.

Where there is no corresponding physical form, a user will read the screen form to determine the input required. The screen must therefore be less full and the questions more explanatory. Help and error messages should be specific to a particular question and the user should be able to request help in response to any question on the form. Support can also be provided by including format details in the questions or answer fields, e.g.

Invoice Date (dd/mm/yy)[   ] or Invoice Date [/   /   ]

It is important not to over-format the input in such cases; the address format

No & Road [   ]
District   [   ]
Town   [   ]
County   [   ]

admits only of a typical suburban address whereas address styles vary widely depending on location. With one particular public utility, it is almost impossible to book a service if you live on a farm — their computerised booking system insists that every house has a number and will not proceed further until the number is input!

A potential problem occurs where a clerical form contains additional fields which are not required to be input. Such areas on the clerical document should be clearly distinguished from those containing data to be input. A clerical form may also contain optional items, or items which are completed only if a given value is entered in an earlier field; ideally, these should occur at the bottom of the form. If this is not possible, the system should automatically skip over any question, corresponding to these optional items, which does not require an answer and should provide confirmation that it has done so.

5.2.3 Implementation

Like the menu structure, the form structure has two main stages: a single display of the form followed by repeated requests for input until the form is complete. The form may be complete either when the user enters a specific form terminator or, if no such terminator is defined, when all the questions have been answered.

A form can be defined as a set of output fields. Unlike a menu, however, there is no single way of subdividing this set into subsidiary structures which will define any form. There may be fields which, in some forms, perform the role of a 'form header' or 'form trailer'; there are fields in Fig. 5.2 which obviously fulfil this role. There are other output fields which specify captions; although these represent questions to the user, they have no significance to the dialogue process. There are also various other outputs such as subheadings and 'decorators' which define the form's outlines. We might consider all these output fields to be 'background' items which define the shape of the form.

Thus a form can be described by a data structure of the type described in Fig. 5.3. Note that a simple boxing of the form could be accomplished merely by adding an attribute, *boxed*, to the FormDIB definition; see Question P1 of Chapter 4. Our FormFieldListType definition allows a more flexible use of decorators.

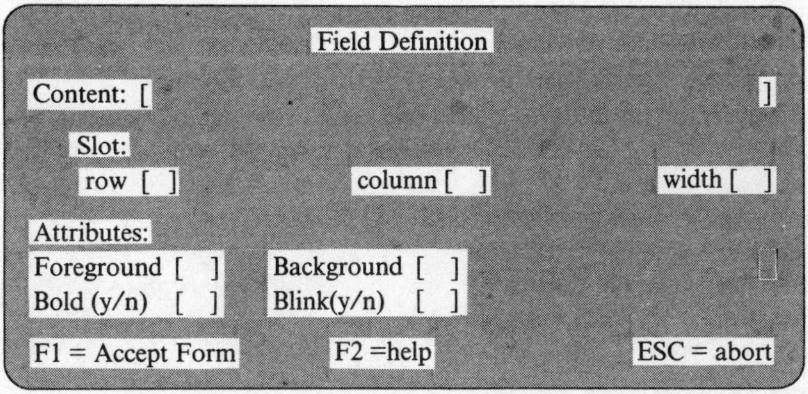

Fig. 5.2. An input form.

```
FormFieldListType = array[1..MaxFormFields] of FieldType;
FormDIBtype = record
                NumberOfFormFields : byte;
                FormFieldList      : FormFieldListType;
              end;
```
Fig. 5.3. A form Dialogue Information Block (FormDIB).

The form in Fig. 5.2 can then be created by the program fragment:

```
with FormDIB do
   begin
   FormOutline:='back=blue,fore=white';
   TLCorner:=chr(201);    TRCorner:=chr(187);
   BLCorner:=chr(200);    BRCorner:=chr(188);
   horizontal:=chr(205); vertical:=chr(186);
   bar:=''; spaces:='';
   for k:=1 to 47 do
      begin
      bar:=concat(bar,horizontal);
      spaces:=concat(spaces,' ');
      end;
   NumberOfFormFields:=15;
   CreateField(FormFieldList[1],concat(TLCorner,bar,TRCorner),
            2,10,49,FormOutline);
   CreateField(FormFieldList[2],
            concat(vertical,
                  '                    Field Definition                    '
                   ,vertical),
            3,10,49,FormOutline);
   CreateField(FormFieldList[3],concat(vertical,spaces,vertical),
            4,10,49,FormOutline);
   CreateField(FormFieldList[4],
            concat(vertical,
                  '     Content: [                                        ] '
                   ,vertical),
            5,10,49,FormOutline);
   ........................................................................
   CreateField(FormFieldList[15],concat(BLCorner,bar,BRCorner),
            16,10,49,FormOutline);
   end;
```

The form can be displayed on the screen by the procedure DisplayForm illustrated in Fig. 5.4.

```
procedure DisplayForm(FormDIB:FormDIBtype);
var k : byte;
begin
ClearScreen;
with FormDIB do
   begin
   for k:= 1 to NumberOfFormFields do
      DisplayField(FormFieldList[k]);
   end;
end; {DisplayForm}
```

Fig. 5.4. Defining and displaying a form.

What parameters are required to define the 'foreground' of the form? The foreground represents the answers which the user supplies to the questions on the form. The display of the questions themselves has been taken care of implicitly in the form background; as with the menu structure, a question will not normally be redisplayed when a particular answer is requested. There is no possibility of implementing a form in 'teletype' mode. However, it is conceivable that some indication, other than the input echo, of the current question may be displayed. For example, the question or a subheading might be highlighted. We will allow the possibility of an explicit question when each answer is requested.

Thus, to process the user's answer to the question requires the same parameters as in the Q&A or the menu structures, i.e. those parameters which were specified in the QandA_DIB data structure. Since the values of these parameters are likely to be different for different questions, there will be a separate QandA_DIB for each question within the form. The foreground of the form is represented by a set of QandA_DIBs as in Fig. 5.5.

```
QandAListType       = array[1..MaxQuestions] of QandA_DIBtype;
QandASet_DIBtype    = record
                        NumberOfQuestions : byte;
                        QandAList         : QandAListType;
                        CurrentQuestion   : byte;
                      end;
```
Fig. 5.5. Dialogue Information Block for form input.

In practice, there are more efficient storage mechanisms than the structures comprising arrays of arrays of fields which we have used, e.g. arrays of pointers or linked lists. We will continue to use array structures for list structures in the descriptions because of their conceptual simplicity.

A ControlDIB must be initialised with values which control how the input will be handled by the input/output processes for each Q&A step; the need for consistency dictates that these values will be the same for all items on the form. Additional control characters are needed to allow the user to skip over a question, to go back to a previous question and to hand the completed form back to the dialogue process. These values occupy three of the previously undefined elements of the ControlDIBtype data structure as illustrated in Fig. 5.6.

PointNextField and *PointPriorField* allow the user to scroll around the questions on the form; *AcceptForm* provides a facility for the user to confirm completion of the form by pressing a specific key. If the ReadField process receives any of these characters, it terminates immediately and returns the

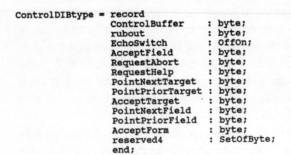

```
ControlDIBtype = record
                  ControlBuffer    : byte;
                  rubout           : byte;
                  EchoSwitch       : OffOn;
                  AcceptField      : byte;
                  RequestAbort     : byte;
                  RequestHelp      : byte;
                  PointNextTarget  : byte;
                  PointPriorTarget : byte;
                  AcceptTarget     : byte;
                  PointNextField   : byte;
                  PointPriorField  : byte;
                  AcceptForm       : byte;
                  reserved4        : SetOfByte;
                end;
```

Fig. 5.6. The ControlDIB with forms controls.

control character in ControlBuffer so that the dialogue process can take any necessary action. If both PointNextField and PointPriorField are null, the user is constrained to answer the questions in order; if AcceptForm is null, the dialogue will assume that the form is complete when the last question in the set has been answered.

The user also proceeds to the next question when he completes the current one. A question can be completed in two ways: *manual skip* requires the user to enter an explicit terminator character for each answer field; *auto skip* proceeds to the next question as soon as the answer field slot is filled. The ReadField process supports both these mechanisms. If ControlDIB contains a non-null value for AcceptField, this value must be entered to terminate input — a manual skip mechanism. If AcceptField is null, the input will terminate when answer.slot.width characters have been entered — an autoskip mechanism.

Manual skip is to be preferred unless the vast majority of the input is of a fixed length, in which case the need to type fill characters is minimal. What is to be avoided at all costs is a combination of the two, i.e. where a skip to the next field occurs either when the last input position is filled or when a skip character is input. Users will get into the habit of typing a skip character at the end of each input and will do so even where it is of maximum length, causing a double skip. This inconsistency is precluded with our single ControlDIB which controls all input throughout the form. There is another problem with auto skip which concerns the editing of input: if the user is going to make a typing mistake, he had better do it before the last character!

A procedure, FormInputIV, which performs immediate validation of any input which represents selection from a targetlist is illustrated in Appendix I.

```
procedure FormInputDV(var QandASet_DIB:QandASet_DIBtype;
                      var ControlDIB:ControlDIBType);
var complete : boolean;
begin
with ControlDIB,QandASet_DIB do
   begin
   complete:=false;
   repeat
      ArbitraryData(QandAList[CurrentQuestion],ControlDIB);
      QandAList[CurrentQuestion].ErrorFlag:=off;
      if equal(ControlBuffer,RequestAbort)
      or equal(ControlBuffer,AcceptForm)
      or ((CurrentQuestion=NumberOfQuestions) and (AcceptForm=0)) then
         complete:=true
      else  {test for scroll back}
      if equal(ControlBuffer,PointPriorField) then
         if CurrentQuestion=1 then CurrentQuestion:=NumberOfQuestions
                              else CurrentQuestion:=CurrentQuestion-1
      else  {test for scroll forward}
      if equal(ControlBuffer,PointNextField) then
         if CurrentQuestion=NumberOfQuestions then CurrentQuestion:=1
                              else CurrentQuestion:=CurrentQuestion+1
      else {proceed to next outstanding question}
         begin
         while (CurrentQuestion<=NumberOfQuestions)
         and   (QandAList[CurrentQuestion].ErrorFlag=off) do
            CurrentQuestion:=CurrentQuestion+1;
         if CurrentQuestion>NumberOfQuestions then
            if AcceptForm=0 then complete:=true
                            else CurrentQuestion:=1;
         end;
      if not equal(ControlBuffer,RequestAbort) then
         ControlBuffer:=0; {because it has been actioned}
   until complete;
   end;
end; {FormInputDV}
```

Fig. 5.7. Input to a form with deferred validation.

We will consider here a procedure, FormInputDV illustrated in Fig. 5.7, which performs deferred validation. If validation is to be deferred until the form is completed, each input must be treated as an arbitrary data value, i.e. each input field is accepted via procedure ArbitraryData (Fig. 4.5).

When the FormInput procedure returns, the user's response to question k will be contained in QandAlist[k].answer.content. The dialogue must then invoke validation of each of these answers and, if an error is encountered, set the ErrorFlag and ErrorMessage in the QandA_DIB for QandAList[k].

This procedure is called repeatedly until all errors are eliminated as illustrated by the following program fragment:

```
for k:=1 to NumberOfQuestions do
   begin
   {ensure each question is asked the first time through}
   {it's an error initially since he hasn't entered anything}
   QandAList[k].ErrorFlag:=on;
   {but there is no error message to display}
   QandAList[k].ErrorMessage.content:=' ';
   end;
```

```
CurrentQuestion:=1;
complete:=false;
repeat
   FormInputDV(QandASet_DIB,ControlDIB);
   if equal(ControlBuffer,RequestAbort) then
      complete:=true
   else
      begin
      NoErrors:=true;
      for k:=1 to NumberOfQuestions do
         begin
         {validate answer k
          if invalid then
             set ErrorFlag:=on for QandAList[k]
             set ErrorMessage content for QandAList[k]
             if NoErrors then
                NoErrors:=false
                CurrentQuestion:=k}
         end;
      if NoErrors then   complete:=true;
      end;
until complete;
```

Note that the process illustrated in Fig. 5.7 allows the user to change any of the answers, not just those that were flagged as invalid. This reflects clerical form filling; if you are handed back a form to correct, you can change anything on it. By default, the dialogue will request the next outstanding answer — the next one with ErrorFlag set on. To ensure that all answers will be requested the first time through, the dialogue initially sets the ErrorFlag to 'on' in each question.

5.2.4 Summary

Many interactive systems have a requirement for data entry via a standard sequence of questions. The form structure suits such usage, which is common in accounting and order processing applications. It is quicker than Question and Answer, it can handle a wider range of inputs than menus, and it can be used by any level of user. Most people are familiar with the concept of filling in forms even if they claim to abhor doing it! Because it has a sequential rather than a tree structure it is less appropriate for option selection.

Another area where form filling has been used is to specify the parameters for querying databases. The mechanism is called *Query by Example*. The fields on which the database can be searched are displayed as column headings on a form. The user enters in each column the values on which he wishes to search. The values input in a given column are 'ORed' and the columns are 'ANDed', so that an input of:

Grade	Location	Skill
SEC	**LON**	**A**
	BIR	**C**
	MAN	

would select all SECretaries in LONdon, BIRmingham or MANchester and who are classed as having skills A or C. It eliminates the problems caused when parentheses must be used to cater for different precedence in the logical operators, e.g.

(grade=SEC) and ((loc=LON) or (loc=BIR) or (loc=MAN))
and ((skill=A) or (skill=C))

Multiple choice menus are also a type of form filling. With such a menu, the user is presented with a list of options but is not restricted to a single selection; he may make zero or more selections from it. Figure 5.8 illustrates such a menu which is presented to the user of a Terminal Emulator package, a program which enables a microcomputer to be used as a dumb terminal. Each of the options on the list represents a terminal characteristic which may be set or unset by the user. To change a characteristic, the user scrolls to the relevant option and types 'y' to set it, or 'n' to unset it. Thus the menu illustrated in Fig. 5.8 is effectively a form with five questions, each of which expects a yes/no answer; the questions have a default answer and so he need not answer each explicitly. This structure is typical of multiple choice menus. Note that, as with most forms, the user can continue to scroll around the options until he presses the AcceptForm key, function key 1 in this case.

```
┌─────────────────────────────────┐
│  Terminal Configuration         │
├─────────────────────────────────┤
│  Local Echo          [Y]        │
│  Local Print         [N]        │
│  Auto Linefeed       [Y]        │
│  Auto LineWrap       [N]        │
│  VT100 Emulation     [Y]        │
│                                 │
│  press F1 to exit               │
└─────────────────────────────────┘
```

Fig. 5.8. A multichoice menu.

5.3 The Command Language Structure

5.3.1 Features

The *command language* structure is almost as commonplace as the menu structure, primarily because it has been a very common style for computer operating systems. It is at the opposite end of the spectrum from the menu structure. The use of the term 'command' reflects the parade ground analogy upon which it is based; the user is the drill sergeant and the system the subservient private. The private speaks only when he is spoken to. When the drill sergeant speaks he supplies in a single command all the information required to carry out the task he wants accomplished. This involves identifying the task and possibly supplying any data values which the task requires. For example

'Halt'   — task requiring no data values
or 'Peel me a grape'   — task and associated data values

Traditional command language dialogues operate in teletype mode. The system says nothing except to display a constant prompt (such as the ubiquitous 'drive>' of most microcomputer operating systems) to indicate its readiness to obey. Each command is entered on a new line, and is usually terminated by a 'carriage return' or 'enter' character.

A>**dir**
A>**pip b:=a:*.com**
A>**mode com1:9600,e,7,1,p**

The private does not question an order; if told to do something stupid, he proceeds to try to do it. Command languages basically adopt the same approach and assume that the user knows what he is doing. There may not be many cases of soldiers marching off a cliff because the sergeant said 'right wheel' instead of 'left wheel' but there are many cases where, for example, a old version of a file has overwritten a new version because the user got the copy command wrong.

If a command is impossible to carry out, the private may say so without identifying the particular part which is impossible. Similarly, when further processing of the input line is impossible, a command language structure gives up, usually with a fairly non-specific error message, and the whole input must be repeated. For example,

A>**dri a.*.com**
    Bad command or filename   (what is invalid?)

5.3.2 Design Criteria

Like the menu structure, a command language is appropriate for Input Control messages; it can, however, cater for a very wide range of options at any point in the dialogue, and does not require the background tasks to be hierarchically structured. Hence, it is appropriate to applications like operating systems where the background tasks form a flat structure of equal but distinct tasks, a sort of primaeval soup in which the tasks float like croutons waiting to be speared with a command fork!

Although it can support a relatively large set of commands, in practice the number in common usage is normally limited to reduce the load on a user's memory. Command language is the least supportive structure, and is appropriate to experienced and frequent users. Initial training is necessary before a user can use the system and he will only discover the full range of the system's facilities by external instruction rather than by using the system itself. Furthermore, since the system has no way of knowing what the user wishes to do, it is difficult to provide help facilities other than of a very general nature.

Because of the load imposed on a user's memory by the structure, it is important that the command identifiers are chosen so as to have a commonsense interpretation and to be easy to remember. Naming of the commands, or even positioning of command keys, can provide perceptual clues to aid memory. Thus the cursor positioning commands in WordStar reflect their layout on the keyboard.

```
Q  W │ E │ R  T              ctl+E = up a line
   ┌─────────────┐
   │ A  S  D  F │ G          ctl+A = word left       ctl+F = word right
   └─────────────┘           ctl+S = char left       ctl+D = char right
      Z │ X │ C  V           ctl+X = line down
```

This naturalness has not always been obvious in the command dialogues which have been implemented; it is doubtful whether many people who did not work with DEC equipment in the 1960s would immediately associate the PIP (standing for Peripheral Interchange Program) command of CP/M with a copy operation. The UNIX operating system provides some even more exotic examples.

The designer must guard against *excess functionality* resulting from an attempt to cater for every possible combination of task requirements with a *single command line*; that is, against developing a multiplicity of different commands, often performing overlapping functions. Such attempts at 'helpfulness' often result in a bewildering array of command keywords and syntaxes, most of which are seldom used and which confuse the majority of users.

The dialogue must handle data messages. This is typically done in a command language structure by means of compound input messages where the *command keyword* (input control) is followed by a *parameter list* (input data). For example:

PIP newfile=oldfile

contains the command keyword 'PIP' identifying a copy task and the parameter list 'newfile=oldfile' specifying that the contents of the file named 'oldfile' are to overwrite the contents of a file named 'newfile', or to create 'newfile' if it does not already exist. A parameter list may be expressed in one of two formats: positional parameters or parameter keywords.

The meaning of a *positional parameter* value is defined by the relative position it occupies in the command string. Thus, in the example

COPY thisfile newfile

the first parameter is the 'source file' (the file to be copied), and the second parameter is the 'destination file' (the new file to be created). A delimiter such as a comma, a slash or a number of spaces is used to separate one parameter from another.

With *parameter keywords*, each parameter value is preceded by a predefined identifier which specifies its meaning. Thus, in

COPY SOURCE=thisfile DESTINATION=newfile

the kewords SOURCE and DESTINATION identify which filename is which.

Positional parameters reduce the volume of input, but it is obviously essential that the values are entered in their correct order. Since rather unpleasant results can arise if you get the source file and the destination files the wrong way round, it is unfortunate that two widely used operating systems (CP/M and MS-DOS) use different orders in their respective copy commands! Positional parameters become particularly trying when the parameter list is long; some operating system commands take a dozen or more parameters. When parameters can be omitted by entering two separators together at the appropriate position, this complexity is compounded.

Parameter keywords reduce memory load in one respect since order is no longer significant, and optional parameters can simply be omitted; it introduces another load, however, by requiring the user to remember more keywords, and the designer to invent 'meaningful' names for them. This approach also requires more processing by the system to cater for the recognition of keywords, and the flexible order.

In many command languages, the parameter list may also contain *switches* which alter the way in which the command is interpreted. Switches normally may occur anywhere in the parameter list and are denoted by an identifier; the prefix '—' is used in UNIX and the prefix '/' in MS-DOS. Thus, in UNIX (MS-DOS), a short form directory listing is invoked by the command

    ls mydirectory   (dir mydirectory /w)

and an extended directory listing with file sizes and dates by

    ls -l mydirectory   (dir mydirectory)

Many command languages support *macros* as a means of providing increased functionality in a single input without increasing the number of commands. A macro consists of a series of separate command strings stored as individual lines in a text file, called a Submit file in CP/M, a Batch file in MS-DOS and a shell script in UNIX. When the file name is entered, the individual command strings of the macro are executed one after another, as though they had been typed at the keyboard. Symbolic parameters may be specified in the command lines of the macro; these are replaced by the actual values entered as parameters of the macro when it is invoked. Thus if an MS-DOS macro called CLG.BAT contains the lines:

    pas %1.pas
    link %1.obj
    %1

entering the command line 'clg myprog', will cause the execution of

    pas myprog.pas
    link myprog.obj
    myprog

5.3.3 Implementation

There is an obvious similarity between a command input and form input. A Command input can be considered as supplying a series of answers to a series of implicit questions. Thus the input

A>**copy FromFilename ToFilename**

could be considered as answers to the implicit questions

command   : **copy**
source   : **FromFileName**
destination : **ToFileName**

Like the form, there must be some criteria for deciding that the user has completed the input; for a command, CarriageReturn acts as the terminator. However, unlike the form, the set of questions is not known in advance. It is not known until the particular command has been identified or, in some cases, which variant of the particular command. For example, the MS-DOS mode command comes in three different flavours:

mode {integer}   to set the screen mode
mode com1:{BaudRate},{Parity},{DataBits},{StopBits},{Timeout}
                          to configure the serial port characteristics
mode lpt1:={Physical}
                          to assign a physical port to the screen echo

The input process for a command language is usually compared with the parsing of a program statement by a compiler or (more accurately) an interpreter. Although the basic syntax of an input is very rigid, there may be several variants of a command and there is often a good deal of freedom about things like how many, if any, spaces may appear in it. The software to implement it is considerably more complex than that required for the other structures. Instead of matching a single response, the dialogue process must first split the command into its constituent parts (called *tokens*), and carry out a greater number of matching operations to determine what option is required, and what data values are being passed to which parameters.

Figure 5.9 shows possible pseudo-code to implement a Command Language structure. GetResponse gets a string of characters from the keyboard, ending with a terminator character. The ReadField process could be used to accomplish this. GetToken gets the next token from 'Response'. If GetToken is applied four times to a Response of 'PIP newfile=oldfile', it will successively return the tokens 'PIP', 'newfile', '=', and 'oldfile'.

```
repeat
   Display BarePrompt
   GetResponse
   Matched:=true
   Set ValidTokens to possible commands
   while Matched and MoreInput
      GetToken
      Match Token against ValidTokens
      if not Matched
         Display ErrorMessage
      else
         Set ValidTokens to permitted values of next parameter
      endif
   endwhile
   if Matched check if Complete
until Matched and Complete
```

Fig. 5.9. Pseudo-code for a command language structure.

5.3.4 Summary

A command language is potentially the quickest and most flexible of all structures, and the majority of 'natural language' dialogues are basically command language structures with a very extensive vocabulary. Experienced users enjoy the feeling of controlling the system rather than being controlled by it. However, it offers little support and even experienced users find it difficult to utilise the full power; most are familiar only with the very limited subset of facilities which they use regularly.

In fact many of the desirable aspects of a command language may be mimicked with the Q&A structures and processes discussed in the preceding sections. We will return to this topic in Chapter 9.

5.4 Hybrid Dialogues

It should now be apparent that the four basic dialogue structures are not totally distinct but are in fact all variations of the Question and Answer structure.

A menu structure is Question and Answer modified so that a first level help message, the menu, is displayed automatically before the option selection question is asked. A form filling structure displays a sequence of questions, the form, all at once, then asks for answers one at one time. A command language structure, particularly where positional parameters are used, is Question and Answer in which the user makes extensive use of 'answer ahead', i.e. supplies the answers to a series of implicit questions in response to a standard first question, the command prompt. These structures might be referred to as:

Menu	:	help-ahead
Form	:	question-ahead
Command	:	answer-ahead

Recognition of this fact provides some clues as to how a computer dialogue might adapt to different environments; we expand on this in Chapter 9. It also provides reasonable guidelines as to where each version of the Q&A structure might best be used.

A menu structure will be appropriate in cases where:

- the range of possible inputs is sufficiently small that they can be explicitly displayed;
- the user needs the possible inputs to be displayed.

This suggests that a menu should be used where a user who is inexperienced, or who is mainly using a pointing technique, is choosing from a limited range of values, i.e. typically in selecting a task process.

A command language structure will be appropriate in cases where:

- the number of input values is small enough to be remembered;
- a limited number of responses is sufficient both to identify the task required and to supply its data.

This suggests usage by experienced users where there is a fairly flat hierarchy of task processes with limited data input requirements.

A Form structure will be appropriate in cases where:

a standard sequence of inputs can be predicted

suggesting usage for the entry of transaction data.

The basic Question and Answer structure is a reasonable compromise for various levels of user. It can be used to substitute for all of the above, but will be particularly appropriate where:

- the range of input values is too great for a menu structure or too complex for a command language;
- the next question to be asked depends on the reply to the current question.

An obvious problem with the simple classification above is that, even with a given level of user familiarity, the data requirements in different parts of the system will vary. If you examine the dialogue requirements of a simple ledger system it will have aspects which are concerned with

- selecting a task process from a small set ot options, e.g. update the ledger, print reports, maintain customer codes;
- the input of transactions, e.g. entering invoice details;
- answers to an unpredictable sequence of questions with a wide range of possible values, e.g. in specifying selection criteria for reports.

Consequently, whilst most systems have a basic underlying Q&A, menu or command structure, it is rarely possible to produce a dialogue for a complete system using a single structure. Different parts of the dialogue will require different structures depending on their particular characteristics. In other words, most dialogues will represent a *hybrid* comprising several of the basic structures.

5.5 The Spreadsheet

Two applications, the spreadsheet and word processing, reflect this hybrid nature very well. We concentrate here on a typical spreadsheet dialogue, using the popular package Lotus 1-2-3 as an example.

The term spreadsheet derives from the large sheets of paper, ruled into lines and columns, which are used as working documents by accountants. The user is not restricted to fixed screen-sized chunks of 24×80 character positions but can position a screen sized 'window' anywhere over a much larger area. In Lotus 1-2-3, the spreadsheet can have a maximum area of 2048 lines by 256 columns, with each column consisting of several character positions. Both rows and columns are labelled:

rows   : 1 — 2048
columns : A,B,.......,Z,AA,AB,..............,IV

A *cell* is identified by a column and row identifier (for example GF17). Each cell can hold a number, or a string of characters. The width of the cells

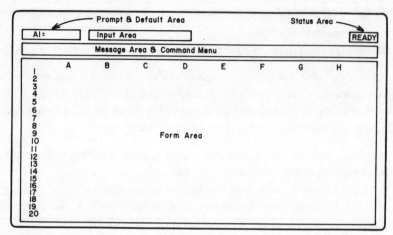

Fig. 5.10.

```
C14:  +C8+C9+C10+C11+C12                                         READ

          A        B        C        D        E        F        G        H
 1                         1985     1986     1987     1988     1989     1990
 2
 3  Sales              1126.77
 4  Cost of Sales       300.77
 5  ---------
 6  Gross Profit        826.00
 7  ---------
 8  Warehousing          15.29
 9  Distribution         20.70
10  Selling              31.45
11  Advertising          48.76
12  Administration       25.98
13  ---------
14  Operating Expenses  142.18
15  ---------
16  Operating Profit
17  Financing Costs
18  ---------
19  Profit before Tax
20  ---------
```

Fig. 5.11.

can be varied. When a spreadsheet is invoked the screen is divided into several
distinct areas, as illustrated in Fig. 5.10. In the top left-hand corner of the
screen is a prompt requesting the contents of the current cell and a prompt of
this type is preserved through the interaction, a basic Question and Answer
structure. In response to this prompt the user may enter:

• a numeric value in various formats;
• a text string;

- a formula such as +B1+ABS(B2) meaning the sum of B1 and the absolute value of B2.

In Fig. 5.11, the formula +C8+C9+C10+C11+C12 has been entered for Cell C14. The computer calculates 15.29+20.70+31.45+48.76+25.98 (the contents of cells C8..C12 respectively), and enters the answer 142.18 in C14. If we were to change the value of C9, the system remembers that C14 is dependent on C9 and changes its value accordingly.

The user may override the prompt with a command by entering a '/' character which will cause a menu bar of possible commands to appear, as shown in Fig. 5.12. Selection from the menu can be accomplished by scrolling through the menu with the cursor control keys and selecting with the return key; the current option is highlighted in inverse video and a description of its features appears on the line below. The user may also select by keying in the unique first character of the option name as an identifier.

Some of the commands require the user to specify a range of cells to which the command is to be applied. For example you may specify an output format such as 'currency' (two decimal places) which is to apply to a group of cells. This can be done either by listing the range of cells in answer to the prompt, or by 'painting' the area with the cursor control keys, i.e. by direct pointing (Fig. 5.13).

There is also a pure command language structure using function keys. You can skip to a particular cell on the spreadsheet directly by depressing function

```
C3:   (F2) 1126.77                                                 ⬦MENU
Worksheet  Range  Copy  Move  File  Print  Graph  Data  Quit
Format, Label-Prefix, Erase, Name, Justify, Protect, Unprotect, Input

            A       B       C       D       E       F       G       H
  1                         1985    1986    1987    1988    1989    1990
  2
  3   Sales               1126.77 1183.11 1242.27 1304.38 1369.60 1438.08
  4   Cost of Sales        300.77  315.81  331.60  348.18  365.59  383.87
  5                       ---------------------------------------------------
  6   Gross Profit         826.00  867.30  910.67  956.20 1004.01 1054.21
  7                       ---------------------------------------------------
  8   Warehousing           15.29   15.29   15.29   15.29   15.29   15.29
  9   Distribution          20.70   20.70   20.70   20.70   20.70   20.70
 10   Selling               31.45   31.45   31.45   31.45   31.45   31.45
 11   Advertising           48.76   48.76   48.76   48.76   48.76   48.76
 12   Administration        25.98   25.98   25.98   25.98   25.98   25.98
 13                       ---------------------------------------------------
 14   Operating Expenses   142.18  142.18  142.18  142.18  142.18  142.18
 15                       ---------------------------------------------------
 16   Operating Profit     683.82  725.12  768.49  814.02  861.83  912.03
 17   Financing Costs      457.90  457.90  457.90  457.90  457.90  457.90
 18                       ---------------------------------------------------
 19   Profit before Tax    225.92  267.22  310.59  356.12  403.93  454.13
 20                       ---------------------------------------------------
```

Fig. 5.12.

```
H19:  (F2) +H16-H17                                                        POINT
Enter range to format: C3..H19

        A        B        C        D        E        F        G        H
1                       1985     1986     1987     1988     1989     1990
2
3    Sales             1126.77  1183.11  1242.27  1304.38  1369.60  1438.08
4    Cost of Sales      300.77   315.81   331.60   348.18   365.59   383.87
5    ---------------------------------------------------------------------
6    Gross Profit       826.00   867.30   910.67   956.20  1004.01  1054.21
7    ---------------------------------------------------------------------
8    Warehousing         15.29    15.29    15.29    15.29    15.29    15.29
9    Distribution        20.70    20.70    20.70    20.70    20.70    20.70
10   Selling             31.45    31.45    31.45    31.45    31.45    31.45
11   Advertising         48.76    48.76    48.76    48.76    48.76    48.76
12   Administration      25.98    25.98    25.98    25.98    25.98    25.98
13   ---------------------------------------------------------------------
14   Operating Expenses 142.18   142.18   142.18   142.18   142.18   142.18
15   ---------------------------------------------------------------------
16   Operating Profit   683.82   725.12   768.49   814.02   861.83   912.03
17   Financing Costs    457.90   457.90   457.90   457.90   457.90   457.90
18   ---------------------------------------------------------------------
19   Profit before Tax  225.92   267.22   310.59   356.12   403.93   454.13
20   ---------------------------------------------------------------------
```

Fig. 5.13.

```
C3:   (F2) 1126.77                                                          EDIT
Enter address to go to: D12

        A        B        C        D        E        F        G        H
1                       1985     1986     1987     1988     1989     1990
2
3    Sales             1126.77  1183.11  1242.27  1304.38  1369.60  1438.08
4    Cost of Sales      300.77   315.81   331.60   348.18   365.59   383.87
5    ---------------------------------------------------------------------
6    Gross Profit       826.00   867.30   910.67   956.20  1004.01  1054.21
7    ---------------------------------------------------------------------
8    Warehousing         15.29    15.29    15.29    15.29    15.29    15.29
9    Distribution        20.70    20.70    20.70    20.70    20.70    20.70
10   Selling             31.45    31.45    31.45    31.45    31.45    31.45
11   Advertising         48.76    48.76    48.76    48.76    48.76    48.76
12   Administration      25.98    25.98    25.98    25.98    25.98    25.98
13   ---------------------------------------------------------------------
14   Operating Expenses 142.18   142.18   142.18   142.18   142.18   142.18
15   ---------------------------------------------------------------------
16   Operating Profit   683.82   725.12   768.49   814.02   861.83   912.03
17   Financing Costs    457.90   457.90   457.90   457.90   457.90   457.90
18   ---------------------------------------------------------------------
19   Profit before Tax  225.92   267.22   310.59   356.12   403.93   454.13
20   ---------------------------------------------------------------------
```

Fig. 5.14.

key F5 followed by the identifier of the target cell. If necessary, the 'window' is moved so that it now includes this cell (Fig. 5.14).

Lotus 1-2-3 was developed in the late 1970s and its dialogue structure is now considered a little old-fashioned; also, a consequence of trying to display as much of the spreadsheet data as possible on a single screen tends to be a somewhat cluttered layout. However, such packages illustrate many principles of good dialogue design. The spreadsheet approach is a *natural* mechanism for the types of application (such as financial analysis) at which it is aimed because it is familiar to its prospective users. Spreadsheets typically form an integrated suite of packages with simple business graphics and file handling, all using a *consistent* approach and with data easily transferred from one to the other. Different dialogue structures have been built around the basic Question and Answer structure to reflect differing input data requirements, and those features of the hardware for which the package is intended are utilised to *minimise* the input effort. There is some *flexibility* in the structure to cater for differing user levels so that where an inexperienced user may well use scroll menus, the experienced user can execute his desired action directly by entering a command string made up of the option identifier. There is no reason why similar features should not be provided in any computer system.

5.6 Implementing a Hybrid Structure

The implementation of a structure like a spreadsheet should not appear too daunting in light of the dialogue processes which we have developed.

Each cell is a field and the spreadsheet is an array of fields, as in a Form. There is an obvious complication in that the number of cells is, in general, too large to display on a single screen; we will consider how this can be overcome in Chapter 10. There is also the complication that a cell may contain, as in the example of Fig. 5.10, not the actual content but an expression specifying how the content may be calculated. If, however, we drop these two requirements, the processes can provide the facilities required.

There is a QandA_DIB for the basic Q&A structure which requests the content of the current cell. As the user moves around the spreadsheet, the content of the question will change to contain the identifier of the current cell:

ChangeFieldContent(QandA_DIB.question,CurrentCellID);

The input will be treated as an arbitrary data value to be validated against a set of templates:

a numeric value
a text string
a '/' indicating that the command menu is to be displayed.

There will be a series of MenuDIBs and associated QandA_DIBs to represent the bar menus. The processes which we have defined so far allow the user to select from these menus either by scrolling or by keying an identifier.

However, this selection mechanism is predefined by the SelectionBy identifier in the QandA_DIB, whereas the example of Fig. 5.11 allows the user to do either. In other words, we need

SelectionBy = (id,scroll,position,key)

where 'key' indicates the input via the keyboard of either an identifier or a scrolling control.

The facilities illustrated in Figs. 5.13 and 5.14 require a slight extension. In the ControlDIB, we defined a number of standard control values which may be input in response to any question; these values include the abort and help request characters and the accept and pointing controls. In the spreadsheet there are additional standard responses, such as the function key commands; these differ from the other controls in that they are specific to a particular application rather than applicable to any dialogue. We can cater for this facility by extending ControlDIB to include these application control values. This is the final element which was reserved in the previous definition of ControlDIB. The generalised ControlDIB now becomes as illustrated in Fig. 5.15.

Whenever an input process receives a control value, it terminates immediately and returns the value to the dialogue via the ControlBuffer of ControlDIB so that it can take whatever action is necessary. These control values are defined by the control set, comprising

ControlSet:=Application Control +
　　　　　　[RequestAbort,RequestHelp,
　　　　　　PointNextTarget,PointPriorTarget,AcceptTarget,
　　　　　　PointNextField,PointPriorField,AcceptForm]

```
ControlDIBtype = record
                ControlBuffer        : byte;
                rubout               : byte;
                EchoSwitch           : OffOn;
                AcceptField          : byte;
                RequestAbort         : byte;
                RequestHelp          : byte;
                PointNextTarget      : byte;
                PointPriorTarget     : byte;
                AcceptTarget         : byte;
                PointNextField       : byte;
                PointPriorField      : byte;
                AcceptForm           : byte;
                ApplicationControl   : SetOfByte;
                end;
```

Fig. 5.15. The general ControlDIB.

```
procedure ReadField(var field:FieldType;
                    DataSet:SetOfByte;
                    var ControlDIB:ControlDIBtype);
var key        : byte;
    ControlSet : SetOfByte;
    EditSet    : SetOfByte;
    filter     : SetOfByte;
    complete   : boolean;
begin
with ControlDIB,field do
   begin
   DisplayField(field);
   ControlSet:=ApplicationControl+
              [RequestAbort,RequestHelp,
               PointNextTarget,PointPriorTarget,AcceptTarget,
               PointNextField,PointPriorField,AcceptForm];
   if slot.width=0 then
      (control characters only)
      ControlBuffer:=GetFilterKey(wait,NoEcho,ControlSet)
   else
      (both control and data)
      begin
      ControlSet:=ControlSet+[AcceptField];
      EditSet:=[rubout];
      filter:=ControlSet+DataSet;                    (nothing to edit)
      if attributes.justification=right then
         CursorTo(slot.row,slot.col+slot.width-1)
      else
         CursorTo(slot.row,slot.col);
      complete:=false;
      key:=GetFilterKey(wait,NoEcho,filter);
      if key in ControlSet then complete:=true
                           else content:='';         (clear answer field)
      while (not complete) do
      ··· begin
         if key in EditSet then delete(content,length(content),1)
                           else content:=concat(content,chr(key));
         if EchoSwitch=on then DisplayField(field);
         if (length(content)=slot.width) and (AcceptField=0) then
            complete:=true
         else
            begin
            CursorTo(slot.row,JustifiedCol(field));
            if length(content)=0 then
               filter:=ControlSet+DataSet              (nothing to edit)
            else if length(content)=slot.width then
               filter:=ControlSet+EditSet              (ignore excess data)
            else
               filter:=ControlSet+DataSet+EditSet;     (allow any)
            key:=GetFilterKey(wait,NoEcho,filter);
            if key in ControlSet then complete:=true;
            end;
         end;
      if key=AcceptField then
         ControlBuffer:=0         (because it has been actioned)
      else
      if key in ControlSet then
         ControlBuffer:=key
      else
         ControlBuffer:=0;        (slot full and AcceptField=0)
      end;
   end;
end; (ReadField)
```

Fig. 5.16. A generalised keyboard input process.

Thus the generalised keyboard input process, ReadField, introduced in
Chapter 3 can be implemented by the procedure of Fig. 5.16. This procedure
repeatedly takes characters from the keyboard until

either a key representing a value in ControlSet is entered, or
if no AcceptField terminator has been specified, the result field content has
been filled.

Data characters specified in the DataSet filter are stored in the content of
the result field and, if echoing is specified, are displayed according to the slot
and attributes defined by the result field. The content of the result field is
edited with the 'rubout' key. On completion of ReadField, the result field
holds any text characters which have been entered, and the keycode of the
control character which caused termination is returned in ControlBuffer.

The function JustifiedCol determines the required cursor position based on
the field justification and the number of characters already entered. Appendix
G contains details of a suitable function.

Since ReadField can cater either for the input of a text string or the input
of control characters we can utilise it to handle selection either by an identifier
or by scrolling within a procedure (described in Appendix H) of the form:

procedure ChooseByKey(var QandA_DIB:QandA_DIBtype;
                      var ControlDIB:ControlDIBtype);

In order to implement selection from the bar menu of Fig. 5.12, we must
define a ControlDIB which contains control values both for keyed identifiers
and for scrolling, and an appropriate QandA_DIB:

```
with ControlDIB do
    begin
    rubout:=0;                       {no editing}
    EchoSwitch:=off;
    AcceptField:=CR;                 {we require a Carriage Return}
    PointNextTarget:=CursorRight;    {keycode 205}
    PointPriorTarget:=CursorLeft;    {keycode 203}
    AcceptTarget:=CR;                {keycode 13}
    end;
with QandA_DIB do
    begin
    CreateField(question,'',0,0,0,'');  {a null question}
    CreateField(answer,' ',0,0,1,'');   {a 1 character input field}
    InvertField(answer);    {defining target highlight as inverse}
    filter:=[ord('w'),ord('r'),ord('c'),... ord('q')];
    ErrorFlag:=off;
    CreateField(ErrorMessage,'',0,0,0,''); {no error message}
    NumberOfTargets:=9;
    CreateField(TargetList[1],'w',2,1,1,'');
    CreateField(TargetList[2],'r',2,12,1,'');
    CreateField(TargetList[3],'c',2,19,1,'');
    .............................................
    CreateField(TargetList[9],'q',2,57,1,'');
    SelectionBy:=key;
    CurrentTarget:=1;
    end;
```

Processing of the input can then be accomplished with the statement:

ChooseByKey(QandA_DIB,ControlDIB);

which will return the ordinal of the option chosen in CurrentTarget and its target name in answer.content, regardless of whether it was chosen by scrolling or by keying the identifier.

5.7 Mode and Modeless Operation

In some hybrid dialogues, the same input message may be interpreted differently according to an internal setting within the dialogue. Such dialogues have different *modes* of operation; the mode determines the context in which the input is interpreted. A *modeless* dialogue is one in which any given input will always be interpreted in the same way.

Consider a word processing package. A user who is editing a piece of text may wish a phrase to be inserted at a particular point, or he may wish the same phrase to replace an existing phrase located at that point. Common implementations of this define two modes of operation for the editor: an insert mode and a replace mode. In the former, any character entered at the keyboard will be interpreted as a request to insert that character immediately prior to the current cursor position; in the latter, the same character will be interpreted as a request to overwrite the current cursor position with that character.

Many packages take this concept of modes much further. A word processor may have two operating modes, edit mode or command mode; a user can usually change from one mode to another by entering a special control character. In edit mode, an input string 'smyfile' will be interpreted as a string of characters to be included in the text at the current position. In command mode, it might be interpreted as a request to quit the word processor and save the current text in a file called 'myfile'.

The obvious advantage of having different modes of operation is that natural identifiers can be used to invoke special control actions. For example, a command can be invoked by an easily memorised keyword like 'save' instead of an obscure, but unique, key sequence or function key; the mode provides a context which renders uniqueness unnecessary. However, it does not require much imagination to appreciate the dangers of this approach. The user must always ensure that he is in the correct mode for the operation he wishes to carry out. It is not unknown for users of such packages inadvertently to delete a file by entering an 'unfortunate' text string whilst in command mode; the number of users who failed to save a file by inserting a string of the form 'shisfile' into the text of the file is legion!

Not surprisingly, all experimental evidence confirms that modeless operation is much to be preferred. Where there is no satisfactory alternative to different dialogue modes (the insert/replace option in text editing is a typical example) the current mode should always be clearly indicated in a status display.

5.8 Input Events — Handling Input from Several Input Processors

So far we have only considered cases where the dialogue process knows at any point from which processor the input will arise. The answer to a question will either come from the keyboard via one of the procedures ChooseById, ChooseByScroll or ChooseByKey, or it will come from a separate pointing device via the procedure ChooseByPosition. Suppose, however, that the user may select an answer using direct pointing or may request help by pressing a function key on the keyboard. Which input driver process should the dialogue process call?

In such a case, there are a number of *input events* (actions on some input processor) which can occur. The dialogue process needs to know when an event has occurred and what type of event it is. We will consider the case where the user's response to a 'question' may come either from the keyboard or from a two-button mouse operating in real mouse mode like that described in Chapter 3; the method is readily extensible to other devices. We assume the existence of the following additional functions in the keyboard and mouse driver processes:

function KeyboardEvent:boolean;external;
function PointerEvent:boolean;external;

These return true if an activity has occurred on the device and false otherwise. The next question to consider is what is meant by an 'activity' or event on the device.

An event might be triggered on the keyboard by the depression of any key. As we saw in Chapter 3, this will typically cause a keycode value to be stored in the keyboard buffer; thus, a keyboard event has occurred if and only if there is something in the keyboard buffer. With most operating systems, low level routines can be provided to inspect this buffer and determine whether it is empty or not. In fact, many operating systems permit a more selective definition of events. An event may be defined as the depression of one of a given subset of keys, i.e. there is a procedure

procedure DefineKeyboardEvent(filter:SetOfByte);external;

such that the function KeyboardEvent returns true only if the user has pressed a key which produces a keycode value in filter. Thus the filter should be defined as the set of keys to which the ReadField process is sensitive:

EventFilter:= QandADIB.filter +
     [rubout,AcceptField,RequestAbort,RequestHelp,
     PointNextTarget,PointPriorTarget,AcceptTarget,
     PointNextField,PointPriorField,AcceptForm] +
     ApplicationControl

i.e. {data characters for a keyed answer} + {ControlDIB input control values} + {any application-specific control values in ControlDIB}

An event might be triggered on the mouse by a movement in a given direction, or by the press or release of a particular button. Again, it is usually possible to define by software which activities or combination of activities trigger an event. For our purposes, it will be sufficient to define a pointer event as triggered by a movement in any direction or a press of any button.

We can now develop routines to test for an input event and return its value to the dialogue process. As with the keyboard processes described in Chapter 3, the dialogue process may wait for an input event to occur, or merely check whether one has occurred. Suitable functions are illustrated in Fig. 5.17. Note that the ordering of the conditional statements means that pointing events take priority over keyboard events; a keyboard event will be reported only after all outstanding pointer events have been reported.

The function, WaitInputEvent, can be used to develop a generalised dialogue process which caters for input from either the keyboard or a pointing device, and for selection by identifier, scrolling or pointing. This Choose process, illustrated in Fig. 5.18, consolidates all the procedures — Choose-ById, ChooseByScroll, ChooseByPosition and ChooseByKey — which we have developed so far.

The Choose procedure insists that the user select a valid target; it will terminate only when a non-zero CurrentTarget has been picked either implicitly or explicitly. With scrolling, only valid targets can be picked but a

```
type SelectionType  = (id,scroll,position,key,any);
     InputEventType  = (null,keyboard,pointer)

function TestInputEvent(selector:SelectionType):InputEventType;
begin
if ((selector=any) or (selector=position)) and PointerEvent then
     TestInputEvent:=pointer
else
if (selector<>position) and KeyboardEvent then
     TestInputEvent:=keyboard
else TestInputEvent:=null;
end; {TestInputEvent}

function WaitInputEvent(selector:SelectionType):InputEventType;
var event : InputEventType;
begin
event:=null;
repeat
     event:=TestInputEvent(selector);
until event<>null;
WaitInputEvent:=event;
end; {WaitInputEvent}
```

Fig. 5.17. Checking for an input event.

user may key an unmatched identifier or may press a mouse button when not pointing at any target. Usually, the dialogue will require that the user select one of the targets; however, some systems which use direct pointing interpret the selection of no target as a request to exit. The minor changes necessary to support this facility are left to the reader.

As a final step, the generalised dialogue input process, Q&A, of Fig. 4.16 can be modified to incorporate the general selection process. This procedure, ilustrated in Fig. 5.19, provides a general input process which can be used with any of the Q&A or menu structured dialogues we have examined, or with any individual question and answer step within a form dialogue structure and will handle any type of input message from the keyboard or from a pointing device.

5.9 Summary

Both the form and the command language structure request a set of answers from the user.

The form structure displays a series of questions and requests the user to supply answers for each; most form dialogues permit the user considerable flexibility in choosing which question to answer next and in editing previous answers. It is a natural and supportive mechanism for the entry of transaction data regardless of whether or not it is based on an existing clerical form.

```
procedure Choose(var QandA_DIB:QandA_DIBtype;
                 var ControlDIB:ControlDIBtype);
var CursorWas   : OffOn;
    complete    : boolean;
    event       : InputEventType;
    PriorTarget : byte;
    row,col     : byte;
begin
with QandA_DIB,ControlDIB do
    begin
    CursorWas:=TestCursor;
    if (CurrentTarget>=1) and (CurrentTarget<=NumberOfTargets) then
        begin
        answer.content:=TargetList[CurrentTarget].content;
        HighlightField(TargetList[CurrentTarget],answer.attributes);
        end;
    if filter=[] then SwitchCursor(off);
    DisplayField(question);
    CursorAt(row,col);
    PointerTo(row,col);
    complete:=false;
    repeat
        if ErrorFlag=on then DisplayField(ErrorMessage);
        ErrorFlag:=off;
        if ControlBuffer=0 then {otherwise there is already something}
            begin
            event:=WaitInputEvent(SelectionBy);
            HideField(ErrorMessage);
            HideField(HelpMessage);
            if event=pointer then
                ReadPointer(row,col,ControlBuffer)
            else
                ReadField(answer,filter,ControlDIB);
            end;
        if equal(ControlBuffer,RequestAbort) then
            complete:=true
        else
            begin
            PriorTarget:=CurrentTarget;
            if event=pointer then
                {***** absolute pointing *****}
                begin
                CurrentTarget:=MatchPosition(row,col,TargetList,
                                             NumberOfTargets);
                CursorTo(row,col);
                if (CurrentTarget<>0) and (AcceptTarget=0) then
                    complete:=true;
                end
            else {event=keyboard}
                begin
                if ControlBuffer=0 then
                    {***** matching keyed data *****}
                    begin
                    CurrentTarget:=MatchString(answer.content,TargetList,
                                               NumberOfTargets);
                    if CurrentTarget<>0 then complete:=true
                                        else ErrorFlag:=on;
                    end
                else
                if (CurrentTarget<>0)
                and ((ControlBuffer=PointNextTarget)
                or   (ControlBuffer=PointPriorTarget)) then
                    {***** relative pointing *****}
                    begin
                    if ControlBuffer=PointNextTarget then
```

Fig. 5.18. A generalised dialogue selection process.

```
                     if PriorTarget=NumberOfTargets then CurrentTarget:=1
                                    else CurrentTarget:=PriorTarget+1
             else
                     if PriorTarget=1 then CurrentTarget:=NumberOfTargets
                                    else CurrentTarget:=PriorTarget-1;
                  ControlBuffer:=0;    {because it has been actioned}
                  {do nothing in the case of AcceptTarget=0}
                  end;
           end;
       if PriorTarget<>CurrentTarget then
           begin
           if PriorTarget<>0 then DisplayField(TargetList[PriorTarget]);
           if CurrentTarget<>0 then
               begin
                  HighlightField(TargetList[CurrentTarget],
                               answer.attributes);
                  CursorAt(row,col);
                  PointerTo(row,col);
                  end;
               end;
          if (not complete) and (ControlBuffer<>0) then
              begin
              if ControlBuffer=AcceptTarget then
                  begin
                  complete:=true;
                  ControlBuffer:=0;    {because it has been actioned}
                  end
              else
              if ControlBuffer=RequestHelp then
                  begin
                  DisplayField(HelpMessage);
                  ControlBuffer:=0;    {because it has been actioned}
                  end
              else
              if ControlBuffer in ApplicationControl+[PointNextField,
                               PointPriorField,AcceptForm] then
                  complete:=true;
              end;
          if CurrentTarget<>0 then
              begin
              answer.content:=TargetList[CurrentTarget].content;
              DisplayField(answer);  {update the display on the screen}
              end
          else
              answer.content:='';
          end;
       if not complete then ControlBuffer:=0;
    until complete;
    if CurrentTarget<>0 then
       begin
       DisplayField(TargetList[CurrentTarget]);
       answer.content:=TargetList[CurrentTarget].content;
       end;
    if CursorWas=on then SwitchCursor(on);
    end;
end; {Choose}
```

Fig. 5.18. (*cont.*)

```
.procedure QandA(var QandA_DIB:QandA_DIBtype;
                    var ControlDIB:ControlDIBtype);
begin
if QandADIB.NumberOfTargets=0 then
   ArbitraryData(QandA_DIB,ControlDIB)
else
   case QandA_DIB.SelectionBy of
      id      : ChooseByID(QandA_DIB,ControlDIB);
      scroll  : ChooseByScroll(QandA_DIB,ControlDIB);
      position: ChooseByPosition(QandA_DIB,ControlDIB);
      key     : ChooseByKey(QandA_DIB,ControlDIB);
      any     : begin
                {define the input events for each device}
                Choose(QandA_DIB,ControlDIB);
                end;
      end; {case}
end; {QandA}
```

Fig. 5.19. A generalised dialogue input process.

The command language structure assumes an experienced user and requires, in response to a standard prompt, the input of a series of answers specifying both a task and its associated data values. The nature of data items required (the format of the command parameters) will typically not be known to the dialogue until after the task has been identified.

All four traditional dialogue structures are variants of the basic Question and Answer structure:

Menu   =   Q&A with help-ahead
Form   =   Q&A with question-ahead
Command   =   Q&A with answer-ahead

In general, no single structure can serve for the whole dialogue of a system; different areas of the system will have characteristics which suit different structures. Although most dialogues have an underlying structure which defines their style, they are usually hybrids consisting of a combination of the basic structures.

In modeless operation, an input will always be interpreted in the same way. Some dialogues support different modes of operation; each mode represents a different context and hence a potentially different interpretation of any input.

The commonality between the structures means that such hybrid structures can be implemented with abstractions based on two data structures:

- A ControlDIB specifying parameters which control the operation of the input process.
- A QandA_DIB specifying parameters which define the interaction for a particular question and response.

A handler for input events, which occur when an activity takes place on an input processor, enables the dialogue process to accept inputs from several input devices without knowing in advance which will provide the input.

This means that it is possible to develop a single dialogue process which can handle a variety of different input mechanisms in a variety of different dialogue structures, and from a variety of input devices. This process provides a strong base for ensuring both consistency and flexibility in a dialogue.

The dialogue structure is a major factor in determining its naturalness, consistency, non-redundancy, supportiveness and flexibility. However, these factors are influenced not only by the structure in which the system requests information from and presents information to a user, but also by the content of the messages exchanged. We consider this aspect in the next chapter.

Discussion Exercises

D1.   In Chapter 2 you were asked to discuss the type of dialogue structure which is best suited the Mailsale application described in Appendix A. A form filling structure would be the normal approach. Should the form filling use immediate or deferred validation? Should it use manual skip or auto skip? Is it necessary for the clerk to be able to edit previous answers on the form?
D2.   In a form filling dialogue, the questions on the form are predetermined and normally an answer is requested for each question. However, it is possible that the answer to a question will cause some later questions to be suppressed because they are now irrelevant. The forms procedures developed in the chapter do not cater for this; suggest what changes are necessary for it to be accommodated.

Programming Exercises

P1.   Implement the library of Q&A routines and the library of MCI routines described in Appendices G and H.
P2.   Develop a program which will accept the following data via a form, with immediate validation

```
Passenger Name   [                        ]
Destination      [              ]
Date             [  /  /  ]
Time             [  .  ]
```

Passenger name can be up to 20 alphabetic characters long. Destination can be any of Calais, Boulogne, Dieppe, Oustreham, Cherbourg or Le Havre; this field is selected via a suppressed menu. Date is in the format dd/mm/yy with today as the default. Time is in 24-hour format but leading zeros can be omitted.

P3.   Develop a procedure to output the following boxed menu

```
┌─────────────────┐
│  dwarf: happy   │
├─────────────────┤
│  happy          │
│  dozy           │
│  lazy           │
│  sleepy         │
│  grumpy         │
└─────────────────┘
```

and allow the user to select from it either by keying the identifier of an option or by scrolling around the menu of options. If the user keys an identifier, it is echoed in the menu header; the default selection is 'happy'. The procedure will return the ordinal of the chosen dwarf.

P4.   Develop a menu design aid program to assist in the design of scroll menus. The program will allow for a menu header field up to 30 characters in length and a maximum 10 menu items up to 15 characters long; all fields in the menu will have the same attributes.

The program will first request the user to specify these attributes. It will then draw a form which contains blank fields for the header and 10 menu items of maximum length; this will be centred in the middle of the screen. The user will overwrite these fields with the relevant contents; the size of the menu fields displayed will be amended to reflect the length of the contents.

The position of the header or the target items can be changed by pointing at the corresponding field and selecting it, moving the cursor to the desired position and selecting it again.

Further Reading

Gittings I. (1985) *Query Languages*, Edward Arnold.

Kraut R.E. *et al.* (1984) 'Command Use and Interface Design', Rosenberg J. 'A Featural Approach to Command Names', both in Janda A. (Ed) *Human Factors in Computing Systems*, North Holland.

Landauer T.K. *et al.* (1983) 'Natural Command Names and Initial Learning: A Study of Text Editing terms', *Comm.ACM*, **26**, 7.

Shneiderman B. (1986) *Designing the User Interface*, Addison Wesley.

Smith S. and Mosier J.L. (1984) *Design Guidelines for User Interface Software*, MITRE Corporation.

Zloof M.M. (1982) 'Office-by-example: A Business Language that Unifies Data and Word Processing and Electronic Mail', *IBM Systems J.*, **21**, 3.

Chapter 6

User support

6.1 Introduction

We saw in the previous two chapters that the structure of a dialogue is one major factor which influences its suitability. However, it is not only the framework within which messages are exchanged that is significant; the content of the messages is equally important to the success of the interchange. The interview format is an acceptable way of eliciting information in many situations; a poor interviewer can render it ineffective by asking obscurely phrased questions.

In a system driven dialogue, the basis of user support is the prompt. In considering the individual structures, we also outlined guidelines for 'phrasing' question prompts, menus and forms. These inform the user what is required from him at each stage in the dialogue. However, what if this basic support is insufficient?

One indication that a user may require additional support is that he enters an unacceptable response to a prompt. In such cases, the dialogue should provide an *error message* which specifies what was unacceptable and what should be done about it.

A certain indication that additional support is required is that the user specifically asks for it. That is, he requests a *help message* to explain further some aspect of the required response.

In this chapter we consider the requirements of these two types of message and also the role of external *user documentation* in an interactive system.

6.2 An Unsuccessful Dialogue

Consider the following extract from an interaction between a user and an electronic mail system, taken from *Breaking the Man–Machine Communication Barrier*, by Hayes, Ball and Reddy. The user is moderately familiar with the system and knows that in order to achieve his purpose — to display the titles of all messages received since May 15 from a user called Robertson —

he needs to use the HEADERS command in conjunction with keyword parameters FROM and SINCE. After considerable time and effort, he finally achieves his goal.

<-haeders from robertson since May 15<CR>
?No such command as "HAEDERS". Type ? for help.
<-headers from robertson since May 15<CR>
?Illegal message sequence at "FROM" — missing quoted string
FROM ROBERTSON SINCE MAY 15
       ^

(robertson should be in quotes — what about the date?.....)

<-haeders from "robertson" since "May 15"<CR>
?No such command as "HAEDERS". Type ? for help.

(Damn! That same mistake again)

<headers from "robertson" since "May 15"<CR>
?Illegal message sequence at "SINCE" — junk at end
FROM "ROBERTSON" SINCE "MAY 15"
                        ^

(perhaps I do need help..........)

<-?<CR>
Type HELP for complete online assistance. Type DOCUMENTATION to enter the editor reading the entire cross-referenced RdMail documentation.
The commands are: <esc>,<lf>,^K,^L,?,!,:,Accept
   Alias, Allocate, *Answer, BBoard, CheckMail, CkMail,
   Classify, Conditional, Context, Create, Current, DeAllocate,
   DeClassify, Delete, Display, Documentation,Echo, Edit, *Exit,
   Forward, From, Goto, *Headers, Help, Kill, *List, Load, Mail,
   Mark, Move, News, Next, Numbers, OverWrite, PConditional,
   PhoneMessage,PopContext,Previous, Print, Profile, Put, QRead,
   *Quit, Read, RebuildDirectory, Remail, Rename, Retry, Sort,
   Topic, *Type, UnDelete, UnMark, Version, Whereis, and
   *WholeHeaders.
*precedes commands that always have single-letter abbreviations

The system attributes are: Answered, Blind, Deleted, Draft,
   Examined, Garbled, New, Newest.

The message sequence keywords are: <class id>, <,>, ~, _,
?, %, ", :, !, *, +, -, All, BackReference, Before,
BodySearch, Classified, Context, Difference, During,
FieldSearch, From, Handled, HeaderSearch, Intersect, Last,
Length, MessageSearch, Minus, Multiple, NextLast, Not, Of,
Processed, Reference, Since, Subject, Union, With
Not (or ~ or _) complements meaning of the following keyword.

(That wasn't awfully helpful so........)

<-help<CR>
Type HELP <topic> for help on <topic>. Type HELP TOPIC for
assistance in using the TOPIC command to search the HELP index.
? gives a list of commands.

<-help since<CR>
SINCE(2 sections, 618 characters)
Want to see it?(Yes,No,Quit)[Yes]:**<CR>**
Section "SINCE" within "Date Searches" within "Searching The Message
File".
Want to see it?(Yes,No,Quit)[Yes]:**<CR>**
SINCE
The SINCE keyword indicates that you wish to search for all messages with
dates after the one you give as an argument.
Section "SINCE" within "Keywords"
Want to see it?(Yes,No,Quit)[Yes]:**<CR>**

SINCE
SINCE takes a quoted string containing a date as a parameter. It represents
all the messages whose DATE fields indicate dates after the given date.
Dates are transformed into a canonical form before being compared, so
that any two date specifications that represent the same moment in time
will compare correctly.

SINCE, message sequence keyword(2 sections, 618 characters)
Want to see it?(Yes,No,Quit)[Yes]:**<CR>**
SINCE
The SINCE keyword indicates that you wish to search for all messages with
dates after the one you give as an argument.
Section "SINCE" within "Keywords"
Want to see it?(Yes,No,Quit)[Yes]:**<CR>**

SINCE

SINCE takes a quoted string containing a date as a parameter. It represents all the messages whose DATE fields indicate dates after the given date. Dates are transformed into a canonical form before being compared, so that any two date specifications that represent the same moment in time will compare correctly.

(Great! lets go and ask somebody!........)

<–headers from "robertson" intersection since "May 15"<CR>
?Illegal message sequence at "ROBERTSON" — unknown symbol
FROM "ROBERTSON" INTERSECTION SINCE "MAY 15"
                            ^

(What did you say it was?...............)

<–haeders from "robertson" intersect since "May 15"<CR>
?No such command as "HAEDERS". Type ? for help.

('*********!!!!'...............)

<–headers from "robertson" intersect since "May 15"<CR>

52 16May80 George Robertson Re:Altos & User Studies (1762)
67 21Jul80 Kamila Robertson Re: faculty research guide (506)
73 25Jul80 Kamila Robertson FRG (973)
(EUREKA!)

(Reprinted courtesy of IEEE Computer Society)

At last the user has his information which the system made available via a single command; of course, this command was entered seven times before the user got it right! It is doubtful if many readers would consider this a successful interaction.

You are asked to discuss the failings of the dialogue which this extract exemplifies in the exercises at the end of the chapter. Note that the user only made four 'mistakes' throughout the interaction:

A trivial typing error ('haeders' for 'headers').

A minor naming error ('intersection' for 'intersect').

A simple syntax error (not realising quotes were necessary around parameter values).

A significant syntax error (not realising that the two keyword parameters must be linked by a logical operator).

The user recognised the first mistake immediately. Of course, he repeated it whenever he stopped concentrating on typing 'headers' and never realising that he didn't actually have to type the whole word. Similarly, he corrected the second and third mistakes immediately and almost in spite of, rather than because of, the system's assistance. It is unlikely that he would ever have discovered his main mistake without outside help.

These problems did not arise simply because a command language structure was chosen for the dialogue; command language is a common choice for applications, such as electronic mail, which users can be expected to access regularly. However, even an experienced user who is happy to use a command language structure will occasionally encounter unfamiliar commands. When the user makes a mistake or gets lost, adequate support must be made available for him to continue. The extract illustrates a singular failure to provide this support.

6.3 Error Messages

6.3.1 What is an Error?

We may consider errors to fall into three classes:

The system crashes.

The system recognises that it is unable to continue processing with the data that it has obtained and asks the user to do something about it.

The system executes a task which produces a result that the user did not intend; for example, it overwrites the latest version of a file with an old version because the user gets the copy command wrong.

Typically all of these arise because of a 'wrong' input by the user. The first class results when the validation checks on input are inadequate to prevent the system attempting to execute an unexecutable instruction. The second class occurs when the validation checks detect that what the user has requested is infeasible. The third class occurs because validation checks can only determine that an input request is feasible, not that it is correct. All systems need a validation mechanism for trapping erroneous input and indicating to the user that it has occurred. An error message is the means by which it is indicated; this typically, but not always, involves the display of a text message.

There are a number of basic causes of user errors. The user may wrongly *perceive* what is being requested, for example by misreading the prompt. These incorrect perceptions can be increased by poor dialogue design. Most people are familiar with the common misreading of the sentence in Fig. 6.1. as 'Paris in the spring' — that is what a human expects to see! If the order of questions in a forms dialogue does not match the source clerical form, similar perceptual errors will occur.

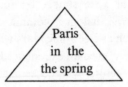

Fig. 6.1.

Even if the user correctly perceives what is requested, he may fail to *comprehend* what is required. Again, this can be increased by obscure phrasing or by inconsistencies in the dialogue. For example, two commands may perform what a user considers to be a similar function but may be entered in different formats. In one variant of the CP/M operating system, the two commands

    copy <ToFilename>=<FromFilename>
    ren <FromFilename> <ToFilename>

are used respectively to copy and to rename a file. Note the reversal of the parameter list order.

Finally, a user may perceive and comprehend what is required, but may fail to take the correct *action* — the brain wanted to type CAN but the fingers insisted on CAM!

6.3.2 What should be done about Errors?

It is worth noting that the majority of 'errors' which users make would not be errors in the clerical performance of a similar task but reflect an inability by the user to conform to the limitations of the computer system. A date of '32 May 1987' is invalid; a date in the form '31 May 1987' is not invalid; it may be an unacceptable input, whilst one in the form '31/05/87' is acceptable, but only in the sense that the dialogue designer was prepared to implement one but not the other.

The input process, except perhaps in a game, should not be an obstacle course; it should be hard for the user to fail. The dialogue should not encourage perception or comprehension errors and should be as tolerant as possible of user input. Of course, toleration must always have limits; how far off the expected format can the input be and still be accepted? We can consider any input to fall into one of the following categories:

1. Immediately usable in that it conforms exactly to what is expected.
2. Usable after a highly probable correction such as a single typing error. In the electronic mail extract, the command 'headers' was a highly probable correction of the input 'haeders'.
3. Usable only after a questionable correction. In the electronic mail example, the automatic insertion of quotes after the keyword 'from' is questionable. Does the user require messages from an individual called 'Robertson' or from a member of the long established May dynasty, namely 'Robertson Since May XV'. People can be called some pretty weird names!
4. Incomprehensible garbage.

The majority of current systems only accept input which falls into Category 1. It is possible to implement a dialogue which is tolerant of input in Category 2 by adopting a 'best fit' rather than a 'perfect fit' approach; the input is compared with all possible responses, and the closest response accepted. This technique is used by the police in the Soundex code for matching surnames by their sound rather than by their spelling; an example is given in Chapter 9.

The problem with tolerating input in Category 3 (and to some extent in Category 2) is that the system cannot be *certain* of its interpretation. If the acceptable responses are ADD, MOD, DEL or PRI, an input of NOD is likely to be MOD but may have been ADD input by an extremely ham-fisted typist! Consequently the system will often require the user to confirm that its interpretation is what he intended. This may be more tedious than re-entering the input.

Thus, the most effective way of providing tolerance in a system is to increase the range of inputs which fall into Category 1. If the system is flexible enough to accept dates in a variety of formats, it is less likely that an input date will be unacceptable. We consider some techniques by which this can be accomplished in Chapter 9.

Note, however, that this does not reduce the incidence of errors where the user enters an input which causes a result he did not intend; it may in fact increase them. The system can only ever check that the input is *feasible* not that it is *correct*. It cannot be sure that the user who selected 'delete all files' really intended to do that, nor that he wanted customer code C101:Clegg as opposed to C110:Cluff? In such cases only the user can confirm the correctness.

The dialogue can reduce the incidence of such mistakes by, for example, ensuring that identifiers are sufficiently distinct that a simple keying error in one command name does not produce another command. However, wherever an irreversible action such as deletion would result, the user should be asked to confirm the input. Wherever a coded identifier is input, the system should display the description so that a visual check is available to the user.

A similar case arises when an input data item is to be checked for a value lying within an acceptable range. Consider the case of an order entry system where the quantity of a product ordered is to be subject to such a check. In general, the maximum quantity ordered will be less than 100, but in very rare cases it may be as high as 2000 items. Obviously, an input of 200 cannot be rejected automatically; equally, it does not make sense to set the test to check only values over 2000 since in that way a large number of errors will be missed. The system should accept all quantities less than 100, and it should ask the user to confirm any values above this limit by issuing a *warning message* to that effect.

Errors will arise no matter how tolerant the system. It should be as easy for the user to recover from the error as to make it. Many operating systems provide a facility for editing a previous command line; the user can recall the previous input line by pressing a function key, edit it and then re-execute it.

An increasing number of systems provide an *undo* facility. A 'snapshot' copy is taken of the system state before a task is executed; the user can restore the system to this state after the task has been executed by pressing an undo key. The provision of such a facility poses several problems. It assumes that all actions are reversible. It may consume a large amount of computing resources to maintain and restore the system state. Also, what is an undo of an undo?

The first step towards recovery is for the user to recognise the error he has made. Recognition of a simple action error, such as miskeying, should be straightforward; hence an error message is seldom necessary with a menu structure. However, a user will require an explanation of perceptual or comprehension errors; this implies a need for the dialogue to provide suitable error messages.

6.3.3 What is a Good Error Message?

A timesharing service with customers throughout the world, many of whom were fairly inexperienced clerical users, produced what is probably the all-time classic error message. When its central computer system failed, proudly displayed in upper case on every terminal was the message:

AWAITING FUNCTION FOUR

This message managed to convey to the users precisely nothing about the nature of the problem, or what action they should take. It did, however, provide hours of employment for support analysts explaining to perplexed Europeans that on the operator's console there were these function keys, and if the operator pressed the fourth one....

An error message is not intended for the designer or the programmer of the system; it should be *informative to the user*. The 'AWAITING FUNCTION FOUR' message could so easily have been replaced by:

'The service is temporarily unavailable — please try again later'

Thus the message should be couched in terms and refer to concepts which reflect the user's model of the task. A programmer expects the error messages produced by a compiler to be expressed in source coding concepts not in terms of the compiler operation. However, it is easy for the designer who has specified the validation to slip into the trap of phrasing the error message in terms of the computer processing which it involved.

If error messages are to be informative, they must be *complete*, and not a code which must be looked up in a manual. IBM's OS operating system produced run-time failure codes of the form OCn, e.g. OC1, OC7; OC stood for Operating Code. If you looked up OC7, the manual told you that you had a 'data exception' which wiser colleagues knew to mean a type mismatch such as alphabetics in a datafield defined as numeric. Of course, the system could have told you this directly!

Ideally, the message should *accurately diagnose* the cause of the error. The electronic mail system in Section 6.2 made no attempt to diagnose the user's error as a missing connector even though it had encountered two successive selection keywords FROM and SINCE; it is not surprising that the user could not diagnose it from the message

'?Illegal message sequence at "SINCE" — junk at end'

It must be admitted that such diagnosis may not be easy; examine a compiler's attempt at diagnosis if you leave an END out of a PASCAL source program. However, this does not free the designer to resort to vague generalisations. Phrases like 'syntax error' or 'invalid format' convey little information. An error message should always attempt *specific identification* of the error, and should illustrate the input format required, as for example in:

21May85 is an unrecognised date — enter in dd/mm/yy format

The message should explain *how to recover*, and what the effect of this will be. When a popular word-processing package runs out of disk space for saving the current file, it comes up with the message:

Disk full — press ESCape

If the user has just entered ten pages of text, he wants to know what will happen when he presses the ESCape key. Will he then be able to insert a new disk and save? Or will it simply flush out his ten pages of text? The user can get very stressed just thinking about it; this stress could have been avoided with a message of the form:

Disk full — unable to save current file
Press ESCAPE and insert new disk to save

or perhaps

Disk full — press ESCAPE and cry!!

The message should be *timely*. This does not necessarily mean that it should be output as soon as the erroneous input is entered. In a menu or question-and-answer structure this would appear to be desirable; in form-filling mode it might be better to wait until the whole form has been input, to avoid disrupting the user. Where a compound input is entered, such as in a command string or a form, the system should try to identify all the errors that have occurred. This is particularly true of command strings where it is infuriating to key in four or five words and have the system identify an error in the first and then, after retyping, the system reports that the second word was also wrong. For example:

>haeders from robertson since May 15
?No such command as "HAEDERS". Type ? for help.

>headers from robertson since May 15
?illegal message sequence at "FROM" — missing quoted string

FROM ROBERTSON SINCE MAY 15

In such cases, it is not unusual for a user to repeat the first keying error when correcting the second. With a form dialogue, it may not be possible to report all the errors at once because of lack of space on the screen, but this is often not significant since less retyping is needed.

Error identification should be *non-threatening*; an input is very seldom 'ILLEGAL' and there are even fewer cases where an error is 'FATAL', yet these adjectives are used in many error messages. A user's attention can be drawn to an error with a *low key* highlight on the field in error and consistent positioning of the error messages. There is no need to simulate the eruption of Krakatoa with red and green flashing video. It is possible to lock the keyboard for a short interval, although the desirability of this is debatable. The messages themselves should be *non-patronising*. A simple statement of what is wrong is preferable to levity ('not like that, dummy') or condescension ('sorry, but I only recognise dates in the form dd/mm/yy').

Error messages do not have to be negative in approach (i.e. of the form 'X is wrong because of Y, so re-enter in the form Z'). Consider the case of a command to copy a file, whose syntax is:

>**COPY destination = source**

Suppose a new user enters the keyword COPY correctly, but gets the rest of the command wrong. A negative approach would merely ask the user to re-enter the command string correctly. However, the system knows that the user wants to copy, it just does not know what is to be copied, and to where. It could therefore ask for this information in the form:

>**COPY bav6sgvghnjnjshcfd565ga**
copy from?   **a:file1**
copy to?   **b:file2**

rather than just request complete re-input; we examine how this can be implemented in Chapter 9. Note however that this mechanism is most suitable where the error resulted from a failure to understand what input was required. It could be very infuriating to an experienced user who had made a simple keying error.

6.3.4 Implementation

We will now examine how error handling can be implemented with the different dialogue structures described in Chapters 4 and 5. For any structure, each input step in the dialogue can be specified by a QandA_DIB as illustrated in Fig. 6.2.

Associated with each QandA_DIB is an ErrorMessage field and an ErrorFlag. The dialogue input process checks the ErrorFlag on entry and, if set, displays the content in the slot and with the attributes specified by ErrorMessage. When the user has entered a new input, the flag is unset and the message cleared from the screen.

Where the input represents selection from a TargetList, a single error message is sufficient to explain any error. With a menu structure, the possible inputs have been listed; the only cause of error is a miskeying which requires either a null error message or a standard request to re-select. With the other structures, the error may arise either from miskeying or because the user has not remembered the TargetList values; a standard message indicating the possible responses will suffice. The dialogue processes of Chapters 4 and 5 for choosing from a TargetList assume that ErrorMessage has been defined before the process is entered. This message is displayed each time an unacceptable input is received and the process terminates only when a valid selection from the TargetList has been made.

Validation of an arbitrary data item is considerably more involved; an input may be unacceptable for a number of reasons:

- It has a unacceptable *format*; this may be a simple format check such as being numeric or alphabetic which can be implemented via the input filter, or a more complex format such as that for a date or a filename.
- It is *inconsistent* within itself; e.g. a date of '29/02/87' or a code containing

```
QandA_DIBtype = record
                    question         : FieldType;
                    answer           : FieldType;
                    filter           : SetOfByte;
                    HelpMessage      : FieldType;
                    validation       : string;
                    ErrorFlag        : OffOn;
                    ErrorMessage     : FieldType;
                    NumberOfTargets  : byte;
                    TargetList       : TargetListType;
                    matching         : TypeOfMatching;
                    CurrentTarget    : byte;
                    SelectionBy      : SelectionType;
                    end;
```

Fig. 6.2. Error handling in the Q&A Dialogue Information Block.

a check-digit which does not tally with the rest of the code.

* It is *incompatible* with other inputs; e.g. on a form for the input of invoice details, the Total Due should equal the Net Invoice Amount plus the VAT Amount.

* It represents an identifier for a *non-existent* item; e.g. there is no record on the Customer File which is identified by the customer code which has been entered.

Since an input may be unacceptable for a number of reasons, a similar number of different error messages are necessary to identify the specific reason for the error. To be precise, there will be a different ErrorMessage.content corresponding to each reason; the need for consistency implies that the slot and attributes will be the same. Furthermore, different inputs will require a different validation process; it may be possible for the dialogue to carry out format and consistency checking but compatibility and existence checking will require an application task process.

The dialogue input process ArbitraryData (Fig. 4.5) does not incorporate any validation. When ArbitraryData terminates, the users input is contained in the answer.content of QandADIB; the dialogue must validate this and, if necessary, re-invoke ArbitraryData.

How can we specify what this validation involves? Ideally we would like to specify the name of a *validation procedure* in QandADIB; in some languages it is possible to store a pointer to a procedure name but unfortunately PASCAL is not one of these. One possibility is to define a generalised procedure

procedure CheckInput(var QandA_DIB:QandA_DIBtype)

which performs the validation of all inputs to the system; the particular validation to be undertaken in any instance is specified by the *validation* parameter of QandA—DIB. To illustrate how this might be accomplished, consider the following program fragment:

```
procedure CheckDate(var InString:string;
                    var ErrorFlag:OffOn;var msg:string);
begin
ErrorFlag:=on;
{check for an acceptable format}
if not ValidDateFormat(InString) then
   msg:='unrecognised date format - enter in format 29/05/86'
else
{check for number of days in month etc.}
if not ValidDateContent(InString) then
   msg:='impossible date value - re-enter a revised  value'
else
if FutureDate(InString) then
```

```
    msg:='future dated invoices are not accepted - please re-enter'
else
{convert to canonical form}
    begin
    ErrorFlag:=off;
    InString:=CanonicalForm(InString);
    end;
end; {CheckDate}

procedure CheckInput(var QandA_DIB:QandA_DIBtype);
.............
begin
with QandA_DIB do
    ...................
    if validation='Date' then
        CheckDate(answer.content,ErrorFlag,ErrorMessage.content)
    else
    if validation='InvoiceNumber' then
        CheckInvoice(answer.content,ErrorFlag,ErrorMessage.content)
    else
    ............
  end; {CheckInput}

..........................
QandA_DIB.ErrorFlag:=off;
repeat
    ArbitraryData(QandA_DIB,ControlDIB);
    CheckInput(QandA_DIB);
until QandA_DIB.ErrorFlag=off;
```

Thus when the validation process returns, the dialogue can inspect the ErrorFlag to determine whether the input was acceptable. If the input must be re-entered, ArbitraryData will be invoked again; since the ErrorFlag is set to on, the relevant ErrorMessage will be displayed.

This mechanism preserves, to some extent, the separation between dialogue process and task processes which we discussed in Chapter 2. With languages which permit procedures to be called by pointer variable, the mechanism is elegant; with a language like PASCAL, however, it may result in an unwieldy general validation procedure. A designer must make a tradeoff based on the software facilities he has avaiiable.

6.4 Help Messages

6.4.1 What is a Good Help Message?

The requirement for concise prompts means that no matter how clear a prompt is, it is unlikely to be successful with every user. There will be occasions when the explicit support provided is inadequate because the user has forgotten the precise format of the input or is unfamiliar with that area of the system. The menu may tell you that 'Moules Farcies aux Noix' is available but it does not tell you whether it contains onions! To cover these cases, supplementary information which expands and explains that contained in the prompt should be available to the user *on request*. It is unreasonable to expect a user to consult a manual for this information whilst sitting at his workstation.

In computer-driven dialogues this help facility may be invoked via a standard response (help, SOS, ?) entered when the system prompts for input. This will be a valid reply on any menu, and to any question or for any field on a form – as illustrated in Fig. 6.3. In a user-driven structure, a help command may exist; it is normally implemented in the same way as other commands, i.e. there will be an executable file with the name <help>. This command may take parameters which refine the help required.

Help messages and error messages have much in common. If the user makes an error he may have a comprehension problem; if he requests help, the system can be sure he has a comprehension problem. It is self-evident that help messages should be *informative*, and expressed in terms the user can understand. Consider the following help message from the extract in Section 6.2:

> SINCE takes a quoted string containing a date as a parameter. It represents all the messages whose DATE fields indicate dates after the given date. Dates are transformed into a canonical form before being compared, so that any two date specifications that represent the same moment in time will compare correctly.

Did you realise that this message means:

> SINCE selects all messages sent or received after a given date. The date may be expressed in any format, but must be enclosed in quote marks, e.g. SINCE "June 20" or SINCE "20/6/83".

This is a classic case of the creator of the message being seduced by the specification of the internal processing. How many users would care that the system converts these various formats on input to the 'canonical form', YYMMDD, even if they understood what it meant? Examples of acceptable inputs are more effective in conveying what is required.

The help provided must be *timely* in that it is provided when, and only when, it is required. Some systems provide a screen or more of help automatically at the beginning of the dialogue. Anyone who needs to read this information will almost certainly have forgotten it by the time they come to use it.

Q&A Structure   Port   : **aux**
                          Handshake : **?**
                              Possible handshakes are
                                  N = None
                                  D = DTR/DSR
                                  X = XON/XOFF
                                  E = ETX/ACK
                          Handshake :

Menu Structure   Handshake Settings
                              None
                              DTR/DSR
                              XON/XOFF
                              ETX/ACK
                          Option : **?**
DTR/DSR   implies flow control by active signals on RS232 pin 20
                 (out) and pin 6 (in)
XON/XOFF   is normal ASCII character flow control
ETX/ACK   is.....

Command Language   >? setport
The SETPORT command configures a serial port.
The syntax is:
SETPORT<port>,<baud>,<parity>,<data>,<stop>,<handshake>
e.g. SETPORT aux,9600,e,7,1,n

Form Filling   Port   [**aux**]
                          Baud Rate [**9600**]
                          Parity   [**e**]
                          Data Bits   [**7**]
                          StopBits   [**1**]
                          Handshake [**?**]
                          Possible handshakes are
                              N = None
                              D = DTR/DSR
                              X = XON/XOFF
                              E = ETX/ACK

Fig. 6.3. Help provision in different structures.

This implies that help should be available at every point in the system *without exception*. In one interactive system, users could print reports off-line by completing a form with their name and department, which would be printed on the banner page of the listing. The system provided a help facility for report selection but not for filling in the Form. In the first week of operation, several reports were produced with banner pages indicating that they were for somebody called 'help' in the 'help' department!

The help should be specific to the user's particular problem; it should be *sensitive to the context* in which the help was requested. A user who has forgotten the syntax of the COPY command does not want an essay on the facilities of the operating system. Similarly, a user who has merely forgotten the precise answer to a question needs a list of the possible answers; where the choice is large, the help message should be formatted so that the user can easily pick out the items which are relevant.

Note how in Fig. 6.3 the level of help varies with the dialogue structure. For the Q&A and the form structure, the help indicates the possible responses. In the menu structure, this information has already been provided by the help-ahead of the menu itself; a request for help indicates that the user requires an explanation of what each response implies. In the command structure, the help merely indicates what implicit questions the user is expected to answer with the command input and the syntax of these answers; it does not detail the possible values for each answer.

This is symptomatic of the need for a general *multi-level* help to give the user more detailed assistance each time he requests help. In most systems only a limited number of levels are desirable; a point is bound to be reached where it is likely that anyone who needs that much help shouldn't be using the system!

A further problem occurs with the command language structure. Help will be context-sensitive provided specific help messages are associated with individual questions; this happens in a standard Q&A, menu or form dialogue where the background task structure provides a dialogue context. However, if a user requests help in a command language, the system has no idea of the context in which the user requires help unless the user supplies additional parameters to refine the request.

The normal approach is to provide a *hierarchical* help facility in such cases. The available commands are grouped into categories, each of which represents a class of activity which the user might want to carry out; this approach enables a user to identify which command he requires from the task he wishes to carry out. This approach is illustrated in Fig. 6.4.

Level 1 Help
      type **Help Edit**   for standard editing operations
      type **Help Screen**   for commands which adjust the text display
      type **Help Format**   for commands which adjust the printed output
      type **Help Block**   for commands which manipulate blocks of text
Level 2 Help
      Press **F7** to enter/leave Block Mode
      Type   **S**   to mark the start of a block
            F   to mark the end of a block
            C   to copy the marked block to the current position
            M to move the marked block to the current position
            E   to erase the marked block
      Type **Help Blockmode** for details of block operations
Level 3 Help
      Block Manipulation Commands

Blocks of text can only be manipulated in the Block Mode of operation. This enables any group of characters — words, phrases, sentences, paragraphs — in the text to be moved, copied or deleted.

To enter Block Mode, press the F7 key; the message 'Block Mode' will appear in the heading line.

To return to normal Edit Mode from Block Mode, press the F7 key again.

Before you enter any command to manipulate a block of text, you must mark the start and finish points of the block.

To mark the start of a block, move the cursor to the first character of the block and type S.

To mark the finish of a block, move the cursor to the last character of the block and type F.

To change the start (finish) of a block which has been marked, just mark the new start (end) positions.

To COPY a block, move the cursor to the position at which the copy is to start at type C.

To MOVE a block, move the cursor to the new position at which the block is to start and type M.

To ERASE a block, type E.

Fig. 6.4. Hierarchical help.

6.4.2 Implementation

The QandA_DIB data structure contains a parameter HelpMessage of type FieldType and the ControlDIB data structure contains a parameter Request-Help defining a keycode by which help can be invoked. Whenever the dialogue input process receives this keycode, it displays the HelpMessage and requests the user to enter his response to the prompt. Following the entry of the response, the help message display is cleared.

There are two problems with this implementation. First, a single field provides very limited space for the message content; this could be overcome by defining the slot as a rectangular area, several columns wide and several rows high. Second, the provision of help messages at every point where input is requested will result in a substantial amount of text; amending this text will be very tedious if it is incorporated within source programs.

The solution is to store the help messages in a file with each help message individually addressable. One possible file structure holds each message as a separate record. A message is assigned a unique number such that message N, together with its slot and attributes, is stored in the Nth record. The HelpMessage parameter in the QandA_DIB would then contain the identifier N; the corresponding message would be displayed by the system reading Record N and writing its content to the screen.

This method has the merit of simplicity, but can be very wasteful of disk storage with messages of very different lengths. An alternative is to split the help message into a series of field-sized chunks each occupying a record; the first field is in Record N, with the remaining chunks in records which form a linked list starting at Record N. When help is requested, the dialogue displays each field from the file in turn until it reaches the end of the list, as illustrated in Fig. 6.5.

The content of the message can be created with a text editor; the output of the editor provides the input to a program which structures the help file. We will return to this topic in Chapter 9 and consider how it can be extended to provide a multi-level help.

As was discussed in Chapter 1, there is no adequate way of testing the quality of the messages other than by having real users interact with the system. The ideal is that an unfamiliar user can perform reasonably well whilst an experienced user is not irritated by an oversupply of supporting information.

6.5 Documentation

Users need support for three main purposes:

To introduce them to the system, and to explain its facilities and underlying concepts.

To provide instruction on how to operate the system so that they can achieve their objective.

To provide assistance and a source of reference whilst operating the system.

We have considered how the provision of suitable error and help messages supports the user from within the dialogue itself. The question arises as to whether all the support facilities that are needed can be provided by the system itself or whether there is a requirement for external hard-copy documentation as well.

There are two extreme viewpoints on this question. The first is exemplified by the salesman of a software package who claims 'Of course you don't need manuals with X, it's really user friendly'. The second is exemplified by the traditional batch data processing approach, which seems to consider that documentation is 'good for the soul': the more you produce, the better!

Interactive systems do not need the same type of documentation as batch computer systems. This is true both of user documentation and of technical

```
procedure GiveHelp(StartAt:integer);
type HelpRecordType = record
                          HelpField        : FieldType;
                          NextRecord       : integer;
                          end;
     HelpFileType    = file of HelpRecordType;
var  RecordNumber   : integer;
     HelpRecord     : HelpRecordType;
     HelpFile       : HelpFileType;
begin
RecordNumber:=StartAt;
while RecordNumber<>0 do
   begin
   ReadIn(HelpFile,RecordNumber,HelpRecord);
   with HelpRecord do
      begin
      DisplayField(HelpField);
      RecordNumber:=NextRecord;
      end;
   end;
end; {GiveHelp}
```

Fig. 6.5. Displaying a help message.

documentation. Since there is no way that a user can realistically make use of a voluminous User Manual whilst seated at his workstation, there seems less justification for systems staff to produce one. On the other hand, internal help facilities, no matter how extensive, do not make the hard-copy User Manual redundant. The truth of this should be obvious from consideration of the type of information which the user needs.

The first requirement is for a *general overview* which describes what the system can do, explains any application concepts which are necessary for an appreciation of the system and relates them to any underlying concepts in the computer system. This type of information is often the hardest for a user (or new systems staff) to extract from extensive detailed documentation. Most commercial software for microcomputers is accompanied by voluminous and expensively bound documentation; many training organisations generate a comfortable income providing perplexed businessmen with an overview drawn from such documentation. Since it is unlikely that a designer would want a user to attempt to use the system with no conception of its basic features, this material is best provided by a book or brochure. Nobody is going to remember (or even read) a large tome, so the designer should aim at around ten pages for this overview.

Once the user appreciates what the system can do, he needs some basic information on *how to get started*: how to manipulate the workstation, how to log-on, and so forth. Hardware service engineers claim that whenever they receive a fault-call by telephone from a new customer, their first step is to check that the equipment has been switched on! 'How to get started' information is best provided by training users on the actual equipment. However, memories may still need to be jogged. On one local area network, the order in which two pieces of equipment are switched on is extremely significant. They break if you get it wrong! This type of information is included in a manual; in most installations there is also a large *notice on the workstation*.

The user will need to know *what to do when something goes wrong*. A checklist is often useful to help the user identify the type of failure: software, communications or a hardware fault, for example. Perhaps a contact name may be provided for fault reporting. Since this information is needed when the system has crashed, there is no point in holding it within the system. This is another case where notices around the workstation are beneficial.

Since consistency is a major design criterion there will be a number of *standard features* which are applicable throughout the system. Examples of such features might include editing, pointing, picking and the use of answer-ahead or abbreviation. This type of information can be contained within the system. For example, function key interpretations are often displayed on the bottom line of the screen. However, this both clogs up the screen and provides help when it may not be required. Although it could be included in a traditional manual, there are benefits in holding the information on a 'shirt pocket guide' such as a *reference card* or a *pocket book*; these may also provide a summary of the facilities available. Figure 6.6 illustrates a 3 × 4 in plastic reference card for use by communications personnel. Similar summary guides exist for the syntax of programming languages, for the facilities provided by an electronic mail system, and so on.

Users will need help on *individual facilities* with which they are not familiar. Initially, this is best provided by training on the system supported by an individual who is already familiar with its operation. Tutorial facilities can be included within the system; it is usually desirable to segregate these facilities from normal system operation, for example by developing a special tutorial version.

In most applications, support in day-to-day operation will be required even after initial training. Typically, this will be provided by help messages within the dialogue; these should be the primary source even if a hard-copy manual is available. The manual should follow the same hierarchical structure as the system but should be indexed so that the information on any given function can be accessed directly. The User Manual for the UNIX operating system is

CASE **V24 BINARY DATA AND CONTROL INTERCHANGE CIRCUITS**

Pin	Name	RS232 circuit	V24 circuit	Function
1	FG	AA	101	Protective Ground
2	TD	BA	103	Transmitted Data
3	RD	BB	104	Received Data
4	RTS	CA	105	Request To Send
5	CTS	CB	106	Clear To Send
6	DSR	CC	107	Data Set Ready
7	SG	AB	102	Signal Ground
8	DCD	CF	109	Received Line Signal Detector
9				Reserved - Positive DC test voltage
10				Reserved - Negative DC test voltage
11	QM			Spare - Equaliser mode
12	SDCD	SCF	122	Secondary Received Line Signal Detect
13	SCTS	SCB	121	Secondary Clear To Send
14	STD	SBA	118	Secondary Transmitted Data
15	TXC	DB	114	Tx Timing (from modem)
16	SRD	SBB	119	Secondary Received Data
17	RXC	DD	115	Rx Timing (from modem)
18				Spare
19	SRTS	SCA	120	Secondary Request To Send
20	DTR	CD	108.2	Data Terminal Ready
21	SQ	CG	110	Signal Quality Detector
22	RI	CE	125	Ring Indicator
23	DRS	CH/CI	111/112	Data Rate Selector
24	TXCE	DA	113	Tx Timing (from terminal)
25	BSY			Busy

Note: V24 pins positive = binary zero, space or control ON
negative = binary one, mark or control OFF

TABLE OF THE ISO 7–BIT CODED CHARACTER SET

b_4	b_3	b_2	b_1	Row \ Column (b_7 b_6 b_5)	0 (0 0 0)	1 (0 0 1)	2 (0 1 0)	3 (0 1 1)	4 (1 0 0)	5 (1 0 1)	6 (1 1 0)	7 (1 1 1)
0	0	0	0	0	NUL	(TC_7)DLE	SP	0	(@)	P		p
0	0	0	1	1	(TC_1)SOH	DC_1	!	1	A	Q	a	q
0	0	1	0	2	(TC_2)STX	DC_2	"	2	B	R	b	r
0	0	1	1	3	(TC_3)ETX	DC_3	£	3	C	S	c	s
0	1	0	0	4	(TC_4)EOT	DC_4	$	4	D	T	d	t
0	1	0	1	5	(TC_5)ENQ	(TC_8)	%	5	E	U	e	u
0	1	1	0	6	(TC_6)ACK	(TC_9)SYN	&	6	F	V	f	v
0	1	1	1	7	BEL	(TC_{10})ETB	'	7	G	W	g	w
1	0	0	0	8	FE_0(BS)	CAN	(	8	H	X	h	x
1	0	0	1	9	FE_1(HT)	EM	)	9	I	Y	i	y
1	0	1	0	10	FE_2(LF)	SUB	*		J	Z	j	z
1	0	1	1	11	FE_3(VT)	ESC	+	;	K	[	k	{
1	1	0	0	12	FE_4(FF)	IS_4(FS)	,	<	L	\	l	|
1	1	0	1	13	FE_5(CR)	IS_3(GS)	-	=	M	]	m	}
1	1	1	0	14	SO	IS_2(RS)	.	>	N	^	n	~
1	1	1	1	15	SI	IS_1(US)	/	?	O	_	o	DEL

CASE, a British company, is a leading international manufacturer of data communications equipment and message switching systems. UK corporate headquarters and development laboratories are at Watford, Hertfordshire with international offices, and a network of distributors, providing sales and support throughout the world.

CASE
COMMUNICATIONS LTD
PO Box 254, Caxton Way, Watford Business Park, Watford, Herts WD1 8XH, England
Telephone 0923-68000. Telex 923325 CASE G. Facsimile 0923-60829

Fig. 6.6. A typical 'shirt pocket guide'. (Reproduced by courtesy of CASE Communications Ltd.)

normally held on line, and the contents pertaining to a particular command can be displayed via the command:

$man <command>

The reader can decide for himself the value of this technique.

Finally, the user may need a source of reference for *data values*. The most common example of such references are lists of codes. Suppose the system issues a prompt for the input of a product but the user cannot remember the code. It may be possible to display a list of possible codes in response to a request for help. However, there may be many thousands of products and the only definition of a valid product code is that there is a record on the product file with that identifier. How suitable assistance may be provided is left as an exercise for the reader's imagination. If the codes are relatively static, there may be an argument for producing a hard-copy list; Prestel provides such a reference list for the pages of information which it contains even though a user may be guided to it by progressing through the system's menu hierarchy.

6.6 Codes

Codes are an important factor in the ease of input to a system, and an aspect which influences the need for user support. Computer systems need codes to enable the efficient identification and (possibly) retrieval of the coded item, which may be a command or a data item such as a particular customer's record from a file. Coding is necessary because names and descriptions are typically highly ambiguous, highly redundant and extremely variable in format. A surname like Fitzgerald is a poor identifier of a particular individual (there are twenty-eight entries under that name in the Leicester telephone directory) and yet a code of much less than 10 characters provides enough room to identify uniquely every individual in the world! Descriptions of items are even worse in this respect: the label '1 inch No 8 chipboard screw' is significantly larger than the item it describes!

In order to provide efficient identification a code must fulfil a number of criteria:

Precision
Clear structure
Allowance for growth
Shortness
Meaningfulness

Precision requires that the code be unique, i.e. that it identifies one and only one item. It also requires that the code is unambiguous both visually and aurally, so that errors in perception are minimised. Some character shapes and sounds are commonly confused; these should be avoided as far as possible when designing a code. Tables of offending combinations are available.

A *clear structure* means that there are well defined rules for constructing a code, so that users can recognise a well formed code value. Such a rule is that exemplified by the driver number on a driving licence:

1–5   First 5 characters of name
6–11   Date of birth, in form YMMDDY. If the licence holder is female, 5 is added to the first digit of the month. For example, the 14th December 1953 would be 562143 for a female, and 512143 for a male.
12–14 Initials.

Any unused character position is filled with a 9. For example, RACHEL BRENDA HUNT born on the 14th December 1953 would have a driver number of:

HUNT9 562143 RB9

A clear structure does not necessitate a complicated rule; it may be as simple as 'take the next number from a list'. Designers can be remarkably imaginative in creating codes. The hours spent thinking them up are matched only by the hours required to use them. Complexity in part arises from attempts to make the code itself convey information about the item it identifies (for example, the driver number tells you the sex and age of the driver) instead of being a purely arbitrary identifier (such as a passport number which conveys no information about the holder). Codes such as driver number are called *facetted* codes because the code is divided into a number of parts (facets) which convey some information about the item identified.

Allowance for growth is needed since the items which are identified are seldom static. Allowing one character position for sex in driver number seems a fairly safe bet. However, several companies in the 1960s designed a 2-digit facet to identify country in their customer codes. A large number of new countries gained their independence in the early 1970s, and these companies hit a major problem with their computer systems when they started trading with their hundred-and-first country.

Shortness: the more frequently a word is used, the shorter it is (try it with some common words!) and long words or phrases tend to become shortened as they increase in popularity (TV instead of TeleVision, VDU instead of Visual Display Unit). Although people express no strong preference for short codes, they make more mistakes in long codes (particularly in the later positions). Of course, the requirement for shortness to some extent runs contrary to the previous requirement for growth allowance, especially if the code is to convey information about the item. How many of us can remember our gas or electricity account numbers?

Finally, codes are more easily remembered if they are *meaningful*, i.e. if the user can easily associate the code with the object it identifies. Note that this is not the same as facetting, in which the the code value specifies particular attributes of the item identified. It helps if the code is similar to natural language so that it can be pronounced. Mnemonic codes which bear some relationship to the item name are also more easily remembered. This is particularly appropriate when designing codes for commands. Sensible abbreviation can often provide a good code, e.g. CAN for cancel. However, the designer should be careful not to fall into the trap of assigning unnatural names to commands merely to derive a convenient abbreviation. The relative positioning of the individual letters on the keyboard should also be considered so that a simple typing error does not corrupt one code into another. The code should be drawn from a limited character set both because it will be more memorable and because it simplifies keying. Codes which are all alphabetic (VDU) are easier to remember than mixed alphabetic and numeric (P45), and these are easier than codes containing punctuation (P/45-7).

Perhaps the best advice that can be given to the code designer is to keep it simple. Remember that the primary function of a code is to serve as an identifier for the item; do not try to make it do too much. So long as the system can find the item, the other characteristics can easily be made available. The code designer has another major asset on his side. People get used to even the most awful codes and, with frequent usage, treat completely arbitrary codes (such as P45,UB40) almost as mnemonics.

6.7 Summary

No structure can provide adequate support to all users in all areas of the system. There will always be a need for additional assistance which expands on the prompts.

Users will need additional support when they make input errors. The designer can reduce the incidence of such errors but cannot eliminate them. Error messages provide the information which enables a user to recognise and to recover from an error.

The dialogue can be certain that the user has a comprehension problem if he explicitly asks for help. It should always be possible for the user to obtain an explanatory help message to overcome this. Since the type of explanation a user needs will depend on his lack of understanding, a multi-level help facility is required.

There is a need for documentation external to the dialogue which provides information on what the system does, how to get started and how to recover from crashes. External documentation is not synonymous with large printed manuals; a mix of different media is likely to be more effective.

At least some part of the input to any system will consist of coded values. Coding structures provide tempting opportunities for the exercise of ingenuity; these should be avoided. Users will require less support to operate a coding system with a simple and easily understood structure.

Messages have been defined as of type FieldType, i.e. they are specified by a content, a slot and a set of attributes. In this chapter we have considered guidelines for the content of messages. In the next we consider some guidelines covering the layout of a screen, i.e. the choice of slot and attributes for the message.

Discussion Exercises

D1.   Outline the types of errors which could arise in using Mailsale, describe how they should be handled, and draft out suitable messages. What help facilities are required within the MailSale system?

D2.   Outline the types of errors which could arise in using the Ariel system specified in Appendix C, and describe:

(a) how they could be minimised;
(b) how they should be handled if they occur.

What help facilities should be incorporated into the Ariel dialogue? Discuss how the addressees of messages should be identified in the Ariel system, and design a coding system to support this.

D3.   Discuss the failings of the system described in Section 6.2 on the evidence of the extract illustrated. Comment specifically on:

(a) the choice of dialogue structure
(b) the choice of code and vocabulary
(c) the handling of errors
(d) the help provision

D4. Many recent systems provide an 'undo' key which reverses the effect of the previous input. Discuss how the following 'undo' facilities might be implemented:

command line recall, i.e. when the undo key is pressed the previous input is restored; pressing the undo key again recalls the input before that and so on;
'undeleting' a file;
undoing the effect of previous changes during text editing.

Programming exercises

P1. It was suggested in Section 6.3.3 that error messages need not be negative, and an example was given as to how an erroneous command string might be corrected. Produce a program which implements this approach for the 'file copy' command in the operating system which you use. For example, the command could take the form:

COPY from to

but if 'from' and 'to' are omitted, or erroneously specified, the system will change to a Q&A form:

COPY
from file? :
to file?   :

P2. Produce a program which will provide a help facility for a common subset of the operating system commands you use (for example, in CP/M, you might choose DIR, STAT, PIP, ERA, TYPE,DATE,TIME,REN). It should be possible for the user to obtain help either on the general facilities or on the operation of a particular command.

P3. The dialogue abstractions developed Chapters 4 and 5 only allow a single Help message of type FieldType. Incorporate suitable changes in these abstractions and in the processes by which they are implemented to support the type of help structure illustrated in Fig. 6.5.

Further Reading

Bailey R.W. (1982) *Human Error in Computer Systems*, Prentice Hall.

Brown P.J. (1983) 'Error Messages: The Neglected Area of the Man/Machine Interface?', *Comm.ACM*, **26**, 4.

Dean M. (1982) 'How a Computer Should Talk to People', *IBM Systems J.*, **21**, 4.

Hayes P. *et al.* (1981) 'Breaking the Man–Machine Communication Barrier', *IEEE Computer*, **14**, 3.

Houghton R.C. (1984) 'On-line Help Systems: a Conspectus', *Comm.ACM*, **27**, 2.

Isa B.S. *et al.* (1984) 'A Methodology for Objectively Evaluating Error Messages', (1984) in Janda A. (Ed) *Human Factors and Computing Systems*, ACM/North Holland.

Norman D.A. (1983) 'Design Rules Based on Analysis of Human Error', *Comm.ACM*, **26**, 4.

Relles N. *et al.* (1981) 'A Unified Approach to On-line Assistance', *AFIPS*, **50**.

Sohr B. (1983) 'Better Software Manuals', *BYTE*, **8**, 5.

Chapter 7

Screen formatting

7.1 Introduction

We saw in Chapter 4 that effective interaction between user and system requires a dialogue which is:

natural
consistent
non-redundant
supportive
flexible.

These criteria apply not only to the basic structure of the dialogue and to the content of the displayed messages, but equally to how they physically appear on the screen. The physical appearance of the screen depends on what message fields are displayed and on the choice of slot and of attributes for each of these.

The design process for any screen may be summarised as follows:

decide *what information*, i.e. what fields, will appear on the screen
decide *the basic format* of this information
decide *where it is to appear* on the screen, i.e. the slot for each field
decide *what highlighting is required*, i.e. what attributes are necessary for each field
develop a *draft screen* layout
evaluate the effectiveness of the layout

and repeat the process until both you and the prospective users are satisfied with the results.

We will illustrate this process by considering a design for a form filling input screen based on the document in Fig. 7.1. This covers most of the principles common to all screen design.

CAR FERRY RESERVATION FORM

	OUTWARD VOYAGE	INWARD VOYAGE	RESERVED ACCOMMODATION				
First choice	From	From		OUTWARD		INWARD	
Date	To	To	Type of cabin preferred *delete as applicable*	Night/Day*		Night/Day*	
Sailing Time			If whole cabin is not required. No. of Berths/Couchettes* *delete as applicable*	Male	Female	Male	Female
Second choice	From	From					
	To	To					
Date			No. of Reclining Seats				
Sailing Time			No. of Club Class Seats				

NAME AND ADDRESS (Block capitals please)
Name

VEHICLE DETAILS
Reg. No.

Address (or Agent's stamp)

Overall length (inc. roof-top luggage) ____ m　Height under 1.83m*/over 1.83m* (inc. roof-top luggage) *delete as applicable*

CARAVAN*/TRAILER* DETAILS *delete as applicable*

Overall length (inc. Tow Bar) ____ m　Height under 1.83m*/over 1.83m* *delete as applicable*

Post Code

Motorcycle Reg. No.　Solo/Combination* *delete as applicable*

Telephone No.

PASSENGERS
No. of Adults (inc. driver)　No. of Children (4 and under 14)

CHALET/CARAVAN/CAMPING SITE

please tick appropriate box.

☐ Tent Rental
☐ Chalet
☐ Caravan/Camping Site

INSURANCE

Holiday Insurance ☐　Vehicle Cover Extension* ☐　Caravan/Trailer Cover Extension† ☐

Car make　Car model

Date of Return if not stated above　Age of Vehicle if personalised number plate

Please tick box if cover required for Winter Sports activities ☐

Fig. 7.1. Ferry reservation document.

7.2 General Guidelines for Screen Layouts

The clerical form illustrated in Fig. 7.1 is used for booking a ferry reservation. The booking clerk in a travel agency will either complete, or ask the customer to complete, a copy of the form. The clerk will then enter the relevant details, using a standard VDU and keyboard, into the ferry operator's computer booking system and wait for the booking to be confirmed. Although at first sight it may seem as though there is duplication of effort in completing the form rather than keying the customers answers directly into the system, it is often quicker and more accurate to do this where information such as name and address or registration numbers, which are susceptible to mishearing or misspelling, are involved.

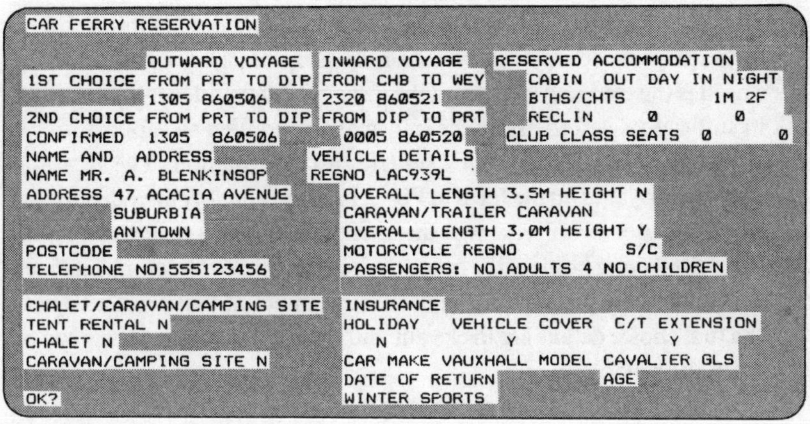

```
CAR FERRY RESERVATION

              OUTWARD VOYAGE   INWARD VOYAGE    RESERVED ACCOMMODATION
1ST CHOICE  FROM PRT TO DIP   FROM CHB TO WEY     CABIN  OUT DAY IN NIGHT
            1305  860506       2320 860521        BTHS/CHTS        1M 2F
2ND CHOICE  FROM PRT TO DIP   FROM DIP TO PRT     RECLIN      0        0
CONFIRMED   1305   860506      0005 860520        CLUB CLASS SEATS  0         0
NAME AND   ADDRESS            VEHICLE DETAILS
NAME MR. A. BLENKINSOP        REGNO LAC939L
ADDRESS 47 ACACIA AVENUE      OVERALL LENGTH 3.5M HEIGHT N
        SUBURBIA              CARAVAN/TRAILER CARAVAN
        ANYTOWN               OVERALL LENGTH 3.0M HEIGHT Y
POSTCODE                      MOTORCYCLE REGNO            S/C
TELEPHONE NO:555123456        PASSENGERS: NO.ADULTS 4 NO.CHILDREN

CHALET/CARAVAN/CAMPING SITE   INSURANCE
TENT RENTAL N                 HOLIDAY    VEHICLE COVER   C/T EXTENSION
CHALET N                         N           Y              Y
CARAVAN/CAMPING SITE N        CAR MAKE VAUXHALL MODEL CAVALIER GLS
                              DATE OF RETURN           AGE
OK?                           WINTER SPORTS
```

Figure 7.2 A poor screen layout

Examine the screen layout in Fig. 7.2 which displays a completed input screen for a particular booking. Hopefully, most readers will feel that a number of improvements are possible in this layout which represents a slavish following of the actual clerical document in Fig. 7.1. Although existing clerical input and output documents provide many pointers to the desired format (the relative order of screen input and source document should be the same), they do not eliminate the need for a conscious process of screen design.

The layout should be such that the user can scan the screen in a logical order and can easily:

extract the information which he is seeking;
identify related groups of information;
distinguish exceptional items (such as error or warning messages);
determine what action (if any) is necessary on his part to continue with the task.

A user will find it very difficult to manage any of these with the layout of Fig. 7.2. We will attempt to produce a more satifactory layout by following the design process.

7.3 What Information Should be Displayed on the Screen?

Non-redundancy implies that the layout contains *only the information which is relevant* to the user at that point in the dialogue. The fact that other information is available, or is stored together with the necessary information, or that there is room for more information on the screen is not significant. The user's need is the deciding factor and the designer must understand the user's task in sufficient detail to assess the information required to support it.

The layout in Fig. 7.2 contains superfluous information. The first and second choice voyages on the form in Fig. 7.1 are presumably intended for the case where the user is not present at the time the booking is made; there is no reason for displaying both on the output, when a particular booking has been made. The clerk will presumably input the first choice; if this is not accepted, then the first choice details are irrelevant and the second choice details can be entered in their place.

A similar argument applies to the layout of a menu. A menu should only list options, which the user can select, regardless of whether it is a traditional menu or a command bar of the type described for spreadsheets in Chapter 5. This is a common failing of many existing packages. In Prestel, a user is presented with a menu of all the possible options even though some choices are restricted to a subset of particular users, and many hybrid dialogues display the same command menu throughout, regardless of whether a given command is available at that point. In both cases, options which are unavailable may be indicated by some highlighting attribute.

Although the screen should not swamp the user with superfluous information, it is equally important to display *all the information relevant* to the user at that point. A user should not be expected to remember information from one screen so as to be able to process the information on a later screen. If all the items from a clerical document will not fit on a single screen, certain items may need to be repeated on all screens to preserve continuity. Thus, if a clerk is required to refer continually to a customer's name while undertaking a set of transactions which occupy several related screens, the customer name should appear in a consistent position on all the screens.

As well as deciding which individual items of information are required, the designer must consider how these items relate to each other. A *logical group*, a set of information which must be viewed as a composite entity in order to achieve the task purposes, should not be split across a screen boundary. Obviously, there can be no fixed rules for deciding what comprises a logical group; this will depend on the nature of the application. A number of data items may be logically related because they describe the same aspect of a task, because they occur from the same source, and so forth. A designer who understands the nature of the user's task and of the data which is involved should not find this a major problem. Very often, the format of existing clerical inputs and outputs will provide strong clues to the groupings.

At first sight there appear to be six main logical groupings of the information in Fig. 7.1:

1. the voyage
2. reserved accommodation
3. vehicles and passengers
4. customer name and address
5. campsite reservation
6. insurances

The first two of these can be subdivided into an outward and an inward passage. The ferry company seems to assume that the same vehicles and number of passengers will be involved in each direction!

As a result of this process, the designer should be able to produce, for a particular task, a list of the required data items in their dependent groups, and to indicate whether these are optional(O) or mandatory(X). This is illustrated in Fig. 7.3, in which dependencies are denoted by indentation; thus registration number, length, height and caravan details are all dependent on a car being booked.

Thus the user must specify all the items in the 'Voyage Group'. No vehicles need be specified in a booking but there must be at least one adult passenger; there need be no child passengers. A car is specified by the input of a registration number; if no car is specified, there is no requirement for the input of the vehicle length and height, or for details of caravan or trailer. There is no need to distinguish between caravans and other types of trailer.

If accommodation can only be reserved on certain routes, there may seem little point in displaying these fields for routes on which it is inapplicable. We could choose to suppress the display of this information unless the user inputs a route on which it is applicable. However, accommodation may not be reserved even if it is available. As we saw in Chapter 5, this suppression or automatic skipping of input fields is not very compatible with the question-ahead nature of form filling and is desirable only if it reflects how the user would naturally scan the form. It may be better to provide a consistent input mechanism by always displaying these items.

There would seem to be little requirement for instructions on how to complete the form in our example. There will obviously be a requirement to confirm that the details are correct; it may be necessary to allow space for messages explaining how a user can edit the form if they are not.

Voyage	(1 group for Outward sailing and 1 for Inward)
From Port	X
To Port	X
On Date	X
At Time	X
Accommodation	(1 group for Outward sailing and 1 for Inward)
Cabin	
Type	O
Berths/Couchettes — Male	O
— Female	O
Seats — Reclining	O
— Club Class	O
Vehicles and Passengers	
Car	
Registration	O
Length	O
Over 1.83 m high	O
Caravan	
Length	O
Over 1.83 m high	O
Motorcycle	
Registration	O
Solo/Combination	O
Passengers	
No. of Adults	X
No. of Children	O
Customer Name and Address	
Name	X
Address (× 3 lines)	X
Post Code and Telephone Number	O
Campsite Reservation	O
Insurances	
Holiday Cover (yes/no)	O
Vehicle Cover (yes/no)	O
Trailer Extension (yes/no)	O
Car Make	O
Car Model	O
Date of Return	O
Age	O
Winter Sports	O

Fig. 7.3 Listing the items for the display.

7.4 How Should the Information be Displayed?

Having decided what items are necessary for the task, the next step is to decide the format in which they should appear. This provides the designer both with an indication of the slot size and of any special attributes which are desirable for each field.

Naturalness implies that the information is presented in *immediately usable* form. The user should not be required to manipulate the information, e.g. by looking up codes, or by computing row or column subtotals outside the system. Figure 7.2 does not confirm the input of a port code with a port name; this may be acceptable in this particular example, given the limited number of ferry ports. Dates and times should be formatted to normal conventions, not, as in Fig. 7.2, displayed in internal system representation. The designer should consider whether a textual presentation is immediately usable; for example, an impression of a sales trend is gained much better from a graph than from a table of figures.

The use of normal *upper and lower case* conventions improves the readability of text. Road signs display place names in both upper and lower case: the shape Birmingham conveys much more than the shape 'BIR-MINGHAM'. The example in Fig. 7.2. was obviously produced by an old-fashioned programmer who even thinks in upper case! Accountants are accustomed to recognising as negative values which are enclosed in brackets or displayed in red, rather than preceded by a minus sign.

Caption fields identify the meaning of individual input and output data fields. They should clearly indicate the content of the corresponding data field and be well differentiated from the data values. This can be accomplished with the guidelines in Fig. 7.4.

Figure 7.2 contains a number of examples of the misuse of captions. Some data fields (notably the sailing times and dates) have no captions. Several seem needlessly verbose (CHALET/CARAVAN/CAMPING SITE) whilst others are arbitrarily abbreviated (RECLIN). Some captions fail to convey the meaning of the data field: HEIGHT YES is meaningless. Furthermore, it is almost impossible to distinguish between captions and the data values they are supposed to identify; captions appear alongside most data fields but above them in the Insurance section.

As a result of this process, the designer will be able to extend the list in Fig. 7.3 to include provisional lengths for the various input fields and provisional caption fields; this is illustrated in Fig. 7.5.

Caption names as brief as possible but without arbitrary abbreviation.

Captions distinguished from data fields by emphasising data values with any combination of

> punctuation, decorators or case e.g.
> > Date: 6 May 86 or Date [6 May 86] or date 6 MAY 86

> 'weaker' attributes in the caption e.g.
> > Date **6 May 86**

Captions positioned in a natural and consistent physical relationship to the corresponding data field

> on the same line and to the left for single occurrence fields, e.g.

> > Invoice Number: [**123456**]
> > Invoice Date : [**25/01/86**]

> as column headings above the corresponding data field for multiple occurrence fields, e.g.

Part Number	Description	Stock Level
123456	**widget**	**750**
234567	**sprodget bucket**	**23**
376890	**something else again**	**7**

> for heading information common to a number of items, such as a logically related group, centred above the group of fields

	Nominal Account Allocation	
Cost Centre	Account No.	Amount
123	**12345**	**140.79**
126	**12345**	**79.80**
999	**99000**	**32.17**

Fig. 7.4 Guidelines for captions.

Group Caption Field	Size and Format	
1. Voyage Details	Outward	Inward
From	Code(3) Name(15)	Code(3) Name(15)
To	Code(3) Name(15)	Code(3) Name(15)
Date	(dd/mm/yy)	(dd/mm/yy)
Time	(hh.mm)	(hh.mm)
2. Accommodation		
Cabin	(D, N or null)	(D, N or null)
Berths — M	(nn or null)	(nn or null)
— F	(nn or null)	(nn or null)
Seats — R	(nn or null)	(nn or null)
— C	(nn or null)	(nn or null)
3. Vehicle Details		
Car Registration	(8 alphameric or null)	
Length	(99.9)	
Over1.83m	(y/n)	
Caravan Length	(99.9 or null)	
Over1.83m	(y/n)	
or		
M/C Registration	(8 alphameric or null)	
Solo/Combination	(s/c)	
4. Passenger Details		
Adults	(nn)	
Children	(nn or null)	
5. Customer Details		
Name	(20 alpha)	
Address (× 3 lines)	(3×20 alpha)	
Post Code	(8 alphameric or null)	
Telephone Number	(12 alphameric or null)	
6. Campsite Reservation	(T/C/S or null)	
7. Insurances		
Holiday	(y/n)	
Vehicle	(y/n or null)	
Trailer	(y/n)	
Car Make	(10 alpha)	
Model	(15 alpha)	
Return Date	(dd/mm/yy)	
Age of Vehicle	(nn years)	
Winter Sports	(y/n)	

Fig. 7.5 Adding the item formats.

7.5 Where should the Information be Displayed?

7.5.1 General Guidelines on Positioning

Having decided what items to display and in what format, the next stage is to position these into the available space on the physical screen. This is not just a case of squeezing them in wherever they will fit!

So much information is displayed in Fig. 7.2 that it is difficult to identify individual items or groups of items. *Clutter* is a subjective measure; whether a particular layout seems cluttered will depend on the individual user and the task which the screen is designed to assist. For example, a screen used for data entry from source documents by trained key operators can be more crowded than one designed for the display of output data messages or for input by an untrained operator. However, there are a number of rules of thumb concerning spacing which provide guidance:

leave approximately half of the total screen area blank;
leave a blank line after every fifth row of a tabular format;
leave four or five spaces between the columns of a columnar format.

These rules of thumb are precisely that, they should be used merely as guidelines, not followed slavishly. Whilst it is quite possible to produce an acceptable format in particular cases which does not follow them, a conscious design decision should have been taken to contradict them.

Where items must be split across more than one screen, the split should occur at a natural break, if such exists. Not only should the break not occur within a logical group, all groups required for a particular decision should also appear on a single screen. Consider what happens if a ferry booking is not accepted. This may occur either because the desired accommodation is not available or because there is insufficient vehicle space; it can be assumed that there is always sufficient passenger space. The customer may change his voyage or may forgo the desired accommodation or both. Thus the clerk requires voyage, accommodation and vehicle details to be displayed on a single screen. It is not essential that the other groups appear on this screen since they do not affect the success of the booking. This analysis also suggests seven logical groups as indicated in Fig. 7.5 rather than the six groups of Fig. 7.3.

On any screen, logical groups should be clearly identifiable as separate entities. This can be achieved by leaving several spaces around the borders of

Voyage Details	Outward	Inward
From	**dve** Dover East	**ost** Ostende
To	**blg** Boulogne	**flk** Folkestone
Date	**26.10.86**	**31.10.86**
Time	**14.05**	**17.50**

Fig. 7.6 Using 'boxing' to delimit logical groups.

each group or by explicitly 'boxing' with vertical and horizontal line segments (as in Fig. 7.6) with different attributes for fields in different groups.

The users's eye should be guided through the screen by the physical patterns created by the blocks of text. These blocks should be *balanced*. Fields should not be tucked up against the margins of the screen but centred about the vertical and horizontal axes. In cases such as menu screens where only a relatively small amount of information is to be displayed, it should appear centred in the leftmost two thirds of the screen. To reinforce this symmetry, data fields and captions should be aligned vertically within a logical group; where possible, this alignment should be preserved across all logical groups.

There should be an obvious *starting point*. The normal convention is to start at the top left hand corner and proceed left to right and top to bottom. Although boxing can suggest other conventions, it should only be changed as the result of a conscious design decision. The same type of information should appear in a *consistent and predictable relative position* on the screen throughout the application.

Aesthetics are important. A screen that is attractively presented is likely to invoke a positive response from a user and be easier to follow. You cannot reasonably expect a user to take more trouble completing a form on the screen than the designer took developing it!

7.5.2 A Template for Screen Layouts

If screen layouts are to be consistent both within and across applications, they must all be based on a common template. Figure 7.7 illustrates such a template.

The top two or three lines of the screen are reserved for *title and status information*. Titling information often includes a description of the

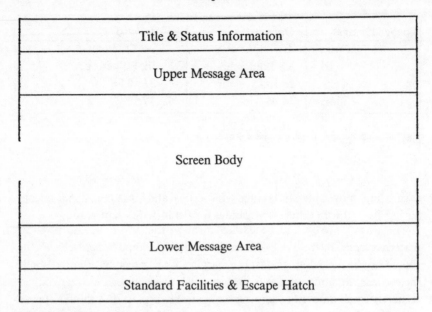

Fig. 7.7 A screen template.

GL301	General Ledger System	13 Jan 86
post/sales/invoices	posting to ledger ... PLEASE WAIT	

Fig. 7.8 Where am I? Is it still working?

application and/or particular task within it to which the screen relates. The current date and time may be displayed towards the right-hand margin. It is also common for each screen to be assigned a unique reference number; if a user encounters any problems with the system, this reference provides a convenient way for systems staff to identify the precise point at which the problem occurred.

The title area can be used to confirm the position in the system which the user has reached. In a menu hierarchy, the status area may indicate the path he has taken through the system by displaying the options chosen on previous menus, as in Fig. 7.8. It can also be used to provide confirmation that the system is still operating.

Optional *upper* and *lower message areas* provide consistent locations for messages which give instruction to the user or indicate exceptional conditions.

```
C3:   (F2) 1126.77                                              MENU
Worksheet  Range  Copy  Move  File  Print  Graph  Data  Quit
Format, Label-Prefix, Erase, Name, Justify, Protect, Unprotect, Input

          A         B       C        D        E        F        G        H
1                          1985     1986     1987     1988     1989     1990
2
3      Sales            1126.77  1183.11  1242.27  1304.38  1369.60  1438.08
4      Cost of Sales     300.77   315.81   331.60   348.18   365.59   383.87
5                      ─────────────────────────────────────────────────────
6      Gross Profit      826.00   867.30   910.67   956.20  1004.01  1054.21
7                      ─────────────────────────────────────────────────────
8      Warehousing        15.29    15.29    15.29    15.29    15.29    15.29
9      Distribution       20.70    20.70    20.70    20.70    20.70    20.70
10     Selling            31.45    31.45    31.45    31.45    31.45    31.45
11     Advertising        48.76    48.76    48.76    48.76    48.76    48.76
12     Administration     25.98    25.98    25.98    25.98    25.98    25.98
13                     ─────────────────────────────────────────────────────
14     Operating Expenses 142.18   142.18   142.18   142.18   142.18   142.18
15                     ─────────────────────────────────────────────────────
16     Operating Profit   683.82   725.12   768.49   814.02   861.83   912.03
17     Financing Costs    457.90   457.90   457.90   457.90   457.90   457.90
18                     ─────────────────────────────────────────────────────
19     Profit before Tax  225.92   267.22   310.59   356.12   403.93   454.13
20                     ─────────────────────────────────────────────────────
```

Fig. 7.9 Status and message areas in a spreadsheet structure.

Instructions which pertain to how the screen should be processed appear in the upper area; those which pertain to how it is disposed appear in the lower area. You need to know 'how to do it' before you start and 'what to do with it afterwards' when you have finished! Either area can be used for help or error messages. It is more common to display help messages in the upper portion of the screen and error messages in the lower. Messages requiring action by the user (e.g. to confirm the values input in form filling) would normally appear in the lower area. The use of an upper message area is well illustrated by hybrid dialogue structures. This area is used for the display both of command menus and of error messages (see Fig. 7.9)

The *screen body* contains the main information which the screen is seeking to impart. In a menu structure, it contains the list of options; the menu header might be considered to appear in either the upper message area or the screen body. In our form filling example, it is the area within which the form is displayed and the input fields echoed. In a hybrid dialogue, such as the spreadsheet illustrated in Fig. 7.9, it contains the cells of the spreadsheet.

One or two lines are reserved at the bottom of the screen to display *standard facilities* which are available on all screens. The message areas contain instructions specific to that particular screen body. A possible use of this area, to indicate the meaning of function key input, is illustrated in Fig. 7.10. It is called an *escape hatch* because it often contains a facility which enables the user to 'escape' from the normal processing flow.

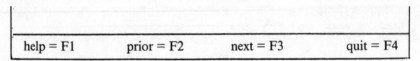

| help = F1 | prior = F2 | next = F3 | quit = F4 |

Fig. 7.10 The Escape Hatch.

This particular template splits the screen horizontally into a number of fixed 'windows'; it is a simple example of the techniques discussed in Chapter 10 for handling dynamic windows. The fact that the layout of every screen consistently conforms to *some* recognised template is more important than which particular template is chosen.

7.5.3 Positioning Error Messages

With a Question and Answer structure, the error message is normally displayed alongside or underneath the answer field. For example,

From: **dvx** Port code not recognised

An error message is usually unnecessary in a menu structure since the most likely cause of error is miskeying or a slip with a pointing device. If an error message is to be displayed, it usually appears below the list of options and in the lower message area.

In both the command language and the forms structure, a number of answers are input and so there are potentially a number of error messages. Most command language structures stop after detecting the first error and hence will display a single error message. In teletype mode, this message is displayed below the input line and the dialogue advances to the next line with a request for reinput. The display of error messages is slightly more problematical in a form structure. The user usually completes the form and returns to edit any fields in error. Therefore, the layout must accommodate the display of a variable number of error messages.

With a simple form, such as that in Fig. 7.11, it may be possible to display an error message alongside the field in error. This is the normal way to display a confirmation message, such as the description corresponding to a code.

This approach is seldom possible with a highly formatted form. In our ferry booking example, an attempt to leave space for a possible error message alongside each input field is likely to destroy the balance of the screen. It is improbable that sufficient space can be reserved in a single area, such as the

Invoice Number: [**V12345**]
Invoice Date   [**12/11/89**]   **Postdated Invoices not accepted**
Customer Code : [**C23**]   Clough Brothers Ltd.
Invoice Amount: [**100.00**]
VAT Amount   : [**15.00**]
Invoice Total   : [**151.00**]   **Invoice Total does not tally**

Fig. 7.11 A simple form with error messages shown alongside fields.

lower message area, to display all the possible error messages simultaneously. As we saw in Chapter 5, the system usually flags the input fields in error, positions the cursor at the first field in error and displays the corresponding message. As each input field is re-entered, the cursor moves to the next one in error and displays its error message.

7.6 Highlighting

Highlighting is the use of 'strong' attributes to make a particular area stand out from the rest of the screen and thereby attract the user's attention to it. Clearly the user's attention can only be attracted to a limited number of areas and if highlighting is overused, it becomes confusing rather than helpful. This is fine if the designer's objective (as in a video game) is to prevent the input process being too easy but it is unlikely to be desirable in most applications.

Initially the designer should specify a layout without any highlights and then go through each field asking himself what positive advantage would arise from the addition of a highlight. If the system only displays the information which is relevant to the user, there should be limited need for emphasis. Many existing systems demonstrate the temptation of highlighting; it is very easy to add just that bit more...

We have defined the attributes of a field in terms of a *foreground* colour, a *background* colour, a *bold* contrast level and a *blink* setting. These various features have different attention-getting powers; some are harder to ignore than others. To avoid diluting their impact, use only the minimum highlighting necessary to attract the user's attention. A person's attention can be attracted with a delicate nudge rather than a punch in the ribs, provided that they have not been subjected to constant battering! A combination of highlighting features is needed only when an exceptional emphasis is required.

A blinking foreground is the strongest visual attention-getter and hence potentially the most distracting. It is best restricted to a single character position alongside the field to be highlighted. Blinking the text of a message is a good way of making it difficult to read!

Colour is the next strongest attention getter. Different colours in the spectrum have different *warmths* and *perceived brightnesses*. Areas shaded with backgrounds in the warmer colours at the red end of the spectrum appear larger than those shaded in colours at the blue end of the spectrum. Areas with backgrounds in white and colours towards the middle of the spectrum appear brighter and are easier to view under a wide range of ambient lighting. The best separation of two areas occurs when one is shaded in black or a colour from near one end of this spectrum and one is shaded in white or a colour from near the middle. The same consideration applies to distinguishing foreground content from the background of a field.

Users like the use of colour. Humans can distinguish many thousands of different colours but can cope with only a limited number at one time. There is also a danger in applying guidelines from colour printing to a screen. Much of the impact of colour printing arises from its use of subtle hues; the brash palette of colours provided by most colour screens does not permit such subtlety and there can be wide variations in the same colour produced on different screens. Certain juxtapositions of these colours, like a blue foreground on a red background, are positively unpleasant to the eye. The only real way of assessing how the colours will appear is to view them on the screen.

The implications of colour blindness can be overstated; it is typically an inability to discriminate between two very specific shades of these colours, accentuated by particular ambient lighting conditions. More important is the fact that all humans bring expectations of the meaning of different colours — red means stop, danger, etc.; colour coding within the system should be consistent with these expectations. A system which uses red for status messages that confirm everything is satisfactory and green for error messages is likely to be confusing.

The consequences of the above for the use of colour on a screen are summarised in Fig. 7.12.

On many monochrome screens, the effect of different colour attributes is to produce different shades of the screen's base colour; thus, on a green screen, different background colours might result in different intensities of green. The eye is less able to distinguish different contrast levels than different colours and the designer should beware of unwanted and nauseous highlights occurring when a system is ported from a colour to a monochrome device.

- Use the minimum of number of colours and not more than three or four on any screen.
- Use background colours in large blocks.
- Use bright colours for emphasis and weaker colours for background areas.
- To distinguish two areas of background, or to distinguish foreground and background, contrast black or a shade from one end of the spectrum with white or a second shade from near the middle.
- Use colour coding consistent with the user's expectation.
- Try it out on the actual screen.

Fig. 7.12 Guidelines for using colour.

Good results can be achieved with two levels, using the higher intensity background to 'box' the area to be emphasised. Inverse video is an example of this effect which is commonly used to highlight messages indicating exceptional conditions such as an input error; the area with the lighter background draws the user's eye. A number of upmarket workstations with black and white displays present a completely inversed image — printing is black on white! However, there is a danger of a 'shimmering' effect from large areas of inverse video which is very tiring on the eyes; it should be possible for a user to select normal or inverse presentation.

The use of different foreground intensities is the least intrusive attention getter. It is particularly effective for distinguishing data fields from output messages such as prompts and captions; the field to be emphasised has the bold attribute set on. A designer is usually spared any temptation to use multiple intensities since most screens support only two levels — bold off (normal) and on (high).

Other highlighting features are possible on some displays. The content of a field may be underscored or displayed in a variety of type styles or sizes; the characters of any given type font are specified as a pattern of bits which correspond to on/off settings of the pixels in a character position. Neither technique has the same impact that it does in hard copy and a multiplicity of fonts hinders rather than helps discrimination and may increase the sense of clutter on the screen.

Finally there is sound. Anyone who has sat in a room with a large number of terminals 'beeping' for input like hungry chicks, or in an amusement arcade full of video games endlessly repeating snatches of electronic Wagner, will appreciate the crass intrusiveness of sound as an attention getter. Sound is effective where it is really important to attract the attention of a user who may not be watching the screen and is therefore not susceptible to a visual highlight. Tests on aircraft cockpit warning systems have shown that its effect is rapidly diluted. Frustrated composers should ensure that they have included an 'off switch' for silent running in their design.

There appears to be little need for highlighting in our ferry booking example. Blinking will be used only as a single character block cursor to indicate the current cursor position. Different foreground intensities will be used to distinguish input fields from captions in the screen body and from the other template areas; a similar effect could be obtained by using two colours but there is no real need for colour. Error input fields will be indicated by using a different background intensity or inverse video; these will be associated with the error message in the lower message area by using the same highlight for the error message. No sound will be used.

7.7 Producing a Draft Design

Having decided the information to be displayed, its format, how it is to be grouped on the screen and what highlighting is required, it is time to start producing some pictures.

A number of clerical forms to assist the design of screen layouts have been produced; these have merits in terms of providing a documentary record but all have a major drawback: what the layout looks like on paper bears little ressemblance to how it will appear on the screen. The form is covered in a matrix of squares indicating the character positions and, in most cases, the aspect ratio of the form differs from that of the screen. The font, which will probably be handwritten, will be different; in fact, the forms seem to encourage many people to use upper case exclusively. Furthermore, there is no way to create the effect of highlights. The only way to get a true impression is to display the draft design on the screen.

A proposed layout for the screen is illustrated in Fig. 7.13. Two lines are reserved at the top of the screen for titling information. There is no upper message area since it is assumed that the existence of a source document renders completion instructions redundant. The body of the screen contains the three logical groups necessary to confirm a booking, and also the passenger details; these logical groups are differentiated by position and spacing.

Captions are aligned within groups and input fields are delimited by bracketing; note how several captions have been changed from the initial proposals in Fig. 7.5. A lower message area of three lines is reserved for the display, in a different background contrast, of error messages and confirmation by the system of the booking. The bottom line displays the interpretation of function/cursor keys.

After the completion of input, the screen appears as in Fig. 7.14. Input fields are echoed with the bold attribute set to 'on'. The port names are alongside the input codes. Coded input and the registration number are displayed in upper case regardless of how they were input. The lower message area contains a confirmation by the system that the booking has been accepted; this appears after the user has pressed the F1 key to confirm the input (provided no errors have been encountered). If the booking could not be accepted because of insufficient space, a corresponding message would be displayed and the cursor returned to the first input field.

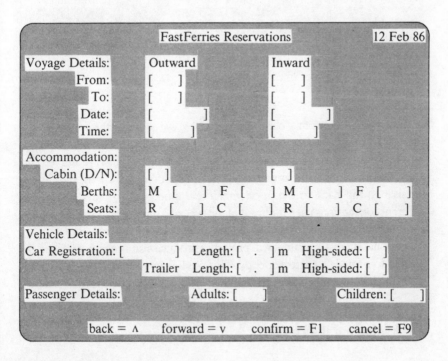

Fig. 7.13 A draft layout.

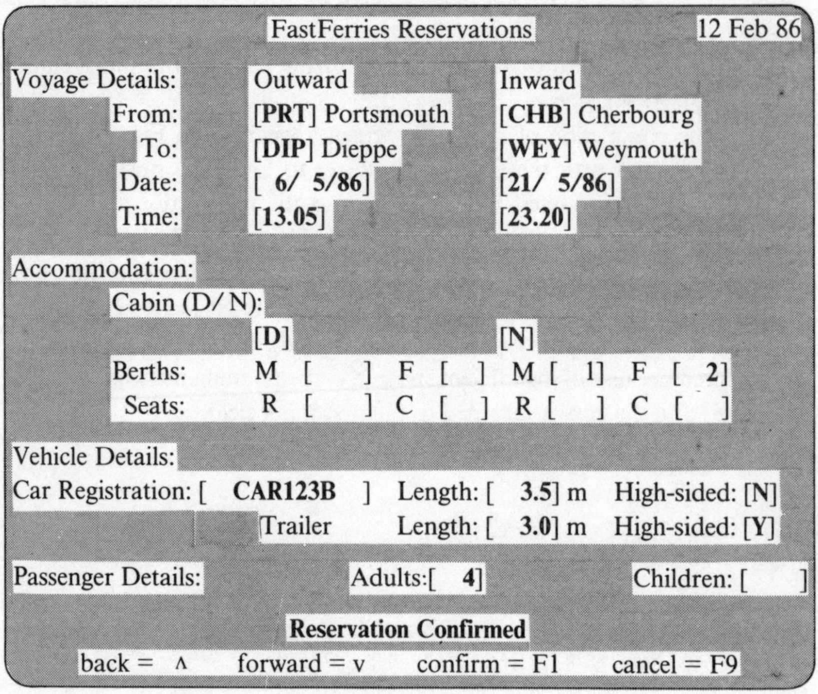

```
┌─────────────────────────────────────────────────────────────────────┐
│                      FastFerries Reservations              12 Feb 86 │
│ Voyage Details:       Outward                Inward                   │
│          From:        [PRT] Portsmouth       [CHB] Cherbourg          │
│            To:        [DIP] Dieppe           [WEY] Weymouth           │
│          Date:        [ 6/ 5/86]             [21/ 5/86]               │
│          Time:        [13.05]                [23.20]                  │
│                                                                       │
│ Accommodation:                                                        │
│          Cabin (D/ N):                                                │
│                       [D]                    [N]                      │
│      Berths:          M [    ]  F [ ]  M [ 1]  F [  2]                │
│      Seats:           R [    ]  C [ ]  R [  ]  C [  ]                 │
│ Vehicle Details:                                                      │
│ Car Registration: [   CAR123B   ]  Length: [  3.5] m  High-sided: [N]│
│                   [Trailer          Length: [  3.0] m  High-sided: [Y]│
│ Passenger Details:              Adults:[  4]          Children: [    ]│
│                         Reservation Confirmed                         │
│     back = ∧        forward = v       confirm = F1     cancel = F9    │
└─────────────────────────────────────────────────────────────────────┘
```

Fig. 7.14 The screen after completion of input.

Once the booking has been confirmed by the system, the screen body changes so that the other logical groups can be entered. This is illustrated in Fig. 7.15. Note that the group containing the voyage details is preserved for information, and that the options in the escape hatch have changed to allow the user to flip back to the prior screen and amend it if desired. Note the different conventions used for input of the type of camping reservation (which are mutually exclusive) and of the types of insurance (which are not).

As a final stage, the system will probably produce a summary which can be printed to provide a customer copy. This obviously no longer needs to have the same layout as the form. Its design is left as an exercise for the reader.

7.8 Evaluating the Design

These layouts are not presented as the optimum solution but merely as an

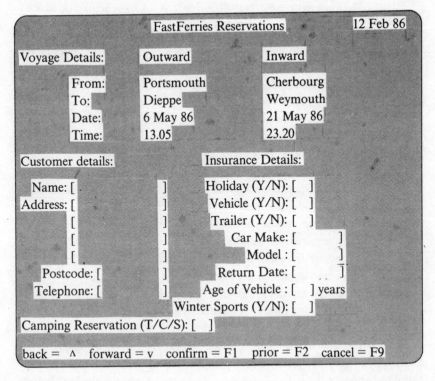

Fig. 7.15 The screen for the remaining logical groups.

illustration of the process; hopefully, they represent an acceptable starting point. The next stage is to evaluate the proposed design and repeat the process until an acceptable format is achieved. How can a screen layout be evaluated? Are there any objective measures which we can apply to test whether the screen is uncluttered, balanced and so forth?

The answer to this latter question is strictly neither yes nor no; a number of general mechanisms have been suggested but are not yet completely formulated. One problem is that the viewer of a screen is heavily influenced by the information content, which tends to cloud his judgement of the presentation. A general mechanism would divorce the content from the format; two suggestions for achieving this are boxing analysis and hot spot analysis.

Boxing analysis divides the screen up into physical groups; a group is an area of text characters with at least one blank space all around its perimeter. The smallest possible rectangle is drawn around each group, dividing the screen into a set of boxes. Drawing axes about the centre of the screen gives an impression of the balance of the layout. The number and size of boxes gives an impression of the 'business' of the layout; a large number of small boxes suggests a 'fussy' layout.

Hot spot analysis attempts to identify the parts of the screen to which a viewer's eye would be drawn by the 'intensity' of the image at that point. The intensity at each point is computed as a moving average of the number of non-blank character positions around that point; increasing density is displayed by using characters which 'switch on' an increasing number of dots in the character matrix or increasing background intensities. One would expect a small number of hot spots symmetrically positioned about the central axes.

These mechanisms are described and illustrated in the reference quoted in the bibliography at the end of the chapter. However, even these techniques lack a quantitative measure: What is a 'large number' or a 'small box'? Is a point surrounded by the character '.' hotter than one surrounded by the character 'W'? These questions are yet to be answered.

Another argument against the general approach suggests that the attempt to divorce content from format is mistaken; a layout should be judged by fitness for its particular purpose rather than as an abstract piece of graphic design. By this token, the only way that the layout can be evaluated is by prospective users actually interacting with that screen. Although general techniques may be useful to a designer in eliminating some design flaws before the user evaluation takes place, there is no substitute for this type of evaluation.

Screen layout, like all aspects of the interface design, is an iterative process. A large number of layouts may need to be modified many times before an acceptable version of the system is produced. If the designer must produce individual code to generate an example of each layout, this will be an unacceptably lengthy process; an automated mechanism, a *screen design aid*, is required to support this.

7.9 Screen Design Aids

The output processes described in Chapter 3 go some way to reducing the effort of generating a screen layout. Rather than coding all the statements necessary to display output from scratch, the designer has merely to assign values to field data structures. A reader who has attempted any of the exercises will be assured of the savings this involves. However, it is still fairly time-consuming. To define a field the user must specify

- the content (not difficult);
- the slot; this means that the designer must already have checked this out roughly;
- the attributes; the effect of these must be a guess.

When this has been done for all fields, the code containing these assignments must be compiled, linked with library routines and executed. Any change in any aspect of any field definition means that the whole process must be repeated. Unfortunately, the designer is unlikely to have a real idea of what the screen looks like until the code is executed. It would be considerably easier if the designer could sit in front of a screen and 'paint' the proposed layout on it; he could then evaluate the screen's appearance as it develops. Figure 7.16 illustrates a screen design aid of this type.

The screen is divided into three parts. The upper message area contains information on the current cursor position and the current values of the attributes. The lower message area contains a menu bar which, among other things, allows the attributes to be changed. The screen body contains the screen that is being designed. The user enters text at any position by moving the cursor to that position and keying; this overwrites the character already there. Attributes can be changed by selecting Option 3 from the menu bar, and scrolling through the attributes in the upper message area, changing individual values to taste. To paint the attributes into an existing field, the designer positions the cursor to the start of the slot and presses a control key; another control key is used to indicate the end. The slot thus marked is redisplayed with the new attributes. The same effect can be produced with a mouse by pointing the mouse at the start of the field, pressing a button and dragging the mouse to the end of the field keeping the button pressed. New fields will take the existing values of the attributes.

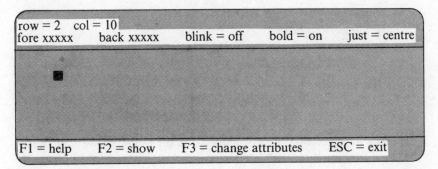

Fig. 7.16 A screen design aid.

Because some of the rows of the screen are taken up with information relating to the screen design aid, it would appear that no screen can be designed that uses these particular lines. One way round this problem is to allow the designer to scroll the screen body up and down, thus allowing the screen to be larger than the screen body. The full screen as it would appear in an application program can be displayed by selecting Option 2 of the menu bar. This is a toggle-switch; selecting it again redisplays the menu bars.

A screen design aid provides the designer with immediate feedback on the visual effect of the screen as he creates it. Changes can be effected simply by overpainting. The minimum requirement of a screen design aid is for it to provide facilities for creating, storing, retrieving and editing 'static' layouts. Further facilities are useful: a mechanism for naming the fields created by the screen design aid, and for linking these names to variables in the application program that is to use these screens; a mechanism for specifying the filtering and validation that is to take place at each field, and for automatically generating the appropriate code. Such facilities mean that the values of the various parameters in QandA_DIBs which define the dialogue can be specified by painting them on the screen. A number of proprietary packages exist which support some or all of these features and many installations have also developed their own. If such facilities do not already exist, their provision should be a high priority to any designer.

7.10 Summary

The screen design process involves:

    deciding what information is to appear;
    deciding how and where each field will appear;
    deciding what highlighting is required;
    developing a draft layout;
    evaluating the effectiveness of the layout.

To ensure consistency, the overall layout of all screens should conform to a standard screen template. This template should identify the position of the information whose communication is the primary purpose of the display and of supplementary information (titling, status and instructions) which support the user's interpretation and manipulation of the primary information.

The screen should contain all the information needed by the user at that point and only that information. The information should be organised so that its physical positioning reflects its logical grouping and is presented in an immediately usable format. The designer must understand the task in order to be able to assess these requirements.

A cluttered screen will impede the user's reception of the information which it contains; there are a number of standard guidelines covering the format and spacing of messages which are applicable. Where related information must be split across several physical screens, care must be taken that each screen still contains all the information necessary to process that particular screen.

Highlights attract a user's attention to particular areas of the screen and help to classify the information displayed in different areas. There are guidelines which can prevent the misuse or overuse of highlighting; intended highlights must still be tested on the screen on which they will be used because of wide variations in the way they are implemented.

Although some objective measures for evaluating screen designs have been suggested, these cannot replace trials with the intended users.

In order to support these trials and rapidly reflect their results in the design, a screen design aid is an invaluable tool.

Discussion Exercises

D1. Design the screen layouts which you feel are necessary to support the processing by a mail sale clerk of a telephone order from an existing agent. The layout(s) should contain explicit illustrations for the handling both of items which are in stock and of items which are unavailable. Illustrate how erroneous input will be handled and give examples of error messages and any help facilities which you feel are necessary.

D2. Several companies have expressed interest in the use of Prestel for direct sales to the public. A single product, 'Bert Blogg's Biggest Hits', available on record or cassette at the giveaway price of £3.99, will be advertised on TV. Members of the public, who subscribe to the Prestel service and have a full alphanumeric keyboard, can obtain any number of copies of the product by completing a Prestel response frame. Prestel allows full screen addressing, all the common highlighting features and simple graphics. It is designed to utilise a 20 line by 40 column colour TV monitor. If you have never encountered Prestel, an idea of the *display* facilities can be obtained by watching the Teletext services such as Ceefax or Oracle. For a Prestel response frame, input fields can be defined with simple validation checks.

Design the layout of a response frame which will enable users to order the product by specifying their name, address and credit card number (Visa, MasterCard and American Express are the only cards accepted).

D3. A software package is required to assist junior-school teachers in the development of vocabulary in slow learners; these are typically 9–10 year olds with a reading age of 5–6. The teacher will define a set of simple graphic representations (for example, a boat, a window or a flower) and will associate with each drawing a list of 5 words of 8 or less letters. A child sitting at a microcomputer will see the picture displayed and must choose the appropriate word. Pupils progress independently through a series of ten pictures.

The software will run on a typical home computer with a standard keyboard and 22 × 40 colour monitor. The pictures and wordsets will be stored on a disk. Design the screen layout which a pupil will see displayed and indicate how a word can be selected. Discuss what should happen if an incorrect choice is made.

Programming Exercises

P1. Determine the effect of different video attributes on the device you are using by producing a colour matrix which displays the possible combinations of background and foreground colour. The FieldType definition assumes 8 colours, so the matrix should be an 8 × 8 array of fields; the field in position (i,j) will have background colour[i] and foreground colour[j]. This exercise produces quite interesting effects even with a monochrome screen.

P2. Program the mail sale system for a single clerk. You need random access via a key to both the agents file and the products file. If your language supports indexed sequential files, then implement the files as:

Agents File   : organisation — indexed
                  access method — dynamic
Products File   : organisation — indexed
                  access method — dynamic

If your language only supports relative files, then use agency numbers of A1, A2, A3,... and have the file self-indexed (i.e. record A1 is stored at record position 1, record A2 at record position 2, and so on). Similarly for the products file, with product codes of P1, P2,...

Design your program so that the order is built up in memory, with the individual lines of the order being stored in the elements of an array. Implement 'Send Order to Picking/Invoicing' simply as a procedure that prints the order in an appropriate format.

Further Reading

Bass L. J. (1985) 'A Generalized User Interface for Applications Programs', *Comm.ACM*, **28**, 6.

Galitz W.O. (1981) *Handbook of Screen Format Design*, QED.

Mason R. E. A. and Carey T. T. (1983) 'Prototyping Interactive Systems', *Comm.ACM*, **26**, 5.

Mehlmann M. (1981) *When People Use Computers*, Prentice Hall.

Pakin S. E. and Wray P. (1982) 'Designing Screens for People to Use Easily', *Data Man.*, July.

Smith S. and Mosier J. L. (1984) *Design Guidelines for User Interface Software*, MITRE Corporation.

Streveler D. J. and Wasserman A. I. (1984) 'Quantitative Measures of the Spatial Properties of Screen Designs', *INTERACT '84*.

Chapter 8

Response time

8.1 What is Response Time?

A system's response time is defined as

the interval between an event and the system's response to that event.

It provides a measure of the delay which the system imposes on the user before he can proceed with the next step of the task. However, this definition can be interpreted in several ways. Consider the example illustrated in Fig. 8.1.

A user sitting at a UNIX workstation linked to a central file server, decides (time A) that he wants to list the contents of a particular directory. After a moment's thought (time B), he starts to type the command 'ls mydir'; at the end of the line (time C), he presses CarriageReturn. Following a short pause (time D), his input scrolls up a line on the screen indicating that the command has been accepted. After a further pause (time E), the first entry in the directory starts to appear on the screen and some time later (time F), the complete directory is displayed on the screen. At what time did 'the event' occur and at what time did the 'system response' occur?

Most readers would agree that the system's response should not be measured from time A or time B since it is unreasonable to include the user's thinking and keying time (the user's response) in the system response time. The most common interpretation is that response time is measured from time C, the entry of the last 'character' of the user's input message, typically depressing the Carriage Return or Enter key.

When does the response time interval end? Although the output may not be usable until the display has been completed at time F, this interval is dependent on the size of the output and the speed of the output device. The most common interpretation is that response time is the interval CE, i.e. from the last input character until the system displays the first 'character' of the resulting output message.

user	types		input line	first entry	directory list
thinks	ls mydir	<CR>	scrolls up	appears	complete
A	B	C	D	E	F

Fig. 8.1. Where is response time measured.

200

However, this interpretation also causes problems. You would expect the interval CE to be shorter for a command requesting a directory listing than for a command requesting the compilation of a PASCAL source program; the second command has a lot more work to do! Would you expect the interval CD, often called the *trivial response* to be different also?

This distinction is important because response time is an obvious criterion against which an interface can be measured; using the interval CE in the example above means that the criterion must take account of the different processing requirements of different tasks. The importance of response time has been recognised since the earliest attempts at on-line systems in the 1960s and it has been widely studied. Poor response is probably the first aspect that users will criticise; everyone agrees that fast response , like motherhood and apple pie, is 'a good thing' because:

- Fast response is impressive; it projects a good image of the system to all those who come into contact with it.
- It may produce tangible benefits; customers may actually be lost if a system responds so slowly that they have to wait an unacceptable length of time, or if by the time the air traffic control system tells the pilot that the glide path is too low, the 747 is a few feet below ground level!
- Poor response may impair a user's effectiveness in carrying out a task by failing to meet his psychological needs in completing the task.

8.2. Psychological Implications of Response

Having agreed that fast response is essential, the obvious question is what does 'fast' mean? Again the answer is far from trivial.

Consider the cases of a clerk whose job is solely based around interaction with a computer system, and a manager whose use of the system is incidental to his primary tasks, and envisage the following:

(a) The clerk entering a series of transactions into a ledger system in the middle of the morning; when one transaction has been accepted by the system, the next one can be input.

(b) The clerk undertaking the same task as (a) but trying to complete a batch of transactions just before work finishes in the afternoon.

(c) The clerk requesting the balance on a particular account in the ledger in order to check a query.

(d) The manager requesting the balance on a particular account in the ledger in order to complete an urgent report he is in the middle of writing.

A response which is acceptable in case (a) is likely to be unacceptably slow in the other cases. Equally, a response acceptable for case (b) may be unnecessarily and undesirably fast for case (a). Cases (c) and (d) involve the same set of actions being carried out by two different users but a response time which is acceptable to the clerk may be totally unacceptable to the manager. However, if in case (c) the customer with the query was actually standing beside him, the clerk would feel more urgency, and require a faster response from the system.

The requirement varies with the type of user, with what he wants the system to do, and with how his interaction with the system affects any associated tasks. Watch the behaviour of counter staff in Post Offices and banks where a single-queue system has been implemented to reduce customer waiting time; the customer at the head of the queue goes to whichever counter position is free. Have you ever noticed that as you reach the counter, the clerk feels a desperate need to do something else, like counting a pile of notes, before serving you? The clerk is slowing down the response of the system to provide an acceptable work rhythm for himself.

This demonstrates that it is possible for the response to be too fast. Some experiments, described in the bibliography, have demonstrated that, for response times below a given level, accuracy of menu selection increased as response time increased; this is not merely a reflection of the fact that users will try awfully hard to get the answer right if you make them waste 30 seconds every time they make a simple typing mistake! It has also been pointed out that novice users may feel threatened if, after spending several minutes typing an input message, the system instantaneously responds with an error message.

You should be able to recognise the same symptoms in your own interaction with computer systems. What response would you accept:

waiting to enter the next source line into the editor?
waiting for compilation to complete?

The response time, just like the other aspects of the interface, must match both the users' expectations and their natural work rhythm.

In human conversation, people expect a response (even if it is only a nod or a grunt) within about two seconds, and they bring this expectation with them to interactions with a computer system. Their expectations are influenced by their metabolism and by their motivation. The stereotype clerk whose primary function is data entry to a computer system will be more patient than the stereotype manager described above and will accept a longer response time (although there are some laid back managers and some highly strung clerks).

Since a user's expectations are strongly influenced by his previous experience with the system, a *consistent* and *predictable* response is also important. Users can detect quite small variations in response but normally do not worry about small fluctuations. However, whenever a system which usually responds within two seconds takes ten seconds, there will be a lot of users pressing keys to check if the system has crashed. This can be a marvellously self-fulfilling activity; if it had not crashed before, when all those keys are pressed...

There is a famous rule that a human can maintain 7 ± 2 things in short term memory at any instant. Consider how telephone numbers are organised into groups of digits so that dialling a telephone number consists of a series of clumps of information. It is also believed that short term memory is limited in units of time and that we can store two seconds worth of speech segment. Humans tend to organise their activity into clumps consistent with what they can maintain in their short term memory. Completion of a clump is called a *closure*. Our brains breathe a metaphorical sigh of relief when we achieve a closure, with the size of the sigh reflecting the significance of the closure. The last group in the telephone number, for example, will be greeted with a bigger sigh than completion of the area code.

Delays prior to closure are very frustrating and stressful since the contents of short term memory need to be continuously refreshed and are easily corrupted by external stimuli; similar delays may be quite acceptable after a closure has been reached. Most people readily accept a delay of several seconds between the end of dialling a number, and the telephone connection being made. Would you be happy to accept a delay between entering each digit on a push-button phone?

Interaction with a computer system imposes similar requirements. An experienced user will treat the entry of a complex query involving a number of related prompts and responses as a single clump, with closure being the completion of the query. Thus, whereas a ten second response may be acceptable for a simple query, or following the completion of a complex query, response times of ten seconds to answers within the complex query will be totally unacceptable. Functions which humans are willing or are able to perform change if the response much exceeds two seconds; the human has to alter his work rhythm just as you would have to change the way you approach telephone dialling if a delay was necessary between digits.

Much of the early work on response time was undertaken by R. B. Miller, who summarised the implications (reproduced from the AFIPS 1985 National Computer Conference Proceedings):

"There is not a straight-line decrease in efficiency as the response increases, rather sudden drops in mental efficiency occur when delays exceed a given point. These sudden drops at given points can be thought of as psychological step-down discontinuities.

"The greater the closure, the longer the acceptable delay in preparing for and receiving the next response following that closure. A general rule for guidance would be:

for good communications with humans, response delays of more than two seconds should follow only a condition of task closure as perceived by, or structured for, the human."

8.3 Recommendations on Acceptable Response Times

Response times requirements can be classified into:

0.1 – 0.2 second: confirmation of physical actions

When a key is depressed, the user expects feedback that the action has taken place (for example, an audible click). If this feedback is not forthcoming almost instantaneously the user will assume that the key has not been accepted, and press it again. Similar response times are necessary for confirmation of pointing. Imagine drawing on the screen with a light pen if the line being traced lagged the position of the pen by one second!

0.5 – 1.0 second: response to simple commands

Response times of this order of magnitude are acceptable between a user requesting some simple manipulation like 'next page', or selecting the next menu level, and the new screen being displayed.

1.0 – 2.0 seconds: chained interaction

Where a user must retain information within short term memory in order to answer a series of related prompts (i.e. where the user perceives the series of prompts as a single clump) the delay between successive prompts should not exceed this level. In fact, ideally, the overall delay for the series should not much exceed two seconds. Response times for simple enquiries (such as listing a disk directory) should not exceed this sort of time.

2.0 – 4.0 seconds: transaction oriented

Whilst this level of response is in general unacceptable for conversational interaction, it may be satisfactory following the entry of a complex query, or transaction input in form-filling mode. In fact, delays of up to ten seconds may be acceptable to some types of user if the delay does not impact any associated activity.

Greater than 10.0 seconds: 'batch-type' activities

In situations where the user perceives the task as a major closure involving a significant amount of processing (e.g. compilation or report generation), the user will accept and probably welcome a fairly substantial delay. However, there is an unofficial rule-of-thumb that

if you can't do it in 20 seconds, it's not interactive

and the user should be free to leave the task and turn to some other activity, returning for the results when it is convenient for him.

8.4 Why is Acceptable Response hard to Achieve?

The response time of a system is made up of a number of different components, as illustrated in Fig. 8.2. Time will be consumed by the dialogue processor in evaluating the user's input and in any task processing which this invokes. This processing may consist of CPU time and/or file subsystem time. File access is frequently a major contributor to response time both because of the relatively long access times and because, in multi-user systems, it represents a relatively scarce resource. The organisation of a file can also have a significant impact on response. For example, indexed sequential organisation is generally unsuitable for on-line query systems requiring a response within two seconds, because of the several accesses to an index necessary to locate a particular record.

If usage is via a network, then the response time of the network must also be included: transmission time including any retransmissions for error recovery, switching delays and other delays included in accessing the link, such as polling.

What can be said for certain about all systems is that the response will degrade exponentially with increasing load. Notice how the time it takes to get through a supermarket checkout lengthens with load on Friday evenings. As the load (the number of shoppers, and how full their trollies are) increases, the utilisation of the checkout assistants increases and queues start to form. The sensitivity of different systems to increasing load varies, but in all systems response degrades rapidly as utilisation approaches 80%.

Response times depend on utilisation of system resources:
>File access time
>CPU time
>Network transmission time.

As the load on a system increases:
>Utilisation increases
>Queues form
>Response degrades (exponentially for utilisations > 80%).

Reaction to load depends on
>Average number of tasks
>Average 'size' of tasks
>Variability in task size.

'Faster' means more processing power, so more cost.
Response times can be estimated, but only in idealised cases. In multi-user systems, response may depend not only on the number and size of tasks which are executing, but on the variability in their sizes and even on the order in which they were requested. For this reason batch and interactive processing can seldom be run successfully on the same machine.

Fig. 8.2. Summary of why fast response is hard to achieve.

In a dedicated single-user system, the problem is merely (!) one of ensuring that the response is acceptable for all the different activities within the system. Except for a very small class of applications, this can be achieved by increasing processing power. As soon as any element of sharing is introduced, even just access to a common hard disk, the problem becomes intractable since the designer has little or no control over the usage, and hence over the response.

Response time can be made acceptable if utilisation can be kept low. However, even today, the provision of this power may be an expensive trade-off. This is particularly galling since users react strongly to poor response but seldom notice good response unless there is a sudden and dramatic improvement.

There is one bright spot in this tale of doom: response time and utilisation are to some extent self-regulating. As response time degrades, users who do not have to use the system will tend to limit their usage. Hence utilisation may well reduce to a level where the response time becomes satisfactory. Time sharing bureaux have been known to take advantage of this phenomenon to regulate their equipment upgrades. When a bureau replaces its computer with one of significantly greater power, the utilisation decreases and the response time improves overnight. This dramatic improvement in response may encourage increased usage to the point where the response degrades again, perhaps to a worse level than before the upgrade. The record time for this to happen is rumoured to be about three weeks.

The bureau receives greatly increased revenue but at the cost of dissatisfied customers, and needs another upgrade. Since no organisation can handle the installation of new equipment more frequently than about every six months, it has been known for some of the initial improvement in processing to be mopped up with a background loop. Thus, when the upgrade is installed, the users see only a small improvement in response. Usage increases more slowly and as it does so, the priority of the loop is gradually reduced so that it has progressively less impact. The result is happy users, increased revenue, and evenly spaced upgrades — at least in theory!

8.5 What Can be Done to Alleviate these Problems?

The *background loop* technique described in the previous section degrades response deliberately rather than improving it. It should provide a more consistent response and hence prevent users forming expectations of response time which cannot be maintained. It is however a crude technique and assumes a multi-user system which supports varying priority levels.

The techniques described in this section aim at reducing the negative effects on the user of poor response rather than improving the response time itself. They all consume some processing power in achieving this and therefore increase the load on the system. Hence, the designer must ensure that the increased processing requirement does not aggravate the response problems. These techniques fall into two classes: the first provides reassurance that the system is still operating, and the second enables the user to structure his closures independently of system response constraints.

8.5.1. Providing Reassurance of Continuing Operation

This is most commonly done by displaying a status message indicating that the system is 'busy'. One popular word processor displays the message WAIT in a status line at the top line of the screen whenever it makes a disk access. The message can be represented graphically; some systems display a clock face and a popular desktop package converts the cursor symbol to an hourglass.

If the response delay is lengthy, this message must be regularly refreshed to provide reassurance of continuing operation; you might display the message immediately and refresh it every two or three seconds. A 'ticking' hand on a clockface is popular, and one system displays a cartoon bee which buzzes busily over the screen.

How can the message be refreshed regularly? On many systems you can use the hardware clock to interrupt the task process regularly so that the display can be updated. However, this is a non-trivial exercise for most high level languages and may not be possible at all. Fortunately, many of the task processes where response is a problem involve the repeated execution of a sequence of instructions such as reading a set of records from a file to calculate a report

    while some condition is true do
            read next record
            ....
            ....

Additional instructions can easily be incorporated into this loop to refresh the message every k iterations. In such a case it seems a little pointless to refresh the same message when the system could actually inform the user of the *task status*:

now processing record 100
now processing record 200 etc.

If the number of repetitions is known, the system could indicate how much of the task had been completed. For example,

'formatting/verifying track 8 of 40'
or 'format 20% complete'
or some graphical representation such as a 'gauge'

Incorporating this type of status tracking into a loop-structured task is easily done.

```
NumberOfIterations:=...;
StatusPoint:=rounded(NumberOfIterations/5); {every 20%}
for i:=1 to NumberofIterations do
        begin
        .....................
        'task instructions'
        .....................
        if (i mod StatusPoint)=0 then
          status:= (100*i) div NumberOfIterations;
        end;
status:= 100;
```

Although the tracking of status points is easy to implement, there is a problem with implementing status reporting in our model of a system. Status tracking is done within the relevant task process whereas status reporting is done by the dialogue process. In our system model, we have separated the dialogue process from the task process; these are two independent processes. How will a task process communicate its status to the dialogue process?

One possibility is to subdivide the task processes into smaller processing units so that status need only be reported at the end of each unit. Thus in the disk formatting example above, the task process unit is 'format a particular track of a disk' not 'format all tracks on a disk'. The dialogue process will keep invoking this task process until all tracks have been formatted and will report the current status to the user at the end of each invocation.

In the more general case, as each status point was reached the task process would relinquish control to the dialogue process for it to report the status to the user, and would then resume. This could be accomplished by running the dialogue and task processes concurrently or by running them asynchronously, in a similar way to that described for handling keyboard inputs described in Chapter 3.

It would be desirable for the system to give the user an indication at the start of a long task of the expected response for that task. The user could then decide whether to go and do something else. However, this is subject to the same problems as estimating response in the first place. Even if it takes k seconds to complete 20% of the task, an estimate of 5k seconds for the complete task may be inaccurate.

8.5.2 Allowing the User to Structure Closures

Response time problems occur because queues form to utilise scarce resources. One reason for resources being scarce is that they have to be shared amongst a number of different tasks and so one way to reduce response time problems is to reduce this sharing. Thus many upmarket workstations will contain a separate display processor so that response for task processing is not degraded by sharing it with the processing required for frequent screen redrawing. In a terminal network, users can be partly shielded from the central system response by replacing dumb terminals by intelligent devices so that some of the processing can be carried out locally. Thus with a form filling dialogue, the input and editing of the form may be accomplished locally rather than by transmitting each field of the form for central validation as it is entered; all fields will be transmitted only when the transaction has been completed. Since this should represent a 'closure' for the user, a longer response will then be acceptable.

Many applications have aspects which are amenable to local processing and this option has become more cost-effective as the cost of microcomputers has reduced to the level of dumb terminals. It can never provide a total solution since many systems are multi-user specifically so that several users can share access to common resources such as files. However, this idea of batching processing locally can be extended even to these applications.

One opportunity for doing this occurs when the task involves calculating a lengthy report. Users seem to have a fatal fascination for watching output lines appear on the screen or a printer no matter how slowly they appear; you may have noticed this trait in yourself. With tasks of this kind, many programmers write lines directly to the output device as they are calculated. There are then three possible causes of delay:

reading records from file to provide report line data;
processor time calculating and formatting the line;
writing the output to the device.

Instead of writing directly to the output device, the program can *spool output* to a disk file; in most high level languages this merely involves reassigning the output file to a different device. Delays may be as long, or even longer, but since no output will be displayed until the end, the user can go and do something else safe in the knowledge that the printer won't screw up the paper feed while his back is turned. He can return later to dump his report from disk.

Report No: **1**
Products : **ALL**
....
delay while report is calculated and spooled
....
report reference 1234 ready for printing
Option : **type 1234**

The designer can also organise input to the system so that the user can achieve a closure independent of the system response time. This means there must be no delays within what the user considers to be a single clump of activity. It implies that the system will not start processing the input required for that clump until the user has entered all the data message required; examples of this, which were described in Chapter 5, include form filling with deferred validation and the use of *macros* for Command Languages . A generalisation of this approach, called *answer-ahead*, can be applied to other dialogue structures. If a user can answer ahead, i.e. can input a string of responses without waiting for the system to request them, he can achieve a closure which is not impacted by the system's response time. He may still be affected adversely by the delay which follows while the system processes that clump, but this should be less onerous. Answer ahead is described in more detail in the following chapter.

8.6 Summary

System response time is the interval between an event and the system's response to that event. This can be interpreted in a number of different ways, resulting in different definitions of response.

Response time is significant since poor response will impair a user's performance by failing to reflect his psychological needs for closure in completing a task. The response must not only be adequately fast but also relatively consistent to avoid confusing user expectations.

There is no single acceptable response time but a set of acceptable response times which vary with the nature of the user, the type of task and how the system task relates to associated processing external to the system.

The provision of acceptable response is difficult since it depends on the utilisation of processing resources and, in most cases, such utilisation cannot be accurately predicted or modelled.

As a minimum, the dialogue should reassure the user, by means of regularly refreshed status messages, that response delays are not the result of the system crashing.

The sharing of resources can be reduced by the provision of local processing power but this is not usually sufficient to eliminate response problems. However, by allowing the facility for 'batching' lengthy input and output tasks, the user can form his own closures rather than having them imposed by the system.

Discussion Exercises

D1. Discuss where closures will occur in the activities which the clerk undertakes when taking a customer order in the mail sale case study. What response times do you feel would be acceptable following these closures? What technical problems might arise in providing this response?

D2. Discuss the closures which will occur in the sending and receiving of messages using the electronic mail system described in the Ariel case study of Appendix C. It is generally accepted that such systems must provide very fast response — why?

D3. What response times do you think a user would reasonably tolerate for the following?

(a) moving from one option to the next on a scroll menu using the space bar;

(b) as above but using a mouse for positioning;

(c) display of an error message;

(d) logging on to a multi-user computer system;

(e) logging off from a multi-user computer system;

(f) scrolling a new portion of a spreadsheet onto the screen;

(g) obtaining your bank account balance from an automatic till;

(h) displaying the next page of information on Prestel;

(i) a computer manager requesting a report of the monthly analysis of usage of a multi-user computer system.

Programming Exercises

P1. Construct a procedure which implements a software delay loop of the form delay(n:integer) to provide a delay of approximately n seconds. Incorporate this into different dialogue structures which you have implemented and investigate the effect of varying the delay on different actions and on someone who is familiar with the dialogue and with someone who is not. For example, you might experiment with the effect of delays in highlighting the current option in a scroll menu.

P2. Using the DisplayField procedure described in earlier chapters, implement a procedure DisplayStatus(status:percentage), which will output the percentage complete in the form of a gauge.

Further Reading

Barber R. E. and Lucas H.C. (1983) 'System Response Time. Operator Productivity and Job Satisfaction' *Comm.ACM*, **26**, 11.

Bevan N. (1981) 'Is There an Optimum Speed for Presenting Text on a VDU?', *Int.J.Man-Machine Studies*, **14**, 1.

Carbonnel J.R. *et al.* (1968) 'On the Psychological Importance of Response Time in a Timesharing System' *Human Factors*, **10**, 2.

Martin J. (1972) *Systems Analysis for Data Transmission*, Prentice Hall.

Miller G.A. (1956) 'The Magic Number Seven, Plus or Minus Two: Some Limits on our Capability for Processing Information', *Psych. Sc.*, **63**.

Miller R.B. (1968) 'Response Time in Man-Computer Conversational Transactions', *AFIPS*, **33**.

Myers B. (1985) 'The Importance of Percent-done Progress Indicators for Computer–Human Interfaces', in Borman L. and Curtis B. (Eds) *Human Factors in Computing Systems II* ACM/North Holland.

Shneiderman B. (1980) *Software Psychology*, Little, Brown & Co.

Chapter 9

Simple adaptation

9.1 Introduction

We have seen that it is important for the dialogue to match the expectations and psychological limitations of the user; these depend both on the nature of the task being undertaken and on the nature and level of experience of the user. The use of hybrid dialogue structures, as discussed in Chapter 5, lessens the problem of a system encompassing a variety of different tasks. However, it is seldom sufficient to cater for the fact that any of these tasks can be undertaken by a variety of users whose levels of experience span the spectrum from beginner to expert. It is extremely desirable, therefore, that there be sufficient flexibility in the dialogue that it is capable of being adapted, or of adapting itself, to accommodate a potentially wide spread of user experience. Adaptability in dialogues can be categorised into three types: fixed, full and cosmetic.

With *fixed adaptation* the user explicitly chooses the level of dialogue support. The need to provide some type of adaptation was recognised early on; it is self-evident that a beginner needs more support than an expert, and early work focussed on fulfilling this particular need. It was typified by a *rule of two* in which a system provided two forms of dialogue:

a *verbose* form providing explicit support for the beginner;
a *brief* form aimed at the expert, offering little or no support.

A menu structure can be considered a verbose form, and a Q&A structure a brief form. The 'Rule of Two' has been extended to a 'rule of N', and a number of popular packages allow the user *explicitly* to choose one of N levels of dialogue. For example, one well known word processor provides four levels of help which can be set by the user. There are several limitations in this approach:

- It does not recognise a continuous spectrum of user skill; users do not change from beginner to expert in discrete jumps.
- A user may be an expert in one area of the system, and a complete novice in other areas.

- How does the system decide whether the user is novice or expert? One common approach is for the system to ask the user to choose the desired level at the outset. Surely any way of phrasing such a question is likely to elicit an answer which tells you more about the user's self-confidence than his competance!

With *full adaptation* the dialogue attempts to maintain a model of the user which changes with his usage of the system, and which controls the style of dialogue, adapting automatically as a result of these changes. But what predictors should the dialogue use when deciding about changes to the model? The time that it takes a user to respond? The number of errors he makes? The number of times he requests help? The nature of the errors and the type of help required? Recognising the characteristics of the user is one of the major problem areas in implementing adaptation in the dialogue; it assumes that the dialogue has a knowledge both of potential users and of the tasks. Much recent research has focussed on how the interface can develop and maintain models of its users as a basis for adaptation, utilising techniques of Artificial Intelligence.

Cosmetic adaptation seeks to provide flexibility of dialogue styles without either attempting to react to the user's behaviour or explicitly requiring him to select a particular style. It achieves this by providing shortcuts (called *accelerators*) such as

   abbreviation and partial matching
   synonyms
   type ahead and answer ahead
   default answers and macros
   multi-level help

which an experienced user can utilise if he wishes. They are cosmetic in the sense that, like cosmetics, they represent essentially superficial enhancements to the basic structure but are, nevertheless, valuable in reducing tedium and in permitting limited personalisation of the interface. In this chapter we consider how such features can be incorporated into the dialogue.

9.2 Flexibility in Matching

As we have seen, selection inputs involve matching the user's input message against a list of possible targets represented as

```
type  TargetListType    = array[1..MaxTargets] of FieldType;
var   NumberOfTargets : byte;
      TargetList        : TargetListType;
```

The matching itself can be undertaken in a number of ways; the type of matching to be used at any point is specified by a parameter in the relevant QandA_DIB.

9.2.1 Normal Matching

The MatchString algorithm reproduced in Fig. 9.1 requires an *exact* match between the subject and one of the targets. It is the designer's responsibility to ensure that the targets are all unique. If they are not, then MatchString will select the first match.

9.2.2 Abbreviated Matching

Abbreviation has the obvious merit of reducing the volume of input. This might appear to favour inexperienced users who are likely to be less competent with the keyboard. However, abbreviation may impair the learning afforded to a novice through using the full input. Abbreviations tend to develop with usage — in the 1950s, that domestic novelty now known as the TV was still called a television. Some systems automatically *complete* the input i.e. they echo the complete target, rather than the abbreviation which the user entered.

```
function MatchString(subject:string;
                     TargetList:TargetListType;
                     NumberOfTargets:integer):byte;
var k,match : byte;
begin
match:=0;
k:=1;
while (k<=NumberOfTargets) and (match=0) do
   if TargetList[k].content=subject then match:=k
                                    else k:=k+1;
MatchString:=match;
end; {MatchString}
```

Fig. 9.1. Normal matching.

If natural item descriptions can be chosen so that a single character uniquely identifies each item, this is undoubtedly desirable. If, however, opaque or eccentric names or abbreviation rules have to be invented to permit single character abbreviations, any gain from the abbreviation is likely to be offset by a loss of naturalness.

Where abbreviations are permitted, there should be a consistent rule for creating them which pertains throughout the system. For example:

a valid abbreviation is any number of characters greater than or equal to the minimum necessary to identify uniquely the item required.

Figure 9.2 shows the abbreviations by which some options may be identified. In abbreviated matching the number of characters in the input string governs how many characters take part in the comparison. Because of this, it may match more than one target. For example, the abbreviation 'p' would match both 'property' and 'personal'. So there are three possible outcomes of this matching:

no match   — does not match any of the targets
unique match   — matches one and only one target
ambiguous match — matches more than one target

We will use a PASCAL 'set'

MatchSet : SetOfByte;

to record the ordinal numbers of the items of TargetList which matched the input string. If MatchSet is empty we have the 'no match' case; if MatchSet contains a single value, we have the 'unique match' case; and if MatchSet contains more than one value, we have the 'ambiguous match' case.

The AbbreviatedMatch procedure shown in Fig. 9.3 utilises the QandA_DIB, matching the content of the 'answer' field against the TargetList.

item						
				valid abbreviations		
motor		mo	mot	moto		
contents	c	co	con	cont	conte	conten	content
property		pr	pro	prop	prope	proper	propert
personal		pe	per	pers	perso	person	persona
life	l	li	lif			
miscellaneous		mi	mis	misc	misce	miscel	miscell–
end	e	en				

Figure 9.2

```
procedure AbbreviatedMatch(QandA_DIB:QandA_DIBtype;
                           var MatchSet:SetOfByte);
var k:byte;
begin
with QandA_DIB do
   begin
   MatchSet:=[];
   if length(answer.content)<>0 then
      for k:=1 to NumberOfTargets do
         if length(answer.content)<=length(TargetList[k].content) then
            if answer.content=copy(TargetList[k].content,1,
                                   length(answer.content)) then
               MatchSet:=MatchSet+[k];
   end;
end; {AbbreviatedMatch}
```
Fig. 9.3.

```
   if count(MatchSet)=0 then
      begin
      ChangeFieldContent(ErrorMessage,
         'Please re-enter - valid replies are ......');
      DisplayField(ErrorMessage);
      end
   else
   if count(MatchSet)>1 then
      begin
      ChangeFieldContent(ErrorMessage,
         'Choice is ambiguous - which of ......');
      DisplayField(ErrorMessage);
      end;

where
      function count(MatchSet:SetOfByte):byte;
      {returns the number of entries in MatchSet}
      var counter,k : byte;
      begin
      counter:=0;
      for k:=1 to MaxTargets do
         if (k in MatchSet) then counter:=counter+1;
      count:=counter;
      end; {count}
```
Fig. 9.4.

The input routine will keep requesting input until an option is 'matched', i.e. until a unique match is obtained. However, the error handling routine may well wish to distinguish between invalid and ambiguous inputs. In particular we may wish to display different messages to reflect these different types of error, as illustrated by the code fragment in Fig. 9.4.

Another form of abbreviation which is adopted for file names by many operating systems is the *wild card* technique. For example, both CP/M and MS-DOS interpret the string:

B:XX*.??Y

as identifying all files on drive B whose names start with the characters XX followed by any number of characters and with an extension which consists of any two characters followed by a Y. The matching process in such cases is more complicated than the example given and is more akin to parsing a command string.

9.2.3 Partial Matching

Abbreviation provides a mechanism for accelerating input and reducing potential typing errors. But it can hardly be considered a mechanism for error tolerance as discussed in Chapter 6. An error tolerant approach would cater in the matching process for simple typing or spelling errors. If MatchSet is empty at the end of the matching, the dialogue may simply tell the user that his response is incorrect, and ask him to re-enter it. Alternatively, it could try a 'partial' match on his current response.

On the assumption that errors are more likely to be made in the later input characters, you might progressively reduce the strictness of the match. One simple method is to delete the rightmost character of the 'subject', and then compare the new 'subject' with each of the match strings. This is repeated until either match(es) are found or 'subject' is reduced to a single character. This method may also produce an ambiguous match. A procedure for partial matching is shown in Fig. 9.5.

This partial matching algorithm has the advantage that it will still match correctly when the user types in more than enough uniquely to identify an item, and makes a mistake in the non-significant characters, e.g. by typing 'prpo' rather than 'prop'. Both the normal matching algorithm and the abbreviated matching algorithm will reject such a case as invalid.

```
procedure PartialMatch(QandA_DIB:QandA_DIBtype;
                       var MatchSet:SetOfByte);
var k:byte;
begin
with QandA_DIB do
   begin
   MatchSet:=[];
   while (length(answer.content)<>0) and (count(MatchSet)=0) do
      begin
      AbbreviatedMatch(QandA_DIB,MatchSet);
      delete(answer.content,length(answer.content),1);
      end;
   end;
end; {PartialMatch}
```
Fig. 9.5.

A number of more general approaches for implementing partial matching exist, all of which rely on establishing a metric so that the 'distance' of the input from each of the possible responses can be measured. The response(s) selected are those which are 'closest' to the input. Partial matching is particularly appropriate where the input consists of names (notorious for their eccentric spellings) or narrative input (for example, in searching a database by keyword) is involved. The Soundex system is one example of matching names based on their sound.

The name input is converted as follows:

remove all non-alphabetic characters (such as '–')
retain the first letter of the name
drop all vowels A E I O U and the letters W H and Y
assign the following numbers to the remaining letters:

1 = B F P V
2 = C G J K Q S X Z
3 = D T
4 = L
5 = M N
6 = R

coalesce adjacent identical numbers to a single number
form the code from the original first letter and the first three of the numbers; if less than 3 numbers remain, pad out with zeros

Thus FARBES, FFORBES, and FORBOUYS which all convert to F612, would all match an input of FORBES but so would FAIRPIECE. This illustrates both an advantage of such a mechanism and a drawback; it tends to result in ambiguous matches which require the system to ask for confirmation from the user. The Soundex system is clearly based on the 'phonetic' closeness of different characters; a similar 'metric' might be applied to the relative closeness of keys on a keyboard.

9.3 Synonyms

A dialogue which supports *synonyms* allows an object to be 'named' by a number of different identifiers, in a variety of formats, or by a variety of mechanisms. For example, MS-DOS allows both DEL and ERASE as equivalent command names for deleting files and also allows DEL to be 'spelt' del. We have seen in Chapter 5 that it is easy to implement menus in which the user may select an option either by scrolling or by keying its identifier.

The merit of synonyms is that a user can use the identifier which seems most natural to him and hence the one which he is most likely to remember. The drawback is that this multiplicity can both confuse the user and complicate the processing required for matching; in particular it can slow down the response of the system if a large number of alternate names must be scanned. Another point to consider is whether there is much rationale for alternate identifiers unless the user can choose his own. This immediately leads to the problem of what happens if different users choose the same identifier for different objects, e.g. 'list' both to display on the screen and for printer output.

It is easy to build a limited and standard set of synonymous identifiers into the dialogue. One method is to associate a translation table with the TargetList of valid responses, as in Fig. 9.6. When the matching routine returns the ordinal of the choice, this is used as an index into the table; consequently both 'delete' and 'erase' would return option 2.

Another possibility is to use a cover routine for each synonym which calls the basic option. For example

```
procedure erase(files:filename);
begin
delete(files);
end; {erase}
```

	TargetList	Translation
1	copy	1
2	delete	2
3	erase	2
4	.....	.

CurrentTarget:=MatchString(subject,TargetList,NumberOfTargets);
if CurrentTarget<>0 then
        TranslatedTarget:=Translation(CurrentTarget);

Fig. 9.6.

One form of synonym which should always be supported (unless there is a specific reason not to do so) is to allow input in any combination of upper and lower case so that, for example, both 'property' and 'pRoPErTy' would match 'Property'. Novice users, and some not so novice, encounter problems with *case sensitive* input, by inadvertently leaving the Caps Lock key on. Even though UNIX is very generous with synonyms, it is case sensitive; for example, 'ls' causes a directory listing and 'LS' a search for a user defined object with that name. Of course, if you have already reserved most of the good names for the operating system, you may feel that you should restrict their influence! Converting an uppercase character to its lowercase equivalent, or vice versa, is trivial since

ord(UpperCaseChar) = ord(LowerCaseChar)+N

where N is an integer which depends on the particular character set.

A single space (or a combination of spaces) is often used as a delimiter to separate the various elements of a command language string. Input should be insensitive to the actual number of spaces entered, and so multiple spaces should be reduced to a single space. (There are exercises at the end of the chapter to convert case and to remove redundant spaces.)

9.4 Defaults

The essence of a *default* value is that the system will assume a particular response unless the user specifically types a different one. Thus, in cases where the user frequently enters the same answer to a particular request, the input can be reduced to the single keystroke necessary to confirm the default value.

Situations requiring a standard answer arise frequently. For example, when entering transaction data into an accounting system, a unique posting reference number and posting date are usually supplied. The reference number is typically the next integer in sequence and the date is typically the current date; it is unnecessary for the user to input these explicitly unless they are different from this assumption. Similar examples apply in command languages. The command DIR in CP/M and MS-DOS lists the directory of the current drive unless the user explicitly specifies a different drive.

The user must be aware of what default value the system is assuming. In Q&A and form filling structures, the default can be displayed with the prompt or field caption

Posting Reference [**1047**]?
Posting Date [**26/10/85**]?

or in the position which the response would occupy

Posting date	26	10	85

Since some users find overtyping existing values confusing, the ReadField keyboard process of Chapter 5 displays the default in the answer field, but clears the field as soon as the user enters the first character of the reply.

In a menu structure, the default is usually indicated by its position (the first item on a menu organised by frequency of use) or by a video highlight. In a scroll menu, moving round the options could be considered as temporarily changing the default value.

In a command language, there is no way to display a default value and so the user must remember it. However, since a command language is aimed at experienced users who have to remember the command syntax anyway....

The commonest way for a user to accept the default value is to enter a null input, i.e. just press the 'Carriage Return' or 'Enter' key. If command language with positional parameters is being used, the user simply omits the entry, which results in two adjacent separators

MODE COM1:9600,,8,1

This would be interpreted as a null reply for the fourth token, leading to the default value (even parity in this example) being used. In a command language with keyword parameters, a default value is selected simply by omitting the relevant parameter keyword and value.

Since users often get the habit of pressing the return key almost automatically, the default value in cases where the outcome is irreversible is customarily the one that preserves the status quo. Thus NO would be the default response to

A>**era** *.*
  Sure [Y/N]?

Defaults assume that one answer will be the most common; it is foolish to implement a default value which is constantly being overridden. A major problem is that, like everything else in the dialogue, the most common answer is likely to change with the user and over time. Thus there must be some mechanism for changing the default values within the system; if these values are coded into a program source such changes will be very tedious! The reader may care to consider how this might be overcome; we will return to it in a later section.

The dialogue processes of Chapters 4 and 5 use the following mechanism for defaults. The default answer for a particular QandA_DIB is stored in the answer field of that DIB. When the Q&A procedure is invoked to accept input via this DIB, the current content of the answer field is displayed. If the AcceptField key is pressed immediately, this default content is accepted; pressing any other valid key causes the field to be cleared, and input which falls within the filter is accepted and displayed in the field.

The user may not just provide the same answers to isolated questions; his usage of the system may be such that he commonly traverses the same paths, i.e. he regularly inputs the same sequence of answers. For example, he may often select a report using the same selection criteria. This could be achieved by repeatedly pressing the return key to accept each default.

Report No [1]   : <CR>
Products [ALL]: <CR>
Markets [EUR] : <CR>
Sources [UK]   : <CR>
. . . .

but it would be tedious. What is needed is a mechanism for 'cataloguing' a series of standard responses such as that provided by operating systems, e.g. BAT files of MS-DOS. *Macros* provide such a mechanism. The user stores his responses for selecting a commonly used report under some name, e.g. MYREPORT. The user responds to the first prompt with the name of the macro (and some indication that it is a macro) and the stored answers are individually fed to each prompt and processed as though they came directly from the keyboard:

Report No [1] : ***MYREPORT**

How this may be accomplished should become apparent in the next section.

9.5 Type ahead and Answer ahead

9.5.1 Type ahead

We saw in Chapter 3 that, for most devices, if the user presses a key while the

CPU is executing a task process, the system will generate an *interrupt* which will:

- cause the CPU to suspend execution of the task process;
- start execution of the keyboard I/O process; this will take the character typed, store it in the keyboard buffer, and on completion of this;
- cause the CPU to resume execution of the suspended task process.

Users who follow regular paths through a system soon become familiar with the sequences of questions and possible responses. Suppose the user types m o t o r <carriage return> while a task process is executing. On completion of the task process the buffer will contain:

If the next request for input requires the user to select from a menu of 'motor, contents .... ,end', the options will be displayed and the user asked to choose. However, the system will find the answer already in the buffer since the user typed it ahead of being asked (hence *type ahead*) and will continue immediately. There is little point in subjecting the user to a display of the menu or prompt if his answer is already in the buffer. Ideally this would only apply to complete answers; a partial answer would be processed in the usual way. Figure 9.7 illustrates the type ahead mechanism.

The advantage of type-ahead is that the user can form his own 'input closures' independent of the timing of prompts from the system. One

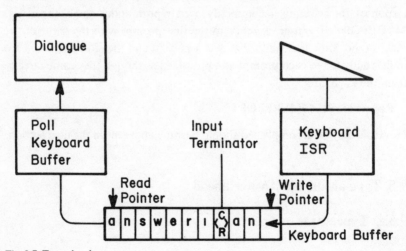

Fig. 9.7. Type ahead.

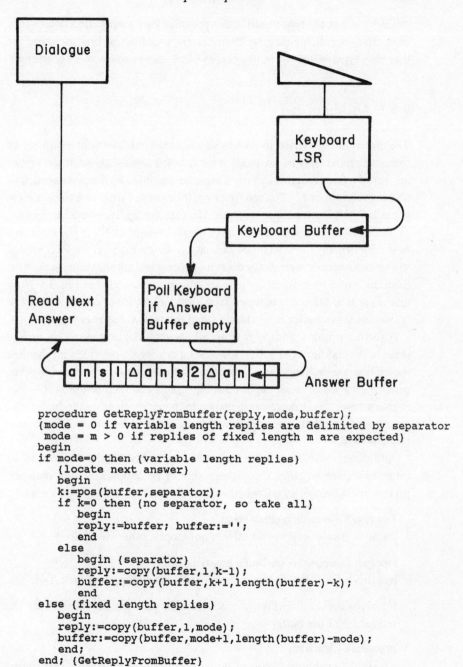

```
procedure GetReplyFromBuffer(reply,mode,buffer);
{mode = 0 if variable length replies are delimited by separator
 mode = m > 0 if replies of fixed length m are expected}
begin
if mode=0 then {variable length replies}
   {locate next answer}
   begin
   k:=pos(buffer,separator);
   if k=0 then {no separator, so take all}
      begin
      reply:=buffer; buffer:='';
      end
   else
      begin {separator}
      reply:=copy(buffer,1,k-1);
      buffer:=copy(buffer,k+1,length(buffer)-k);
      end
else {fixed length replies}
   begin
   reply:=copy(buffer,1,mode);
   buffer:=copy(buffer,mode+1,length(buffer)-mode);
   end;
end; {GetReplyFromBuffer}
```

Fig. 9.8. Answer ahead.

difficulty is that the type ahead buffer provided by the operating system may be relatively small, for example 15 characters, thus limiting how far ahead the user may type. When the buffer becomes full, excess characters are ignored.

9.5.2 Answer ahead

The user is not restricted to answering only the next question; a number of sucessive replies may be provided. This is called *answer ahead*. If the replies are not of a fixed length, each reply must be delimited by a *separator* such as Carriage Return or '/'. The separator must be chosen with care since it must not occur in the normal input stream. To ease typing, it should ideally be a single unshifted character (or at least a single keystroke). Since the keyboard buffer is normally of very limited capacity, a *dialogue answer buffer* is needed to implement answer ahead; the dialogue process will take each answer in turn from the buffer by locating the next separator, as illustrated in Fig. 9.8. Note that there is a difference between type ahead and answer ahead in that the dialogue answer buffer is filled only when the system requests input.

A further problem with answer ahead occurs if the user enters an invalid input in the middle of the buffer. It would be possible to provide a mechanism for editing the buffer after it has been input — many interactive systems provide a means to recall the last line input, edit and then resubmit it — but in many cases this is more cumbersome than merely clearing the buffer and restarting from that point. The buffer should also be cleared if the user requests help.

Additional routines are needed to support type ahead and answer ahead. In order to decide whether the prompt should be suppressed, the dialogue process must be able to test whether the user has typed/answered ahead:

function KeyboardEvent:boolean;
{returns 'true' if keyboard buffer is not empty, otherwise 'false'}

function DialogueAnswerBufferEmpty:boolean;
{returns 'true' if the dialogue answer buffer is empty, otherwise 'false'}

If a type/answer ahead is incorrect, the dialogue must be able to flush the remainder of the buffer

procedure ClearKbd;
{clears the keyboard buffer of any characters that may have been typed ahead of them being requested}

procedure ClearAnswerBuffer;
{clears the dialogue answer buffer}

9.6 Command Language as Answer ahead

Suppose we have a QandA_DIB which prompts for a command name:

command?

The user input is matched against TargetList which holds the permitted commands. When matched, a sequence of QandA_DIBs is processed to accept the parameters for that command. For example:

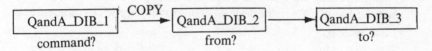

A typical dialogue might be:

command?   **COPY**
from?   **A:FILE1**
to?   **C:FILE2**

Compare this with the following 'command language' string:

command?   **COPY bb A:file1 bbbbb c:FILE2**

If the string is preprocessed to a standard format by converting all letters to the same case (e.g. upper case), and removing superfluous blanks, we obtain:

This can be considered as an answer ahead to the previous sequence of

QandA_DIBs with space as the delimiter. Because the answers to the 'from?' and 'to?' questions have been provided ahead of the questions being asked, these prompts have been suppressed. Hence, a command dialogue can be viewed as *question-and-answer with answer ahead*. The example chosen has used positional parameters but a similar argument will handle keyword parameters and the inclusion of 'switches' in the command string. Recognition of this fact can guide us when designing a command language.

With a command language, the user has the sensation of *being in control*: – the dialogue is user-driven. Because answer-ahead places greater demands on short-term memory, consistency and memorability are extremely important:

- The names assigned to commands should be meaningful, and easy to remember. Wherever possible, congruent pairs of names should be used (for example, GET and PUT, INSERT and DELETE, and so on).
- A standard delimiter (such as space or comma) should be adopted, and used consistently. Thus, the designer should avoid capricious differences in syntax such as

    pip newfile=oldfile
    ren newfile oldfile

- A standard escape convention should be used.

In the hands of experienced users, a well designed command language can lead to fast interaction; many computer professionals are very skilled at interacting with operating systems via command languages. However, it can take a long time to become proficient, and relearning can be a major exercise after an extensive interval away from the system.

If the command language is designed on the basis of Q&A with answer ahead, then it can cater for a range of user skills. For an experienced user, 'closure' will occur at the end of a complete command string; for an inexperienced or 'rusty' user, it may occur within a command string. If the user types only part of the answer, (perhaps because he doesn't know the full format of the command, or perhaps because he has forgotten it after some time away from the system) then some questions will be unanswered, and so the system can prompt him for the remaining answers. For example, if the user types:

    command? **COPY**

and then presses Carriage Return, or a Help key system or pauses for a given interval, the system can prompt with a form requesting the remainder of the information:

from? **A:FILE1**   to? **C:FILE2**

By regarding it as a special case of Q&A, a command language can be made more flexible; in fact, we have introduced an *implicit* Rule of two. On the one hand, experienced users using answer ahead see the dialogue as a traditional command language; on the other hand, novices can be given the syntax of the commands, and specific help can be provided for each parameter. This mechanism can be extended further to an implicit rule of N. The possible values for command parameters could be scrolled through each answer box; a user may either type in a parameter value or scroll through the possible options using the supressed menu technique described in Chapter 4.

9.7 Multi-level Help

We saw in Chapter 6 that a good help message must be specific to the user's problem. This implies that a series of help messages are necessary at each point where input is requested from the user, rather than a single all-embracing message.

As a minimum, the system should distinguish between a user who has merely forgotten the precise 'phrasing' of the response (i.e. who requires a menu of the available options or formats) and a user who does not understand what input is being requested. This distinction can be achieved by implementing two different help requests. For example, an input of MENU displays the available options (the TargetList from the QandA_DIB), and an input of HELP provides a message which displays not only the options but a brief explanation of what each does.

However, like the rule of two, this is a rather crude distinction; a more subtle mechanism would allow N levels, although not all N would necessarily be appropriate at all points in the dialogue. Equally, the systems designer is likely to feel that there is some N above which more dramatic assistance is needed than can be supplied automatically.

One method of supplying multi-level help is based on displaying a first-level help message and then asking the user if he requires more. This process is repeated until either the user is satisfied or there is no more help that can be given. The sample dialogue at the start of Chapter 6 uses this approach which effectively introduces a Help sub-dialogue with a Q&A structure.

Option? : **HELP**

.... first level help ....

....

More? : **Y**

.... second level help.........

....

A more elegant mechanism relies on the system tracking the number of times the user has requested help at that point in the dialogue, for example by maintaining a CurrentHelpLevel, as shown in Fig. 9.9.

```
if reply=help then
   begin
   if CurrentHelpLevel>MaxHelpLevel then
      begin
      ChangeFieldContent(HelpMessage,'no more help available');
      DisplayField(HelpMessage);
      end
   else
      begin
      GiveHelp(StartAt[CurrentHelpLevel]);   {See Figure 6.5}
      CurrentHelpLevel:=CurrentHelpLevel+1;
      end;
   Buffer:='';   {can't answer-ahead!}
   end;
```

Fig. 9.9. Multi-level help.

The mechanism described in Section 6.4.2 can be easily extended to incorporate multi-level help. Instead of containing a single value N pointing at the first record of a single help message, the help message parameter in the QandA_DIB would contain an array of first-record pointers, one for each level of help, and its own current and maximum help levels.

CurrentHelpLevel : byte;
MaxHelpLevel   : byte;
StartAt   : array[1..GlobalMaxHelpLevel] of integer;

9.8 Multi-language Considerations

Amongst the earliest people to recognise the desirability of separating the interface from the task processing in a system were systems designers working in multinational companies in the 1960s. Systems which had been developed at great cost in North America or the UK were appropriate for operations elsewhere in the world but were difficult to transport because the prospective users, who were not fluent in English, found difficulty in understanding the messages. Changing these messages was difficult as they were scattered as literals throughout the programs making up the system. Therefore a programmer was needed to go through the source programs, locating and changing these to produce a new source for the European location; of course it helped if this programmer knew French, German, Italian . . . or alternatively if there was a translator who knew COBOL.

Life would have been much easier if all these messages — prompts, help messages, error messages — had been held on a data file divorced from the syntax of the programming language involved. Then a translator could have been given a listing of the file to translate, and data preparation staff could have keyed in this translation to create another file. The literals could be referenced in the program via a number, for example:

    Retrieve(MessageFile,MsgNo,Message);
    DisplayField(Message);

There is litle point in displaying output in the user's native language if he still has to respond in English; the valid responses must also be held on file for ease of translation.

    Ledger? : **sales**   =====>   Livre? : **clients**

We have already seen the desirability of holding help messages on file. Combining this with the multi-language capability requires a file which contains a record or group of records associated with each input request which details

    the prompt message
    the series of help messages
    the TargetList of valid responses
    the error message to be displayed if the response is invalid.

Since we have abstracted the parameters associated with any input request into a QandA_DIB data structure, this is equivalent to saying that the data values associated with each QandA_DIB must be held on file. Records are also needed for the other types of message, e.g. output data messages such as report titles, status messages, etc. The structure of the dialogue procedure can be adjusted to reflect this requirement, by including a routine to set up the DIB associated with any input step from the relevant file.

This mechanism enables the designer to allow for personalised dialogues. We have considered it from the point of view of providing a native language facility in systems which are to run at a variety of installations. However it need not be restricted to providing the same dialogue in English or French or some other language. There is no reason why, where a clerk and a manager both use the same system for different functions, a different dialogue should not be provided merely by supplying a different data file which will run with the same dialogue process and the same background tasks.

A user can be restricted to a particular subset of the system's facilities by defining only that subset on the dialogue file. For example, a user who is allowed to read but not amend a personnel database would never see any reference to updating facilities, since the TargetList on his dialogue file would not contain the response 'update'. Different default values can be supported for different users and even the default paths described in Section 9.4 could be stored on this file.

On a terminal-based system, the required file can be identified automatically by some mechanism such as a log-in code, and on a stand-alone based system by providing the user with a diskette containing his personal dialogue. A little thought should indicate the undesirability of asking the user which dialogue he requires: if it is a choice of language, in which language do you ask for the choice?

It is also possible that the character used in answer ahead, and ControlDIB values such as the 'standard' response which users input to request the default or to request help, may vary for different users. These can also be held on the dialogue file but since they are the same at each input request, they do not need to be stored for every individual request and could be held in a header record at the start of the file.

The mechanism is not without drawbacks. We have already mentioned the problem of efficient storage. There will also be some degradation in response since a number of retrievals from file will be needed to set up the messages. In Chapter 11 we discuss how these reservations can be overcome, and consider how all the various dialogue structures and facilities can be accommodated in a generalised dialogue manager.

9.9 Summary

The dialogue must incorporate some element of adaptability to cater for varying levels of expertise in different users and in the same user in different parts of the system.

Fixed adaption is a crude mechanism since it requires the user to choose a particular level of support explicitly. Full (or automatic) adaption is extremely difficult to implement since it requires the system to recognise a user's characteristics from his inputs. Cosmetic adaption provides accelerators which can, but need not, be utilised by an experienced user and provide a limited amount of personalisation.

Rather than requiring an exact match with an entry in the TargetList, the system may accept abbreviated or partial matches. Partial matches provide some error tolerance but it is often difficult to define a metric for deciding which target has been matched and such metrics often result in ambiguity.

Synonyms allow a user to identify system objects by a variety of identifiers, in a variety of formats or by a variety of mechanisms. They permit personalisation of the dialogue but may confuse rather than assist novice users.

Defaults reduce the input load by enabling a user to select a common response or set of responses (a macro) with a single input.

With type ahead and answer ahead, a user may supply a series of responses without waiting for the system to prompt for them individually. This allows a user to form his own closures rather than having closures imposed by the system.

Interpreting a command language structure as a Q&A structure with answer ahead, suggests both guidelines for the design of command languages and ways in which such a structure can adapt to cater for both novice and expert users.

A multi-level help facility is necessary to provide support which is specific to a user's problem. Such a mechanism is easily implemented by storing pointers to the relevant message levels in the QandA_DIB.

We saw earlier that developing a common abstraction (the QandA_DIB) facilitated the production of generalised processes which could implement any dialogue structure. Holding the values for these data structures on a dialogue file enables personalised dialogues to be produced for any group of users.

Discussion Exercises

D1. Two common keying errors are:

- the transposition of 2 letters e.g. TSET for TEST;
- the substitution of one letter by another e.g. TWST for TEST, often by hitting an adjacent key to the one intended.

Suggest a possible partial matching metric which could be used to handle these cases.

D2. An alternative way of implementing multi-level help is to superimpose multiple messages onto the structure described in Section 6.4.2 (a single pointer in the HelpMessage field of the QandA_DIB pointing to the first record of the first-level help message).

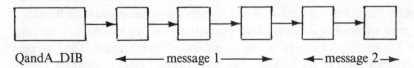

QandA_DIB   ◄———— message 1————►   ◄—message 2—►

Messages can be assumed to occupy an integral number of records. However, some mechanism is needed to distinguish between the various messages. Initially the QandA_DIB pointer points to the first record of the first message. After one call for help, this pointer will be left pointing at the first record of the second message. And so on.

What are the advantages and disadvantages of this approach?

D3. Dialogue files provide a mechanism for supporting personalised dialogues for different users. Discuss the record format which is needed for such a file.

Programming Exercises

P1. Implement a routine to convert all ASCII lowercase alphabetics in an input string to uppercase.

P2. Implement a routine which will remove all redundant spaces from an input string, i.e. convert all multiple spaces within the string to single spaces and remove any leading or trailing spaces.

P3. Many operating systems support a macro facility whereby a series of command lines can be stored in a 'batch' file. When the batch file is invoked, the sequence of commands is executed as though they had been typed at the keyboard.

Suggest how such a facility can be used to support synonyms; for example, to provide a variant of the intrinsic file copy function by one with a different name and different parameter order.

P4. Amend the ReadField keyboard process to incorporate an answer-ahead .

mechanism which is independent of the operating system keyboard buffer. The dialogue process will maintain a global variable as a buffer. (How long should this buffer be?) Whenever a user is requested for input, he may type as many successive answers as he likes; this input string is read into the buffer. A prompt will be displayed and input requested only if the buffer is empty. Assume that the user terminates each input with a carriage return.

P5. If in Question P2 all the valid responses were single character replies, it would be silly to insist on a carriage return being typed either after a single reply or after a string of answer-ahead replies. How else could the system determine if the user had completed entering the answer-ahead string?

Further Reading

Benbasat A. *et al.* (1984) 'Command Abbreviation Behaviour in Human–Computer Interaction', *Comm.ACM*, **27**, 4.

Durham I. *et al.* (1983) 'Spelling Correction in User Interfaces', *Comm.ACM*, **26**, 10.

Good D. M. *et al.* (1984) 'Building a User Derived Interface', *Comm.ACM*, **27**, 10.

Mozeico H. (1982) 'A Human/Computer Interface to Accommodate User Learning Stages', *Comm.ACM*, **25**, 2.

Schneider M.L. *et al.* (1984) 'An Experimental Evaluation of Delimiters in a Command Language Syntax', *Int.J.Man–Machine Studies*, **20**, 6.

Wasserman T. (1973) 'The Design of Idiot-Proof Interactive Systems', *AFIPS*, **42**.

Chapter 10

WIMPs

10.1 Introduction

Command language interfaces have enjoyed continuing popularity for many years. They reflect the sense of control which an experienced user feels when interacting with a system. However, the last few years have seen a number of significant developments in the interfaces between computer systems and their users. These have mainly concentrated on interfaces for inexperienced or infrequent users, particularly in office automation applications, and are tending to replace the traditional menu structure dialogue.

The *WIMP* interface is typical of these developments. Such an interface

W — presents information to users via multiple *Windows* on the display;

I — representing pictorially as *Icons* the data objects with which the system is concerned

M — using a *Mouse* to select from;

P — menus which *Pop-up* automatically on the screen or which a user can *Pull down* from a menu bar at the top of the screen.

Any relationship between the acronym and characteristics of the users at which it is aimed is, of course, purely coincidental!

These developments result from work carried out in the early 1970s at Xerox Corporation's Palo Alto Research Center, but their recent popularity results from the increased power of typical business microcomputers. In particular, they require workstations which have

* sufficient RAM to support a screen map several times the size of the physical screen, allowing parts of the display to be 'overlapped';
* a medium- or high-resolution bit-mapped screen to support the display of graphic representations such as icons;
* adequate processing power to redraw the screen rapidly and to support at least a limited amount of multi-tasking.

WIMP interfaces are exemplified by operating systems such as the Apple Mackintosh, Digital Research Graphics Environment Manager (GEM), MicroSoft Windows and IBM's TopView, and by an increasing number of application software packages which conform to the same conventions. In this chapter, we examine the various elements which make up a WIMP interface; first, however, we consider the philosophy which underlies them.

10.2 The Underlying Analogies

The main thrust towards the development of these interfaces arose when computing started to invade the office, particularly the executive office. This involved a significant change both from the traditional transaction processing type of application and from the traditional dedicated clerical user. Designers were faced with an environment in which a single user might spend his time on a number of different but related applications: text processing, simple calculation, simple graphics. Furthermore, these are activities which represent only part of any task on which the user is engaged, where computer usage is discretionary, and for which the user is unlikely to accept more than minimal computer training.

In an attempt to provide an interface which was natural, consistent and supportive of such users, designers looked for analogies in the clerical performance of similar tasks. Although there are dangers in basing a computer system too closely on a clerical analogy, we have seen that such analogies can provide useful guidelines. Three main analogies underly the WIMP philosophy.

10.2.1 The 'Concrete Object' Metaphor

Traditional interfaces require the user to manipulate strings of symbols in order to specify operations and the data items to which these operations are to be applied. Thus, storing a file in a directory might be achieved by the command

copy myfile /MyDirectory

A user must learn both the computer system semantics (the strings, the computer system objects which they represent and how these relate to task objects) and the computer systems command syntax.

In the clerical performance of a similar task, the items are represented by physical (i.e. 'concrete') objects. Files are sheaves of paper or folders, directories are drawers in a filing cabinet and so forth. Clerical operations involve physical actions on these objects. Thus, to store a file, the human will pick up the sheaf of papers, walk across to the filing cabinet, open the drawer and place the file inside. To rename a file, a human will erase the old name and write in the new one.

The concrete object metaphor seeks to eliminate the dichotomy between the syntax and semantics of the task and the syntax and semantics of the computer system by modelling the interface on the natural human performance of the task. A file might be copied by dragging it with the mouse to the relevant directory icon. There are a number of ramifications in this approach, called *direct manipulation*, to which we return later in the chapter.

10.2.2 'What You See Is What You Get'

If you underline a portion of text on a page, you immediately see the result of your action as a line on the paper. Similarly, if you copy a paper file you see both the original and the copy before you.

This has traditionally not been the case when carrying out the computer equivalent of these tasks. Highlighting features in word processing packages were often indicated on the screen by a control character embedded in the text; the result of the action appeared only when the text was printed. Many users have been irritated to discover on printing that, by forgetting to turn off the highlight, they had highlighted large blocks of text. It has also been noted that many inexperienced users check, by redisplaying the directory, that their commands to copy and delete files have been interpreted correctly.

What You See Is What You Get (abbreviated to WYSIWYG and pronounced 'wizzy-wig') describes interfaces in which the actual effect of any action is reflected upon the display immediately. This implies that the screen can mimic the facilities of a hardcopy device since, if a user marks a piece of text for printing in italic, it will appear on the screen in italic style. If a file is deleted, the user will see the file disappear from a list of files displayed on the screen.

The interface is effectively providing a natural status message confirming that the action has been carried out. It has been pointed out, therefore, that it is more accurately described as 'what you see is what you *have got*'.

10.2.3 The 'Desktop' and 'Clipboard' Metaphors

A human sitting at a desk has a number of sources of information available to him. The desktop will hold documents in a variety of formats: text, tables of figures, graphs, pictures and so forth. The documents may relate to different tasks or to different aspects of the same task. At any point, the human can pick up and leaf through any of these documents, make notes on or take extracts from them, or compare one with another. He will probably have access to a clock, a diary, an address book and a calculator. Most of the activities he undertakes, such as writing reports, answering correspondence and formulating plans, will require the use of a number of different documents and tools.

The Desktop metaphor suggests that the interface should provide the user with similar flexibility. It should permit ready access to a variety of different information sources and formats and allow the user to switch easily between one and another — to 'shuffle the papers on the desk'. It should be easy both to swop from one type of task (a spreadsheet for financial planning) and another (a wordprocessor for report writing) and to transfer information between such tasks. Tools (a calculator, clock , diary, notepad) should also be available.

The multiple sources of information are provided by different windows on the physical screen. The information in any window may consist of text, of

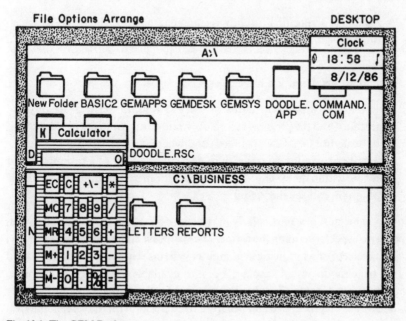

Fig. 10.1. The GEM Desktop.

graphics or of a combination of these. The information in different windows may all arise from a single task or from different tasks. An example of such an interface is illustrated in Fig. 10.1.

A human can transfer information from one document to another by cutting out the relevant sections of one document and pasting them into their repective positions in the new document. Before wordprocessors, this was the traditional way of minimising retyping; the cut sections could be temporarily stored on a clipboard until required. WIMPs usually provide a similar *cut and paste* facility but with a 'magical' clipboard which enables copies of the same item to be pasted as many times as desired.

10.3 Windows

10.3.1 What is a Window?

If you look through the window of a house, you obtain a particular view of the outside world; if you look through a different window, you obtain a different view of the world. The word 'window' in computer systems arises from this analogy.

A *window* is a specified (usually rectangular) area of the physical screen through which a user views a particular aspect of his interaction with a particular task.

Note that this definition has two aspects:

It describes a window in terms of the relationship between its physical appearance and the physical screen. A window in a room may be described by its structure (e.g. bow, pebbled) and where it is situated on the wall.
It describes a window in terms of its content as a view of a task process or data item within the system. A window in a room may be described in terms of what you can see through it.

In fact some authors, particularly in computer graphics, distinguish between these two aspects, defining the former as a *viewpoint* and the latter as a *window*.

The concept of windowing in computer systems is not new; it has been used since page-mode visual displays became available. The screen template, introduced in Chapter 7, splits the screen into a number of windows. The windows are of a fixed size and occupy a fixed position on the screen; they are often referred to as *tiles*.

Tiling was a common technique in the early wordprocessing and spreadsheet packages developed for microcomputers. Figure 10.2 illustrates the four window tiles displayed by WordStar during text editing.

The top line of the screen is a *status window* which displays the name of the text file being edited, the current position within it, and whether any input will be inserted into or will overwrite the current text at that position.

Lines 2 through 9 of the screen form an *instruction window* which displays a menu of editing commands.

Line 10 contains the *rulerline window* showing the text margins and the tab stops.

The remainder of the screen is a *text window* showing the portion of the text which can be edited currently. This window demonstrates a general aspect of windowing. Since it is unlikely that the complete text could be displayed at once, there must be a mechanism by which a user can move the window over the text (or the text under the window) to bring another portion of text into view.

Wordprocessing can be thought of as a type of form filling; the text window is a trivial form where the next question is always a request for the next text string. However, at any point in the editing process, the user may want to override this request with a command to do something else, such as reposition the cursor, include some formatting details, save the text, and so on. Execution of a command often causes a further level of menu to be displayed in the instruction window. It some cases, it may also cause a Question and Answer structure to be invoked in a fifth window, the *response window*.

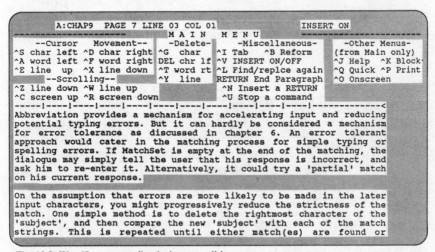

Fig. 10.2. WordStar screen tiles during text editing.

A user has little control over tiles. WordStar supports a rule of four type of adaption; the user can suppress the instruction window by choosing a less supportive level of dialogue and hence provide a larger text window. With type ahead, the user can suppress the response window. However, in general the user cannot change the position or size of the windows displayed. This means that areas of the screen are reserved for information which may not be necessary, reducing the area available for information which may be needed, such as additional text. The rule of N approach does not overcome this problem, since suppressing the instruction window at the start means that instructions may not be available when they are needed.

Dynamic windows appear when needed and disappear when the user has finished with them. Although consistency dictates that these windows appear in a predictable position, it is desirable for the user to be able to change the size and positions of the windows, perhaps overlaying one window over others. These features are typically provided by recent window-based interfaces.

10.3.2 Window Definition

Superficially, a window is a simple extension of the FieldType data structure used by screen output procedures like DisplayField. Viewed from the physical screen, a window can be defined by the data structure:

```
WindowDetailsType       =  record
                           content    : ContentType;      [what]
                           slot       : SlotType;         [where]
                           attributes : AttributesType;   [how]
                           end;
```

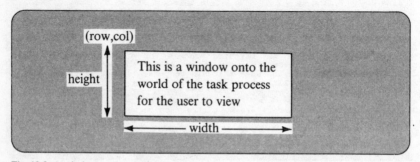

Fig. 10.3. A window as a part of the screen.

The *slot* which a window occupies on the screen is usually a rectangular area (Fig. 10.3) and hence can be described by the data structure

```
SlotType              = record
                        TLRow,TLCol  : byte; (top left corner)
                        width        : byte; (size across screen)
                        height       : byte; (size down screen)
                        end;
```

Since we are restricting discussion in this book to text-mode operation, windows always start on a character position boundary and contain an integral number of character positions. In graphics mode operation, windows may start and end on individual pixel boundaries.

The attributes describe the default format in which information within the window is displayed; for example, the content of the window might be diplayed in inverse video. Thus, the attributes will specify default background and foreground colours and a default intensity; 'blinking' the whole window is so undesirable that we will not consider it as a default attribute.

There are additional attributes which apply to a window. How will the window be delimited? The standard convention is to draw a *border* around it with line segments but a window may have a different border style or no border; we will introduce a type, *Border Type* which enumerates the different border styles. It is also common to display a legend or *label* describing the

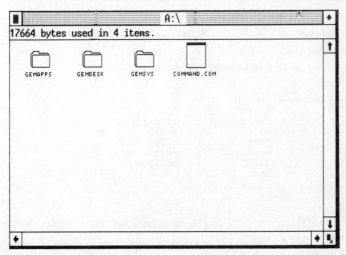

Fig. 10.4. A GEM window with border and label. (Reproduced by courtesy of Digital Research Inc.)

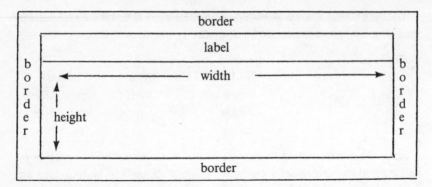

Let b = number of character positions occupied by each border element and
1 = number of rows occupied by the label

$$Slot.TLRow > b + 1$$
$$Slot.TLRow + Slot.\ height + b\ < MaxScreenRows$$
$$Slot.TLCol\ > b$$
$$Slot.TLCol + b\ < MaxScreenCols$$

Fig. 10.5.

purpose of the window; if a label is specified, the convention is to display it at
the top of the window. Figure 10.4 illustrates a bordered, labelled window.

We must also decide whether the border and label lie within or outside the
window; we will adopt the convention that they lie outside the window.
Hence, for a window to fit the physical screen, the inequalities of Fig. 10.5
must be satisfied.

Combining these requirements yields the definition

```
AttributesType = record
                   foreground,
                   background : colours;
                   bold       : OffOn;
                   font       : FontType;
                   border     : BorderType;
                   label      : LabelType;
                   end;
```

The physical screen itself might be considered as a single, borderless,
unlabelled window starting in (1,1) and of width MaxScreenCols and height
MaxScreenRows. Single screen operation is considered by some authors as
the degenerate case of windowing.

We have yet to consider the content of a window. Can it be specified, as in a field, merely as a string of characters? We defined a window as something which provides the user with a 'particular view of his interaction with a particular task'. Therefore the window may contain messages fulfilling any of the dialogue functions: a prompt, an echo of user input, output data, help, error or status messages. A prompt may be of any form, a menu, a question, a form or a command prompt. This suggests a more structured content than a simple character string.

10.3.3 Windows and Pads

In a non-windowing environment, output processes write directly to the area of memory reserved for the physical screen map. Thus,

DisplayField(field)

writes the string specified by field.content into the screen map starting at the position corresponding to (row,col) in field.slot, and sets the corresponding attributes to the values specified in field.attributes.

Windowing environments typically introduce an intermediate step, as illustrated in Fig. 10.6. Rather than writing to the area of memory reserved for the screen map, an output process writes to a buffer — a *virtual screen*.

Divorcing the output process from the physical screen map removes the constraint to contain output within the limits of the physical screen. A system can maintain a number of separate virtual screen buffers simultaneously; an output process can write to any of these buffers. Furthermore, these buffers may be of any size and may be located at any convenient point in memory, on disk or partly in memory and partly on disk. We will refer to these buffers as *pads*.

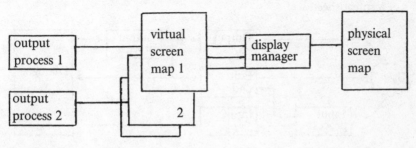

Fig. 10.6.

Output processes manipulate pads. Whenever an output process like DisplayField is invoked, it must specify not only the field but also the pad to which it is to be output:

procedure DisplayField(pad:PadHandle;field:FieldType)

The field.slot specifies the position of the field relative to the origin of the pad rather than relative to the origin of the screen.

In a single-tasking environment, tasks are executed sequentially, i.e. each task runs to completion before the next starts. In such environments there may be a number of pads associated with the interface; for example, the dialogue may output prompts to one pad, help messages to another pad, output data messages to a third pad, and so forth.

In a multi-tasking environment, tasks can be executed concurrently by allocating each task a slice of the processor in turn (see Biggerstaffe (1986) for a description of how simplified multi-tasking can be implemented on an IBM-PC). In such environments there may be a number of distinct pads associated with each concurrent task.

Corresponding to the output pads for output processes are input pads for input processes. These are merely the input buffers which we have discussed in earlier chapters. Since there is a single physical keyboard buffer, a number of virtual buffers are needed to support input to a number of concurrent tasks.

Pads may be classified, as illustrated in Fig. 10.7, in terms of the access which they provide to the user and to the dialogue:

Output pads are pads which the dialogue writes to via an output process; the user cannot alter the contents of such a pad.

Input pads are pads in which the user supplies the content via an input process such as ReadField.

Edit pads are pads in which both the user and the dialogue may alter the contents; typical examples are the text pad of a wordprocessor or the cells of a spreadsheet.

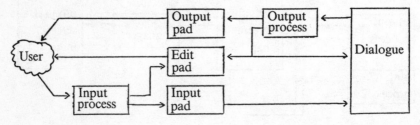

Fig. 10.7. Pad classifications.

Some authors define a further type of pad which is a special case of an output pad. It is possible to mimic teletype operation within a window. In such cases, the dialogue writes output line-by-line to a single output pad; interspersed with the output are echoes of all the users input. Such a pad is called a *transcript pad* since it contains a sequential record (a transcript) of the interaction.

In a non-windowing environment, the operating system maintains a record of the current output position, the *cursor position*, in the screen map. Any output written to the screen starts at the current cursor position, and procedures like DisplayField write to a specific position by first changing the cursor position. In a windowing environment, the dialogue must maintain a record of which pads are open and of the current position in each of these, i.e. it must maintain a list which details for each pad:

Pad id: an identifier by which input and output processes can select the particular pad.
Pad buffer: a pointer to the location of the buffer area.
Pad class: i.e. input, output or edit.
Current position: the position (PadRow,PadCol) at which output will be written to an output pad or read from an input pad.

What is the relationship between a pad and a window? We defined a window as providing a particular view of a user's interaction with a task. The interaction is made up of messages exchanged via input and output processes; these output processes write the messages to pads. Therefore we can consider a window to be the *echo of a particular portion of a particular pad onto the physical screen*. This implies that we can specify the content of a window as a pointer to a position in a specified pad, i.e.

```
ContentType = record
          PadId     : PadIdType;
          RowOffset : integer;
          ColOffset : integer;
          end;
```

Since the offset of any point in the window from the position in the pad to which it corresponds is invariant, we need only specify the offset of one point in the window, e.g. the top left corner.

Every window has one pad with which it is associated, but a single pad may have a number of different windows over it. If each window has a different offset into the pad, it will provide a different view. Such an approach is often

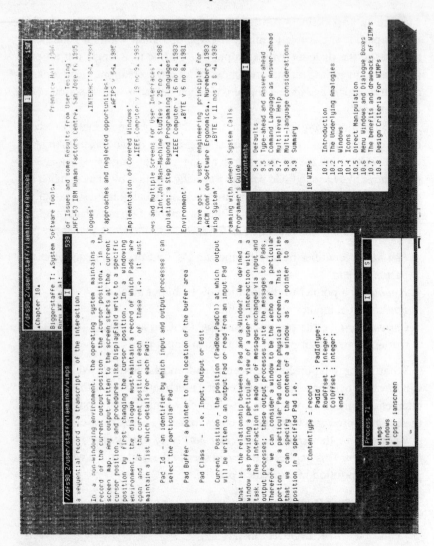

Fig. 10.8. Multiple 'browsing' windows on a text pad.

used to provide a hierarchical browsing facility through a large text. For example, suppose a text pad consists of an academic paper. One window could be positioned over the synopsis presented at the start of the paper, another window could be positioned over the text in the body of the paper, and a third window over the bibliography at the end. This is illustrated in Fig. 10.8.

Note that although the pad in the above case is conceptually a single buffer, it need not be implemented as a single contiguous area of memory. Efficiency considerations may dictate that a separate buffer area is reserved for each window and that pad storage is split between memory and disk.

10.3.4 Display Manager Functions

Responsibility for echoing to the physical screen the contents of those parts of pads lying under windows must be assigned to a process; we call this process the *display manager*. It provides functions to

> open and close a window
> move a window relative to its pad
> move a window relative to the screen
> change the size or attributes of a window

If any of these functions are invoked, the display manager will effect the necessary changes by redrawing the physical screen. When an output process changes the contents of a portion of a pad which lies under a window, the display manager echoes these changes in the corresponding window.

It accomplishes this by maintaining a WindowList detailing all current windows. Each entry in the list defines a single window by specifying an identifier for the window, its content in terms of an offset into a particular pad, its slot relative to the screen and its attributes:

```
WindowListType :        array[1..MaxWindows] of WindowType
    WindowType|=        record
                        WindowId         : WindowIdType;
                        WindowDetails    : WindowDetailsType;
                        end;
```

All windows cannot have an equal priority. For example, if two slots overlap then one window must appear on the top. This is known as the *active window*. Even if windows do not overlap, there must be some rule for associating keyboard input with a particular pad. By convention, the head of the WindowList specifies the active window.

Opening a window is equivalent to adding it to the head of the WindowList. The display manager must be informed of the pad to which the window relates, its slot relative to the screen and its attributes. Normally when a window is opened it points to the start of its associated pad, although this

is not essential. The display manager must inform the dialogue of the
identifier of the new window. Hence, we need a procedure of the form:

> **procedure OpenWindow(var WindowId:WindowIdType;**
> **var status:ErrorCode;**
> **PadId:PadIdType;**
> **WindowSlot:SlotType;**
> **WindowAttributes:AttributesType)**

The operation of the OpenWindow procedure is summarised in Fig. 10.9.
Note that we have assumed that the associated pad already exists. Obviously
the system must include functions for opening and closing pads. These
functions may be separate routines, similar to the CreateField procedure,
which are invoked by the dialogue processes themselves. Alternatively, the
OpenWindow procedure may implicitly open a new pad if it does not already
exist. Since each pad requires a buffer area to be reserved, the system must
check that sufficient buffer space is available.

```
procedure OpenWindow(var WindowId:WindowIdType;
                         var Status:ErrorCode;
                         WindowPad:PadIdType;
                         WindowSlot:SlotType;
                         WindowAttributes:AttributesType);
{global variable WindowList}
var NewWindow:WindowType;
begin
Status:=OK;
{check that another window is allowed}
if NumberOfWindows=MaxWindows then Status:=TooManyWindows;
{check for valid window specification}
if not CheckPad(WindowPad) then Status:=NoPad;
if not ValidAttrbutes(WindowAttributes) then Status:=BadFormat;
if not WithinScreen(WindowSlot,WindowAttributes) then
   Status:=TooBig;
if Status:=OK then
{add NewWindow to the WindowList and ReDraw screen}
   with NewWindow.WindowDetails do
      begin
      content.PadId:=WindowPad;
      content.RowOffset:=0;
      content.ColOffset:=0;
      slot:=WindowSlot;
      attributes:=WindowAttributes;
      AddWindow(NewWindow,WindowList);
      WindowId:=NewWindow.WindowId;
      DrawBorder(NewWindow);
      LabelWindow(NewWindow);
      DrawContent(NewWindow);
      end;
end;{OpenWindow}
```
Fig. 10.9. Opening a window.

If the window can be opened then the screen must be redrawn. Note that redrawing the contents of the window involves statements of the form:

```
with WindowDetails.Content,WindowDetails.Slot do
   begin
   for i:=0 to height-1 do
      begin
      CursorTo(TLRow+i,TLCol);
      for j:=0 to width-1 do
         begin
         GetPad(PadId,RowOffset+i,ColOffset+j,ch,attributes);
         WriteVideoMap(ch,attributes);
         end;
      end;
   end;
```

where GetPad(p,r,c,ch,att) returns the character (ch) and attributes (att) at position (r,c) of pad p.

Closing a window deletes its entry from the WindowList

procedure CloseWindow(WindowId:WindowIdType
var status:ErrorCode)

Rather than specifying the window explicitly, the display manager may only allow the window which is currently active to be closed. The next window in the WindowList then becomes the active window and the screen must be redrawn to reflect this. If pads can be opened implicitly by opening a window, the question also arises as to whether a pad should be closed when the final window open on that pad is also closed.

With our convention, the last window opened becomes the active window. However, it must be possible to make another window active. A particular window can be specified by pointing at and picking it; for example, by moving the input cursor into a window over an edit pad and starting to type, or by pressing a 'Pop' key or mouse button. This implies the existence of a procedure

procedure PopWindow(WindowId:WindowIdType;
var status:ErrorCode)

Popping a window (as illustrated in Fig. 10.10) moves the specified window to the head of the WindowList. The screen must be redrawn so that the new active window is not overlapped. Some systems also allow a user to scroll round the WindowList, via a 'NextWindow' button, so that the next window in the list becomes the active window.

When a window is opened, it points to the origin of the associated pad. Since the window slot may be too small to echo the whole of the pad, the pad contents will be clipped to fit the slot. It must be possible to move the window relative to its pad (i.e. to change the offset of the top left corner of the window) so as to view another part of the pad; this change must be reflected by redrawing the area of the screen which the window occupies. This can be accomplished with a procedure of the form:

procedure ScrollWindow(WindowId:WindowIdType;
                        var status:ErrorCode
                        direction:UpDownLeftRight;
                        amount:integer)

The way in which a window can be moved relative to its pad may be restricted. *Teletype windows* can only be scrolled down by one line. A typical application is a window over an input pad; as each new input line is entered the previous line is scrolled out of the window. *Frame windows* can only be scrolled up or down in fixed window-sized chunks; effectively the pad is divided into frames and the window can only be moved to a frame boundary. Such windows are often used for output pads containing menu or forms

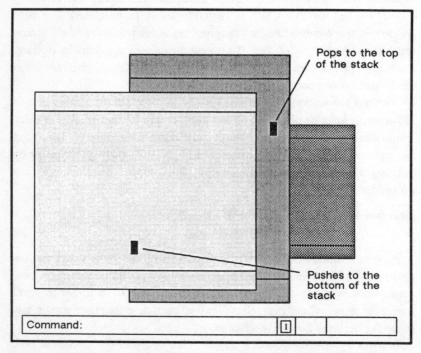

Fig. 10.10. Popping windows. (Reproduced by courtesy of Apollo Computer Inc.)

dialogue prompts. In general, a window can be scrolled by an arbitrary amount in any direction; there may be special cases of the procedure to handle movement by one line or by a frame. This type is typical of the text window in a wordprocessor or the data window in a spreadsheet.

Moving a window relative to the screen has two aspects: the origin of the window may be changed, the size of the window may be changed, or both. This can be implemented by a procedure of the form:

> **procedure MoveWindow(WindowId:WindowIdType;**
> **var status:ErrorCode;**
> **NewWindowSlot:SlotType)**

In many systems only the active window can be moved, in which case the window identifier is implicit. Like OpenWindow, MoveWindow must check that the NewWindowSlot is within the physical limits of the screen.

Movement relative to the screen may be restricted. *Tiles* are fixed in position and in size, and typically split the screen vertically as in Fig. 10.2. *2-D windows* can be moved and resized but may not overlap another window; this restriction simplifies the redrawing of the screen but MoveWindow must check the slots of all windows in the WindowList to ensure that the restriction is not flouted. In more general systems, a window may be moved anywhere on the screen and changed to any size which does not exceed the physical screen limits. It may overlap other windows or it may be totally covered by other windows.

The global attributes of a window may be changed (e.g. to remove the border or change the background) by a procedure of the form

> **procedure ChangeWindow(WindowId:WindowIdType;**
> **var status:ErrorCode;**
> **NewWindowAttribute:AttributesType)**

If the user is able to invoke directly the changes described above, the dialogue will require routines to inquire about the status of the interface. These will include:

> **function GetActiveWindowId:WindowIdType;**
> **function GetNumberOfWindows:integer;**
> **procedure GetWindowDetails(WindowId:WindowIdType;**
> **var WindowDetails:WindowDetailsType)**

The display manager must redraw the physical screen whenever an input/output process writes to a portion of a pad which is covered by the active window;

a window is opened, closed, moved relative to the pad or to the screen, has its attributes changed, or becomes active.

Only that area of the screen occupied by the window need be overwritten when a window is opened, or it is moved relative to its pad, or the pad contents change. In other cases, large areas of the screen may need to be redrawn to ensure that windows overlap correctly. The display manager may accomplish this simply, if somewhat inefficiently, by clearing that area of the screen occupied by the relevant window and then redrawing each window starting from the *tail* of the WindowList.

Note that related information may be displayed in several windows; for example, one window may display a table of figures whilst another window displays a graphical representation of the table. When the content of the pad underlying the first window changes, it should trigger corresponding changes in the pad underlying the others. With many display managers, these related changes will not be echoed to the display immediately but will appear only as the corresponding window becomes active. Some authorities claim that this staggered triggering is desirable since it can be perceived by the user as a cause–effect relationship.

Up to now, we have concentrated on the maintenance of the display. However, a process is also required to manage the buffers. A *pad manager* ensures that the buffer space occupied by pads is reserved and released as pads are opened and closed; this may be a separate process or may be invoked implicitly by the display manager. It may also provide facilities for changing the pad type so that an input or an output pad can be converted to an edit pad.

Since output processes now write to the pad rather than to the screen map, we need equivalents of the CursorTo and CursorAt functions of Chapter 3 to test and reposition the current output position in a pad:

procedure PadCursorTo(PadId:PadIdType;row,col:integer)
procedure PadCursorAt(PadId:PadIdtype;var row,col:integer)

Note that such repositioning may not be trivial to implement if the pad is held partly in memory and partly on disk, e.g. where a text file is being edited in a window. In such cases the pad manager will need to swop blocks between memory and disk whenever the cursor position moves outside the portion of the pad currently in memory.

The dialogue process invokes display manager and pad manager functions

```
procedure OpenWindow(var WindowId:WindowIdType;
                         var status:ErrorCode;
                         PadId:PadIdType;
                         WindowSlot:SlotType;
                         WindowAttributes:AttributesType);
procedure CloseWindow(WindowId:WindowIdType
                         var status:ErrorCode);
procedure PopWindow(WindowId:WindowIdType
                         var status:ErrorCode);
procedure ScrollWindow(WindowId:WindowIdType;
                         var status:ErrorCode
                         direction:UpDownLeftRight;
                         amount:integer);
procedure MoveWindow(WindowId:WindowIdType;
                         var status:ErrorCode;
                         NewWindowSlot:SlotType);
procedure ChangeWindow(WindowId:WindowIdType;
                         var status:ErrorCode;
                         NewWindowAttribute:AttributesType);

procedure OpenPad(var PadId:PadIdType;
                     var PadLocation:^buffer;
                     var status:ErrorCode;
                     pathname:string;
                     PadClass:InOutEdit);
procedure ClosePad(PadId:PadIdType;
                     var status:ErrorCode);
procedure PadCursorTo(PadId:PadIdType;row,col:integer);
procedure PadCursorAt(PadId:PadIdType;var row,col:integer);
```

Fig. 10.11. Display manager and pad manager functions.

by calling system procedures of the form described above; these are summarised in Fig. 10.11. However, if the user is to be able to control the interface, he requires a mechanism for invoking these functions. User control may be implemented by means of a command language using either command strings e.g. 'MoveWindow WindowIdentifier Row Col', or by interpreting function keys e.g. the F9 key is interpreted as 'close the active window'.

In WIMP interfaces, it is more common to implement this control by means of *direct manipulation*, i.e. by physically manipulating windows on the screen with a pointing device. We consider how this is achieved in a later section. First, however, we consider a special type of window, an *icon*.

10.4 Icons

An icon is a small window which often displays a pictorial representation of the pad contents into which it provides a view. Figure 10.12 illustrates the icons which are displayed when the GEM Desktop package is invoked.

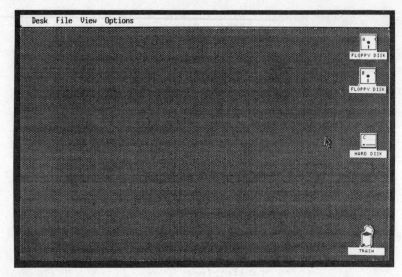

Fig. 10.12. The GEM Desktop in icon format. (Reproduced by courtesy of Digital Research Inc.)

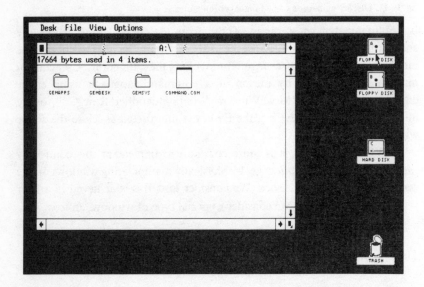

Fig. 10.13. Expanding an icon to a window. (Reproduced by courtesy of Digital Research Inc.)

There are pads open for each of these icons, but to save display space the content of these pads is not currently echoed. If the icon is expanded, the corresponding pad content will appear in a normal size window. For example, if the icon for disk drive A is expanded, a window will appear containing a series of icons which represent the contents of the disk on the A drive; this is illustrated in Fig. 10.13. If one of these icons is expanded, a further window will appear containing its contents, and so forth.

The icon in the bottom right-hand corner represents the waste bin; files are deleted by putting them in this bin. The pad underlying this window might be considered as a transcript pad containing the names of all files which have been deleted during the session.

Most WIMPs allow the designer to specify his own icons as a bit map which defines the pictorial representation required. They also provide a set of predefined icons like those illustrated in Fig. 10.14 which are provided with the GEM Desktop. The icon on the left of each group represents executable files and that on the right represents data files produced by using an executable file from that group. Thus a wordprocessing package would be represented by a 'typewriter' and text files produced with it will be represented as pages of typescript.

This implies the need for another window attribute: its pictorial representation as an icon. Each entry in the WindowList must also contain a flag indicating whether the corresponding window currently appears as an icon or

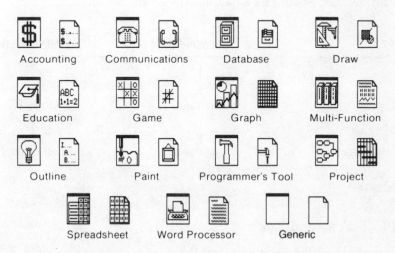

Fig. 10.14. GEM's predefined icons. (Reproduced by courtesy of Digital Research Inc.)

as a normal window. Two more display manager functions are required:

procedure MakeIcon(WindowId:WindowIdType;
IconSlot:SlotType)
procedure ExpandIcon(WindowId:WindowIdType;
WindowSlot:SlotType;
WindowAttributes:AttributesType)

An icon does not occupy much space on the screen. However, it serves as a reminder of a potentially large amount of information. In effect, icons provide a pictorial menu of currently available items. We now consider how icon and other window operations can be invoked by direct manipulation.

10.5 Direct Manipulation

Direct manpulation is a consequence of the concrete object metaphor; if windows, pads and the other data items in the system are concrete entities they can be manipulated by physical actions rather than by command strings. Thus the string of symbols in the command to copy a file to another directory would be replaced by actions, illustrated in Fig. 10.15, in a direct manipulation interface.

Physical operations are implemented by a variety of mechanisms. Usually, although not necessarily, these utilise a pointing device such as a mouse and are represented by different mouse movements and button clicks.

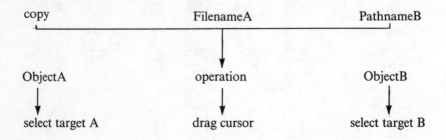

Fig. 10.15.

10.5.1 Point and Pick

In Chapter 3 we considered point and pick operations for selecting targets; the input cursor is positioned to the relevant target and a key pressed or button clicked to select it.

Any area of the screen may be considered a target. Thus, a user can specify a particular window as the active window by moving the input cursor into it and clicking. An icon can be expanded into a window by clicking on it; since no position or size is specified explicitly, the new window will occupy a default position and size. A pad can be opened for a file, and a default window opened over this pad, by selecting a particular filename from a directory listing. If the file is a text file, an edit pad may be opened; if the file is executable, it may be invoked and input and output pads may be opened to manage its execution. GEM utilises all these techniques; a single click selects and a double-click opens.

Pointing is also used to position the pad cursor. As the input cursor moves around a window, the pad cursor can be tied to it since, if the current cursor position (row,col) is within a window W with slot (TLRow, TLCol,width,height) then

PadRow:= row + RowOffset – TLRow

and

PadCol:= col + ColOffset – TLCol.

10.5.2 Dragging and Rubber Banding

Dragging is typical of move and copy operations. A target is selected and dragged across to a new position where it is deselected. Thus a user may move a window or an icon relative to the screen by pointing somewhere within it and pressing a button to select it. The user then moves the pointer, keeping the button held down until the desired position is reached — the item is 'dragged' across the screen with the cursor.

Let the original slot occupied by the window be (TLRow, TLCol,width,height). Suppose the cursor position on selection is (row1,col1) and the final cursor position is (row2,col2). Then, the new slot for the window is given by

(TLRow+row2-row1,TLCol+col2-col1,width,height)

A file can be copied into a directory by dragging the target which represents the file onto the target which represents the directory. A file can be deleted by dragging it onto the trash icon.

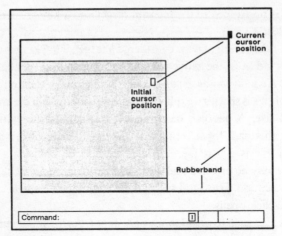

Fig. 10.16. Changing the size of a window with a rubber band. (Reproduced by courtesy of Apollo Computer Inc.)

Rubber banding is a special case of dragging used to resize a window. The user moves the input cursor to a corner of the window and holds down a button or presses a 'Grow' key; a flexible 'rubber band' appears around the perimeter of the window as illustrated in Fig. 10.16. Keeping the button down, the user moves the cursor, thereby stretching the rubber band; moving the cursor perpendicular to a window edge causes only that edge to move. When the required size is reached, the button is released or a 'Mark' key pressed.

Let the original slot occupied by the window be (TLRow, TLCol,width,height). Suppose the cursor position on selection is (row1,col1) and the final cursor position is (row2,col2). Then, the new slot for the window is given by

(TLRow,TLCol,width+col2-col1,height+row2-row1)

Rubber banding is also used to copy or delete groups of files; a rubber band is stretched around all the target areas representing those files.

10.5.3 Screen Buttons and Slide Bars

The previous mechanisms utilise mouse buttons or keys to identify operations like select. The number of operations which can be coded in this way is limited by the number of mouse buttons; using the keyboard to supplement the mouse buttons is unattractive since it causes the user to switch from one

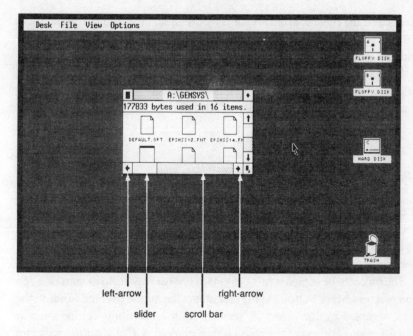

left-arrow   right-arrow

slider   scroll bar

Fig. 10.17. GEM Desktop screen buttons and slide bars. (Reproduced by courtesy of Digital Research Inc.)

device to the other. The number of 'buttons' can be increased by displaying them as targets on the display; such a screen button can be pressed by clicking on its target.

In the real world, buttons operate in discrete steps whereas a sliding bar enables input to be varied continuously. A slide bar may also be represented on the display as a target; the user drags the bar with the mouse instead of clicking on it.

Both mechanisms are often used to scroll a pad under its associated window. Figure 10.17 illustrates screen buttons and slide bars displayed within the border of a GEM window.

When the mouse is clicked on the *arrow* buttons the pad scrolls left/right or up/down in fixed 'pages'; when objects are displayed as icons in the window, an icon occupies one 'page'.

GEM uses two terms to define a slide bar. A *slider* indicates the position of the window over the pad and a *scroll bar* is used to adjust this position. The horizontal slider in Fig. 10.17 is at the left-hand side indicating that the window is currently echoing the leftmost portion of the pad. The pad may be scrolled to the right in arbitrary units by dragging the scroll bar to the right.

If the mouse is clicked on the close button in the top left of the border, the window is closed.

Another common usage of screen buttons arises when the image of a calculator is displayed on the screen. A user operates the calculator by clicking the mouse on the calculator buttons.

10.5.4 Cut and Paste

A complete pad can be copied by dragging the associated source target to the destination target, but there are cases where a user will wish to copy only part of a pad. For example, a user may wish to incorporate a graph displayed in one window into a block of text displayed in another.

The object to be copied is first delimited. The user points to its start position and presses a Mark button. As the user moves the mouse over the window, the area occupied by the object is 'painted' with an attribute setting such as inverse video. The end of the object is then marked; a 'Copy' button indicates a copy is to be transferred, a 'Cut' button that it is to be removed from the original.

The contents of the delimited area are stored in a temporary buffer, called a *clipboard* or a *paste buffer*. The user transfers the object from the clipboard by pointing to the destination location and pressing a 'paste' button.

10.5.5 Overwriting

The point and pick mechanism is an inefficient way of supplying the arbitrary values required by a number of common operations. In many cases, such inputs can be supplied by overwriting the 'label' of a target on the display.

Consider the standard operating system commands for setting current date and time. Anyone who has set a digital alarm clock will appreciate that scrolling through all the possible values is a tedious and error-prone mechanism. In a direct manipulation interface, the user types the desired values into a clock/calendar window as illustrated in Fig. 10.18. Similarly a file can be renamed, or the working directory changed, by overtyping the original name in the directory listing or the icon label.

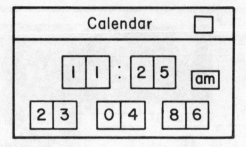

Fig. 10.18. Calendar setting.

10.6 Menu Windows and Dialogue Boxes

There is insufficient space on a physical screen to display permanently all the icons and screen buttons necessary to activate all the possible operations and supply all the data values for an operating system or application system. To overcome this limitation, WIMPs utilise dynamic windows to prompt for user input via a menu, Q&A, or a form filling dialogue.

A *popup menu* is a window which appears, usually in the middle of the display, requesting the user to select from a menu block. The user selects by scrolling through the options and the window disappears when the selection is made.

Permanently available functions may be classified into groups and the group headings displayed as the options of a *menu bar*. This bar is normally displayed in a window at the top of the screen; the options within each group are displayed in subsidiary menu blocks below the relevant bar entry, as illustrated in Fig. 10.19. To invoke the subsidiary menu, the user positions the input cursor to the corresponding option in the menu bar; there are then two distinct mechanisms.

Dropdown menus appear automatically; thus as user moves along the bar a subsidiary menu block will 'drop down' under each heading. *Pulldown* menus appear only if the user actively selects an entry in the bar by clicking on it. In both cases, a user selects from the subsidiary menu by pointing and picking; the menu window disappears when the user selects an option from the menu, moves the cursor to another entry on the menu bar, or selects a null option by clicking on an area of the screen outside the menu.

The dialogue process to implement a popup menu is identical to that for the scroll menus described in Chapter 4 except that, instead of clearing the screen, a window is opened on the dialogue output pad at the start of the process and

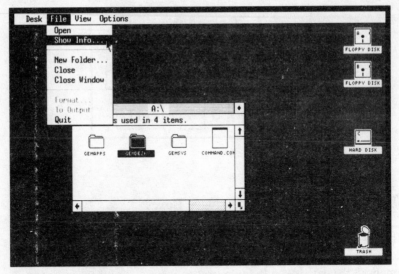

Fig. 10.19. A GEM dropdown menu. (Reproduced by courtesy of Digital Research Inc.)

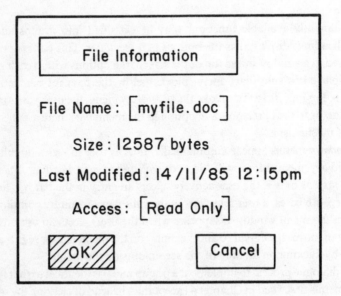

Fig. 10.20. A dialogue box.

closed at the end. Pulldown and Dropdown menus differ slightly since the user can select from the subsidiary menu options, the main menu bar options or a null option; suitable processes are detailed in Appendix I.

Arbitrary input data values cannot be supplied via a menu dialogue. A user selecting to open a new folder from the menu in Fig. 10.19, must supply a name for the folder. This can be accomplished by 'popping' a window with a prompt for the name onto the screen; where a number of predetermined questions must be answered, the window will contain a form rather than a single question. Such a window, as illustrated in Fig. 10.20, is called a *dialogue box*.

10.7 The Benefits and Drawbacks of WIMPs

10.7.1 The Benefits and Drawbacks of Multiple Windows

Multiple windows provide a user with ready access to *more information* than is possible with a single frame. Tiling may permit an increased density of information on the screen; a user can infer from overlapping windows that more information is available in the background and that this can easily be moved to the foreground.

They allow access to *multiple sources* of information. The user may *integrate* information from several sources. For example, a graphic image produced with a drawing package may be incorporated into text produced with a wordprocessing package; two map windows illustrating the levels of house prices and of unemployment in different regions may be overlaid onto each other to check for a correlation. Related information may be viewed from different *perspectives*. In Fig. 10.21 a program is being run via a debug utility so that its execution can be controlled and traced; multiple windows are used to display the debug utility input and output, the program input and output and the source instructions code which are being executed. The user may examine the same information at different *levels of detail*. One window may display a graph showing a sales trend whilst another contains the detailed figures from which the graphs were compiled; average performance ratios for a complete market sector may be displayed in one window whilst a user scrolls the ratios for individual companies in that sector through another.

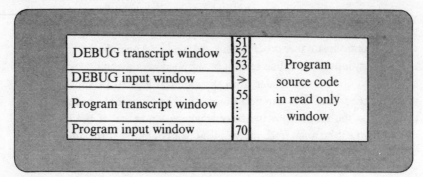

Fig. 10.21. Multiple windows for a debug facility.

Windows and icons offer the possibility of extending the user's memory and provide effective *attention getters*. A window which has been partially overlapped still *reminds* the user of that information; menu bars and icons are reminders of options which are available. Equally, a user can hardly fail to notice a window containing a status or error message which suddenly pops up in the middle of the screen.

In a multi-tasking environment, the association of different pads with different tasks enables a user to control multiple *concurrent tasks*. The input and output of each task is echoed in different windows, allowing the user to focus on each task as required.

Multiple windows increase the user's perceived viewing space — there is more to look at! — but they do not necessarily increase the amount of information which the user is able to absorb from this viewing space. As we saw in Chapter 7, a cluttered or disorganised screen may well decrease the amount of information which a user obtains. With window tiles, the layout of the screen is under the designer's control but a general display manager allows users to control window position and size; should the interface try to prevent the user creating a *confusion* of multiple windows? Is the desktop metaphor only an analogy with a tidy desk, or do we allow untidy desktops as well?

Where a user can control multiple windows there is also a danger that the user will spend large amounts of time manipulating the display rather than on task activity. When his desk is swamped by mounds of documents, a human will expend a lot of effort shuffling the documents to obtain the required information.

10.7.2 The Benefits and Drawbacks of Icons

Icons are a useful reminder mechanism. Since they occupy a small area they can be permanently displayed on the screen and provide a handle which can be expanded to access large amounts of information.

The benefit of pictorial representation in icons, rather than text labels, is more debatable. Proponents claim that pictorial images provide an effective classification of system objects which utilises human visual memory. In a traditional interface this classification is effected by naming conventions; for example, PASCAL files carry the extension '.pas' and assembler files the extension '.asm'. Opponents claim that replacing this convention with a picture is a gimmick, used merely because a bit-mapped display can support it. Some of the icon images illustrated in Fig. 10.14 are natural, others require rather greater imagination; the naturalness of a picture like the trash icon, which needs a text label to explain it because neither the image nor its context are sufficient, is dubious.

10.7.3 The Benefits and Drawbacks of Direct Manipulation

The major benefit claimed for direct manipulation is that it eliminates the need for a user to learn special computer semantics (command keywords) and syntax (parameter list structures) in order to interact with the system. Since the manipulations are natural ways of operating, the system should also be easier to learn and to remember.

Direct manipulation interfaces also score heavily on consistency; Section 10.5 illustrated that a wide variety of operations can be implemented with a very small set of mechanisms. Where a family of applications software has been designed specifically for such an environment, all applications are managed in an identical way, input and output formats are the same, and data is easily transferred between applications.

There are two consequences of direct manipulation which increase the supportiveness of the interface. Such interfaces normally imply a WYSIWYG style of presentation which provides excellent confirmation of input actions. They also normally imply the provision of an *undo* facility to reverse previous actions. If an object can be deleted by throwing a piece of paper into the waste bin, it should be possible to 'undelete' it by taking it back out of the bin, at least until the cleaners come round and empty the bin!

Direct manipulation is not necessarily the least redundant type of interface.

Although an operation can be effected with point and pick operations, in many cases it may be quicker for an experienced user to key the operation directly using a traditional command structure. The rubber-band grouping of files is a slower and less powerful selection mechanism than the 'wildcard' feature offered by most command languages.

These limitations also impact the flexibility of the dialogue. Since it is essentially based on a menu structure, it provides a high level of support. This may involve providing more support than an experienced user requires and will certainly constrain the way in which he interacts with the system.

10.8 Design Criteria for WIMPs

Researchers are still developing guidelines for use with WIMP interfaces but a number of criteria can be derived from those for traditional screen layouts and dialogue structures.

Windows are an effective way of grouping information on the screen. Thus, the contents of a window should form a logically related group, and the borders of each window should be clearly delimited. The designer should try to avoid filling the screen with a multiplicity of small windows and windows should appear initially in a consistent position and have a consistent size. Ideally, the system should adjust this default initial position and size to reflect any user preference, perhaps by positioning them in the slot to which the user moved them the last time they appeared.

The layout within an individual window should be designed subject to the criteria discussed in Chapter 7 for the screen as a whole. The contents should reflect a logical ordering, consistent format and utilise the minimum highlighting necessary for emphasis. However, these criteria must also be applied to the screen as a whole. The spatial positioning of windows on the screen should reflect a logical order and the number of different highlights used across all windows should be kept to a minimum. There is no point in restricting any window to two colours if several windows displayed on the screen each use a different pair of colours.

In fact, since windows are dynamic, the sense of animation obtained from windows 'popping' onto and off the screen should reduce the need to use different video attributes for highlighting. Similarly, when changes in one window trigger changes in the content of a second, the user's attention can be attracted to the second window by staggering the redrawing of its content.

The input mechanism should be consistent. The various software packages being developed to support WIMP environments are starting to form *de facto* conventions for these, although copyright restrictions have meant that some suppliers have been forced to adopt slightly different conventions e.g., dropdown as opposed to pulldown menus. The designer should also avoid complicated coding of mouse buttons (such as simultaneous depression of several buttons) or involved sequences of button presses.

To support experienced users, the interface should permit shortcuts such as the direct keying of a menu identifier as well as scrolling, and the use of command strings/function keys as alternatives to pointing.

Finally, the designer should ensure that the workstation configuration is of adequate power to support the interface. Pad buffers can be held on disk but the response time implications of manipulating such disk buffers are considerable. Seeing the screen redrawn can induce a sense of animation; it can also induce a sense of tedium if it happens too often or too slowly. It is possible to use cursor keys for a type of direct manipulation; it is not comfortable!

10.9 Summary

In a windowing system, input and output processes write to virtual screen buffers, called pads, rather than to the physical screen. This removes the constraints of physical screen size on the output and permits multiple overlapped virtual screens.

A window echoes the contents of a particular portion of a particular pad to the physical screen. A window is associated with one pad but one pad may have many windows, each presenting a different view, associated with it. The echoing is effected by a display manager process which provides functions to

open and close a window
select the window which is currently active
move a window relative to its pad
move a window relative to the screen
change the attributes of a window.

A pad manager process is required to manage the virtual screen buffers which may be in memory, on disk or split between the two.

Icons are small windows which can be expanded to display potentially large amounts of information. They serve as reminders and are often, but not always, described by a pictorial label.

The dialogue process invokes display manager and pad manager functions via external system calls. A user may invoke them either via a command language structure or by direct manipulation. Direct manipulation treats data items as concrete objects which can be physically manipulated by techniques such as point and pick, dragging, screen buttons and overwriting.

Multiple windows provide the user with access to more information, possibly from multiple sources or from multiple tasks. The advantages of this seem to outweigh the potential confusion and effort in manipulating such windows.

Direct manipulation provides an interface which is natural, consistent and highly supportive of novice users. It may however be redundant, inflexible and overly supportive of an expert user.

These *iconic operating environments* have been held up as exemplars of how the man–computer interface should be implemented. They have proved very successful with inexperienced users for office automation applications and there is a rapidly growing range of application software based around them. These facilities are increasingly being incorporated within operating systems and there is a move towards standardisation based upon 'X Windows'.

They are perhaps best considered as providing a powerful set of mechanisms for 'formatting' output messages and for supporting pick and point input. There are dangers in basing a computerised mechanism too closely on the clerical performance of a similar task; attempts to produce flying machines based on an analogy with the operation of a bird's wings have not proved a great success! Such interfaces are not, in themselves, a total solution to the problems of interface design.

Further Reading

Biggerstaffe T. (1986) *System Software Tools*, Prentice Hall.

Bury K. F. *et al.* (1985) 'Window Management: Review of Issues and some Results from User Testing', *HFC-53* IBM, Human Factors Centre, San Jose, Ca.

Card S. K. *et al.* (1984) 'Window-Based Computer Dialogues', *INTERACT '84*.

Konsynski B. R. *et al.* (1985) 'A View on Windows: Current Approaches and Neglected Opportunities', *AFIPS*, **54**.

Myers B. (1986) 'A Complete and Efficient Implementation of Covered Windows', *IEEE Computer*, **19**, 9.

Norman K. L. *et al.* (1986) Cognitive Layouts of Windows and Multiple Screens for User Interfaces', *Int.J.Man-Machine Studies*, **25**, 2.

Scheifler R. W. *et al.* (1986) 'The X Window System', Transactions on Graphics #63, Special Issue on User Interface Software, ACM.

Shneiderman B. (1983) 'Direct Manipulation: a Step Beyond Programming Languages', *IEEE Computer*, **16**, 8.

Tessler L. (1981) 'The SMALLTALK Environment', *BYTE*, **6**, 8.

Thimbleby H. (1983) 'What You See is What You Have Got — a User Engineering Principle for Manipulative Display', *ACM Conf on Software Ergonomics*, Nuremberg.

Webster B. (1986) 'A Simple Windowing System', *BYTE*, **11**, 3 and 4.

Apollo Computer Inc: *Programming with General System Calls*.

Digital Research Inc: *GEM Programmer's Guide*.

Chapter 11

Dialogue specification

11.1 Introduction

The traditional way of representing dialogues was by screen layout definitions — forms illustrating the relevant field positions and formats. However, a screen layout presents a snapshot of the dialogue at a particular point; even if the layouts are filed hierarchically they provide a poor representation of how the dialogue progresses from one point to another. Some improvement can be made by supplementing the layouts with supporting narrative, but narrative is verbose and frequently imprecise.

A notation is required which can convey the dynamics of the dialogue precisely and concisely. Such representation is the first step towards automating the generation of dialogues.

11.2 Transition Networks

The progress of a dialogue can be viewed as a series of transitions from one state to another. The dialogue may be in a particular state awaiting input from the user, and it will progress to one of several next states depending on the nature of the input received. This can be represented as a *transition network* (also called a *state diagram*) as illustrated in Fig. 11.1. Each state is represented by a *node*, denoted N ; we will consider a node to be any point at which the dialogue outputs a message to the user or requests an input from the user. Transitions between nodes are indicated by directed *arcs* connecting the

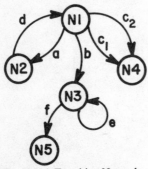

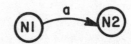

if dialogue is in state NI and
condition a is satisfied then
dialogue progresses to state N2

Fig. 11.1. A Transition Network

274

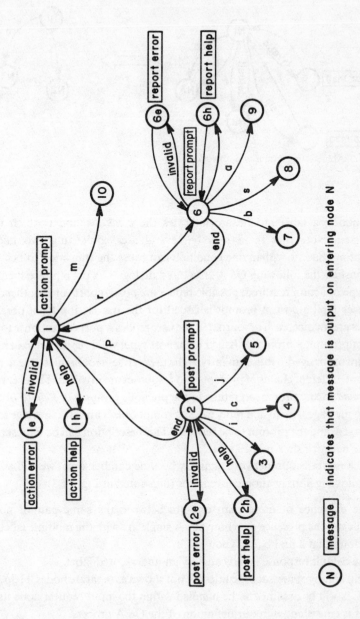

Fig. 11.2. A Transition Network for a Q&A-structured dialogue.

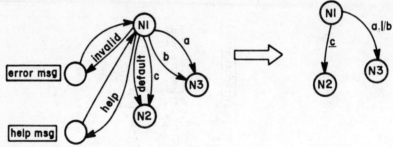

Fig. 11.3. Abbreviating a transition network.

two nodes; a label on the arc indicates the *condition* under which it is traversed. Note that there 'may be several arcs connecting two nodes, indicating that more than one condition can cause the transition to occur.

Consider the following Q&A-structured dialogue. A prompt is issued for the type of action required; possible replies are *post*, *reports* or *monthend*. If the user replies *post*, a prompt is issued for the transaction type; possible replies are *invoice*, *cash* or *journal*. If the user replies *reports* in response to the action prompt, a prompt is issued for report type; valid replies are *balances*, *statements* or *aged*-debts. Similarly, if the user replies *monthend* to the action prompt, different chains of prompts and responses are invoked. The user may reply *end* to any prompt to return to the previous prompt, or *help* to obtain a help message. An invalid reply to any prompt causes an error message to be displayed, and the prompt to be reissued. This description can be represented by the network shown in Fig. 11.2.

Because transition networks quickly become cumbersome, we will adopt the following abbreviation conventions (illustrated in Fig. 11.3):

- The existence of more than one arc between the same pair of nodes indicates the presence of synonyms. A single arc with the multiple label a|b denotes that a and b are synonyms.
- The default response is indicated by an underscored label.
- Help and error message facilities are not shown as separate nodes. Help and errors will be assumed to be handled within the input request node itself; this is consistent with our definition of the Q&A process.

In a Q&A structure, the dialogue progresses by issuing a question prompt and selecting the arc to be traversed on the basis of the response; the question and valid responses are defined by a QandA_DIB. What happens in the case

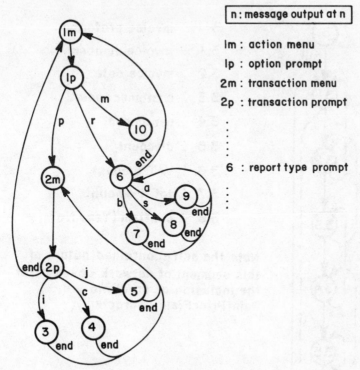

Fig. 11.4. Transition network for a menu structure.

of menu structure where there is a Menu-DIB as well as a QandA_DIB? There is no input corresponding to the output of the menu itself upon which a choice of arc can be made. In fact, this is an example of a more general case of nodes where there is an output message without a corresponding input.

Output without a corresponding input can be represented as an automatic transition from one node to another via a single unlabelled arc. Figure 11.4 illustrates this by describing a dialogue where the Q&A selection of action and transaction type in Fig. 11.2 has been replaced by menu selection. There are also cases where no output message is associated with a node even though there are input messages which determine transitions from that node. The reader is invited to suggest circumstances under which this can occur.

The examples considered so far have all been concerned with selecting a path through a hierarchy — all the inputs have represented selection from an explicit TargetList. How does the transition network cater for nodes which request the input of arbitrary data? This can be illustrated by developing the ledger application of Fig. 11.2. After the user has selected 'invoice', an invoice

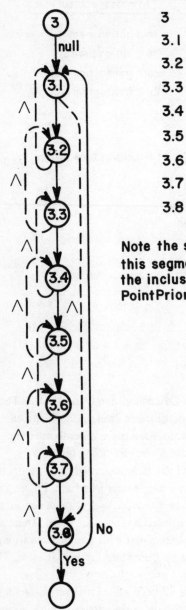

3   : invoice proforma

3.1 : invoice number

3.2 : invoice date

3.3 : customer code

3.4 : net amount

3.5 : discount

3.6 : VAT amount

3.7 : total amount

3.8 : confirm (Yes/No)

Note the self-contained nature of this segment of network – even after the inclusion of scrolling via PointPriorField character ∧

Fig. 11.5. Transition network with a proforma for form filling.

proforma is displayed for the user to complete by form filling (see Fig. 11.5). In this example, fields are not validated on input. Each node is connected to a single next node by a single arc indicating that an unconditional transition to this node will occur regardless of the content of the input.

Transition networks provide a precise representation of the dynamics of a dialogue but the diagrams become cluttered after only a small number of nodes. This is a significant problem since the interface to a simple application may contain hundreds of nodes. The problem can be reduced by introducing the concept of a *subnetwork* (often abbreviated to *subnet*) for any self-contained portion of a network which can be treated as a separate entity. The network shown in Fig. 11.5 is an example of a subnet; it is simply an expansion of Node 3 of Fig. 11.4. In this sense, expressing networks as nodes which themselves can be expanded into networks is akin to the *stepwise refinement* method of software engineering.

The concept of a subnetwork is particularly useful where common node sequences occur in several places in the dialogue; it is analogous to a subprogram in programming. Figure 11.6 shows part of the transition network for an operating system dialogue; note how this representation illustrates the 'flat' hierarchy of a command language dialogue. The subnet for the input of a valid pathname is invoked at a number of points in the network. In fact, a subnet can be called by itself, just as a subprogram may call itself. As in programming, this is called 'recursion', and a network with this feature is called a *Recursive Transition Network* (RTN).

Suppose that this operating system dialogue allows the user to echo all input and output to an attached printer as well as to the screen; in CP/M and MS-DOS, this echo can be 'toggled' on and off by pressing the Control and the P key simultaneously. If the echo is on, the dialogue must make additional

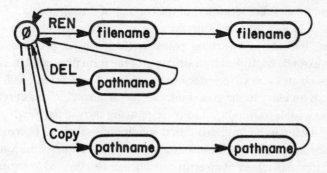

Fig. 11.6. Transition network with two calls to the same subnet.

transitions to nodes which effect the echo; the network must therefore 'remember' whether the echo has been 'toggled' on or not.

This is an example of multi-mode operation which we encountered in Chapter 5; if a dialogue operates in several modes, an input may be interpreted differently depending on the context established by the current mode. Thus, the same input may cause different transitions depending on the current context. A network which needs a 'memory' to store the context is called an *Augmented Transition Network* (ATN).

11.3 Dialogue Processing at a Node

The discussion so far has encompassed three types of node:
1. A node at which a message is output to the user requesting input. The transition to an adjacent node is dependent on the content of the input message. A typical example is a node (1p in Fig. 11.4) which requests an input control message such as option selection.
2. A node at which a message is output to the user with no request for input, followed by an automatic transition to an adjacent node. A typical example is a node (1m in Fig. 11.4) which displays a form or menu.
3. A node at which a message is output to the user requesting input, followed by an unconditional transition to an adjacent node. A typical example is a node (3.3 in Fig. 11.5) which requests an input data message on which no validation is undertaken by the dialogue process, or on which all validation is performed within the node.

Note the distinction beween type 2 and type 3 above. In type 2, the transition is automatic, i.e. it takes place without any input being supplied. In type 3, no transition takes place until input has been supplied but the same transition then occurs regardless of the content of the input data.

Each node in a transition network represents a particular state in the dialogue. It forms a switching point in the dialogue progression. The switching can be controlled by a structure of the form illustrated in Fig. 11.7 which associates a NextNode destination with each of a set of conditions.

There is an entry in the condition stub for each specific condition which defines a possible transition, and a corresponding entry in the NextNode stub defining the arc to be traversed if that condition is satisfied. There is also a NextNode entry defining the transition which applies if none of the conditions are met; this may represent an error case but can also be used to represent an unconditional transition. Figure 11.8 illustrates the contents of the switching control structure for two different types of node.

Condition	NextNode
C(1)	N(1)
C(2)	N(2)
....	....
C(k)	N(k)
else	N(k+1)

Fig. 11.7. Node routing control structure.

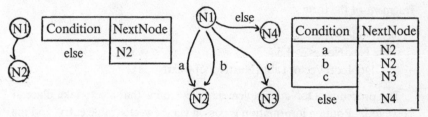

Fig. 11.8.

Thus, the different types of node in the transition network for the accounting example of Fig. 11.2 are characterised by different control structures. The condition stub is empty for nodes at which the contents of a menu_ or Form_DIB are displayed. A node at which selection from an explicit list is required will have a non-empty condition stub. There will be an entry corresponding to each value in the TargetList and the transition will depend on which of these values is matched by the input.

The processing at a node is defined by the appropriate QandA_DIB; we saw in Chapter 5 how the data values of the QandA_DIB parameters control the operation of any Q&A process. Since this already holds the matching conditions, we need some way of representing the routing information of the transition network.

We can associate an exit vector with each node of a network:

```
ExitVectorType =   record
                   AbortExit          :  NodeID;
                   UnconditionalExit  :  NodeID;
                   ConditionalExitList :  array[1..MaxTargets] of NodeID;
                   end;
```

where ConditionalExitList holds the destination nodes corresponding to the entries in the TargetList of the QandA_DIB; AbortExit holds the destination node if the dialogue is aborted; and UnconditionalExit contains the destination node if this node has no conditions attached.

The routing of an entire transition network can now be represented by a vector table of the form:

VectorTableType = array[1..MaxNodes] of ExitVectorType;

Illustrated in Fig. 11.9 is the vector table corresponding to the accounting network of Fig. 11.4.

Processing the nodes of a transition network can be performed by a code fragment of the form:

NextNode:=1;
while NextNode<>0 do
    DoNode(VectorTable[NextNode],NextNode);

The procedure DoNode implements the actions that are to take place at NextNode. Routing information is passed via the vector table entry, and the conditions that pertain on exiting the procedure determine which of these exit nodes is to be the next destination node. This is returned via NextNode.

11.4 Transitions based on Input Format

The condition on an arc defines what input *token* will cause a transition from

NodeID	Abort exit	Uncond exit	Conditional exits									
			1	2	3	4	5	6	7	8	9	10
1m	—	1p	—	—	—	—	—	—	—	—	—	—
1p	0	—	2m	6	10	—	—	—	—	—	—	—
2m	—	2p	—	—	—	—	—	—	—	—	—	—
2p	1m	—	3	4	5	—	—	—	—	—	—	—
3	2m	2m	—	—	—	—	—	—	—	—	—	—
4	2m	2m	—	—	—	—	—	—	—	—	—	—
5	2m	2m	—	—	—	—	—	—	—	—	—	—
6	1m	—	7	8	9	—	—	—	—	—	—	—
7	6	6	—	—	—	—	—	—	—	—	—	—
8	6	6	—	—	—	—	—	—	—	—	—	—
9	6	6	—	—	—	—	—	—	—	—	—	—
10	.	.	—	—	—	—	—	—	—	—	—	—
..	.	.	—	—	—	—	—	—	—	—	—	—

'Abort' transfers back to the previous level.

Fig. 11.9. Routing vector table for the accounting application.

one node to the next. A token is the smallest element of an input message which has meaning to the dialogue process. An input message may contain a single token, or in a command language or answer ahead string, may contain several tokens. Each token may be the result of a single input action (e.g. a single character) or a number of input actions.

The TargetList in a QandA_DIB defines a set of valid tokens as an explicit list of literal values. At nodes where the user is required to select from an explicit list, the transition depends on which value in the list is matched by the input token. Tokens may also be expressed in terms of an acceptable data format; as we saw in Chapter 2, valid dates can be specified by producing an explicit list of all acceptable date values, but are expressed much more concisely by a format specification. This format specification partitions the possible inputs into classes.

An arbitrary data value input at a node may be an instance of one of several possible classes of token, with the transition to the next node dependent on which class of token is entered. Suppose, for example, that the user is required to enter a customer code and the subsequent dialogue depends on whether a wholesale or a retail customer code is input. Wholesale customers have codes which consist of the character 'W' followed by any number of numeric digits followed by two alphabetics; retail customers have codes consisting of one or more numeric digits followed by the letter 'R'.

In such a case, the label on the arc will specify a class of token rather than a literal value. We represent a token class by the notation <TOKEN> and a token literal by the notation TOKEN, as illustrated in Fig. 11.10. The label TOKEN denotes that the transition will occur if, and only if, the input matches the string 'TOKEN'; the label <TOKEN> that the transition will occur if, and only if, the format of the input matches the specification of the class TOKEN.

The specification of a token class can also be represented by a transition network. Figure 11.11 illustrates the definition of the wholesale and retail customer code classes described above.

Each network has an initial state, denoted node 0. An input string is recognised by the network if the input satisfies a series of conditions which yield a transition from node 0 to an accepting (or final) state, denoted node n. As we saw, such a network can be implemented by a conditional structure; for example, Fig. 11.11(a) might be implemented by:

```
node0:  ch:= GetNextCharacter;
        if ch='W' then goto nodel else fail;
```

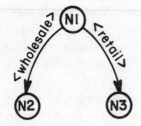 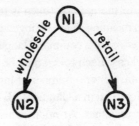

NI : 'customer code :'
expects input in either
wholesale or retail
format

NI : 'type of sale :'
expects input either of literal
'wholesale' or of literal 'retail'

Fig. 11.10.

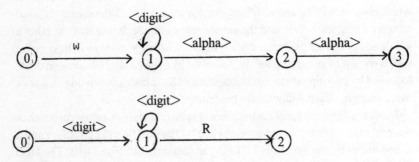

Fig. 11.11. Transition networks to represent token classes; (a) wholesale customer code; (b) retail customer code.

```
node1:  ch:= GetNextCharacter;
        if ch in [0..9] then goto node1
        else
        if ch in [A..Z] then goto node2
        else fail;
node2:  ch:=GetNextCharacter;
        if ch in [A..Z] then goto node3 else fail;
node3:  if EndOfInput then accept (wholesale) else fail;
```

'fail' will reposition the input pointer to the start of the string so that the system can test whether it will be recognised by another transition network, e.g. as a retail customer code.

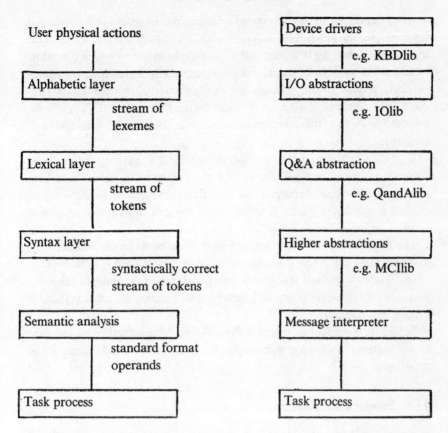

Fig. 11.2. The interface hierarchy.

11.5 The Dialogue Hierarchy

Thus a condition for a transition within a transition network may itself be represented by another transition network. This reflects the hierarchical nature of the elements which make up the interface illustrated in Fig. 11.12.

The basic elements of the dialogue form an alphabet of *lexemes* — primitive information carrying units, just as the English language is constructed from an alphabet of characters. Device dependent driver routines convert a physical act, such as a key depression, into the corresponding lexeme. An input process, like ReadField in Chapter 3, builds these individual lexemes into meaningful tokens, just as individual letters are combined into English words.

Q&A processes are not interested in individual lexemes but in combinations of lexemes which form tokens; for example, they are interested in the input of the token 'COPY', not in the individual characters which constitute its name. The purpose of lexical analysis is to chop the input up into a stream of tokens and to convert them to some standard internal representation. Thus the Choose process of Chapter 5 might convert the token 'COPY' to the ordinal 5, indicating that it represents selection of the fifth alternative from an explicit list.

English words can be combined in specified ways to produce valid sentences. Syntax analysis checks the sequencing of a series of tokens produced by the lexical analyser to ensure that they produce a valid sentence of the dialogue language; for example, that a string of input tokens represents a valid command line string or form input.

The English sentence must then be 'understood' by its reader. Similarly the interface must determine from the sequence of tokens what is to be done to what. Semantic analysis is concerned with assigning a meaning to the input and invoking the appropriate task process with a parameter list that the task process can handle.

Before we consider this aspect of the dialogue process further, we examine an alternative notation for representing the lexical and syntactic structure of a dialogue.

11.6 Production Systems

The purpose of syntax analysis is to check that the series of tokens produced by the lexical analyser is permitted within the specification of the language. *Production systems* are particularly suited to describing the syntax of valid inputs of a command language, although they can also be used instead of any transition networks (other than an augmented network) to describe any other dialogue structures.

The *grammar* of a language is the set of rules which governs the constructs that are permitted in that language. In general, a grammar involves three quantities : terminals, non-terminals and productions.

The *terminals* of a language are the basic atomic symbols (the tokens) from which more complex structures are constructed. In English, for example, the terminals are words such as 'basic' and 'atomic'. In an operating system command language, example terminals are keywords such as CHECK and COPY, or punctuation symbols such as ':' and '.'.

The terminals of a command language are grouped together to form compound structures analogous to the sentences of the English language. *Non-terminals* are special symbols used to describe these compound constructs. Different authors use different notations; we have adopted the notation of representing a non-terminal by a name enclosed within the < and > symbols, for example <letter>.

The *production rules* define the ways in which non-terminals may be constructed, and hence define the legal constructs in the language. For example, in English, a sentence might be defined as consisting of a subject, followed by a verb, followed by an object. The production rules for the 'checkdisk' command in a command language might be:

<checkdisk>	$\longrightarrow$	CHECK | CHECK <pathname>
<pathname>	$\longrightarrow$	<drive>:<filename> | <drive>: |
		<filename>
<drive>	$\longrightarrow$	A | B
<filename>	$\longrightarrow$	<name>.<extension> | <name>
<name>	$\longrightarrow$	<letter> | <name> <character>
<extension>	$\longrightarrow$	<character> | <extension> <character>
<character>	$\longrightarrow$	<letter> | <digit>
<letter>	$\longrightarrow$	A | B | C | ... | Z
<digit>	$\longrightarrow$	0 | 1 | 2 | ... | 9

The symbol $\longrightarrow$ means 'is defined by'. Hence,

<left-hand side> $\longrightarrow$ <right-hand side>

means the left-hand side is defined in terms of the right-hand side.

Interpreting the vertical bar as 'or', the production rule

<letter> $\longrightarrow$ A \| B \| C \| ... \| Z

means 'a letter is defined as an 'A' or a 'B' or ... or a 'Z'', and the production rule

<character> $\longrightarrow$ <letter> \| <digit>

means 'a character is defined as either a letter or a digit'.

The production rule

<name> $\longrightarrow$ <letter> \| <name> <character>

is recursive, in that <name> is defined in terms of itself. The rule means 'a name consists of either a single letter, or a <name> followed by a character'. Valid names are:

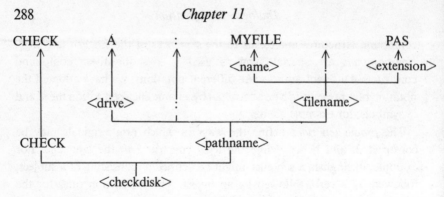

Fig. 11.13. Parse tree for the string CHECKDISK A:MYFILE.PAS.

X   — a single letter
X1   — the <name> 'X' followed by the character '1'
XX   — the <name> 'X' followed by the character 'X'
XX1 — the <name> 'XX' followed by the character '1'

Hence, on this definition, a name is defined to be a letter followed by zero or more characters.

The production rules determine the constructs that are permitted in the language. *Parsing* is the term given to the process of checking a sequence of tokens to see if it conforms to the production rules. For example, to check that CHECK A:MYFILE.PAS is a valid construct, the system builds the *parse tree* shown in Fig. 11.13. In practice the tokens would be in a tokenised format produced by the lexical analyser. Working from the production rules for <checkdisk>:

<checkdisk>	consists of the keyword CHECK followed by the non-terminal <pathname>
CHECK	maps onto the 'CHECK' token in the input string
<pathname>	consists of <drive> followed by ':' followed by <filename>
<drive>	maps onto the 'A' token in the input string
:	maps onto the ':' token in the input string
<filename>	consists of <name> followed by '.' followed by <extension>
<name>	maps onto the 'MYFILE' token in the input string
.	maps onto the '.' token in the input string
<extension>	maps onto the 'PAS' token in the input string

Hence, the input string is deemed to be valid because a parse tree can be drawn from <checkdisk> to the string, utilising all the tokens.

Production rules are a very compact way of specifying the permitted formats of a language. They are commonly used to specify valid expressions in a programming language, and so are particularly appropriate for specifying the permitted constructs of the commands of an application program. They do not convey the same visual impression of the dynamics of a highly structured dialogue as does a transition network.

They can also be used at the lexical level to specify the format of token classes. A general 'matching' process can be produced by replacing the explicit match strings in a TargetList with a set of production rules which define a format rather than a value to be matched.

11.7 Implementation Considerations

11.7.1 Presentation and Control

Throughout this book we have stressed the importance of separating the user interface from the application. This enables the designer to abstract the two major aspects of the interface (illustrated in Fig. 11.14): the presentation of the information exchanged between the user and the background task processes, and the control of the dynamics of the interaction.

The *presentation* component of the dialogue process is concerned with the format in which the information is exchanged. To a user this encompasses the external aspects of the interface that he sees. These include the images that appear on the screen, and the reading of raw data from the input devices. We have developed libraries of routines at different levels of abstraction, reflecting the dialogue hierarchy of Fig. 11.12, that can assist with presentation. The routines provided in these libraries are described in the appendices:

Appendix F : VDU, KBD and mouse drivers

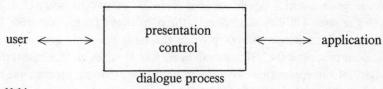

Fig. 11.14.

Appendix G : input/output library
Appendix H : Question-and-Answer library
 Appendix I : MCI library.

For example, to provide a menu-structured dialogue we set up Menu_ and QandA_DIBs, then invoke the Q&A routine. Presentation details are taken care of by Q&A, guided by the specified data values in the QandA_DIB parameters. Raw data accepted from an input device may have to be converted to a standard format by the presentation component, before being passed to the application. This could involve the recognition of tokens using production rules, as described in Section 11.6. Likewise, raw data received from the application may have to be transformed into a format appropriate to the user before being displayed on the screen.

The *control* component of the dialogue process defines the structure of the dialogue between the user and the application. It can be viewed as an intermediary, routing the sequences of tokens received from both the presentation component and the application to their respective destinations.

In terms of the transition networks described in this chapter, the presentation aspects of the dialogue are primarily determined by the actions that take place *within* a node. On the other hand, the control aspects of a dialogue are determined by the routings *between* the nodes of the network. How can we implement such a network in practice? We have seen that we can write specific routines to implement the actions needed at the various nodes, drawing on routines in our libraries, and that we can navigate around a network using the ExitVector mechanism. However, if we wanted to change the dialogue style, perhaps from a menu to a command language to cater for increasing proficiency in the user, the node routines themselves would have to be altered, which is undesirable.

One solution is to specify the node processing in terms of data, rather than specifying it as a routine, and have an invariant process, the *table-driven dialogue process*, interpret the data and take the appropriate actions. The data could be changed easily, either at the outset (installing a dialogue appropriate to a particular user) or whilst a dialogue is running (if some way can be found to recognise a user's experience level from his usage). In either case, the dialogue style will vary according to the particular data encountered. The Dialogue Information Blocks provide the basis for such a table-driven dialogue process; if the DIB data values are held in tables on files, rather than baked into an application as constants within the program, the dialogue can be changed merely by loading new tables.

11.7.2 Message Handling

In the previous section we considered the dialogue process to be an intermediary between the user and the application. But what do we mean by the application? In Chapter 2 we introduced the idea of a pool of task processes being available to implement the processing needed for a specific task. Developing this idea further leads to the notion of the application being a message handler, switching messages between the user and the task processes needed to fulfil that application, as illustrated in Fig. 11.15.

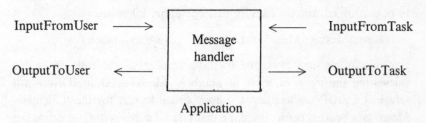

Fig. 11.15.

```
repeat
        ReceiveMessage (UserInputDriver,operation/ListOfNumbers)
        case operation of
            mean :  TransmitMessage(MeanTaskOutputDriver,ListOfNumbers)
                    ReceiveMessage(MeanTaskInputDriver,Mean)
                    TransitMessage(UserOutputDriver,Mean)
          median :  TransmitMessage(MedianTaskOutputDriver,ListOfNumbers)
                    ReceiveMessage(MedianTaskInputDriver,Median)
                    TransmitMessage(UserOutputDriver,Median)
            mode :  TransmitMessage(ModeTaskOutputDriver,ListOfNumbers)
                    ReceiveMessage(ModeTaskInputDriver,Mode)
                    TransmitMessage(UserOutputDriver,Mode)
            end {case}
    until operation=end
    TransmitMessage(UserOutputDriver,TerminationMessage)
```

Fig. 11.16. Message handler for the mean/median/mode application.

We can specify an application in terms of the messages transmitted to and received from the user and to and from the tasks comprising the system. For example, Fig. 11.16 is an outline of the mean/median/mode application introduced in Chapter 2, in which the user selects the operation he wants performing (mean, median or mode), and provides the data for that operation (a list of numbers).

The message handler receives input via input drivers, and transmits output via output drivers. For example,

ReceiveMessage(UserInputDriver,operation/ListOfNumbers)

receives a message from the user input driver regarding the type of operation to be performed, and the data for that operation. Likewise,

TransmitMessage(MeanTaskOutputDriver,ListOfNumbers)

transmits a message from the message handler to the task driver for calculating the mean of a set of numbers. MeanTaskOutputDriver will reformat ListOfNumbers into the appropriate format for the 'Calculate-Mean' task process before invoking that task. If a different CalculateMean task process were to be used (possibly expecting input in a slightly different format) a new MeanTaskOutputDriver would be needed. Again, the message handler would not need changing.

The drivers for user input and user output are analogous to device drivers; different users need to be driven in different ways. The driver is in fact the dialogue process described in Section 11.7.1, encompassing the presentation and control components of the dialogue. To change from a 'novice' dialogue to an 'expert' dialogue one could simply exchange the drivers. Adaptation could be achieved by changes in the data controlling the table-driven dialogue process or by linking a different user driver routine.

Notice the inherent symmetry of the message handler. Both the user and the task processes transmit messages to, and respond to messages from, the message handler. The user drivers and the task drivers can be replaced by alternative drivers to accommodate respective differences in the user or the task processes. The user and task drivers are responsible for the semantic analysis of the messages and for their conversion to a standardised form which can be switched by the message handler.

The logic of the handler described so far implies a simple application involving a single window and one input/output device. To cater for multiple windows (perhaps associated with concurrent processes, and with input from multiple sources), we need to specify solutions in terms of events (for example, the mouse cursor has been moved into a new window), with special event handlers to provide the actions associated with each event. An event handler needs to be able to pass tokens to other event handlers, and to wait for specific events to occur. Events were introduced in Chapter 5, where we allow both keyboard and mouse input in our general 'choose' routine. We employ a simple polling strategy to determine whether a keyboard or a mouse event has occurred; an interrupt driven system would, in practice, be more effective. This type of processing is akin to the concurrent processing of multi-user operating systems; it is beyond the scope of this book to take this topic further.

11.7.3 User Interface Management Systems

Much current research effort is directed towards *user interface management systems* (UIMS), which are packages to support the implementation of user interfaces. A UIMS is analogous to a *database management system* (DBMS) in that a UIMS mediates between the application and the user, whilst a DBMS mediates between an application and the physical format of the database. Both aim to improve portability as well as encourage consistency.

Fundamental to UIMS is the concept of strict separation of the interface from the application, so that the user and the application do not communicate directly, but only via the UIMS. Ideally, it should support all dialogue styles, and simplify the construction of complex interfaces. A UIMS will provide an *interface definition language* for representing the dialogue required and a *generator* which automatically produces the necessary code from a source definition in this language; it functions like a compiler or interpreter for a programming language. Typical development tools provided with it are likely to include screen generation tools, a graphics package, and editors for help messages, error messages, prompts, forms, icons, graphics, and so on. Typical runtime facilities are likely to include management of complex multi-window windows, conversion of user input to semantic function, and conversion of task output to user representation.

There are a number of advantages to developing interfaces via a UIMS. The resulting interfaces should be more robust and conform to a greater degree of standardisation. Above all, interfaces are likely to take less time to develop; this facilitates a prototyping approach whereby the designer can test and modify interfaces quickly and easily, can compare alternatives and intended users can evaluate the interface and suggest changes. By automating the implementation of the types of abstraction which we have developed, UIMS provide the mechanisms which support the design strategy introduced in Chapter 1.

11.8 Summary

Both transition networks and production systems are widely used for representing dialogues.

The transition network reflects the dynamics of a dialogue but rapidly becomes unwieldy; the production system, on the other hand, is more compact, but does not illustrate the dynamics. Neither technique conveys an impression of the visual appearance of output. Hence, they should be thought of as representational tools which are a supplement to, rather than a substitute for, screen layouts.

Since the dialogue can be specified in terms of either transition networks or production rules, it is possible to generalise any dialogue in terms of a processor dealing with transition tables or production rules.

User interface management systems (UIMSs) are packages to support the implementation of user interfaces by automating the generation of executable code from a source definition of the dialogue.

In the final chapter, we briefly consider approaches which seek to incorporate a knowledge of the task domain within the interface and thus increase the extent to which it co-operates with a user in achieving his goals.

Programming Exercises

P1. Produce a transition network which represents the dialogue for the processing of a telephone order in Mailsale.

P2. An integer can be defined as an optional sign (+,−) followed by a number of digits (0...9). Produce both a transition network and a set of Production Rules which define an integer.

Write a routine which will convert an input text string to its integer value. The routine has three parameters:

- the input text string;
- a flag which is set to true if the text string produces a valid integer, and to false otherwise;
- the corresponding numeric value if the flag is true.

P3. Repeat Exercise P2 for a real number, which is defined as an optional sign (+,-) followed by any number of digits (0..9), optionally followed by a decimal point and one or more digits. Do not worry about the number of digits in the integer or decimal parts.

P4. Explain why, in most programming languages, if the dialogue is to allow the user to input a help request character, routines like those in Exercises P2 and P3 are essential.

P5. The inputs to a forecasting system consist of character strings. Each string represents N decimal numbers; if all N numbers have the same value, the user may enter that value just once instead of entering the same value N times. The numbers may be expressed in any valid decimal format, e.g. a line of input might have the form

1.713   23   .56   -.27   +1

Develop a procedure which will validate an input character string and convert it to the corresponding N numeric values.

Further Reading

Edmonds E. A. (1981) 'Adaptive Man Computer Interfaces' in Alty J. L. and Coombs M. J. (Ed) *Computing Skills and the User Interface* Academic Press.

Foley J. D. (1980) 'The structure of Interactive Command Languages', in Guedj R. A. *et al.* (Eds) *Methodology of Interaction*, North Holland.

Good D. M. *et al.* (1984) 'Building a User Derived Interface', *Comm.ACM*, **27**, 10.

Kieras D. and Polson P. G. (1984) 'A Generalised Transition Network Representation for Interactive Systems', in Janda A. (Ed) *Human Factors and Computing Systems*, ACM/North Holland.

Moran T. P. (1981) 'The Command Language Grammar: A Representation for the User Interface of Interactive Computer Systems', *Int.J.Man-Machine Studies*, **5**, 1.

Parnas D. L. (1969) 'On the Use of Transition Diagrams in the Design of a User Interface for an Interactive Computer System', *24th National ACM Conference*.

Pfaff G.E. (1985) (Ed) *User Interface Management Systems*, Springer Verlag.

Schulert A. J. *et al.* 'ADM — A Dialog Manager', in Borman L. and Curtis B. (Eds) *Human Factors in Computing Systems II*, ACM/North Holland.

Chapter 12

Intelligent interfaces

12.1 Introduction

All the interfaces that we have considered so far have been 'dumb'. The transfer of information between the physical input/output processes and the user has involved only a simple mechanistic conversion; pressing key x generates scan code y which is converted by the keyboard handler to a sequence of one or more character codes (Figure 12.1).

Similarly, the dialogue process operates as a purely passive go-between. Regardless of the dialogue structure chosen, input messages received via the input processes are converted mechanically into a form suitable for the relevant task process; output messages from the task process undergo a similar conversion, but in reverse. In dialogues which support different modes of operation, a previous input may have set a *dialogue context* which affects how the current input sequence is to be interpreted, but this interpretation is still mechanical. The interface does not have to *understand* the content of the messages when making the conversion. It needs no knowledge of the nature of the user's behaviour nor of the internal structure of the task processes nor of the data which they manipulate other than some superficial format rules. The 'adaptive' features discussed in Chapter 9 merely provided extensions to these mechanics which a user with particular characteristics is likely to utilise.

The types of interface described in this chapter have a number of common characteristics which might entitle them to be loosely described as *intelligent*. The major characteristic is that the conversions involved in the interface, whilst by definition mechanistic, must be made in the light of a *world context*. The interface must possess some knowledge of the task world in which it and the user are operating (Figure 12.2).

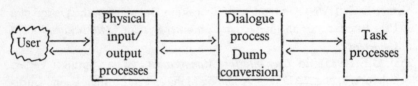

Fig. 12.1.

296

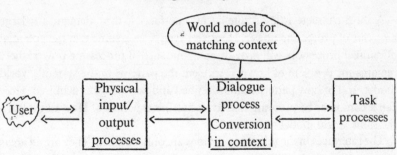

Fig. 12.2.

This happens all the time when humans communicate with each other. If a speaker utters the sentence 'Bert's a bit of a pig', the listener does not take this to mean that Bert is a constituent part of an animal providing pork! Humans acquire and refine their knowledge (their 'world model') continuously. They interpret information which they receive, and phrase information which they output, in the light of this model. The process by which they do this is often described as a form of *pattern recognition*. Incoming information is matched against patterns held in the world model to see which it fits, i.e. which is the preferred interpretation. The listener does not have a model of humans with snouts grovelling in a sty but does have a model which metaphorically relates the appetites of pigs and of certain humans. Of course, if while referring to Bert, the speaker pointed to an object comprising a curly tail, trotters and a pink snout making 'oink' noises, the listener would revise his world model to accommodate that pattern!

A second characteristic of most intelligent interfaces is that they also use a form of pattern recognition to interpret inputs from the user in the light of the system's world model. Two problems arise: the mechanics of the pattern recognition process itself, and second, the provision of a world model which can acquire and store the patterns.

Humans are extremely good at recognising patterns and at 'matching' them against the semantic patterns in long term memory. Because, it is believed, of the high level nature of these stored patterns, they can interpret correctly very scanty and imperfect information — satirical cartoons and impressionistic art depend on this ability for their effectiveness. It requires a great deal of power to process the rules required for a computer system to make a simple decision (such as whether an image of a machine tool bit indicates that the bit is broken) which a human would make almost subconsciously in an instant.

A third characteristic of 'intelligent' interfaces is their demand for large amounts of processing power. However, even if we assume that the potential of parallel processors will provide an abundance of processing power, there remains the problem of how to represent the patterns in the system's world model, and of how patterns can be refined and new patterns acquired. How can a computer be programmed to learn from experience? How can it learn the same world model as its user?

The interfaces in the following sections are only outlined. They are all areas of active research and form a common interest between the fields of man–computer interaction and of artificial intelligence. Although many impressive results have been obtained in limited contexts (i.e. with very restricted world models), much remains to be done. The reader should also note that there is a school of thought which is not convinced of the benefits that the provision of such interfaces will bring for their users.

12.2 Voice and Vision Input and Output

It is often claimed that a truly natural interface between humans and computer systems will be achieved only when the two can talk to each other. The use of additional media such as speech and visual images increases the *bandwidth* available for the communication and hence the rate at which information can be transferred.

Speech output is perhaps the easiest of the problems both conceptually and technically, and a number of chips are available which provide text-to-speech conversion for low cost microcomputers. Speech consists of a series of *phonemes*, or meaningful sounds, and the hardware basis is a sophisticated tone generator which can synthesise a range of suitable sounds. The problem is to provide a set of rules which indicate what phoneme should be produced for a given text syllable; unfortunately, the phoneme depends not only upon the particular syllable but also upon what syllables precede and follow it. The topic has been widely studied by linguists and a number of rules defined. The more comprehensive the rules and the range of tones which can be generated, the less likely the output is to sound like a half-strangled duck! In fact, as with electronic pianos and drum machines, better results are produced if recorded, rather than synthesised, sounds are used. To support comprehensiveness within an adequate response time requires significant processing power. One may question the expenditure of this processing power in normal applications when it is accepted that humans receive about 80% of their sensory input by vision and only about 10% by hearing.

Speech input and vision (the input of images from a camera) are both examples of pattern matching; they are extensions of the process required in a document reader. The patterns against which matching takes place are extremely numerous and complex. Speech input requires the recognition, from continuous speech waveforms, of the correct string of phonemes and their conversion into text syllables depending on the context. In speech output there is no problem in deciding where one word ends and the next begins. Text is conveniently delimited by spaces and punctuation characters. Continuous speech is not so conveniently delimited by pauses; pauses can frequently occur within words! Furthermore, the phonemes themselves will vary with the particular speaker and may be further corrupted by background noise. For an idea of the difficulty, get someone to enunciate the two phrases

'It's hard to recognise speech'
'It's hard to wreck a nice beach'

As the above example illustrates, very different phrases can sound very similar. In fact, many words with different spellings and meanings sound identical; is an input 'read' the past tense of the verb, 'red' the adjective, or 'Red' the proper nickname? In human conversations, the listener has both a context and a variety of supplementary clues such as intonation, expression and gesture to support his interpretation; these supplementary clues are not available to the computer system.

Most commercially available speech input devices recognise only a limited range (200–300 words) of unconnected utterances and must usually be trained to a particular speaker. Effectively, they provide 'voice buttons' analogous to the screen buttons of direct manipulation interfaces. This is obviously relevant to situations in which the hands and/or eyes cannot be used, such as the blind; in these cases total accuracy of input and output, and fast response, may not be essential.

It is a common saying that 'a picture is worth a thousand words'; in fact, the costs in terms of bits required is much more than that. How do you define the many complex and interrelated shapes which make up the picture? In one research project which, from a series of TV pictures, attempts to identify humans walking, the system has been known to identify park benches out for a stroll! The majority of current commercial applications are less ambitious. They concentrate on extracting significant features from an element of the picture and comparing them with a particular pattern; for example, looking for defective products by comparing features of an actual image against those of an acceptable product. Even this requires significant memory and processor power.

Speech and vision input are unlikely to form a major component of most commercial interfaces in the near future. However, a type of vision output, interactive video, has become a realistic and affordable mechanism recently. Although it cannot be considered 'intelligent' it can provide a significant enhancement to the output of visual images.

Interactive Video (Fig. 12.3) enables the output of images from a computer-controlled video disk player. It provides photographic quality output in areas which no level of sophistication in computer graphics could support. It has been used to teach sign language to the deaf by displaying a picture of a human 'signing' superimposed on the word itself. It also provides a mechanism whereby the customer can see images of the hot spots of Torremolinos while the clerk is displaying details of hotel availability!

The video disk is a high capacity storage medium which can be accessed randomly. The video player provides fast access to the disk which can be controlled programatically by sending suitable software sequences; the process is very similar to reading a magnetic disk. The digital output from the video disk can be displayed on a monitor just as though it was a movie but with particular frames being displayed on request. The video player is not extravagantly expensive but the production of the video disk masters can be costly. Therefore the application is best suited to areas where relatively static information is required at a large number of sites, for example travel agents. Just as a microcomputer may use cassette recorders rather than disk drives for backing storage, a video cassette player can be used instead of the video disk; the limitations are the same — slow speed and restriction to sequential access.

The approaches described in this section concentrate on extending the range of input/output processors by which a human user and the system can communicate. In the next section, we examine approaches which seek to

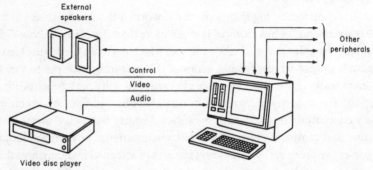

Fig. 12.3. Interactive video configuration.

extend the grammar of the communication; as we shall see, this approach is subject to similar problems.

12.3 Natural Language Processing

A natural language system (NLS) might be considered the culmination of the trend to increasingly higher level languages for programming which, by protecting the user from the machine, reduce the expertise required for interaction. It differs from 'limited English' in the range of inputs which are acceptable; an NLS should interpret correctly any English construct which a human might reasonably be expected to understand. The possibilities of such systems have been under investigation for a long time and have been widely assumed by writers of fiction.

The earliest attempts were made during the 1950s in the field of mechanical translation; input in one language was converted to output in another. These systems relied entirely on a syntactical analysis of input and generation of output, i.e.

the dog $\longrightarrow$ le chien (masculine singular)
the Provençal houses $\longrightarrow$ les maisons provençales (feminine plural)
the old church $\longrightarrow$ l'ancienne église (feminine singular)

The rules of grammar found in any elementary grammar text, together with a simple dictionary, enable translation of a kind. However, this concentration on syntax was soon recognised to have been a failure since there is only a limited likelihood of the output conveying the same meaning as the input in all but trivial sentences. For example, in the translation of a French romantic novel, a heroine who suffers 'un coup de foudre' is likely to be frazzled by 'a blow (bolt) of lightning' rather than smitten by 'love at first sight', the idiomatic usage of the French phrase.

In the 1960s considerable impact was achieved by systems which largely ignored syntactical analysis and concentrated on matching keywords in the input stream; the best known of these, Eliza and Parry, mimic psychoanalysis consultations. The Doctor program developed by Weizenbaum in Eliza holds a consulation with you as patient. If you enter an input such as 'My mother didn't like me', it will respond with the seemingly appropriate response 'Tell me more about your family'. As the conversation continues you begin to notice that the Doctor has rather an obsession with your relations and with emotions such as love, hate, and so forth. It picks out such words and slots them into randomly selected preset responses with simple conversions (you ≫I, my ≫your, etc.). This may impress for a short time but tends to limit the range of conversation.

Such systems were impressive achievements for their time but could hardly be said to possess a world model, even that of a caricature psychoanalyst. In the 1970s, however, this pattern matching technique was allied to sophisticated syntactical analysis in systems which might be considered to hold a model of a very limited world. The best known of these was the SHRDLU system developed by Winograd.

SHRDLU has some 'knowledge' of a world consisting of coloured boxes, cubes and pyramids. For example, it knows that you can put a pyramid on a cube but you can't put a cube on a pyramid. It 'knows' this because it has a set of stored rules of the form:

(x isaCube) and (y isaPyramid) and (y On x)
not ((x isaCube) and (y isaPyramid) and (x On y))

It can 'learn' new rules provided they refer to concepts such as colour and ownership, for which there are rules stored. Thus, if you input 'the red cube is mine', it will subsequently interpret all references to 'my cube' correctly. If an input cannot be resolved unambiguously, it will ask for confirmation.

SHRDLU performs impressively in its little world. It can parse extremely complex syntax more quickly than most humans. It can make subtle interpretations; it will, for example, correctly respond in two different ways to the request:

'put the pyramid on the cube in the box'

depending on which of the two states illustrated in Fig. 12.4 represents the current state of its world. However, its knowledge even of cubes and pyramids is limited. For example, it doesn't know that if there is superglue on the cube,

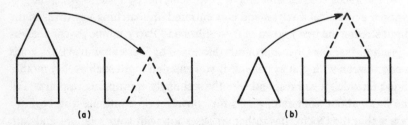

(a)   (b)

Fig. 12.4. 'Put the pyramid on the cube in the box'.

putting a pyramid on it will be a rather permanent move. Additional rules can always be added; to get some impression of how many rules would be needed, just think for a few moments of all the things you know about cubes and pyramids!

This approach has been extended and, in the 1980s, impressive natural language interfaces have been developed for querying databases. Artificial Intelligence Corporation's product Intellect can respond to queries on a personnel database of the form

'Are there any managers in London earning a salary of less than x'.
'Broken down by department print a salary list for these including their age and grade'.

Being able to interact with a system in this manner might seem to be extremely desirable. A novice user would have access to powerful and flexible processing without the need for significant training. There are a number of drawbacks, however, which arise from the fact that all such interfaces are based on a model constrained to a small area of knowledge; humans, even in everyday conversation, draw continuously and subconsciously on a vast and flexible model of the world.

The first disadvantage is that most human discourse does not consist of grammatically correct utterances. People exchange phrases and incomplete sentences, and the listener completes the missing information from the context. For example,

'What is the top speed of the MG Turbo?'
'And the Porche 911?'

Queries to the Intellect system mentioned previously could be expressed more succinctly with the program-like syntax of a command language; for example,

list grade=manager, loc=London, salary$<$x

The verbosity of natural language is fine if you are speaking but is rather tedious if you have to type it.

Natural language can be ambiguous. What interpretation would you place on the statement 'the peasants are revolting'?; there are at least two possible interpretations. Natural language relies on the speaker and the listener having similar world models. Admittedly, not many users will want to discuss revolting peasants with a computer system but imagine the background knowledge that is necessary for a database query system to make the major distinction in meaning which arises from the minor difference in wording of these two statements:

'list all managers who have turned down new accounts because they have too much business'
'list all managers who have turned down new accounts because they have too little business'

There is a danger that the system will interpret input too literally. In Chapter 1, we observed that a system, requested to specify products with a profit percentage below x% , will probably list pages of products satisfying this criterion rather than listing the few exceptions which do not. To complicate matters even further, in human conversations people may well say something whose literal interpretation is the opposite of what they mean. Describing a particularly stupid act as 'really clever!' is called irony; again humans need a context and supplementary clues to recognise it.

Is there any point in allowing a natural language input unless the output is also 'natural'? This is a much harder problem to solve since the system not only has to generate correct syntax but also an acceptable style. It may be grammatically correct to start every sentence of this section 'Natural Language...' but it would hardly be considered a natural style.

A final argument that can be advanced against natural language interfaces is that they may well encourage misconceptions of the system's capabilities. You may know that a computer is only a dumb adding machine, but if it 'understands' your language ...

True natural language interfaces are unlikely to be in common usage commercially for some time to come. They require a sophisticated model of the task world to provide a context for interpretation and input and output processors which reflect the multimedia nature, including gesture and intonation, of human–human interaction and which complement the actual words exchanged.

There are claims that such an interface, even if possible, is undesirable, i.e. that people do not want to talk to machines, nor, in general, do they want machines to talk to them. Speaking instruments in cars have not proved very popular with motorists after the initial novelty has worn off. Using one's hands, rather than voice, to control devices is extremely natural. There was an early television game in which participants had to aim a crossbow by shouting instructions like 'up' or 'left' at a human operator; the difficulty of this can be judged by the fact that a very large sum of money was won by anyone who could do it successfully. Humans may adopt particular phrasings or intonations in order to cajole or bully another human into achieving a particular goal. No-one has yet suggested that computers, unlike humans, pets and even plants, respond to either sweet-talking or abuse!

In the next section, therefore, we consider some suggestions for the interface which, while containing some of its aspects, does not assume a true natural language capability. It does, however, seek to achieve some degree of 'co-operation' by the system with the user.

12.4 Graceful Adaptation and User Models

The interfaces described in the preceding sections require a model of the world to provide them with a context for interpreting inputs and phrasing outputs; their world is the application tasks which they are designed to support. A user has his own model of this application world and uses his model to formulate input to the system and to interpret its outputs. The requirement that the dialogue be natural is another way of saying that the system's model and the user's model of the application world should match. If these models are radically different, misconceptions will give rise to comprehension errors which may jeopardise the success of the interaction.

All interfaces, even 'dumb' ones, contain a model of their application world. The way the dialogue is structured, the phrasing and conventions which are used, all contain assumptions about the world of the application. In a dumb interface, this model reflects the view of the application conceived by the designer when he designed the system. This model is static, and the users must adjust their models to match it if they are to interact successfully with the system.

The early part of this book was largely concerned with guidelines for minimising the obstacles which may be placed inadvertently in the path of this adjustment. For example, an eccentric colour-coding scheme (red for correct and green for erroneous) makes the process of adjustment more difficult. The user has to assimilate both this new convention and the pattern which identifies the context in which it is appropriate, whilst retaining the more common, and already familiar, contexts in which the opposite convention is used.

Many of the least successful man–computer interfaces failed because the model upon which the designer based the system differed greatly from that of the users. To minimise this, great emphasis has been placed on techniques of systems analysis which help the designer to acquire a model similar to that of the user. However, few systems have a single user and even a single user changes over time; on which user and at which point in time should the model be based? Even if one accepts a relatively homogeneous group of users there are likely to be differences between individual models of the application, and so some adjustment is inevitable. Why should the user have to adjust to the system model rather than the system model adapting or being adapted to reflect the user's current model?

Separating the content and presentation of the system messages and valid responses from the dialogue structure can provide a personalised interface to each user. This can be achieved by holding the contents of the DIBs (the parameters which characterise each stage of the dialogue) on file. As we saw in Chapter 9, this personalisation goes some way to reflecting differences between user models; it can, for example, present selected aspects of the overall task by making different task processes available to different classes of users (such as managers and clerks). Different levels of help can be provided, and the format of output messages varied.

The use of dialogue files, together with generalised dialogue processes developed in Chapters 4, 5 and 10, facilitate changes in the dialogue style to correct mismatches at any stage in the system's life. This is particularly important during the design and early stages of implementation. Incorporating accelerators, particularly answer ahead and flexibility in matching, provide a further measure of adaptability; they enable the user to adapt the interface himself. It is also conceivable that a user could modify the contents of the dialogue file himself; for example, he could change the phrasing of prompts and error messages. This poses the problem of what dialogue should be used for the task of updating the dialogue.

We have considered the user adapting to the interface, and adaptation of the interface by the designer and by the user. What about adaptation by the interface itself? In Chapter 5, it was demonstrated that all dialogue structures could be considered as variants of Q&A with

Menu   = help ahead
Command   = answer ahead
Form Filling = question ahead

Suppose we organise the dialogue messages so that the prompt is a standard Q&A prompt and the first-level help message is a more detailed prompt, say a menu. Suppose further that the interface can identify the level of experience of the user by the way he interacts with the system, and stores this in an ExperienceFlag. The same dialogue file can then cater for three different experience levels by adjusting what is loaded from file into the DIBs.

```
Case ExperienceFlag of
     Novice   : question:= 1st level help
     Moderate: question:= Prompt
     Expert   : question:= null
```

Thus an expert user will get only a bare prompt to which he can answer ahead, i.e. a command language dialogue. The inexperienced user will get a menu structure from which he can pick. But how can the interface identify the user's skill level? The user may be an expert in some parts of the system and a novice in others. This is merely one aspect of the general problem of how the interface can infer the user's model of the task process from his inputs. To do this, the interface needs not only a model of the application tasks but also a series of different *user profiles* which can be overlaid on the task model.

The development of user profiles is an area of continuing research and as yet no formalisation exists. The profile is obviously a complex amalgam of a number of factors such as the user's personality traits (e.g. self-confidence), cognitive skill, knowledge of the task, familiarity with the interface itself, and so on. Some of these factors (e.g. personality) are relatively static whilst others (e.g. knowledge base) change rapidly over time. A number of criteria for self-adaptation have been suggested.

Measuring the user's response time (the length of time between the prompt being displayed and the user replying) is a simplistic technique which assumes that competence with a particular input device is proportional to the user's overall expertise. The obvious objection is that if you turn round to take a sip of coffee while running the system, you are relegated from expert to novice.

The incidence of input errors might provide a guide but only if the system can distinguish different types of error; or are all poor typists novice users? How can a comprehension error be distinguished from a simple action error?

The amount of help requested and its converse, the extent to which answer ahead is utilised, provide a better measure. Continuing requests for help suggest that a more supportive dialogue is required and that the value of the ExperienceFlag should be reduced. Answer ahead suggests that a less supportive dialogue is needed and that the value of the ExperienceFlag should be increased.

However, this is not sufficient. Consider two users who both encounter an aspect of the system with which they are unfamiliar; one user is a novice with little experience of any parts of the system, whereas the other has considerable expertise in other areas of the system. These two users do not need the same suppport to achieve their goals; the former needs more than the latter. This suggests that the value of the ExperienceFlag will depend on a complex set of rules which relate the nature of the user's current input, the nature of the particular task within the system and a history of the user's previous usage of the system. The interface needs a rich world model to help it interpret what the user needs.

The term *graceful interaction* has been coined to describe the type of interface which provides a reasonable measure of self-adaptation. Such a system is flexible both in terms of the range of inputs it is prepared to accept and in terms of output presentation. It is capable of personalisation in the ways we have discussed, and can recognise objects, and processes upon these objects, by a number of different user descriptions. Like a well mannered human listener, the system will not disrupt the user's flow but will inform the user of ambiguous and unrecognised inputs, and negotiate with him for their resolution. Thus if the user inputs the request 'display gross margin' and the system does not recognise the identifier 'gross margin', it will request the user to define it in terms of identifiers it can recognise, i.e. 'net sales' 'minus' 'cost of sales'.

Much of this can be achieved with the use of individual dialogue files and accelerators. However, further capabilities are needed for the type of co-operation which takes place in a typical interaction between humans. It must be able to track the focus of the user's attention as it changes between objects and processes. When the user says 'print it', the interface must be able to decide what 'it' refers to. Graceful interaction also implies that the interface can explain its behaviour; for example, why a particular input is required or why a particular action has been taken.

This is not a mechanistic conversion of phrasing on a dialogue file. Such facilities imply that the system can determine the *goals* which underlie the user's input; its task model and user profile must be adequate for it to determine what the user is trying to achieve. This is something with which people sometimes find difficulty in human–human interactions; it is a very tall order for a computer system.

12.5 Summary and Conclusion

'Intelligent' interfaces seek to extend the interaction between human and computer by

- increasing the range of input and output media through which the interaction takes place;
- enriching the grammar of the input and output;
- attempting to co-operate with the user in the achievement of task goals.

These extensions reflect the multi-media nature, rich syntax and semantics and co-operative approach of human-human interaction.

They all require the system to have a model of the task world in which it and the user are operating which corresponds closely with the user's mental model of that world.

Since the system may have many different users and each user's model may change over time, the system must be able to adapt its model to different users by recognising a user profile.

The design strategy introduced in Chapter 1 is a prerequisite for the construction of such interfaces. The interfaces described in this chapter bind together the same 'black box' task processes as the simpler interfaces described in earlier chapters.

We have tried to demonstrate how the interface can be separated from these background task processes and how, by abstracting the elements of the interface, the mechanisms for adaptation can be bolted on. We have not attempted to provide a detailed checklist for the design of the ideal interface since we do not believe that there is a magic formula which can be followed to achieve this. The creative process may be '90% perspiration and 10% inspiration' but that 10% is very important. The rapid increase in hardware and software capabilities offers great scope for the application of this inspiration.

In all design processes, even one as creative as painting, this inspiration can be directed by established guidelines based on known physical and psychological characteristics of humans. Guidelines are not fixed dos and don'ts. Impressionism developed in painting only because the impressionists rejected the accepted guidelines on portraying the effect of light. But guidelines should be rejected only as a result of a conscious design decision, and not through ignorance of their existence.

Since our knowledge of how humans gain understanding in other than rote tasks is so imperfect, it is essential that users experience an interface before its design and construction are completed. Only in this way can we test the correspondence between a user's mental model of the task world and that inherent in the interface. By separating the interface from the task processes, users can experiment with the operation of a system even before these task processes have been constructed. Generalised dialogue processes facilitate this prototyping approach to design and implementation.

There is no substitute for trials by the user when evaluating the suitability of an interface. Equally, for the designer, there is no substitute for practical experience of different interfaces. The artist Hockney once said:

> 'I do not expect an artist always to draw but I certainly mistrust an artist who cannot draw'.

Further Reading

Bolt R. A. (1984) *The Human Interface: Where People and Computers Meet*, Lifelong Learning Publications.

Hayes P. and Reddy D. R. (1984) 'Steps Towards Graceful Interaction in Spoken and Written Man–machine Communication', *Int.J.Man-machine Studies*, **19**, 3.

Kaplan S. J. and Ferris D. (1982) 'Natural Language in the DP World', *Datamation*, August.

Lea W. (Ed) (1980) *Trends in Speech Recognition*, Prentice Hall.

Mason M. V. (1986) 'Adaptive Command Prompting in an On-line Documentation System' *Int.J.Man-Machine Studies*, **25**, 1.

Rich E. (1983) 'Users are Individuals: Individualising User Models', *Int.J.Man-Machine Studies*, **18**, 3.

Rich E. (1984) 'Natural Language Interfaces', *IEEE Computer*, **17**, 9.

Shackel B. (1984) 'Designing for People in the Age of Information', *INTERACT '84*.

Weizenbaum J. (1983) 'ELIZA', reprinted in *Comm.ACM*, **26**, 1.

Winograd T. (1972) *Understanding Natural Language*, Edinburgh University Press.

Appendix A

Mailsale

Mailsale is a mail order company specialising in sales of clothing items. Customers (called agents) order goods from a glossy catalogue which is distributed quarterly; goods are despatched on approval, and must be either paid for or returned within a given period. Currently, orders are received by post on standard order forms as illustrated in Fig. A.1.

The data from these forms is input to a batch computer system which validates the orders and produces:

1. Picking lists for selecting the items from the warehouse.
2. Invoices to be despatched with the goods.

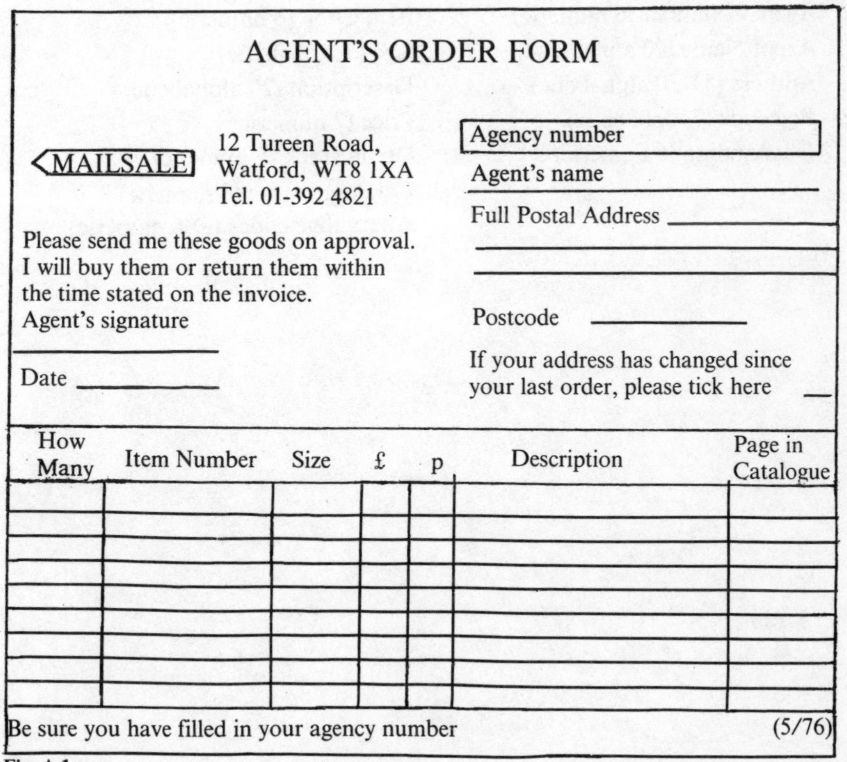

AGENT'S ORDER FORM

◁MAILSALE] 12 Tureen Road,
Watford, WT8 1XA
Tel. 01-392 4821

Agency number

Agent's name

Full Postal Address _____

Please send me these goods on approval.
I will buy them or return them within
the time stated on the invoice.
Agent's signature

_____

Date _____

Postcode _____

If your address has changed since
your last order, please tick here ▔

How Many	Item Number	Size	£	p	Description	Page in Catalogue

Be sure you have filled in your agency number   (5/76)

Fig. A.1.

Mailsale feel that they are losing sales because, when an item is out of stock or has been discontinued, agents are unaware of, or do not bother to reorder, alternative items. As a result, Mailsale are considering introducing a telephone order system (to be called *Hotline*) whereby an agent will telephone in details of any items he wishes to inspect. The call will be taken by one of ten sales clerks who will enter details of the items at a VDU terminal. If an item requested by the agent is in stock, the order line for it will be accepted. If not, the clerk will be able to display a list of alternative items which are available, and try to persuade the agent to substitute one of them. The clerk will also check that the agent's address details are correct, and inspect his credit rating to ensure that goods are not despatched to an agent with unpaid bills. An order detailing all the items selected will be fed automatically into the existing picking/invoicing system.

You may assume that there are files available which contain the following information:

Agents
*Agency Number (6 numeric)
 Agent Name (20 alphabetic)
 Address (5×20 alphabetic)
 Postcode (7 alphabetic)
 Outstanding (6 numeric)

Products
*Item Code (6 numeric)
 Size (2 alphabetic)
 Description (20 alphabetic)
 Price (7 numeric)
 Qty in stock (5 numeric)
 Catalogue page (3 numeric)
 Alternative codes (3×6 numeric)

* indicates a key field.

Appendix B

COWCUT — a retail butcher's carcass-cutting management aid

W.Cowman and Sons is a small firm of butchers. Meat is usually bought either as half an animal (a 'side') or as a quarter of an animal (a 'forequarter' and a 'hindquarter' being the two halves of a side). This meat is then cut into appropriate joints, and sold across the counter of their single retail outlet. Cowmans have developed their own cutting methods to make the best use of the meat from a given weight of carcass. However, setting the price of the various joints is very much a matter of inspiration on the part of management. At present, in order to obtain an historical cost-per-pound figure for each type of joint from a particular carcass, every joint must be physically weighed and a summary sheet produced manually. Time-consuming recalculation is needed if the prices of the various joints are varied. Cowmans have approached you with regard to designing a computer system to assist them in this area of their business.

Item	Weight		Price(£/lb)	Revenue(£)
	lb	oz		
Shin	5	8	1.38	7.59
Shoulder	6	4	1.38	8.62
Thick rib	13	0	1.65	21.45
Blade	6	8	1.65	10.72
Neck	6	6	1.38	8.80
Chuck	32	0	1.55	49.60
Chine	6	9	1.75	11.48
Skirts	3	9	1.30	4.62
Mince	5	0	1.10	5.50
Brisket	11	9	1.40	16.18
	96	5		144.56
Scrap	38	11		
	135	0		

Fig. B.1. Joint information for a 135 lb forequarter.

During early interviews, the directors indicated the sort of system they desire. The output is to be a 'spreadsheet' type of display which will allow experimentation with a variety of retail prices, the system responding by showing the total revenue and profit resulting from these policies.

Suppose Cowmans bought a 'beef forequarter' weighing 135 lb for £74.25. The forequarter would be cut into joints, with typical weights and prices, as shown in Fig. B.1. In the computer system envisaged by Cowmans the user would enter an overall carcass weight (e.g. 135 lb forequarter). The system would then display the various joints associated with a forequarter (shin, shoulder, ... brisket) together with the weights, prices and revenues. Also displayed would be total weight of carcass, total weight of joints, scrap, total revenue, total profit, initial cost and overall profit percentage.

Adding the individual item weights together gives a *total weight of joints* of 96 lb 5 oz — there are 16 ounces (oz) in a pound weight (lb). Subtracting this figure from the *total weight* of 135 lb gives a *scrap* of 38 lb 11 oz. The revenue for each joint is calculated by multiplying the weight by the price-per-pound for each item. Adding the column of revenues gives a *total revenue* of £144.56. The *total profit* is obtained by subtracting the *initial cost* (£74.25) from the total revenue (£144.56), giving £70.31. The *overall profit percentage* is (70.31/144.56) × 100 = 48.63%.

The user is to be permitted the following operations:

- He can select the 'price-per-pound' field for one of the joints (e.g. blade) and change the value in this field (e.g. from £1.65 to £1.70). The system will automatically recalculate the joint revenue and redisplay the new value. The total revenue, total profit and overall profit percentage will also be recalculated and redisplayed.
- He can select the 'overall profit percentage' field and change its value. The system recalculates and redisplays all the items affected by this change. The change in the total joint revenue is distributed over the individual joint revenues in proportion to their current values.
- During the previous alterations the user can choose to *hold* some joint revenues, so that the revised total revenue is distributed over the remaining joints.

Cowmans envisage using a theoretical model to predict an estimate of the joint weights from a given overall carcass weight. However, there is no simple relationship between overall carcass weight and individual joint weights. The proposed solution is to create a number of 'standard profiles' relating joint weights to a range of overall carcass weights. The table of standard profiles will be created by physically weighing the joints from a number of actual carcasses. Joint weights of a particular carcass can then be estimated by using a weighted average of joint weights in the standard profiles just above and just below the particular carcass. This is shown in Fig. B.2.

Item	A	B	C	D
Chuck	26	30	34	38
Mince	37	42	48	54
Brisket	42	49	55	61
	..	..	..	..
Overall weight	125	140	155	170

Fig. B.2. Standard profiles.

This illustration uses four profiles. In practice there may be up to ten profiles for any carcass. A to D represent profiles for beef forequarters. An estimate is to be made for a new forequarter weighing 150 lb. This overall weight falls between standard profiles B and C. To obtain the weighted average for each joint, the following formula is used:

$$\text{Joint weight} = \text{Joint weight}_B + (\text{Joint weight}_C - \text{Joint weight}_B)$$

$$\frac{150 - \text{Total weight}_B}{\text{Total weight}_C - \text{Total weight}_B}$$

This formula is then applied to each individual joint (chuck, mince, brisket, ...) in turn.

Cowmans would like you to design a prototype computer system based on 'beef forequarter' carcasses. If the system proves successful, it will be extended at a later date to include other types of carcass. You should bear this extension in mind when you design the screen layout — beef forequarters have ten different types of joint, but other carcasses may have up to thirteen types of joint. The 'profiles' should also cater for this possible extension.

Appendix C

Ariel — an electronic mail system

A large company wishes to install an electronic mail facility on its in-house computer network. The network consists of a minicomputer in each of the company's branch locations to which a single high speed printer and a number of VDU terminals are attached. The minis are linked to a medium sized mainframe at the company's head office which provides via VDU terminals processing and consolidation facilities for head office staff, and which works as a central file store for the network as a whole. There is at least one VDU in each department throughout the company; typically, these are medium quality VT100-type terminals, and some have a slave character-printer attached.

Each authorised user of the system will be assigned an unique 'mailbox' by which messages sent to him will be addressed. Typical users will include departmental secretaries handling normal interdepartmental correspondence, and managers with their own mailboxes for personal correspondence with their colleagues. It is estimated that there will be around forty of the former, and sixty of the latter.

A message may be of any length. The average will be five lines, but the length is extremely variable and may extend up to several pages. It may be sent to any number of authorised users by specifying the mailboxes of the intended recipient(s). A message may be edited after it has been entered but before it has been sent. The precise nature of the editing facilities is at the discretion of the designer.

Once a message has been sent, it will be stored until retrieved by the intended recipient(s). A user may display a list of all outstanding messages in his mailbox, and may choose to display the full text of any of these messages. Facilities will also be provided for a 'hardcopy' of the message to be produced, and for the user to 'file' the message in his own personal file and/ or 'forward' it to another authorised user.

Messages will not be removed from the system until a user explicitly requests deletion. Users may have any number of messages outstanding. An average departmental mailbox will receive about ten, and personal mailboxes about five, messages per day.

Appendix D

Libraries

D.1 Introduction

Programmers often find that the same routines are used in a number of different programs. The development process can be quickened by keeping these commonly used routines in libraries, from which they can be incorporated into any program that needs to use them. This avoids reinventing the wheel every time a particular function is required. The following are typical examples:

STRING_LIB   : a library of string-handling routines
VDU_LIB   : a library of screen-handling routines
KBD_LIB   : a library of keyboard routines
MOUSE_LIB   : a library of mouse-handling routines
IO_LIB   : a library of device-independent I/O routines
QandA_LIB   : a library of Question and Answer routines
MCL_LIB   : a library of dialogue routines

These routines are described in detail in the following appendices. The way in which routines from a library are incorporated into a program under development depends on the programming language being used.

Suppose we develop a collection of routines (procedures and functions) related to creating fields, accepting input via these fields, and sending output to the screen via the fields. We could code these routines in any language, thus creating a *source library*. This source library could then be compiled to produce an *object library*. Most languages provide at least one of the following mechanisms for incorporating selected routines from these libraries into a program being developed.

- The source code of the particular library routines can be included into the program source code at the editing stage, by using an appropriate editor command.
- The source code of the particular library routines can be included into the program source code at the compilation stage, by using an appropriate compiler directive.

317

- The object code of the particular library routines can be combined with the program object code at the linking stage, by using an appropriate linker directive. This method needs some statements in the source code of the program under development, to inform the compiler that the named routines are external, and will be provided at the linking stage. This is explained in Section D.4.

D.2 Hierarchy of Libraries

The libraries used by the examples in this book are not independent, but build on routines contained in other libraries, as illustrated in Fig. D.1.

At the lowest level are the device drivers:

VDU library   : containing routines to drive the screen
KBD library   : containing routines to drive the keyboard
MOUSE library : containing routines to drive a mouse.

The routines in the I/O library make use of routines in the VDU and KBD libraries. For example, the I/O library contains a routine ReadField which calls the routine GetFilterKey from the KBD library. In turn, the routines in the Q&A library make use of routines in the field library. For example, the Q&A library contains a routine ChooseByKey which calls ReadField and

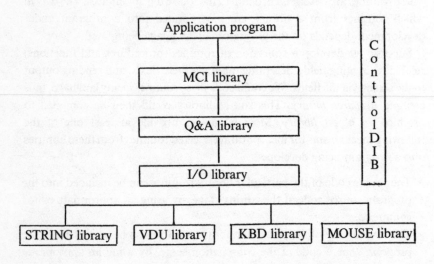

Fig. D.1.

DisplayField from the I/O library. Application programs will normally make use of routines from the higher libraries (for example, Q&A and MCI), but they can in fact use any of the routines in the lower libraries.

This modular approach depends on the functionality of each routine being well defined, and on there being well defined interfaces between the routines. So long as the interfaces and the functionality are not changed, changes can be made to a particular routine in one library (altering how the functionality is achieved) without affecting routines in other libraries which call that routine. In other words, calling routines are not concerned with the detail of how called modules are implemented.

D.3 Dialogue Parameters

Routines normally communicate with each other by passing data via parameter lists, and this is the mechanism we have adopted. However, the routines in the MCI, Q&A and I/O libraries are data-driven in the sense that the application program can specify the particular key that is to be used for a particular function. For example, one application might use function key 1 for 'requesting help', whereas another might use the letter 'h'. There are a number of these dialogue parameters which are needed by many of the routines at several levels, and so should be available globally. We hold the dialogue parameters in a Dialogue Information Block called ControlDIB. Because there is no standard mechanism in PASCAL for allowing separately compiled routines to have access to common data, we have chosen to pass ControlDIB as a parameter to those routines that require it.

The type definition of ControlDIB is:

```
ControlDIBtype    = record
                    ControlBuffer        : byte;
                    rubout               : byte;
                    EchoSwitch           : OffOn;
                    AcceptField          : byte;
                    RequestAbort         : byte;
                    RequestHelp          : byte;
                    PointNextTarget      : byte;
                    PointPriorTarget     : byte;
                    AcceptTarget         : byte;
                    PointNextField       : byte;
                    PointPriorField      : byte;
                    AcceptForm           : byte;
                    ApplicationControl   : SetOfByte;
                    end;
```

```
where
  byte                = 0..255;
  OffOn               = (Off,On);
  SetOfByte           = set of byte;
```

These dialogue parameters play an important part in controlling the dialogue. The detailed purpose of each is explained in the subsequent appendices when that parameter is encountered. In general, though, if a dialogue parameter is set to 0 (representing null), it becomes inoperative. For example:

RequestAbort   : determines the key which will cause the dialogue to be aborted. If set to null, then no key will cause an abort condition.

AcceptField   : determines the key which signifies that the operator has finished keying data into a field. If set to null then the width of the field determines the end of keyed input into that field — input terminates when the field is full.

D.4 Include-files

Most languages allow statements from a source library to be *included* by the compiler into a program being compiled. This is usually accommodated by including a statement of the form

    {$I b:mciconst.inc}

at the point where the statements are to be included. In this example, when the compiler encounters this 'include' directive, it will go to the file mciconst.inc on drive B, read all the statements in this file, and incorporate them into the program being compiled.

There are a number of constants which are used by all the libraries.

ScreenRows
ScreenCols
MaxTargets   {in a Q&A selection from targets}
MaxOptions   {in a menu}
MaxQuestions   {on a form}
MaxFormFields {on a form}

These are stored in the file called mciconst.inc, and included in whatever program needs them. Storing them in a include-file in this way ensures consistency.

As mentioned in Section D.2, the compiler needs information about all external routines. This can be achieved in the same way, by storing statements of the form

procedure DisplayField(field:FieldType);external;

in an 'include' file (say b:ioproc.inc), and incorporating them into a program by a statement of the form

{$I b:ioproc.inc}

at the appropriate point in the program. Include-files for each of the libraries are provided in the appendix describing that library.

Appendix E

STRING library

Most programming languages provide facilities for handling strings of characters, either as part of the language or as an extension to the standard. We assume that string handling is available in the language you are using, and so no include-files are needed.

Declaring a string. For example : var ThisString : string
Assigning a value to a string   : ThisString:='abcde'

The following basic string handling routines form a useful library. They have been used in the programs contained in this book.

function concat(s1,s2,...:string):string;external;
{Returns the string resulting from appending strings s2, s3,... to the end of s1. Concat can take 2 or more parameters.}

function copy(s1:string;index,count:integer):string;external;
{Returns the string resulting from taking 'count' characters from s1, starting at position 'index'.}

procedure insert(s1,s2:string;index:integer);external;
{Inserts s2 into s1, starting at position 'index'.}

procedure delete(s1:string;index,count:integer);external;
{Deletes 'count' characters from s1, starting at position 'index'.}

function length(s1:string):integer;external;
{Returns the number of characters in s1.}

function pos(s1,s2:string):integer;external;
{Searches s1 for the first occurrence of s2. If found, the position is returned via the function, otherwise 0 is returned.}

function asc(s1:string):integer;external;
{Returns the numeric value that is the ASCII code of the first character of s1.}

function chr(k:integer):string;external;
{Returns a one-character string whose ASCII code is the value in k.}

function str(x:real):string;external;
{Converts the number in x into text form, and returns it via the function.}

function val(s1:string):real;external;
{Converts the string representation of s1 to its numeric value, and returns it via the function.}

Appendix F

Device driver library

This appendix provides functional descriptions of typical driver routines for VDUs, keyboards and mice. The descriptions take the form of procedure headings, descriptive text and specification of data types. It is expected that readers will be able to write the equivalent routines for their particular devices. The procedure headings and descriptive text together constitute the include-files for these libraries.

F.1 VDU Library

```
type
     byte            = 0..255;
     OffOn           = (off,on);
     colours         = (black,blue,green,cyan,red,magenta,yellow,white);
     CursorValue     = (FullBlock,HalfBlock);
     LeftCentreRight = (left,centre,right);
     AttributesType  = record
                       foreground  : colours;
                       background  : colours;
                       blink       : OffOn;
                       bold        : OffOn;
                       justification : LeftCentreRight;
                       end;
```

procedure SwitchCursor(switch:OffOn);external;
{Makes the text cursor invisible (off) or visible (on). See Section 3.2.2.}

function TestCursor:OffOn;external;
{Returns 'off' if the text cursor is invisible and 'on' if visible. See Section 3.2.2.}

procedure DefineCursor(cursor:CursorValue);external;
{The text cursor is defined by an array of pixels. The width of the cursor block is fixed, but by varying the values of the 'bottom' and 'top' pixel lines,

the height of the cursor, and its position relative to the centre line of the character position in which it appears, can be adjusted. Typical default values are bottom=2, top=13. If bottom is greater than 13, the cursor will be invisible. Bottom=2 and top=7 defines a half-block cursor.}

procedure CursorTo(row,col:byte);external;
{Moves the cursor to position (row,col). See Section 3.2.2.}

procedure CursorAt(var row,col:byte);external;
{Returns the current position of the cursor in row and col. See Section 3.2.2.}

procedure ReadVideoMap(var ch:char;var attributes:AttributesType);
                                    external;
{Returns the character at the current cursor position via the variable 'ch', and its attributes via the variable 'attributes'. See Section 3.2.3.}

procedure WriteVideoMap(ch:char;attributes:AttributesType);external;
{Displays the character in 'ch' at the current character position with the attributes specified in 'attributes'. See Section 3.2.3.}

procedure DisplayString(content:string;attributes:AttributesType);external;
{Displays the string with the specified attributes, starting at the current cursor position. See Section 3.2.3.}

F.2 KBD Library

type
    WaitType   = (wait,NoWait);
    EchoType   = (echo,NoEcho);
    SetOfByte   = set of byte;

function GetKeyChar(WaitSwitch:WaitType;EchoSwitch:EchoType):
                                    byte;external;
{If WaitSwitch is set to 'wait' this function will continually interrogate the keyboard until a key is pressed. The character code corresponding to the key will be returned. The character will only be echoed to the screen if EchoSwitch is set to 'echo'. If WaitSwitch is set to 'NoWait' the function will interrogate the keyboard once, returning the code of any key that has been pressed, or returning null (ASCII 0) if no key has been pressed. See section 3.3.2.}

procedure GetKeyScan(WaitSwitch:WaitType;EchoSwitch:EchoType;
var scan,ascii:byte);external;
{Operates in a similar way to GetKeyChar, except that it returns values for
both the scan code and an ASCII interpretation of this code

Scan	ASCII	Meaning
0		no key pressed
<>0	0	special key pressed (scan contains code)
<>0	<>0	normal key pressed (ASCII contains code)

See Section 3.3.3.}

function GetAnyKey(WaitSwitch:WaitType;EchoSwitch:EchoType):byte;
external;
{Converts the scan and ASCII codes of GetKeyScan into standard
keycodes. Normal characters have their standard ASCII value (in the range
32..127). Special keys (such as function or cursor keys) are allocated a
keycode in the range 1..31 or 128..255. The specific keycodes used in this
book are listed in the following section. See Section 3.3.3.}

function GetFilterKey(WaitSwitch:WaitType;EchoSwitch:EchoType;
filter:SetOfByte):byte;external;
{Similar to GetAnyKey, except that only keys whose corresponding
keycodes are specified in the filter are active. All other keys are filtered out.
See Section 3.3.3.}

procedure ClearKbd;external;
{Clears the keyboard buffer of any characters that may have been typed
ahead of them being needed. See Section 9.5.2.}

function KeyboardEvent:boolean;external;
{Returns 'true' if a key has been pressed, otherwise 'false'. The character is
not removed from the keyboard buffer. See Section 5.8.}

F.3 Keycodes used in this Book

The following keycodes refer to a PC with 18 function keys (F1..F18), and
SHIFT, CONTROL and ALT keys. These keycodes are stored in an include
file called 'keycodes.inc'.

const

null	=	0;	PGUP	=	201;
BS	=	8;	CursorLeft	=	203;
tab	=	9;	CursorRight	=	205;
CR	=	13;	ENDkey	=	207;
ESC	=	27;	CursorDown	=	208;
tilde	=	126;	PGDN	=	209;
home	=	199;	INS	=	210;
CursorUp	=	200;	DEL	=	211;

F1	=	187;	ShftF1	=	212; {Same as F11}
F2	=	188;	Shftf2	=	213; {Same as F12}
F3	=	189;	Shft3	=	214; {Same as F13}
F4	=	190;	ShftF4	=	215; {Same as F14}
F5	=	191;	ShftF5	=	216; {Same as F15}
F6	=	192;	ShftF6	=	217; {Same as F16}
F7	=	193;	ShftF7	=	218; {Same as F17}
F8	=	194;	ShftF8	=	219; {Same as F18}
F9	=	195;	ShftF9	=	220;
F10	=	196;	Shft10	=	221;

CtrlF1	=	222;	AltF1	=	232;
Ctr1F2	=	223;	AltF2	=	233;
CtrlF3	=	224;	AltF3	=	234;
CtrlF4	=	225;	AltF4	=	235;
CtrlF5	=	226;	AltF5	=	236;
CtrlF6	=	227;	AltF6	=	237;
CtrlF7	=	228;	AltF7	=	238;
CtrlF8	=	229;	AltF8	=	239;
CtrlF9	=	230;	AltF9	=	240;
CtrlF10	=	231;	AltF10	=	241;

F.4 Mouse Library

type

```
CursorValue  =  (FullBlock,HalfBlock);
rectangle    =  record
                  TopLeftRow : byte;
                  TopLeftCol  : byte;
```

```
                width : byte;
                height : byte;
                end;
ButtonType  =   (LeftButton,RightButton); {for 2-button mouse}
ReportType  =   record
                count : byte;
                  row : byte;
                  col : byte;
                  end;
```

procedure SetPointerCursor(cursor:CursorValue);external;
{Defines the 'shape' of the cursor associated with the pointing device. See Section 3.4.3.}

procedure SwitchPointerCursor(switch:OffOn);external;
{Makes the pointer cursor invisible (off) or visible (on). See Section 3.4.3.}

procedure SetPointerLimits(limits:rectangle);external;
{Constrains the pointer to movement within the specified rectangular area. See Section 3.4.3.}

procedure PointerTo(row,col:byte);external;
{Moves the pointer cursor to position (row,col). See Section 3.4.3.}

procedure PointerAt(var row,col:byte);external;
{Returns the current position of the pointer cursor in row and col. See Section 3.4.3.}

procedure ReadPress(button:ButtonType;var report:ReportType);external;
{Returns the number of presses of the specified button, and the position at which the last press occurred. See Section 3.4.3.}

procedure ReadRelease(button:ButtonType;var report:ReportType);external;
{Returns the number of releases of the specified button, and the position at which the last release occurred. See Section 3.4.3.}

procedure ReadPointer(var row,col:byte;var action:byte);external;
{Returns the position of the pointer in row and column, and what activity has taken place since the pointing device was last interrogated (such as target picked, abort button pressed). The corresponding keycode is returned in 'action'. See Section 3.4.3.}

function PointerEvent:boolean;external;
{Returns 'true' if some activity has taken place, such as a button being pressed, or movement. See Section 5.8.}

F.5 Device Initialisation

Many devices can operate in a number of modes. For example, the screen can operate in various graphics and text modes, the mouse may be able to operate in either Keyboard Emulation mode or Real Mouse mode, and the keycodes generated by special keys may be alterable. Each device must be initialised by setting the relevant mode with procedures of the form:

> **procedure InitialiseVDU;external;**
> **procedure InitialiseKBD;external;**
> **procedure InitialiseMouse;external;**

if different values than those provided as operating system defaults are required.

Appendix G

Input/output library

This appendix provides functional descriptions of typical input/output routines. A full listing of the routines is provided at the end of the appendix. Preceding sections describe individual routines, and how to use them.

G.1 Input/Output routines

The following statements constitute the procedure declarations include-file for the input/output library. The routines themselves are explained in the subsequent sections of this appendix.

```
procedure CreateField(var field:FieldType;
            message:string;
            row,col,width:byte;
            AttributesString:string);external;
procedure DisplayField(field:FieldType);external;
procedure ReadField(var field:FieldType;
            DataSet:SetOfByte;
            var ControlDIB:ControlDIBtype);external;
procedure ChangeFieldContent(var field:FieldType;
            NewContent:string);external;
procedure ChangeFieldSlot(var field:FieldType;
            row,col,width:byte);external;
procedure ChangeFieldAttributes(var field:FieldType;
            AttributesString:string);external;
procedure ClearField(field:FieldType);external;
procedure HideField(field:FieldType);external;
procedure HighlightField(field:FieldType;
            HighlightAttributes:AttributesType);external;
procedure InvertField(var field:FieldType);external;
procedure ClearScreen;external;
```

The following routines are explained in the indicated sections of the book.

330

function TestInputEvent(selector:SelectionType):InputEventType;
                              external;
{Tests for an event that is permitted within SelectionType (id, scroll, position, key and any) and returns the type that has occurred — null, keyboard, pointer. See Section 5.8.}

function WaitInputEvent(selector:SelectionType):InputEventType;
                              external;
{Waits for an event that is permitted within SelectionType (id, scroll, position, key and any) and returns the type that has occurred — keyboard or pointer. See Section 5.8.}

function MatchString(subject:string;
                    TargetList:TargetListType;
                    NumberOfTargets:byte);byte;external;
{returns the ordinal number of the target in TargetList whose content is the same as subject, or 0 if no match. See Section 4.3.3.}

function MatchPosition(row,col:byte;
                    TargetList:TargetListType;
                    NumberOfTargets:byte);byte;external;
{Returns the ordinal number of the target in TargetList whose slot contains the position (row,col), or 0 if no match. See Section 3.4.3.}

procedure RelativePick(TargetList:TargetListType;
                    NumberOfTargets:byte;
                    highlight:AttributesType;
                    var ControlDIB:ControlDIBtype;
                    var TargetChosen);external;
{Uses relative positioning to select a target from TargetList. The ordinal is returned in TargetChosen. See Section 3.4.2.}

procedure AbsolutePick(TargetList:TargetListType;
                    NumberOfTargets:byte;
                    highlight:AttributesType;
                    var ControlDIB:ControlDIBtype;
                    var TargetChosen);external;
{Uses absolute positioning to select a target from TargetList. The ordinal is returned in TargetChosen. See Section 3.4.3.}

G.2 Type Declarations Include-File for the Input/Output Library

The following type declarations are needed when using the routines of the input/output library. They are stored in the file 'iotype.inc'.

```
byte              = 0..255;
SetOfByte         = set of byte;
OffOn             = (Off,On);
WaitType          = (Wait,NoWait);
EchoType          = (echo,NoEcho);
colours           = (black,blue,green,cyan,red,magenta,yellow,white);
LeftCentreRight   = (left,centre,right);

SlotType          = record
                      row                 : byte;
                      col                 : byte;
                      width               : byte;
                    end;

AttributesType    = record
                      foreground          : colours;
                      background          : colours;
                      blink               : OffOn;
                      bold                : OffOn;
                      justification       : LeftCentreRight;
                    end;

FieldType         = record
                      content             : string;
                      slot                : SlotType;
                      attributes          : AttributesType;
                    end;

ControlDIBtype    = record
                      ControlBuffer       : byte;
                      rubout              : byte;
                      EchoSwitch          : OffOn;
                      AcceptField         : byte;
                      RequestAbort        : byte;
                      RequestHelp         : byte;
                      PointNextTarget     : byte;
                      PointPriorTarget    : byte;
                      AcceptTarget        : byte;
                      PointNextField      : byte;
                      PointPriorField     : byte;
                      AcceptForm          : byte;
                      ApplicationControl  : SetOfByte;
                    end;
```

G.3 Fields (see Section 3.2 onwards)

A *slot* is defined as a number of columns of the screen, in a single row, starting at some specified 'row' and 'column'. The top left-hand corner of the screen is taken to be Row 1, Column 1. The PASCAL type definition is:

```
SlotType        = record
                     row          : byte;
                     col          : byte;
                     width        : byte;
                     end;

byte            = 0..255;
```

The display *attributes* of a particular character position are:

foreground colour;
background colour;
blink and bold.

All the character positions within a slot have the same attributes, whose PASCAL type definition is:

```
AttributesType   = record
                      foreground          : colours;
                      background          : colours;
                      blink               : OffOn;
                      bold                : OffOn;
                      justification       : LeftCentreRight;
                      end;

colours          = (black,blue,green,cyan,red,magenta,yellow,white);
OffOn            = (off,on);
LeftCentreRight  = (left,centre,right);
```

A string of characters is displayed in a slot. If the length of the string is less than the width of the slot, then the rest of the slot is filled with spaces. The string may be displayed on the left of the slot, on the right of the slot, or in the centre of the slot, as determined by the 'justification' attribute.

The combination of a slot, its content and its attributes is called a *field*. A field has the following type definition:

```
FieldType        = record
                      content             : string;
                      slot                : SlotType;
                      attributes          : AttributesType;
                      end;
```

G.4 Creating a Field (see Section 3.2.4)

The first step is to declare a variable of type FieldType:

    var field : FieldType;

The 'CreateField' routine provided in the input/output library

    CreateField(var field:Fieldtype;
                content:string;
                row,col,width:byte;
                attributes:string);

initialises the content, the slot and the attributes of a field. The content of the field is set to the value of the 'content' parameter; the slot is defined by the values of the 'row', 'col' and 'width' parameters; and the attributes are initially set to the following defaults:

    background   black
    foreground   white
    blink   off
    bold   off
    justification left

Any attribute values specified in the attribute string change these default settings. The string comprises a number of phrases of the form 'keyword=value' separated by commas. The keyword (fore, back, blink, bold or just) specifies the attribute and the value specifies the setting for that attribute. For example

    'fore=green, back=red, bold=on, blink=on, just=centre'

Any number of phrases (including none) can be combined in any order. Only those attributes that require changing need be specified; the remainder will take their default values. Hence, a null string retains all the defaults. For example:

    CreateField(field,'Customer ID',10,15,20,'back=white,fore=black')

will create a field containing the string 'Customer ID'. When the field is displayed, this string will appear on the screen as a black text foreground on a white background, left justified in a field of width 20, starting at (10,15). By default, bold and blink will be 'off', and the justification is 'left'.

G.5 Displaying a Field (see Section 3.2.4)

A field is displayed on the screen using the 'DisplayField' procedure

DisplayField(Field:FieldType);

For example:

DisplayField(field);

will cause 'field' to be displayed on the screen, providing the slot is physically on the screen, i.e. it lies within the screen's maximum and minimum row and column co-ordinates. A slot whose start position is row 0, column 0 is not on the screen, so the DisplayField procedure will have no effect.

G.6 Changing a Field (see Section 3.2.4)

We may wish to change the content, the slot position and width, or the attributes of an existing field; there are three corresponding routines in the input/output library. The parameters are similar to those for CreateField.

ChangeFieldContent(var field:FieldType;
     NewContent:string);
ChangeFieldSlot(var field:FieldType;
     NewRow,NewCol,NewWidth:byte);
ChangeFieldAttributes(var field:FieldType;
     AttributeChanges:string);

G.7 Reading a Field (see Section 3.3.4)

Input from the keyboard is accepted via a field. The 'ReadField' procedure takes the form:

ReadField(var field:FieldType;
   DataSet:SetOfByte;
   ControlDIB:ControlDIBtype);

The parameter DataSet specifies those characters which are valid 'data' characters; it acts as a filter, only allowing those characters contained in the set to pass through. For example, to accept only numeric values:

DataSet:=[ord('0')..ord('9')];

If a character contained in DataSet is typed, it is appended to the 'content' string of the field.

The precise operation of ReadField is controlled by the values of the variables contained within ControlDIB (which is a record). These variables have special interpretations (e.g. AcceptField, EchoSwitch) and are assigned the keycodes of the keys which are to represent those functions. In cases where a particular special interpretation is inappropriate, that variable is assigned a null value, the keycode 0.

AcceptField   : defines a key which signifies that the operator has finished keying data into a field. If set to null then the width of the field determines the end of keyed input into that field — input terminates when the field is full.

rubout   : defines a key which causes the last key typed to be rubbed out. If set to null it is not possible to rub out previous characters.

EchoSwitch   : specifies whether keyed input is echoed to the screen.

RequestAbort   : defines a key which causes the dialogue to be aborted. If set to null then no key will abort the dialogue.

The way in which ReadField is controlled by the values assigned to these various elements of ControlDIB is illustrated by the following examples; they all assume:

CreateField(answer,'*****',10,20,5,'');
DataSet:=[ord('a')..ord('z'),ord('*')];
RequestAbort:=ESC; {keycode 27}
rubout:=BS;   {keycode 8}

G.7.1 Example: an Input which is Echoed to the Screen and Explicitly Terminated

AcceptField:=CR: {keycode 13}
EchoSwitch:=on;
ReadField(answer,DataSet,ControlDIB);

When ReadField is first invoked, the content of the field *answer* (if it is non-null) is displayed in the slot with whatever attributes have been assigned. If the

AcceptField key is pressed immediately, this value is retained as the content. In other words, a default value can be assigned to the 'content' part of the field before ReadField is invoked; this default is accepted by pressing the AcceptField key immediately. Pressing any other key causes the field to be cleared; any keys which fall within DataSet are echoed on the screen, and appended to the 'content' string. Pressing the 'rubout' key rubs out the last character typed. Characters typed after the field becomes full are ignored. Input terminates when the AcceptField key is pressed. The RequestAbort key causes immediate termination.

On input the 'justification' attribute controls the position in the slot at which input is echoed. If the justification is 'left', then echo of the next character occurs one place to the right of the previous character, with the characters entered so far being displayed left-justified. If the justification is 'right', then echo occurs at the right hand side of the slot, with the characters entered so far being displayed right-justified. Hence, each character typed pushes the string one place to the left, and the rubout key deletes the rightmost character. This is particularly useful when entering numeric data. If the justification is 'centre', then the characters entered so far are displayed in the centre of the field, and input is requested immediately to the right of the last character entered.

G.7.2   Example: an Input which is Echoed to the Screen but Terminated Implicitly

```
AcceptField:=null:         {keycode 0}
EchoSwitch:=on;
ReadField (answer,DataSet,ControlDIB);
```

This case is the same as the previous case, with the exception that input terminates when the slot becomes full. This is useful when an application requires single-key input. If the width of the slot is set to 1, ReadField will accept a single character from those characters specified in DataSet, and terminate immediately.

G.7.3 Example: an Input which is not Echoed to the Screen but Explicitly Terminated

```
AcceptField:=CR;          {keycode 13}
```

```
EchoSwitch:=off;
ReadField(answer,DataSet,ControlDIB);
```

This case is the same as the case G.7.1, with the exception that the keyed characters are not echoed on the screen. This is useful for password protection. In our example, five asterisks will be displayed on the screen. However, characters typed at the keyboard will be invisible, as the EchoSwitch is off. The cursor will still move, showing where input is expected and thus how many characters have been typed.

G.7.4 Example: an Input which is not Echoed to the Screen and which has no Explicit Terminator

```
AcceptField:=null:            {keycode 0}
EchoSwitch:=off;
ReadField(answer,DataSet,ControlDIB);
```

This is the same as the previous case, with the exception that input terminates when the slot becomes full.

G.8 Input Control Parameters (see Section 3.3.4)

The ControlDIB data structure contains values which control the operation of the input process.
```
rubout
AcceptField
RequestAbort
RequestHelp
PointNextTarget
PointPriorTarget
AcceptTarget
PointNextField
PointPriorField
AcceptForm
ApplicationControl
```

Those features required in a particular dialogue, such as 'help' or being able to 'abort' the dialogue, are activated by assigning the corresponding parameter the keycode of a key selected for that feature. For example, if the ESCAPE key is to be used to abort the process, then

ControlDIB.RequestAbort:=ESC;   {keycode 27}

Features not required are assigned null values, for example

ControlDIB.AcceptField:=null;   {keycode 0}

ReadField automatically accepts keys corresponding to ControlDIB parameters which have been set to non-null values; it returns immediately with that keycode held in ControlBuffer (except for 'rubout' which is actioned by ReadField itself). The contents of ControlBuffer are interpreted and acted on by higher level dialogue routines, such as Q&A. These are described in Appendix H.

All the parameters listed above, with the exception of ApplicationControl, are of type 'byte'. ApplicationControl is defined as SetOfByte, and is used to specify characters which may have meaning to a particular dialogue process calling ReadField (rather than being of relevance to a general dialogue process). If one of the keys specified in ApplicationControl is pressed, ReadField exits immediately, with the keycode of the typed key again returned via ControlBuffer. It is the responsibility of the calling program to examine ControlBuffer, and act on it accordingly.

On exit from ReadField, ControlBuffer will be zero if data has been accepted (either terminated explicitly by the AcceptField key being typed, or implicitly by field.width characters being typed). If a control key has terminated input, ControlBuffer will hold the keycode of the corresponding key.

If one of the parameters of ControlDIB is set to a particular keycode value, and the same keycode is included in DataSet, then precedence is given to ControlDIB and the key is treated as control rather than data.

G.9 Clearing a Field (see Section 3.2.4)

There may be occasions when you want to clear the content of a field, for example, to clear an error message after the fault has been corrected. This can be accomplished with the ClearField procedure

ClearField(field:FieldType);

For example:

ClearField(field);

causes 'field' to be cleared to the field's background colour. ClearField effects this by changing the content to spaces and redisplaying the field. This setting is temporary. If DisplayField is called again for the same field, the original content will re-appear.

G.10 Highlighting a Field (see Section 3.4.1)

There may be occasions when you want to highlight a field that has previously been displayed on the screen, for example to show that it is being pointed at. This can be accomplished with the HighlightField procedure

HighlightField(Field:FieldType;Highlighting:AttributesType);

For example:

HighlightField(field,answer.attributes);

causes 'field' to be displayed with the attributes of the field 'answer'. HighlightField effects this by changing the attributes of 'field' to those of 'answer' and redisplaying it. This setting is temporary. If DisplayField is called again for the same field, it will re-appear on the screen with its original attributes.

G.11 Inverting a Field (see Section 4.4.3.3)

HighlightField(field,answer.attributes) causes 'field' to be displayed with the attributes of the field 'answer'. Inverse video is commonly used for highlighting, and so a procedure InvertField is provided to swap a field's foreground and background colours. In the following example, 'field' and 'answer' are both created with default attributes. Answer is then swapped to inverse video by InvertField.

CreateField(field,'displayed in inverse video',5,10,30,");
CreateField(answer,",0,0,0,");
InvertField(answer);
HighlightField(field,answer.attributes);

G.12 Hiding a Field (see Section 3.2.4)

There may be occasions when you want to hide a field completely. This can be done with the HideField procedure, which is the same as ClearField except that the field is cleared to the background colour of the screen rather than to the background colour of the field.

G.13 Clearing the Screen

The ClearScreen procedure clears the screen to its default background colour.

G.14 The Environment

Dialogue routines need to know something about the environment in which they are operating, such as the number of rows and columns on the screen, the default settings of the screen's foreground and background colours, and so on. Ideally, this information would be set up in an EnvironmentDIB at the outset of the dialogue, and made available globally in the routines in the various libraries. Non-standard extensions to PASCAL can be used to facilitate this. However, because there is no standard mechanism for making data globally available to separately compiled procedures in PASCAL, we have elected to 'bake' the environment into our libraries. The input/output library contains

```
const
   ScreenRows          = 24;
   ScreenCols          = 80;

procedure GetDefaultAttributes(var field:FieldType);
begin
with field.attributes do
   begin
   foreground:=white;
   background:=black;
   blink:=off;
   bold:=off;
   just:=left;
   end;
end; {GetDefaultAttributes}
```

G.15 Example Program

The following program fragment creates the screen illustrated in Fig. G.1.
The content and attributes of the field marked by x's can be altered by
entering different strings via the two input fields labelled 'content' and
'attributes'. For example, if you type 'NewContent' and
'blink=on,back=red,just=right', then 'NewContent' will be displayed in the
output field with the specified attributes.

```
Content  .............................
Attributes  ................................................
                    XXXXXXXXXXXXXXXXXXXXXXXXXXXXXXXXXXXX
```

Fig. G.1.

```
var ControlDIB                : ControlDIBtype;
    in1,in2,out1,out2,out3    : FieldType;
    filter                    : SetOfByte;
    aborted                   : boolean;
begin
ClearScreen;
with ControlDIB do
   begin
   RequestAbort:=ESC;      {keycode 27}
   rubout:=BS;             {keycode 8}
   AcceptField:=CR;        {keycode 13}
   EchoSwitch:=on;
   CreateField(in1,'initial message',7,18,30,'');
   CreateField(in2,'back=white,fore=black',9,18,50,'');
   CreateField(out1,'Contents          : ', 7,4,14,'');
   CreateField(out2,'Attributes        : ', 9,4,14,'');
   CreateField(out3,in1.content,13,18,30,in2.content);
   DisplayField(out1);
   DisplayField(out2);
   DisplayField(out3);
   DisplayField(in1);
   DisplayField(in2);
   repeat
       filter:=[ord('a')..ord('z'),ord(' ')];
       ReadField(in1,filter,ControlDIB);
       aborted:=ControlBuffer=RequestAbort;
       ChangeFieldContent(out3,in1.content);
       if not aborted then
          begin
          filter:=[ord('a')..ord('z'),ord('='),ord(',')];
          ReadField(in2,filter,ControlDIB);
          aborted:=ControlBuffer=RequestAbort;
          ChangeFieldAttributes(out3,in2.content);
          end;
       DisplayField(out3);
   until aborted;
   end;
end.
```

G.16 Listings

```
segment IOLib (input, output);
{----------------------------------------------------------------------}
const
    ($I b:mciconst.inc)
type
    ($I b:iotype.inc)
    TypeOfMatching = (exact,abbreviated,partial);
    SelectionType  = (id,scroll,position,key,any);
    InputEventType = (null,keyboard,pointer);
    TargetListType = array[1..MaxTargets] of FieldType;

{----------------------------------------------------------------------}
procedure cls(attributes:AttributesType);external;
procedure CursorTo(row,col:byte);external;
procedure DisplayString(var str:string;
                            attributes:AttributesType);external;
procedure SwitchCursor(switch:OffOn);external;
procedure SwitchPointerCursor(switch:OffOn);external;
procedure PointerTo(row,col:byte);external;
procedure ReadPointer(var row,col:byte;var action:byte);external;
function  equal(ControlBuffer,ControlByte:byte):boolean;external;
function  GetFilterKey(WaitSwitch:WaitType;
                            EchoSwitch:EchoType;
                            filter:SetOfByte):byte;external;
function  PointerEvent:boolean;external;
function  KeyboardEvent:boolean;external;

{----------------------------------------------------------------------}
procedure ConvertToLowerCase(var AttributeString:string);
var ascii,k,size : byte;
begin
size:=length(AttributeString);
for k:=1 to size do
    begin
    ascii:=ord(AttributeString[k]);
    if (ascii>=65) and (ascii<=90) then AttributeString[k]:=chr(ascii+32);
    end;
end; {ConvertToLowerCase}

{----------------------------------------------------------------------}
procedure GetDefaultAttributes(var field:FieldType);
begin
with field.attributes do
    begin
    foreground:=white;
    background:=black;
    blink:=off;
    bold:=off;
    justification:=left;
    end;
end; {GetDefaultAttributes}

{----------------------------------------------------------------------}
procedure justify(field:FieldType;
                    var JustifiedContent:string);
var spare  : byte;
    blanks : string;
begin
blanks:='                                        '
blanks:=concat(blanks,blanks);
with field do
    begin
    if slot.width=0 then
        JustifiedContent:=''
    else if slot.width=length(content) then
        JustifiedContent:=content
    else if slot.width<length(content) then
        JustifiedContent:=copy(content,1,slot.width)
    else
        begin
```

```
        spare:=slot.width-length(content);
        case attributes.justification of
           left: JustifiedContent:=concat(content,
                                  copy(blanks,1,spare));
         centre: JustifiedContent:=concat(copy(blanks,1,spare div 2),
                                  content,
                                  copy(blanks,1,(spare+1) div 2));
          right: JustifiedContent:=concat(copy(blanks,1,spare),
                                  content);
        end; (case)
        end;
    end;
end; (justify)

(-----------------------------------------------------------------------)
function JustifiedCol(field:Fieldtype):byte;
begin
with field do
    begin
    if attributes.justification=left then
        JustifiedCol:=slot.col+length(content)
    else if attributes.justification=right then
        JustifiedCol:=slot.col+slot.width-1
    else    (field.attributes.justification=centre)
      -:.JustifiedCol:=slot.col+length(content)+
                       ((slot.width-length(content)) div 2);
    end;
end; (JustifiedCol)

(-----------------------------------------------------------------------)
function OnScreen(field:FieldType) : boolean;
begin
if (field.slot.row>=1) and (field.slot.row<=ScreenRows) and
   (field.slot.col>=1) and (field.slot.col<=ScreenCols) then
      OnScreen:=true
else
      OnScreen:=false;
end; (OnScreen)

(-----------------------------------------------------------------------)
procedure RemoveSpaces(var AttributeString:string);
begin
while pos(' ',AttributeString)<>0 do
    delete(AttributeString,pos(' ',AttributeString),1);
end; (RemoveSpaces)

(-----------------------------------------------------------------------)
procedure ChangeFieldContent(var field:FieldType;
                             NewContent:string);
begin
field.content:=NewContent;
end; (ChangeFieldContent)

(-----------------------------------------------------------------------)
procedure ChangeFieldSlot(var field:FieldType;
                          row,col,width:byte);
begin
field.slot.row:=row;
field.slot.col:=col;
field.slot.width:=width;
end; (ChangeFieldSlot)

(-----------------------------------------------------------------------)
procedure ChangeFieldAttributes(var field:FieldType;
                                AttributeString:string);
begin
RemoveSpaces(AttributeString);
ConvertToLowerCase(AttributeString);
with field.attributes do
    begin
    if pos('fore=black',  AttributeString)<>0 then foreground:=black;
    if pos('fore=blue',   AttributeString)<>0 then foreground:=blue;
    if pos('fore=green',  AttributeString)<>0 then foreground:=green;
    if pos('fore=cyan',   AttributeString)<>0 then foreground:=cyan;
```

```
       if pos('fore=red',       AttributeString)<>0 then foreground:=red;
       if pos('fore=magenta',   AttributeString)<>0 then foreground:=magenta;
       if pos('fore=yellow',    AttributeString)<>0 then foreground:=yellow;
       if pos('fore=white',     AttributeString)<>0 then foreground:=white;
       if pos('back=black',     AttributeString)<>0 then background:=black;
       if pos('back=blue',      AttributeString)<>0 then background:=blue;
       if pos('back=green',     AttributeString)<>0 then background:=green;
       if pos('back=cyan',      AttributeString)<>0 then background:=cyan;
       if pos('back=red',       AttributeString)<>0 then background:=red;
       if pos('back=magenta',   AttributeString)<>0 then background:=magenta;
       if pos('back=yellow',    AttributeString)<>0 then background:=yellow;
       if pos('back=white',     AttributeString)<>0 then background:=white;

       if pos('blink=off', AttributeString)<>0 then blink:=off;
       if pos('blink=on',  AttributeString)<>0 then blink:=on;

       if pos('bold=off', AttributeString)<>0 then bold:=off;
       if pos('bold=on',  AttributeString)<>0 then bold:=on;

       if pos('just=left',   AttributeString)<>0 then justification:=left;
       if pos('just=centre', AttributeString)<>0 then justification:=centre;
       if pos('just=right',  AttributeString)<>0 then justification:=right;

    end;
end; {ChangeFieldAttributes}

{---------------------------------------------------------------------}
procedure CreateField(var field:FieldType;
                           message:string;
                           row,col,width:byte;
                           AttributeString:string);
begin
ChangeFieldContent(field,message);
ChangeFieldSlot(field,row,col,width);
GetDefaultAttributes(field);
ChangeFieldAttributes(field,AttributeString);
end; {CreateField}

{---------------------------------------------------------------------}
procedure DisplayField(field:FieldType);
var JustifiedContent:string;
begin
if OnScreen(field) then
   begin
   justify(field,JustifiedContent);
   CursorTo(field.slot.row,field.slot.col);
   DisplayString(JustifiedContent,field.attributes);
   end;
end; {DisplayField}

{---------------------------------------------------------------------}
procedure HideField(field:FieldType);
begin
if field.content<>'' then
   begin
   GetDefaultAttributes(field);
   with field.attributes do
      begin
      foreground:=background;
      bold:=off;
      end;
   DisplayField(field);
   end;
end; {HideField}

{---------------------------------------------------------------------}
procedure HighlightField(field:FieldType;
                         HighlightAttributes:AttributesType);
begin
field.attributes:=HighlightAttributes;
DisplayField(field);
end; {HighlightField}

{---------------------------------------------------------------------}
```

```
procedure InvertField(var field:FieldType);
var temp : colours;
begin
with field.attributes do
   begin
   temp:=foreground;
   foreground:=background;
   background:=temp;
   end;
end; (InvertField)

{----------------------------------------------------------------------}
procedure ReadField(var field:FieldType;
                        DataSet:SetOfByte;
                        var ControlDIB:ControlDIBtype);
var key       : byte;
    ControlSet : SetOfByte;
    EditSet    : SetOfByte;
    filter     : SetOfByte;
    complete   : boolean;
begin
with ControlDIB,field do
   begin
   DisplayField(field);
   ControlSet:=ApplicationControl+
              [RequestAbort,RequestHelp,
               PointNextTarget,PointPriorTarget,AcceptTarget,
               PointNextField,PointPriorField,AcceptForm];
   if slot.width=0 then
      {control characters only}
      ControlBuffer:=GetFilterKey(wait,NoEcho,ControlSet)
   else
      {both control and data}
      begin
      ControlSet:=ControlSet+[AcceptField];
      EditSet:=[rubout];
      filter:=ControlSet+DataSet;               (nothing to edit)
      if attributes.justification=right then
         CursorTo(slot.row,slot.col+slot.width-1)
      else
         CursorTo(slot.row,slot.col);
      complete:=false;
      key:=GetFilterKey(wait,NoEcho,filter);
      if key in ControlSet then complete:=true
                           else content:='';     (clear answer field)
      while (not complete) do
         begin
         if key in EditSet then delete(content,length(content),1)
                          else content:=concat(content,chr(key));
         if EchoSwitch=on then DisplayField(field);
         if (length(content)=slot.width) and (AcceptField=0) then
            complete:=true
         else
            begin
            CursorTo(slot.row,JustifiedCol(field));
            if length(content)=0 then
               filter:=ControlSet+DataSet          (nothing to edit)
            else if length(content)=slot.width then
               filter:=ControlSet+EditSet          (ignore excess data)
            else
               filter:=ControlSet+DataSet+EditSet; (allow any)
            key:=GetFilterKey(wait,NoEcho,filter);
            if key in ControlSet then complete:=true;
            end;
         end;
      if key=AcceptField then
         ControlBuffer:=0         (because it has been actioned)
      else
      if key in ControlSet then
         ControlBuffer:=key
      else
         ControlBuffer:=0;       (slot full and AcceptField=0)
      end;
   end;
```

```
end; (ReadField)

{----------------------------------------------------------------------}
procedure ClearField(field:FieldType);
begin
ChangeFieldContent(field,' ');
DisplayField(field);
end; (ClearField)

{----------------------------------------------------------------------}
procedure ClearScreen;
var defaults : FieldType;
begin
CursorTo(1,1);
GetDefaultAttributes(defaults);
cls(defaults.attributes);
CursorTo(1,1);
end; (ClearScreen)

{----------------------------------------------------------------------}
function MatchString(subject:string;
                     TargetList:TargetListType;
                     NumberOfTargets:byte):byte;
var k,match:byte;
begin
match:=0;
k:=1;
while (k<=NumberOfTargets) and (match=0) do
   if TargetList[k].content=subject then match:=k
                                    else k:=k+1;
MatchString:=match;
end; (MatchString)

{----------------------------------------------------------------------}
procedure RelativePick(TargetList:TargetListType;
                       NumberOfTargets:byte;
                       highlight:AttributesType;
                       var ControlDIB:ControlDIBtype;
                       var CurrentTarget:byte);
var
   complete : boolean;
   filter   : SetOfByte;
begin
with ControlDIB do
   begin
   filter:=ApplicationControl+[RequestAbort,RequestHelp,
           PointNextTarget,PointPriorTarget,AcceptTarget,
           PointNextField,PointPriorField,AcceptForm];
   SwitchCursor(off);
   if (CurrentTarget<1) or (CurrentTarget>NumberOfTargets) then
      CurrentTarget:=1;
   HighlightField(TargetList[CurrentTarget],highlight);
   complete:=false;
   repeat
     if ControlBuffer=0 then
        ControlBuffer:=GetFilterKey(Wait,NoEcho,filter);
     {ControlBuffer cannot be zero}
     if ControlBuffer=RequestAbort then
        complete:=true
     else
     if (ControlBuffer=PointNextTarget)
     or (ControlBuffer=PointPriorTarget) then
        begin
        DisplayField(TargetList[CurrentTarget]); {turn off old highlight}
        if ControlBuffer=PointNextTarget then
           if CurrentTarget=NumberOfTargets then CurrentTarget:=1
                                  else CurrentTarget:=CurrentTarget+1
        else
           if CurrentTarget=1 then CurrentTarget:=NumberOfTargets
                           else CurrentTarget:=CurrentTarget-1;
        HighlightField(TargetList[CurrentTarget],highlight);
        ControlBuffer:=0; {because it has been actioned}
        if AcceptTarget=0 {needed for dropdown menus} then
           complete:=true;
```

```
          end
      else
      if ControlBuffer=AcceptTarget then
          begin
          complete:=true;
          ControlBuffer:=0;   {because it has been actioned}
          end
      else
          {ControlBuffer=ApplicationControl,RequestHelp,
                         PointNextField,PointPriorField,AcceptForm}
          complete:=true;
    until complete;
    SwitchCursor(on);
    end;
end; {RelativePick}

{-----------------------------------------------------------------------}
function MatchPosition(row,col:byte;
                         TargetList:TargetListType;
                         NumberOfTargets:byte):byte;
var k,match:byte;
begin
match:=0;
k:=1;
while (k<=NumberOfTargets) and (match=0) do
    if   (row=TargetList[k].slot.row)
    and (col>=TargetList[k].slot.col)
    and (col< TargetList[k].slot.col+TargetList[k].slot.width) then
        match:=k
    else
        k:=k+1;
MatchPosition:=match;
end; {MatchPosition}

{-----------------------------------------------------------------------}
procedure AbsolutePick(TargetList:TargetListType;
                         NumberOfTargets:byte;
                         highlight:AttributesType;
                         var ControlDIB:ControlDIBtype;
                         var CurrentTarget:byte);
var
    complete    : boolean;
    PriorTarget : byte;
    row,col     : byte;

begin
with ControlDIB do
    begin
    SwitchCursor(off); SwitchPointerCursor(on);
    if (CurrentTarget>=1) and (CurrentTarget<=NumberOfTargets) then
        begin
        PointerTo(TargetList[CurrentTarget].slot.row,
                  TargetList[CurrentTarget].slot.col);
        HighlightField(TargetList[CurrentTarget],highlight);
        end;
    complete:=false;
    repeat
        PriorTarget:=CurrentTarget;
        ReadPointer(row,col,ControlBuffer);
        if equal(ControlBuffer,RequestAbort) then
            complete:=true
        else
            begin
            {ControlBuffer may be zero}
            CurrentTarget:=MatchPosition(row,col,TargetList,NumberOfTargets);
            if (CurrentTarget<>0) and (AcceptTarget=0) then
                complete:=true
            else
            if CurrentTarget<>PriorTarget then
                begin
                if PriorTarget<>0 then DisplayField(TargetList[PriorTarget]);
                if CurrentTarget<>0 then HighlightField(TargetList[CurrentTarget
                                                        ,highlight);
                end
```

```
          else
          if (ControlBuffer<>0) and (ControlBuffer in ApplicationControl+
                                      [AcceptTarget,RequestHelp]) then
              complete:=true;
          end;
   until complete;
   SwitchPointerCursor(off); SwitchCursor(on);
   end;
end; {AbsolutePick}

{------------------------------------------------------------------}
function TestInputEvent(selector:SelectionType):InputEventType;
begin
if ((selector=any) or (selector=position)) and PointerEvent then
   TestInputEvent:=pointer
else
   if (selector<>position) and KeyboardEvent then
       TestInputEvent:=keyboard
   else
       TestInputEvent:=null;
end; {TestInputEvent}

{------------------------------------------------------------------}
function WaitInputEvent(selector:SelectionType):InputEventType;
var event : InputEventType;
    k     : integer;
begin
event:=null;
repeat
   for k:=1 to 10000 do {nothing};
   event:=TestInputEvent(selector);
until event<>null;
WaitInputEvent:=event;
end; {WaitInputEvent}

{------------------------------------------------------------------}
begin {IOLib}
end.
```

Appendix H

Q&A library

This appendix provides descriptions of routines needed to support Q&A-based dialogues. A full listing of the routines is provided at the end of the appendix. Preceding sections describe individual routines, and how to use them.

H.1 Routines in the Q&A Library

procedure QandA(var QandA_DIB:QandA_DIBtype;
var ControlDIB:ControlDIBtype);external;
{Provides a Question-and-Answer dialogue based on the data provided by a QandA_DIB and the ControlDIB. This may involve the entry of arbitrary data, or selection from a list of targets. The following routines in the Q&A library are called by Q&A:

routine	called when
ArbitraryData(QandA_DIB,ControlDIB)	NumberOfTargets=0
ChooseByID(QandA_DIB,ControlDIB)	SelectionBy=id
ChooseByScroll(QandA_DIB,ControlDIB)	SelectionBy=scroll
ChooseByPosition(QandA_DIB,ControlDIB)	SelectionBy=position
ChooseBykey(QandA_DIB,ControlDIB)	SelectionBy=key
Choose(QandA_DIB,ControlDIB)	SelectionBy=any}

procedure SetControlDefaults(var ControlDIB:ControlDIBtype);external;
{Initialises the variables in ControlDIB to null values.}

procedure SetQandADefaults(var QandA_DIB:QandA_DIBtype);external;
{Initialises the variables in the QandA_DIB to null values.}

procedure DisplayMenu(MenuDIB:MenuDIBtype);external;
{Displays the menu specified by MenuDIB.}

procedure SetMenuDefaults(var MenuDIB:MenuDIBtype);external;
{Initialises the variables in MenuDIB to null values.}

H.2 Type Declarations Include-file for the Q&A Library

The following type declarations are needed when using the routines in the Q&A library. They are stored in the file 'qatype.inc'.

```
TargetListType      = array[1..MaxTargets] of FieldType;
TypeOfMatching      = (exact,abbreviated,partial);
SelectionType       = (id,scroll,position,key,any);

QandA_DIBtype       = record
                      question          : FieldType;
                      answer            : FieldType;
                      filter            : SetOfByte;
                      HelpMessage       : FieldType;
                      Validation        : string;
                      ErrorFlag         : OffOn;
                      ErrorMessage      : FieldType;
                      NumberOfTargets   : byte;
                      TargetList        : TargetListType;
                      matching          : TypeOfMatching;
                      CurrentTarget     : byte;
                      SelectionBy       : SelectionType;
                      end;

MenuDIBtype         = record
                      MenuHeader        : FieldType;
                      NumberOfOptions   : byte;
                      TargetList        : TargetListType;
                      SupplementaryList : TargetListType;
                      MenuTrailer       : FieldType;
                      end;
```

H.3 Q&A_DIBs

Question-and-Answer (Q&A) is the basic dialogue mechanism. There are two categories:

Q&A to input arbitrary data
Q&A to select from targets.

The information required for both these categories is held in a Q&A Dialogue Information Block (abbreviated to QandA_DIB), as defined in Section H.2. The first four items are common to both categories.

question   : this field contains the question that is to be asked. If there is no explicit question, then either the content can be set to '', or the slot can be defined to be off the screen.

answer   : this field holds any keyed data that is entered in response to the question. EchoSwitch in ControlDIB is set 'off' if the *keyed data* is not to be displayed. If the *slot* is not to be shown on the screen (for example, with point-and-pick), then it is positioned off the screen.

filter : the set of characters which are valid when using keyed input of data.

HelpMessage : the field containing the help message which is to be displayed when the user presses the RequestHelp key.

The next three items relate to 'input of arbitrary data' and 'matching by keyed identifier'.

validation : a string specifying the validation that is to be carried out on the keyed data entered into answer.

ErrorFlag : set to 'on' if an error has been encountered when entering data via this QandA_DIB, otherwise set 'off'.

ErrorMessage : the field containing the error message that is to be displayed when the user has input invalid data.

The remaining five items relate to selection from targets.

NumberOfTargets: the number of targets associated with this DIB.

TargetList : the list of target fields associated with this DIB; each target may be a string representing an identifier, a slot, or both. To reduce complexity and hence aid understanding we will always represent lists as arrays.

matching : the type of matching that is to be applied between keyed input and the targets. Exact matching is used in the examples in this appendix. If no match is found, ErrorFlag is set 'on' and the ErrorMessage field is displayed.

CurrentTarget : holds the ordinal number of the currently selected target. CurrentTarget may be set initially to any value in the range 1..MaxTargets; if it is outside this range, a default of 1 is assumed.

SelectionBy : specifies the way the selection will be made. The possibilities are:

id : keyed identifier
scroll : scrolling forwards and/or backwards

position	: direct pointing
key	: id and/or scroll
any	: id, scroll and/or position

All the examples provided in the subsequent sections assume the existence of a variable

var QandA_DIB : QandA_DIBtype;

H.4 ControlDIB Settings

It is important to maintain consistency throughout a dialogue. Consistency of the input process can be achieved by assigning values to the ControlDIB variables at the start of the program, and thereafter not altering them. For example:

```
var
   ControlDIB : ControlDIBtype;

SetControlDefaults(ControlDIB);
with ControlDIB do
   begin
   rubout:=BS;                      {keycode 8}
   EchoSwitch:=on;                  {enable echoing}
   AcceptField:=CR;                 {keycode 13}
   RequestAbort:=ESC;               {keycode 27}
   RequestHelp:=F1;                 {keycode 187}
   PointNextTarget:=CursorDown;     {keycode 208}
   PointPriorTarget:=CursorUp;      {keycode 200}
   AcceptTarget:=CR;                {keycode 13}
   end;
```

The procedure SetControlDefaults initialises all the variables in Control-DIB to null values. The required items are then set to specific values, within the 'with' statement. The above ControlDIB is assumed in the following examples.

H.5 Q&A with Arbitrary Data

Input of arbitrary data is illustrated by the following program fragment which accepts a numeric value, validates that it lies in the range 15..20, and finally stores the validated entry in the variable called 'row', which is of type 'byte'.

```
SetQandADefaults(QandA_DIB);
with QandA_DIB do
   begin
   CreateField(question,'row',13,11,6,'');
   CreateField(answer,'15',13,17,2,'just=right');
   filter:=[ord('0')..ord('9')];
   CreateField(HelpMessage,
         'permitted range is 15..20. Press RETURN to accept the value',
         24,1,80,'');
   Validation:='numeric, range 15..20';
   CreateField(ErrorMessage,'',24,1,80,'just=centre');
   InvertField(ErrorMessage);
   NumberOfTargets:=0;
   end;
repeat
   QandA(QandA_DIB,ControlDIB);
   with ControlDIB do aborted:=equal(ControlBuffer,RequestAbort);
   if not aborted then validate(QandA_DIB);
until aborted or (QandA_DIB.ErrorFlag=off);
row:=ConvertStringToByte(QandA_DIB.answer.content);
```

The procedure SetQandADefaults initialises all the variables in the
QandA_DIB to null values. The answer field is defined to be right-justified
because the data to be input is numeric. The filter only permits numeric
characters. NumberOfTargets is set to zero because there are no targets.
Although the Q&A procedure can filter out all but numeric digits, some
combinations of digits are still invalid (14,21,99 for example). These are
rejected by a separate 'validate' procedure outside the Q&A process.

```
procedure validate(var QandA_DIB:QandA_DIBtype);
begin
with QandA_DIB do
   begin
   if Validation='numeric, range 15..20' then
      if not (val(answer.content) in [15..20]) then
         begin
         ChangeFieldContent(ErrorMessage,'not in range 15..20');
         QandA_DIB.ErrorFlag:=on;
         end
      else
         QandA_DIB.ErrorFlag:=off
   else
   if Validation=.............. then
   ...............
   end;
end; {validate}
```

'Validation' in the QandA_DIB tells 'validate' what type of validation is to
be performed. If the validate procedure finds the input unacceptable, it will
plant an appropriate error message into the QandA_DIB, and set ErrorFlag
on. The Q&A procedure will be recalled, the error message will be displayed,
and the user invited to correct the entry. The repeat loop continues until a
valid entry is received.

We have adopted this method of validation because of the limitations of

PASCAL. If the programming language used to implement the Q&A routines allows procedure names as data items, then it is preferable for ValidationCode to hold the name of the validation procedure directly. Validation is a string rather than an enumerated type because the type of validation is not known at the time the library routines are written.

H.6 Q&A Selecting from Targets

The QandA_DIB variable NumberOfTargets determines whether the Q&A is being used for entry of arbitrary data (NumberOfTargets=0) or for selecting from a list of targets (NumberOfTargets<>0), as in a menu. There are three methods for selecting from targets:

keyed identifier	(keyboard)
relative pointing	(keyboard)
absolute pointing	(pointing device, e.g. mouse)

H.6.1 Q&A with Keyed Identifier

Suppose one of the following seven options is to be selected from a menu by typing its identifier.

mtr	Motor
cnt	Contents
prp	Property
prs	Personal
lfe	Life
msc	Miscellaneous
end	End

A MenuDIB is required to define the menu display and a QandA_DIB is required to define the processing of the response.

```
SetQandAdefaults(QandA_DIB);
with QandA_DIB do
   begin
   CreateField(answer,'',15,16,3,'bold=on');
   filter:=[ord('a')..ord('z')];
   CreateField(HelpMessage,
               'enter the 3 character code of the required option',
               24,10,60,'fore=black,back=white,just=centre');
   CreateField(ErrorMessage,'Please re-enter',
```

```
                         24,10,60,'fore=black,back=white,just=centre');
      NumberOfTargets:=7;
      CreateField(TargetList[1],'mtr', 7,10,3,'');
      CreateField(TargetList[2],'cnt', 8,10,3,'');
      CreateField(TargetList[3],'prp', 9,10,3,'');
      CreateField(TargetList[4],'prs.',10,10,3,'');
      CreateField(TargetList[5],'lfe',11,10,3,'');
      CreateField(TargetList[6],'msc',12,10,3,'');
      CreateField(TargetList[7],'end',13,10,3,'');
      SelectionBy:=id;
      end;
```

Note that question, validation, ErrorFlag, matching and CurrentTarget have not been set explicitly, so retain the null values set in SetQandADefaults.

```
with MenuDIB do
   begin
   CreateField(MenuHeader,'Types of insurance',5,8,18,'');
   NumberOfOptions:=7;
   for k:=1 to NumberOfOptions do
      MenuDIB.TargetList[k]:=QandA_DIB.TargetList[k];
   CreateField(SupplementaryList[1],'Motor',7,15,13,'');
   CreateField(SupplementaryList[2],'Contents',8,15,13,'');
   CreateField(SupplementaryList[3],'Property',9,15,13,'');
   CreateField(SupplementaryList[4],'Personal',10,15,13,'');
   CreateField(SupplementaryList[5],'Life',11,15,13,'');
   CreateField(SupplementaryList[6],'Miscellaneous',12,15,13,'');
   CreateField(SupplementaryList[7],'End',13,15,13,'');
   CreateField(MenuTrailer,'Option?',15,8,7,'');
   end;

DisplayMenu(MenuDIB);
QandA(QandA_DIB,ControlDIB);
```

The seven options are displayed on the screen, and the user is invited to enter his choice. If his entry does not match any of the targets an error message is displayed, and the user asked to retype his selection. The Q&A procedure terminates either when a match is made, or the user presses the Escape key to abort.

H.6.2 Q&A with Relative Pointing (Scrolling)

Suppose one of the previous seven options is to be selected by scrolling backwards or forwards through the list, and picking the one required. The operator uses special keys to point at the target he wishes to select. The following ControlDIB variables are used.

PointNextTarget — determines a key which will position to the next target in the list. If left null (0) then scrolling forward will be inoperative.

PointPriorTarget — determines a key which will position to the previous target in the list. If left null (0) then scrolling backwards will be inoperative.

AcceptTarget   determines a key which causes the current target to be picked. If AcceptTarget is null the first target pointed at is picked.

Some highlighting is needed to make the current target stand out. The Q&A procedure adopts the convention of using the attributes of the answer field for this purpose. Hence, the programmer specifies the required highlighting via the attributes of 'answer'.

Only slight modifications are needed to the previous QandA_DIB to effect selection by relative pointing. In practice, the targets are likely to be different, for example 'Motor' instead of 'mtr Motor'.

We will use inverse video for highlighting. We first create the answer field with default attributes, and then invert them:

    CreateField(answer,",15,16,3,'bold=on'); InvertField(answer);

The help message needs modifying.

    CreateField(HelpMessage,
                'down=next target   up=prior target   return=pick',
                24,10,60,'fore=black,back=white,just=centre');

No ErrorMessage is needed.
The method of selection must be changed.

    SelectionBy:=scroll;

The seven options are displayed on the screen, and the first option (Motor) is highlighted. The operator can *point* at the next option by pressing the PointNextTarget key; Motor will revert to normal display, and Contents will become highlighted. The PointPriorTarget key can be used similarly to highlight the previous target. This pointing is continued until the desired target is highlighted. The operator then presses the AcceptTarget key to *pick* that target.

H.6.3 Q&A with both keyed Identifier and Relative Pointing

We can permit both types of selection in the same Q&A, simply by changing SelectionBy to

    SelectionBy:=key;

We would need to restore the error message appropriate for keyed data, and we need a help message that explains both methods of selection.

H.6.4 Q&A with absolute pointing

We can permit absolute pointing (for example, via a mouse) in the same Q&A, simply by changing SelectionBy to

SelectionBy:=position;

We need to change the error message to something appropriate for absolute pointing, and to amend the help message. In practice, the targets are likely to be dispersed around the screen instead of being vertically aligned.

H.6.5 Q&A with keyed Identifier, Relative and Absolute Pointing

We can permit all three methods of selection in the same Q&A, simply by changing SelectionBy to

SelectionBy:=any;

We again need to amend both the help and the error messages.

H.6.6 Listings

```
segment QandALib (input,output);
{ ------------------------------------------------------------------}
const
    {$I b:mciconst.inc}
type
    {$I b:iotype.inc}
    {$I b:qatype.inc}
    InputEventType    = (null,keyboard,pointer);

{ ------------------------------------------------------------------}
procedure ClearScreen;external;
procedure ClearKbd;external;
procedure CursorTo(row,col:byte);external;
procedure CursorAt(var row,col:byte);external;
function  KbdBufferEmpty:boolean;external;
procedure CreateField(var field:FieldType;
                         message:string;
                         row,col,width:byte;
                         AttributeString:string);external;
procedure DisplayField(field:FieldType);external;
procedure HideField(field:FieldType);external;
procedure HighlightField(field:FieldType;
                             HighlightAttributes:AttributesType);external;
```

```pascal
procedure ReadField(var field:FieldType;
                    DataSet:SetOfByte;
                    var ControlDIB:ControlDIBtype);external;
procedure SwitchCursor(switch:OffOn);external;
function  TestCursor:OffOn;external;
function MatchString(subject:string;
                     TargetList:TargetListType;
                     NumberOfTargets:byte):byte;external;
function MatchPosition(row,col:byte;
                       TargetList:TargetListType;
                       NumberOfTargets:byte):byte;external;
procedure RelativePick(TargetList:TargetListType;
                       NumberOfTargets:byte;
                       highlight:AttributesType;
                       var ControlDIB:ControlDIBtype;
                       var TargetChosen:byte);external;
procedure AbsolutePick(TargetList:TargetListType;
                       NumberOfTargets:byte;
                       highlight:AttributesType;
                       var ControlDIB:ControlDIBtype;
                       var TargetChosen:byte);external;
function  WaitInputEvent(selector:SelectionType):InputEventType;external;
procedure ReadPointer(var row,col:byte;var action:byte);external;
procedure SwitchPointerCursor(switch:OffOn);external;
procedure PointerTo(row,col:byte);external;

{-----------------------------------------------------------------------}
function count(MatchSet:SetOfByte):byte;
var counter,k : byte;
begin
counter:=0;
for k:=1 to MaxTargets do
   if (k in MatchSet) then counter:=counter+1;
count:=counter;
end; {count}

{-----------------------------------------------------------------------}
function first(MatchSet:SetOfByte):byte;
var k,kfirst : byte;
begin
kfirst:=0;
for k:=1 to MaxTargets do
   if (k in MatchSet) and (kfirst=0) then kfirst:=k;
first:=kfirst;
end; {first}

{-----------------------------------------------------------------------}
function equal(ControlBuffer,ControlByte:byte):boolean;
begin
if (ControlBuffer<>0) and (ControlBuffer=ControlByte) then
   equal:=true
else
   equal:=false;
end; {equal}

{-----------------------------------------------------------------------}
procedure AbbreviatedMatch(QandA_DIB:QandA_DIBtype;
                           var MatchSet:SetOfByte);
var k:byte;
begin
with QandA_DIB do
   begin
   MatchSet:=[];
   if length(answer.content)<>0 then
      for k:=1 to NumberOfTargets do
         if length(answer.content)<=length(TargetList[k].content) then
```

```
               if answer.content=copy(TargetList[k].content,1,
                                    length(answer.content)) then
                 MatchSet:=MatchSet+[k];
     end;
end; {AbbreviatedMatch}

{-------------------------------------------------------------------}
procedure ExactMatch(QandA_DIB:QandA_DIBtype;
                     var MatchSet:SetOfByte);
var k:byte;
begin
with QandA_DIB do
   begin
   MatchSet:=[];
   if length(answer.content)<>0 then
      for k:=1 to NumberOfTargets do
         if answer.content=TargetList[k].content then
            MatchSet:=MatchSet+[k];
   end;
end; {ExactMatch}

{-------------------------------------------------------------------}
procedure PartialMatch(QandA_DIB:QandA_DIBtype;
                       var MatchSet:SetOfByte);
var k:byte;
begin
with QandA_DIB do
   begin
   MatchSet:=[];
   while (length(answer.content)<>0) and (count(MatchSet)=0) do
      begin
      AbbreviatedMatch(QandA_DIB,MatchSet);
      delete(answer.content,length(answer.content),1);
      end;
   end;
end; {PartialMatch}

{-------------------------------------------------------------------}
procedure DisplayMenu(MenuDIB:MenuDIBtype);
var k:byte;
begin
ClearScreen;
with MenuDIB do
   begin
   DisplayField(MenuHeader);
   for k:=1 to NumberOfOptions do
      begin
      DisplayField(TargetList[k]);
      DisplayField(SupplementaryList[k]);
      end;
   DisplayField(MenuTrailer);
   end;
end; {DisplayMenu}

{-------------------------------------------------------------------}
procedure ArbitraryData(var QandA_DIB:QandA_DIBtype;
                        var ControlDIB:ControlDIBtype);
var
   complete : boolean;
begin
with QandA_DIB,ControlDIB do
   begin
   if ErrorFlag=on then DisplayField(ErrorMessage);
   ErrorFlag:=off;
   complete:=false;
   repeat
```

```
      DisplayField(question);
      ReadField(answer,filter,ControlDIB);
      HideField(ErrorMessage);
      HideField(HelpMessage);
      if equal(ControlBuffer,RequestAbort) then
         complete:=true
      else
      if equal(ControlBuffer,PointNextTarget)
      or equal(ControlBuffer,PointPriorTarget)
      or equal(ControlBuffer,AcceptTarget) then
         ControlBuffer:=0   {ignored by ArbitraryData}
      else
      if equal(ControlBuffer,RequestHelp) then
         begin
         DisplayField(HelpMessage);
         ControlBuffer:=0;   {because it has been actioned}
         end
      else
         {a higher level control character has caused termination}
         complete:=true;
   until complete;
   end;
end; {ArbitraryData}

{------------------------------------------------------------------------}
procedure ChooseByID(var QandA_DIB:QandA_DIBtype;
                     var ControlDIB:ControlDIBtype);
var
   complete   : boolean;
begin
with QandA_DIB,ControlDIB do
   begin
   complete:=false;
   repeat
      if ErrorFlag=on then DisplayField(ErrorMessage);
      ErrorFlag:=off;
      DisplayField(question);
      ReadField(answer,filter,ControlDIB);
      HideField(ErrorMessage);
      HideField(HelpMessage);
      if equal(ControlBuffer,RequestAbort) then
         complete:=true
      else
      if ControlBuffer=0 then
         begin {a text string has been entered}
         CurrentTarget:=MatchString(Answer.content,TargetList,
                                    NumberOfTargets);
         if CurrentTarget<>0 then
            begin
            answer.content:=TargetList[CurrentTarget].content;
            complete:=true;
            end
         else
            ErrorFlag:=on;
         end
      else
      if (ControlBuffer=PointNextTarget)
      or (ControlBuffer=PointPriorTarget)
      or (ControlBuffer=AcceptTarget) then
         ControlBuffer:=0                      {ignored by ChooseById}
      else
      if equal(ControlBuffer,RequestHelp) then
         begin
         DisplayField(HelpMessage);
         ControlBuffer:=0;              {because it has been actioned}
         end
```

```
        else
            {a higher level control character has caused termination}
            complete:=true;
    until complete;
    end;
end; {ChooseByID}

{------------------------------------------------------------------------}
procedure ChooseByScroll(var QandA_DIB:QandA_DIBtype;
                         var ControlDIB:ControlDIBtype);
var
    complete : boolean;
begin
with QandA_DIB,ControlDIB do
    begin
    complete:=false;
    repeat
        DisplayField(question);
        RelativePick(TargetList,NumberOfTargets,answer.attributes,
                     ControlDIB,CurrentTarget);
        answer.content:=TargetList[CurrentTarget].content;
        HideField(HelpMessage);
        if equal(ControlBuffer,RequestAbort) then
            complete:=true
        else
        if equal(ControlBuffer,RequestHelp) then
            begin
            DisplayField(HelpMessage);
            ControlBuffer:=0; `  {becuase it has been actioned}
            end
        else
            complete:=true;
    until complete;
    DisplayField(TargetList[CurrentTarget]);
    end;
end; {ChooseByScroll}

{------------------------------------------------------------------------}
procedure ChooseByPosition(var QandA_DIB:QandA_DIBtype;
                           var ControlDIB:ControlDIBtype);
var
    complete : boolean;
begin
with QandA_DIB,ControlDIB do
    begin
    complete:=false;
    repeat
        DisplayField(question);
        AbsolutePick(TargetList,NumberOfTargets,answer.attributes,
                     ControlDIB,CurrentTarget);
        HideField(HelpMessage);
        HideField(ErrorMessage);
        {ControlBuffer can be zero}
        if equal(ControlBuffer,RequestAbort) then
            complete:=true
        else
        if equal(ControlBuffer,RequestHelp) then
            DisplayField(HelpMessage)
        else
        if CurrentTarget<>0 then
            begin
            answer.content:=TargetList[CurrentTarget].content;
            complete:=true;
            end
        else
            DisplayField(ErrorMessage);
```

```
        until complete;
        if CurrentTarget<>0 then
            begin
            DisplayField(TargetList[CurrentTarget]);
            answer.content:=TargetList[CurrentTarget].content;
            end;
        end;
end; {ChooseByPosition}

{------------------------------------------------------------------------}
procedure ChooseByKey(var QandA_DIB:QandA_DIBtype;
                      var ControlDIB:ControlDIBtype);
var CursorWas   : OffOn;
    MatchSet    : SetOfByte;
    complete    : boolean;
    PriorTarget : byte;
begin
with QandA_DIB,ControlDIB do
    begin
    CursorWas:=TestCursor;
    if (CurrentTarget<1) or (CurrentTarget>NumberOfTargets) then
        CurrentTarget:=1;
    answer.content:=TargetList[CurrentTarget].content;
    HighlightField(TargetList[CurrentTarget],answer.attributes);
    if filter=[] then SwitchCursor(off);
    DisplayField(question);
    complete:=false;
    repeat
        if ErrorFlag=on then DisplayField(ErrorMessage);
        ErrorFlag:=off;
        if ControlBuffer=0 then ReadField(answer,filter,ControlDIB);
        HideField(ErrorMessage);
        HideField(HelpMessage);
        if equal(ControlBuffer,RequestAbort) then
            complete:=true
        else
            begin
            PriorTarget:=CurrentTarget;
            if ControlBuffer=0 then
                (***** matching keyed data *****)
                begin
                case matching of
                    abbreviated : AbbreviatedMatch(QandA_DIB,MatchSet);
                    exact       : ExactMatch(QandA_DIB,MatchSet);
                    partial     : PartialMatch(QandA_DIB,MatchSet);
                end; (case)
                if count(MatchSet)=1 then
                    begin
                    CurrentTarget:=first(MatchSet);
                    complete:=true;
                    end
                else
                    ErrorFlag:=on;
                end
            else
            if (ControlBuffer=PointNextTarget)
            or (ControlBuffer=PointPriorTarget) then
                (***** relative pointing *****)
                begin
                if ControlBuffer=PointNextTarget then
                    if PriorTarget=NumberOfTargets then CurrentTarget:=1
                                     else CurrentTarget:=PriorTarget+1
                else
                    if PriorTarget=1 then CurrentTarget:=NumberOfTargets
                                     else CurrentTarget:=PriorTarget-1;
                ControlBuffer:=0;    (because it has been actioned)
```

```
                    {do nothing in the case of AcceptTarget=0}
                    DisplayField(TargetList[PriorTarget]);
                    HighlightField(TargetList[CurrentTarget],answer.attributes);
                    answer.content:=TargetList[CurrentTarget].content;
                    end;
                if (not complete) and (ControlBuffer<>0) then
                    begin
                    if ControlBuffer=AcceptTarget then
                        begin
                        complete:=true;
                        ControlBuffer:=0;    {because it has been actioned}
                        end
                    else
                    if ControlBuffer=RequestHelp then
                        begin
                        DisplayField(HelpMessage);
                        ControlBuffer:=0;    {because it has been actioned}
                        end
                    else
                    if ControlBuffer in ApplicationControl+[PointNextField,
                                        PointPriorField,AcceptForm] then
                        complete:=true;
                    end;
                end;
        until complete;
        DisplayField(TargetList[CurrentTarget]);
        answer.content:=TargetList[CurrentTarget].content;
        if CursorWas=on then SwitchCursor(on);
        end;
end; {ChooseByKey}
{------------------------------------------------------------------------}
procedure Choose(var QandA_DIB:QandA_DIBtype;
                 var ControlDIB:ControlDIBtype);
var CursorWas    : OffOn;
    MatchSet     : SetOfByte;
    complete     : boolean;
    event        : InputEventType;
    PriorTarget  : byte;
    row,col      : byte;
begin
with QandA_DIB,ControlDIB do
    begin
    CursorWas:=TestCursor;
    if (CurrentTarget>=1) and (CurrentTarget<=NumberOfTargets) then
        begin
        answer.content:=TargetList[CurrentTarget].content;
        HighlightField(TargetList[CurrentTarget],answer.attributes);
        end;
    if filter=[] then SwitchCursor(off);
    DisplayField(question);
    CursorAt(row,col);
    PointerTo(row,col);
    complete:=false;
    repeat
        if ErrorFlag=on then DisplayField(ErrorMessage);
        ErrorFlag:=off;
        if ControlBuffer=0 then {otherwise there is already something}
            begin
            event:=WaitInputEvent(SelectionBy);
            HideField(ErrorMessage);
            HideField(HelpMessage);
            if event=pointer then
                ReadPointer(row,col,ControlBuffer)
            else
                ReadField(answer,filter,ControlDIB);
```

```
      end;
  if equal(ControlBuffer,RequestAbort) then
      complete:=true
  else
      begin
      PriorTarget:=CurrentTarget;
      if event=pointer then
          {***** absolute pointing *****}
          begin
          CurrentTarget:=MatchPosition(row,col,TargetList,
                                       NumberOfTargets);
          CursorTo(row,col);
          if (CurrentTarget<>0) and (AcceptTarget=0) then
              complete:=true;
          end
      else {event=keyboard}
          begin
          if ControlBuffer=0 then
              {***** matching keyed data *****}
              begin
              case matching of
                  abbreviated : AbbreviatedMatch(QandA_DIB,MatchSet);
                  exact       : ExactMatch(QandA_DIB,MatchSet);
                  partial     : PartialMatch(QandA_DIB,MatchSet);
              end; {case}
              if count(MatchSet)=1 then
                  begin
                  CurrentTarget:=first(MatchSet);
                  complete:=true;
                  end
          else
              ErrorFlag:=on;
          end
      else
      if (CurrentTarget<>0)
      and ((ControlBuffer=PointNextTarget)
      or  (ControlBuffer=PointPriorTarget)) then
          {***** relative pointing *****}
          begin
          if ControlBuffer=PointNextTarget then
              if PriorTarget=NumberOfTargets then CurrentTarget:=1
                              else CurrentTarget:=PriorTarget+1
          else
              if PriorTarget=1 then CurrentTarget:=NumberOfTargets
                              else CurrentTarget:=PriorTarget-1;
          ControlBuffer:=0;   {because it has been actioned}
          {do nothing in the case of AcceptTarget=0}
          end;
      end;
  if PriorTarget<>CurrentTarget then
      begin
      if PriorTarget<>0 then DisplayField(TargetList[PriorTarget]);
      if CurrentTarget<>0 then
          begin
          HighlightField(TargetList[CurrentTarget],
                         answer.attributes);
          CursorAt(row,col);
          PointerTo(row,col);
          end;
      end;
  if (not complete) and (ControlBuffer<>0) then
      begin
      if ControlBuffer=AcceptTarget then
          begin
          complete:=true;
          ControlBuffer:=0;   {because it has been actioned}
```

```
                     end
                else
                if ControlBuffer=RequestHelp then
                   begin
                   DisplayField(HelpMessage);
                   ControlBuffer:=0;     {because it has been actioned}
                   end
                else
                if ControlBuffer in ApplicationControl+[PointNextField,
                                 PointPriorField,AcceptForm] then
                   complete:=true;
                end;
           if CurrentTarget<>0 then
              begin
              answer.content:=TargetList[CurrentTarget].content;
              DisplayField(answer);   {update the display on the screen}
              end
           else
              answer.content:='';
           end;
        if not complete then ControlBuffer:=0;
   until complete;
   if CurrentTarget<>0 then
      begin
      DisplayField(TargetList[CurrentTarget]);
      answer.content:=TargetList[CurrentTarget].content;
      end;
      if CursorWas=on then SwitchCursor(on);
      end;
end; {Choose}

{----------------------------------------------------------------------}
procedure SetControlDefaults(var ControlDIB:ControlDIBtype);
begin
with ControlDIB do
   begin
   ControlBuffer:=0;
   rubout:=0;
   EchoSwitch:=off;
   AcceptField:=0;
   RequestAbort:=0;
   RequestHelp:=0;
   PointNextTarget:=0;
   PointPriorTarget:=0;
   AcceptTarget:=0;
   PointNextField:=0;
   PointPriorField:=0;
   AcceptForm:=0;
   ApplicationControl:=[];
   end;
end; {SetControlDefaults}

{----------------------------------------------------------------------}
procedure SetMenuDefaults(var MenuDIB:MenuDIBtype);
var k : byte;
begin
with MenuDIB do
   begin
   CreateField(MenuHeader,'',0,0,0,'');
   for k:=1 to MaxOptions do
      begin
      CreateField(TargetList[k],'',0,0,0,'');
      CreateField(SupplementaryList[k],'',0,0,0,'');
      end;
   NumberOfOptions:=0;
   CreateField(MenuTrailer,'',0,0,0,'');
```

```
    end;
end; {SetMenuDefaults}

{---------------------------------------------------------------------}
procedure SetQandAdefaults(var QandA_DIB:QandA_DIBtype);
var k : byte;
begin
with QandA_DIB do
   begin
   CreateField(question,'',0,0,0,'');
   CreateField(answer,'',0,0,0,'');
   filter:=[];
   CreateField(HelpMessage,'',0,0,0,'');
   validation:='';
   ErrorFlag:=off;
   CreateField(ErrorMessage,'',0,0,0,'');
   NumberOfTargets:=0;
   for k:=1 to MaxTargets do
      CreateField(TargetList[k],'',0,0,0,'');
   matching:=exact;
   CurrentTarget:=0;
   SelectionBy:=id;
   end;
end; {SetQandAdefaults}
{---------------------------------------------------------------------}
procedure QandA(var QandA_DIB:QandA_DIBtype;
                var ControlDIB:ControlDIBtype);
begin
if QandA_DIB.NumberOfTargets=0 then
   ArbitraryData(QandA_DIB,ControlDIB)
else
   case QandA_DIB.SelectionBy of
      id       : ChooseByID(QandA_DIB,ControlDIB);
      scroll   : ChooseByScroll(QandA_DIB,ControlDIB);
      position : ChooseByPosition(QandA_DIB,ControlDIB);
      key      : ChooseByKey(QandA_DIB,ControlDIB);
      any      : Choose(QandA_DIB,ControlDIB);
   end; {case}
end; {QandA}

begin
end.
```

Appendix I

MCI library

The routines described in the previous appendix operate on a single QandA_DIB, requesting a single answer to a single question. In this appendix we examine structures which support a series of answers in the same dialogue step, and their associated routines. A full listing of these routines is provided at the end of the appendix. Preceeding sections describe how to use them.

I.1 Routines in the MCI Library

procedure DisplayForm(FormDIB:FormDIBtype);external;
{Displays a Form.}

procedure FormInputIV(var QandASet_DIB:QandASet_DIBType;
var ControlDIB:ControlDIBtype);external;
{Accepts input via a form, performing immediate validation of keyed input when choosing by keyed identifier from a list of targets.}

procedure FormInputDV(var QandASet_DIB:QandASet_DIBType;
var ControlDIB:ControlDIBtype);external;
{Same as FormInputIV, except that validation is deferred until the form has been accepted.}

I.2 Type Declarations Include-file for the MCI Library

The following type declarations are needed when using the routines of the MCI library. They are stored in the file 'mcitype.inc'.

```
FormFieldListType = array[1..MaxFormFields] of FieldType;
FormDIBtype       = record
                      NumberOfFormFields : byte;
                      FormFieldList      : FormFieldListType;
                    end;

QandAListType     = array[1..MaxQuestions] of QandA_DIBtype;
QandASet_DIBtype  = record
```

368

```
NumberOfQuestions : byte;
QandAList         : QandAListType;
CurrentQuestion   : byte;
end;
```

I.3 Forms

Forms come in many shapes and sizes, containing some or all of headers, trailers, captions, subheadings, and decorators. These are essentially background items which determine the shape of the form. Hence, we define a FormDIB to be a series of output fields. The foreground of a form represents the answers which the user supplies to the questions on the form. The display of the questions themselves is taken care of implicitly in the display of the form background. Hence, we need a set of QandA_DIBs for the answers.

var   FormDIB   : FormDIBtype;
         QandASet_DIB   : QandASet_DIBType;

The form is processed by:

DisplayForm(FormDIB);
FormInputDV(QandASet_DIB,ControlDIB);   {deferred validation}

The following variables in ControlDIB relate specifically to forms:

PointNextField   : defines a key which positions to the next field of a form. If left null (0) then 'next field' positioning is inoperative.

PointPriorField   : defines a key which positions to the previous field of a form. If left null (0) then 'previous field' positioning is inoperative.

AcceptForm   : defines a key which will cause the form to be accepted. If left null (0) then the form will be accepted immediately data has been entered into the last field of the form.

The following program is an elaboration of the program described in Section G.15. It utilises a FormDIB and a QandASet_DIB to accept keyboard data. The program is primarily concerned with displaying an output field. The operator can change the contents, the position of the slot and its width, or the attributes of this output field by entering data via a form (whose outline is shown in Fig. I.1).

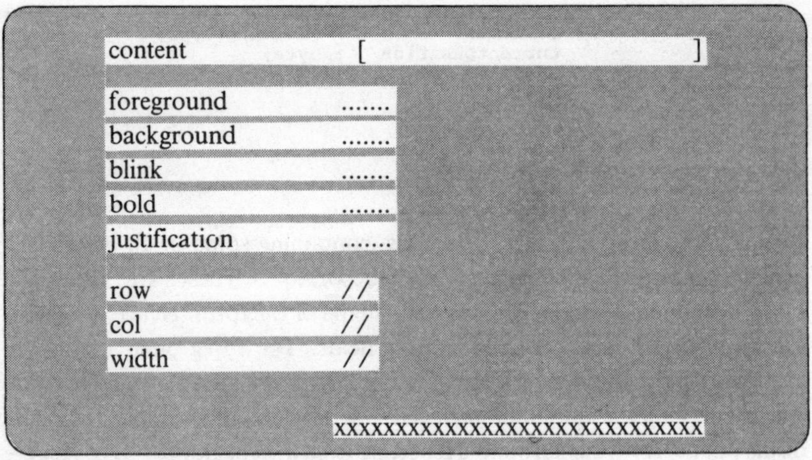

Fig. I.1.

The output field is shown as x's at the bottom of the display. The remaining fields make up a form. The content field is a left-justified keyed data field. The fields marked by dots are all point-and-pick fields. The three fields for entering the row, column and width values are right-justified for accepting numeric digits.

The fields are pointed at using PointNextField and PointPriorField, and the answers altered by retyping. The data is only accepted when the AcceptForm key is pressed. The row, column and width values are then validated. Row must be in the range 15..20, column in the range 1..80, and col+width must not exceed 80. If one or more fields are invalid, appropriate error messages are implanted into the error message fields, and the form reprocessed with the cursor positioned over the first field in error (and its error message displayed). Only when all data values are valid are the changes made to the output field, and it is redisplayed.

In the following program fragment, the output field is called 'out' and the items of QandAList are:

QandAList[1]	content
QandAList[2..6]	foreground, background, blink, bold and justification
QandAList[7..9]	row, col and width

```
DisplayForm(FormDIB);
CreateField(out,QandASet_DIB.QandAList[1].answer.content,17,11,30,
        'back=yellow,fore=black');
```

```
DisplayField(out);

with QandASet_DIB, ControlDIB do
    begin
    CurrentQuestion:=1;
    {display the answer fields}
    DisplayField(QandAList[1].answer);
    for k:=2 to 6 do
        with QandAList[k] do DisplayField(TargetList[CurrentTarget]);
    for k:=7 to 9 do DisplayField(QandAList[k].answer);
    repeat
        repeat
            FormInputIV(QandASet_DIB,ControlDIB);
            aborted:=(ControlBuffer=RequestAbort);
            {validate the fields of the form}
            NoErrors:=true;
            QandAList[7].ErrorFlag:=off;
            row:=value(QandAList[7].answer.content);
            if (row<17) or (row>20) then
                begin
                ChangeFieldContent(QandAList[7].ErrorMessage,
                                   'not in range 17..20');
                QandAList[7].ErrorFlag:=on;
                CurrentQuestion:=7;
                NoErrors:=false;
                end;
            col:=value(QandAList[8].answer.content);
            if (col<1) or (col>80) then
                begin
                ChangeFieldContent(QandAList[8].ErrorMessage,
                                   'not in range 1..80');
                QandAList[8].ErrorFlag:=on;
                if NoErrors then
                    begin
                    CurrentQuestion:=8;
                    NoErrors:=false;
                    end;
                end
            else
                begin
                MaxWidth:=81-col;
                width:=value(QandAList[9].answer.content);
                if (width<1) or (width>MaxWidth) then
                    begin
                    str(MaxWidth,MaxWidthString);
                    ChangeFieldContent(QandAList[9].ErrorMessage,concat(
                                   'not in range 1..',MaxWidthString));
                    QandAList[9].ErrorFlag:=on;
                    if NoErrors then
                        begin
                        CurrentQuestion:=9;
                        NoErrors:=false;
                        end;
                    end;
                end;
        until NoErrors or aborted;
        if not aborted then
            begin
            {process the fields of the form}
            ChangeFieldContent(out,QandAList{1].answer.content);
            ChangeFieldSlot(out,row,col,width);
            ChangeFieldAttributes(out,concat(
                    ' fore=',QandAList[2].
                             TargetList[QandAList[2].CurrentTarget].content,
                    ' back=',QandAList[3].
```

```
                         TargetList[QandAList[3].CurrentTarget].content,
                   ' blink=',QandAList[4].
                         TargetList[QandAList[4].CurrentTarget].content,
                   ' bold=',QandAList[5].
                         TargetList[QandAList[5].CurrentTarget].content,
                   ' just=',QandAList[6].
                         TargetList[QandAList[6].CurrentTarget].content))
            DisplayField(out);
            end;
      until aborted;
      end;
ClearScreen;
```

I.4 Pulldown and Dropdown menus

A menubar is usually displayed in one line across the screen. There may be a subsidiary menu associated with each of the choices of the menubar. If a subsidiary menu appears when we *pick* the option in the menubar, we have a *pulldown menu*; if it appears when we *point* at the option in the menubar, we have a *dropdown menu* (the associated menus drop down automatically when we scroll through the menubar).

To implement pulldown and dropdown menus we need a QandA_DIB for the menubar, and a QandASet_DIB for the associated menus (QandAList[n] is associated with the n'th option of the menubar).

    var Menubar : QandA_DIBtype;
        QandASet_DIB : QandASet_DIBtype;

I.4.1 Pulldown Menus using Relative Pointing

The following program fragment implements pulldown menus from a menubar, using relative pointing via the keyboard. The DisplayTargets and HideTargets procedures respectively display and hide the targets associated with the specified QandA_DIB.

```
{------------------------ pull down ------------------------}
SaveScreen;
with ControlDIB,QandASet_DIB do
   begin
   AcceptTarget:=CR;                              {explicit picking}
   Menubar.CurrentTarget:=1;
   DisplayTargets(Menubar);
   aborted:=false; complete:=false;
   repeat
      {processing the Menubar}
      PointNextTarget:=CursorRight;
      PointPriorTarget:=CursorLeft;
```

```
        ApplicationControl:=[];
        QandA(MenuBar,ControlDIB);
        aborted:=equal(ControlBuffer,RequestAbort);
        if not aborted then
          begin
          {processing the sub-menu}
          DisplayTargets(QandAList[Menubar.CurrentTarget]);
          PointNextTarget:=CursorDown;
          PointPriorTarget:=CursorUp;
          ApplicationControl:=[CursorLeft,CursorRight]; {menubar ctrls}
          QandA(QandAList[Menubar.CurrentTarget],ControlDIB);
          aborted:=equal(ControlBuffer,RequestAbort);
          accepted:=ControlBuffer=0;
          if aborted or accepted then
             complete:=true
          else
             HideTargets(QandAList[Menubar.CurrentTarget]);
          end;
    until aborted or complete;
    end;
```

(On completion QandAList[Menubar.CurrentTarget].CurrentTarget holds
the ordinal of the target that has been selected within the menu associated
with the Menubar.CurrentTarget option of the menubar.)

I.4.2 Dropdown Menus using Relative Pointing

The following program fragment implements dropdown menus from a
menubar, using relative pointing via the keyboard.

```
{------------------------- drop down -------------------------}
SaveScreen;
with ControlDIB,QandASet_DIB do
   begin
   Menubar.CurrentTarget:=1;
   DisplayTargets(Menubar);
   DisplayTargets(QandAList[Menubar.CurrentTarget]);
   aborted:=false; complete:=false;
   repeat
      PointNextTarget:=CursorDown;
      PointPriorTarget:=CursorUp;
      AcceptTarget:=CR;                                   {explicit picking}
      ApplicationControl:=[CursorLeft,CursorRight]; {menubar ctrls}
      QandA(QandAList[Menubar.CurrentTarget],ControlDIB);
      aborted:=equal(ControlBuffer,RequestAbort);
      accepted:=ControlBuffer=0;
      if not (aborted or accepted) then
         begin
         {can only be CursorRight or CursorLeft}
         HideTargets(QandAList[Menubar.CurrentTarget]);
         PointNextTarget:=CursorRight;
         PointPriorTarget:=CursorLeft;
         AcceptTarget:=0;                                 {immediate picking}
         ApplicationControl:=[];
         QandA(MenuBar,ControlDIB);
         DisplayTargets(QandAList[Menubar.CurrentTarget]);
         end;
   until aborted or accepted;
   end;
```

(On completion QandAList[Menubar.CurrentTarget].CurrentTarget holds
the ordinal of the target that has been selected within the menu associated
with the Menubar.CurrentTarget option of the menubar.)

I.4.3 Pulldown and Dropdown Menus using Absolute Pointing

The main difference between absolute pointing with, say, a mouse, and
relative pointing via a keyboard, is that the mouse is not constrained to be
pointing at a target at all times. With both pulldown and dropdown menus,
the cursor follows the movement of the mouse, and if it falls onto a target that
target is highlighted. The differences are:

*Dropdown:*actions are taken when the cursor enters or leaves a target. For
example, if only the menubar is being displayed and the cursor enters Target
3, then the associated sub-menu will drop down automatically (this is
achieved by processing the menubar with AcceptTarget set to null). Sub-
menu targets are highlighted in turn as the cursor moves over them. The
current target is accepted by pressing the AcceptTarget key (using a non-null
AcceptTarget). If the cursor is moved into a blank region of the screen (and
hence outside the targets for sub-menu 3), the sub-menu automatically
disappears. A new sub-menu must now be selected by moving the cursor into
the menubar.

Pulldown: actions only take place when the user presses a key. For example,
if only the menubar is being displayed and the cursor enters Target 3, then the
target will be highlighted. The associated sub-menu will only be displayed if
the AcceptTarget key is pressed. Likewise, if the cursor is moved into a blank
region of the screen (and hence outside the targets for sub-menu 3), the sub-
menu will disappear only when the AcceptTarget key is pressed. Accepting a
target is the same as for dropdown.

I.5 Listings

```
segment MCILib (input,output);
{ ---------------------------------------------------------------------}
const
   {$I b:mciconst.inc}
type
   {$I b:iotype.inc}
```

```
    {$I b:qatype.inc}
    {$I b:mcitype.inc}

{-------------------------------------------------------------------}
procedure ClearScreen;external;
procedure CursorTo(row,col:byte);external;
procedure DisplayField(field:FieldType);external;
procedure HideField(field:FieldType);external;
function  equal(ControlBuffer,ControlByte:byte):boolean;external;
procedure QandA(var QandA_DIB:QandA_DIBtype;
                var ControlDIB:ControlDIBtype);external;
procedure ArbitraryData(var QandA_DIB:QandA_DIBtype;
                        var ControlDIB:ControlDIBtype);external;

{-------------------------------------------------------------------}
procedure HideTargets(QandA_DIB:QandA_DIBtype);
var k : byte;
begin
with QandA_DIB do
   if NumberOfTargets<>0 then
      for k:=NumberOfTargets downto 1 do HideField(TargetList[k]);
end; {HideTargets}

{-------------------------------------------------------------------}
procedure DisplayTargets(QandA_DIB:QandA_DIBtype);
var k : byte;
begin
with QandA_DIB do
   if NumberOfTargets<>0 then
      for k:=1 to NumberOfTargets do DisplayField(TargetList[k]);
end; {DisplayTargets}

{-------------------------------------------------------------------}
procedure DisplayForm(FormDIB:FormDIBtype);
var k : byte;
begin
ClearScreen;
with FormDIB do
   begin
   for k:= 1 to NumberOfFormFields do
      DisplayField(FormFieldList[k]);
   end;
end; {DisplayForm}

{-------------------------------------------------------------------}
procedure FormInputIV(var QandASet_DIB:QandASet_DIBtype;
                      var ControlDIB:ControlDIBtype);
var complete : boolean;
begin
with ControlDIB,QandASet_DIB do
   begin
   complete:=false;
   repeat
      QandA(QandAList[CurrentQuestion],ControlDIB);
      QandAList[CurrentQuestion].ErrorFlag:=off;
      if equal(ControlBuffer,RequestAbort)
      or ((ControlBuffer<>0) and
         (ControlBuffer in ApplicationControl)) then
         complete:=true
      else
      if equal(ControlBuffer,AcceptForm)
      or ((CurrentQuestion=NumberOfQuestions) and (AcceptForm=0)) then
         begin
         ControlBuffer:=0;  {because it has been actioned}
         complete:=true;
         end
```

```
            else  {test for scroll back}
            if equal(ControlBuffer,PointPriorField) then
               if CurrentQuestion=1 then CurrentQuestion:=NumberOfQuestions
                               else CurrentQuestion:=CurrentQuestion-1
            else  {test for scroll forward}
            if equal(ControlBuffer,PointNextField) then
               if CurrentQuestion=NumberOfQuestions then CurrentQuestion:=1
                               else CurrentQuestion:=CurrentQuestion+1
            else  {proceed to next outstanding question}
               begin
               while (CurrentQuestion<=NumberOfQuestions)
               and   (QandAList[CurrentQuestion].ErrorFlag=off) do
                  CurrentQuestion:=CurrentQuestion+1;
               if CurrentQuestion>NumberOfQuestions then
                  if AcceptForm=0 then complete:=true
                               else CurrentQuestion:=1;
               end;
         if not complete then ControlBuffer:=0; {it has been actioned}
      until complete;
      end;
end; {FormInputIV}


{---------------------------------------------------------------------------}
procedure FormInputDV(var QandASet_DIB:QandASet_DIBtype;
                      var ControlDIB:ControlDIBType);
var complete : boolean;
begin
with ControlDIB,QandASet_DIB do
   begin
   complete:=false;
   repeat
      ArbitraryData(QandAList[CurrentQuestion],ControlDIB);
      QandAList[CurrentQuestion].ErrorFlag:=off;
      if equal(ControlBuffer,RequestAbort)
      or ((ControlBuffer<>0) and
         (ControlBuffer in ApplicationControl)) then
         complete:=true
      else
      if equal(ControlBuffer,AcceptForm)
      or ((CurrentQuestion=NumberOfQuestions) and (AcceptForm=0)) then
         begin
         ControlBuffer:=0;  {because it has been actioned}
         complete:=true;
         end
      else  {test for scroll back}
      if equal(ControlBuffer,PointPriorField) then
         if CurrentQuestion=1 then CurrentQuestion:=NumberOfQuestions
                         else CurrentQuestion:=CurrentQuestion-1
      else  {test for scroll forward}
      if equal(ControlBuffer,PointNextField) then
         if CurrentQuestion=NumberOfQuestions then CurrentQuestion:=1
                         else CurrentQuestion:=CurrentQuestion+1
      else {proceed to next outstanding question}
         begin
         while (CurrentQuestion<=NumberOfQuestions)
         and   (QandAList[CurrentQuestion].ErrorFlag=off) do
            CurrentQuestion:=CurrentQuestion+1;
         if CurrentQuestion>NumberOfQuestions then
            if AcceptForm=0 then complete:=true
                         else CurrentQuestion:=1;
         end;
      if not complete then ControlBuffer:=0; {it has been actioned}
   until complete;
   end;
end; {FormInputDV}


{---------------------------------------------------------------------------}
begin {MCILib}
end.
```

Index